The
Gluten-Free
Cookbook

The Gluten-Free Cookbook

Cristian Broglia

Introduction

It is my hope that this collection of 350 naturally gluten-free recipes from over 80 countries will introduce you to a wide range of unfamiliar ingredients, shake up your repertoire of day-to-day dishes, and open your eyes to the exciting possibilities of gluten-free cooking.

Gluten is a protein present in many cereals (like wheat, oats, spelt, barley, rye, bulgur, and freekeh) and in all their derivatives (such as flour, semolina, flakes, and meal). Gluten develops when two specific proteins, glutamine and gliadin, are hydrated and processed either mechanically or manually.

Wheat and other gluten-containing grains have existed since the beginning of civilization. However, the places where these grains were cultivated varied widely, depending upon altitude, climate, farming technology, and economic development. In regions where it was difficult or not cost-effective to grow such grains, alternative staple crops were cultivated, including almonds, chestnuts, cassava, corn, and potatoes. It is thanks to the creativity of cooks in those regions that today we can count on an incredible variety of global gluten-free dishes.

Those who want to eat a gluten-free diet must replace gluten-containing grains with other cereals that are naturally free of gluten, such as rice, corn, millet, buckwheat, quinoa, sorghum, teff, and amaranth. These grains, even when reduced to flour, can be tasty alternatives and can offer a considerable variety of tastes and textures.

The Gluten-Free Cookbook is a collection of recipes that are *naturally* gluten-free. The word naturally was the first criterion for deciding what to include in the book. So, for example, you won't find pasta in the book because pasta contains gluten, and you won't find any store-bought "gluten-free pasta" either. You also won't find recipes for breads or pastries that are commonly made with wheat flour, as we chose not to replicate any classics by using alternative flours. On the other hand, you will find lots of rice dishes in the book, because rice is naturally gluten-free and the original recipes need no modification.

But why produce a collection of 350 naturally gluten-free recipes? Excluding this protein complex from our diet is an increasingly common practice. The reasons for this are many: food allergies or intolerances, desire to change one's diet, or the interest in experimenting with new eating styles. This book is for those who cannot eat gluten, but it is also for those seeking new and interesting dishes from around the world, and for those who host gluten-free eaters.

Collecting and choosing the recipes for this book was quite an exciting task. I was eager to take on the challenge of finding suitable naturally gluten-free recipes because I am intrigued by world flavors and new ingredients. I started my culinary career as a chef in Parma, Italy, home to so many high-quality raw materials. There I learned to handle ingredients with care, to listen to the producers, and to unravel secrets handed down from generation to generation. Italy is of course famous for its pasta, so I learned very soon which type of wheat is best for making pasta, how to cook it perfectly, and what sauce pairs the best with each type of dish.

I then traveled the world to learn about new food cultures and traditions, tasting various dishes and exploring new ingredients. I journeyed throughout Europe and the Caribbean. In the process I refined my culinary art and opened my mind to cuisines that were innovative and creative. When I returned to Parma, I became executive chef and a cooking teacher. And I continued to travel to more countries in Europe, plus Asia, North America, and South America.

I am constantly inspired by global cuisines and food cultures. In my many years of travel, and through my work experience, I have developed a great deal of interest in gluten-free food and recipes. I deepened my research on vegetable proteins, discovering that textures and tastes can be achieved without gluten-containing proteins, all the while respecting tradition. Today my work is a mix between innovation and history, creativity and rigor, respect for the rules and revolution. I can say without a doubt that gluten-free cooking is now a major part of my professional life.

Some may think that gluten-free cooking is not very interesting because of what it excludes. On the contrary, gluten-free cuisine is not boring at all and you will find lots of variety. For example, you can sit at a table in the American South and eat a savory Shrimp and Grits (page 282) or go to Peru and enjoy Ceviche (page 260) served with sweet potatoes and corn. In Ireland you will find there is Irish Beef Stew (page 302) with Colcannon (page 228), and in Italy you would be amazed by a Flourless Chocolate Cake (page 400). In India there are papadum, thin crackers made with legumes, usually black mung beans or chickpeas (see recipes pages 170 and 171).

Searching through my large collection of cookbooks as well as consulting my extensive notes from my travels, I discovered many, many recipes that were already gluten-free. Compiling and cooking through these recipes, I was reminded of the pleasures of my travels, the markets I visited, the restaurants where I dined, the foods and flavors I loved most, and the books I read. Of course, there were also the people that I met along the way and the many who shared stories and recipes from their home kitchens. Thanks to them, I discovered new recipes, for example, Greens and Cheese Corn Pie (page 80) from Albania and Rice Cakes with Vegetables and Coconut Sauce (page 63) from Indonesia.

Alongside the great classics of gluten-free international cuisine—such as Creole Jambalaya (page 195) from the United States, Salmon Sushi Rolls (page 199) from Japan, Cheese Breads (pages 140 and 142) from Brazil and Paraguay, Steamed Tamales (page 84) from Mexico, and Corn Roti (page 157) from India—you will also find in this book many lesser-known regional specialties, such as Injera (page 153) from Ethiopia, Yuca Skillet Cake (page 20) from Bolivia, Farinata (page 154) from Italy, and Steamed Rice Dumplings (page 386) from Nepal. In many countries, gluten has an undisputed starring role in the kitchen (I am thinking, for example, about my Italy with pasta and pizza), but in other places, gluten-free flours, cereals, legumes, and tubers are still preferred. For example, in South America you can find many recipes made with yuca (cassava), plantains, and nuts; and in Asia there are many dishes with rice and seaweed.

There are also signature dishes from various countries that we may forget or not realize are gluten-free. From meat and fish dishes to salads, soups, stews, and desserts. There are Latkes (page 25) from Israel, Sweet Rice Cake Balls (page 412) from Korea, Guacamole with Homemade Tortilla Chips (page 36) from Mexico, Paella Valenciana (page 188) from Spain, Pea and Ham Soup (page 108) from the UK, Tomato and Onion Salad (page 214) from Tanzania, Ratatouille (page 226) from France, Grilled Pike (page 274) from South Africa, Fudge (page 410) from the United States, and Steamed Layer Cake (page 397) from Thailand. I could go on and on.

Reaching a definitive manuscript of naturally gluten-free home-cooking recipes was certainly not a linear process. We started out with a list of over 400 possible recipes. Then by rereading them, trying them again, and looking for their origins, some were eliminated. Others were inserted at the last moment when I realized that there was something missing. But after all the winnowing and testing and tasting, I believe we ended up with a truly special set of dishes.

I have divided the recipes into the following chapters: Breakfast, Starters, Soups, Bread and Wraps, Rice and Noodles, Salads, Vegetables and Legumes, Fish and Shellfish, Meat and Poultry, and Desserts and Sweet Treats. Each recipe is accompanied by a short intro that might describe the dish's history or its place in the cuisine of a region or advice on particular ingredients or cooking techniques. This, together with the recipe itself, should help give you a picture of the food culture the dish comes from and the flavors that characterize it.

Through the process of putting this book together, I have discovered a tremendous amount about gluten-free cooking. I hope that this collection of recipes will also be a discovery for you—about how you can still have a cuisine rich in taste even while gluten-free. At the end of your journey, you will be familiar with many new ingredients and surprising cooking techniques. And once you learn how to use the ingredients, you will be able to create your own new recipes, too.

Enjoy!

Cristian Broglia

Breakfast

Congee

(DF) (NF) (VG) (VT) 5 **China**

Preparation time: 10 minutes
Cooking time: 1 hour 10 minutes
Serves: 6

8½ cups (68 fl oz/2 liters)
    vegetable stock
2½ cups (450 g) sweet
    (glutinous) rice, carefully
    rinsed
1 tablespoon grated fresh ginger
1 teaspoon sea salt
½ scallion (spring onion),
    thinly sliced, for garnish
Sesame oil, for drizzling

This rice porridge is a typical breakfast in China, where it is called congee or *juk*. Many Asian countries have similar dishes, which can be served for lunch or dinner as well as breakfast, and can be sweet or savory. Chinese congee may vary from region to region for the type of rice or the amount of water or stock used, but all are basically a very soft and creamy porridge.

In a soup pot, combine the stock, rice, ginger, and salt. Mix well and bring to a boil over high heat. Reduce the heat to low and simmer, stirring occasionally, until the rice breaks down and the mixture thickens into a creamy porridge, about 1 hour. Add more stock as it cooks if the mixture seems too dry.
   Serve hot, garnished with sliced scallion (spring onions) and drizzled with sesame oil.

Cassava Flour Porridge

(DF) (NF) (VG) (VT) 5 **Angola**

Preparation time: 15 minutes
Cooking time: 1 hour
Serves: 4

Scant 4¼ cups (500 g) cassava
    flour (see Note)

Funje is a traditional Angolan dish served as a breakfast, a side dish, or for lunch and dinner. It has a sticky, smooth, and creamy texture and its flavor is very delicate, so it is the perfect canvas for other strongly flavored ingredients used as toppings. It is important that the mixture be completely lump-free.

Preheat the oven to 350°F (180°C/Gas Mark 4).
   In a saucepan, bring 4 cups (32 fl oz/950 ml) water to a boil.
   Meanwhile, in a bowl, with an electric mixer, beat together the cassava flour and 4 cups (32 fl oz/950 ml) cold water for 10 minutes or until smooth, with no lumps.
   Stir the cassava flour mixture into the boiling water, reduce the heat to medium-low, and cook until cooked through and thickened, about 5 minutes.
   Pour the porridge into an 11-inch (30 cm) Dutch oven (casserole), cover, transfer to the oven, and bake until set and firm, about 45 minutes.
   Serve hot.

Note: Cassava flour, also known as manioc flour, is the dried and ground up root of yuca (cassava). It should not be confused with tapioca, which is a starch derived from yuca root.

Buckwheat Kasha

(NF) (VT) 5

Russia

**Preparation time: 5 minutes,
 plus 20 minutes resting time
Cooking time: 30 minutes
Serves: 4**

1 tablespoon (15 g) unsalted butter
1 egg
1 cup (160 g) kasha (roasted
  buckwheat groats)

Kasha is the name of both a porridge as well as the grain it is made from: buckwheat. Originally from Russia, kasha is common to almost all of Eastern Europe and the Baltic countries. Because cooked kasha was typically served for special occasions, its name became synonymous with celebration.

In a saucepan, bring 2 cups (16 fl oz/475 ml) water to a boil over high heat. Add the butter and remove the pan from the heat. Let it rest, covered, for 5 minutes.

Meanwhile, in a medium bowl, beat the egg lightly with a fork. Add the kasha and stir gently to mix.

Pour the kasha mixture into a large saucepan. Set over medium heat and cook, stirring, until it is lightly toasted and dry, about 10 minutes. Pour in the water/butter mixture, reduce the heat to low, cover, and simmer until all of the liquid is absorbed, about 15 minutes.

Remove from the heat. Uncover and drape with a clean tea towel. Let it rest for 15 minutes and serve.

Ring-Shaped Fried Rice Breads

(NF) (VT)

Nepal

**Preparation time: 15 minutes,
 plus overnight soaking time
Cooking time: 40 minutes
Serves: 4**

Scant 2 cups (350 g) basmati
  or other long-grain white rice
2½ cups (300 g) grated
  palm sugar
Scant 1 cup (7 oz/200 g) ghee
1 small very ripe banana
½ teaspoon ground cardamom
¼ teaspoon ground cloves
⅔ cup (5 fl oz/150 ml) milk
Rice flour, as needed
Vegetable oil, for frying

A traditional Nepalese fried bread, *sel roti* makes an excellent breakfast or snack and is usually served with tea. The cooked breads can be stored at room temperature for up to 20 days.

Rinse the rice until the water runs clear. Put the rice in a pot and add water to cover. Let soak overnight.

Drain and rinse the rice, then drain well. Transfer it to a food processor and add the sugar, ghee, banana, cardamom, and cloves. With the machine running, slowly add the milk, until it turns into a smooth dough that is loose enough to be piped. If the dough is too runny, mix in about 1 tablespoon rice flour. Scrape the dough into a piping bag with a ½-inch (1.5 cm) plain tip (nozzle).

Pour 1 inch (2.5 cm) oil into an 8-inch (20 cm) frying pan and heat over medium heat. Carefully drop a half teaspoonful of batter into the oil. If it sizzles, it is the right temperature.

Squeeze some of the dough into the oil in a circle 6 inches (15 cm) wide. Fry until golden brown. Drain on paper towels. Repeat until you have used all the dough. Serve warm or at room temperature.

Shakshuka

Preparation time: 10 minutes
Cooking Time: 40 minutes
Serves: 4

1 tablespoon olive oil
½ onion, diced
1 clove garlic, minced
1 red bell pepper, chopped
4 cups (720 g) diced tomatoes
2 tablespoons tomato paste
    (tomato purée)
1 teaspoon mild chili powder
1 teaspoon ground cumin
1 teaspoon paprika
Pinch of cayenne pepper
Pinch of sugar
Sea salt and freshly ground
    black pepper
8 eggs
½ tablespoon chopped fresh
    parsley, for garnish (optional)

Shakshuka is a North African dish, nowadays popular all over the Middle East, especially in Israel, where it was imported by Maghrebi Jews who immigrated to that country. The name of the dish comes from a Berber word that means "mixture." It can be breakfast, lunch, or dinner, but in Israel it is often breakfast served with warm crusty bread for dipping into the sauce. By tradition it is served straight out of the terra-cotta pan it is cooked in, placed in the center of the table.

In a large frying pan, heat the oil over medium heat. Add the onion and sauté until translucent, 4–5 minutes. Add the garlic and sauté until fragrant. Add the bell pepper and sauté until softened, about 12 minutes.

Stir in the tomatoes, tomato paste (tomato purée), chili powder, cumin, paprika, cayenne, sugar, and salt and black pepper to taste. Stir and simmer over medium heat until it starts to reduce, about 10 minutes.

Crack the eggs into the tomato mixture, spreading them evenly. When you add the eggs will depend on if you want the eggs cooked soft, medium, or hard.

For hard-cooked eggs: Cover the pan and simmer until the eggs are fully cooked, 10–15 minutes. Keep an eye on the sauce to make sure it doesn't reduce too much, which can lead to burning.

For soft to medium eggs: Let the sauce reduce for a few minutes uncovered, before cracking the eggs on top. Cover the pan and cook for 7 minutes for medium eggs, 5 minutes for soft eggs with runny yolks.

Serve hot. Garnish with chopped parsley, if desired.

Poached Eggs and Skillet Hash

Preparation time: 15 minutes
Cooking time: 50 minutes
Serves: 4

4 large yellow potatoes, peeled
    and cut into chunks
2 tablespoons extra-virgin olive oil
2 onions, cubed
1 lb 2 oz (500 g) green beans,
    cut into small pieces
Generous 1 cup (9 oz/250 g)
    green peas
Sea salt and freshly ground
    black pepper
Dried oregano
9 oz (250 g) slab bacon, diced,
    or lardons
3 tablespoons distilled white
    vinegar
4 eggs

In Belgium as well as parts of Central Europe there are many variations on the dish called *poêlée*, which translates to "cooked in a frying pan." This example from Belgium is a simple preparation, with a good amount of protein, thanks to bacon, legumes, and eggs. Because the eggs are poached and the yolks are just barely cooked, it is important to choose very fresh eggs, preferably organic.

In a vegetable steamer, cook the potato chunks until tender, about 20 minutes.

In a cast-iron skillet, heat the oil over medium heat. Add the onions, green beans, and peas and cook until the vegetables start to sizzle, about 5 minutes. Season to taste with salt, pepper, and oregano. Cook, stirring occasionally, until the green beans are softened, about 20 minutes. If the pan looks dry, add a little bit of water. Add the potatoes and stir, then remove from the heat.

In a separate frying pan, cook the bacon over medium heat until golden and crispy, about 8 minutes. Drain on paper towels.

In a shallow pot, bring 3 cups (24 fl oz/710 ml) water and the vinegar to a boil. Reduce to a simmer and carefully break the eggs into the water one at a time. Let them cook for 2 minutes (the yolks should still be runny) and remove them with a skimmer.

Divide the vegetable hash onto four plates. Top each with a poached egg and a sprinkle of bacon. Serve hot.

Bacon, Eggs, and Beans

**Preparation time: 20 minutes,
plus overnight soaking time
Cooking time: 1 hour 40 minutes
Serves: 4**

3 cups dried white kidney beans,
  soaked overnight
4 tablespoons sunflower oil
1 yellow onion, chopped
1⅔ cups (400 g) passata
  (unseasoned tomato sauce)
2 tablespoons sugar
1 tablespoon Worcestershire sauce
1 teaspoon mustard powder
Sea salt
8 slices smoked back bacon
  (see Note)
4 eggs

The British have been dining on this hearty breakfast dish since the sixteenth century, though the first recipes for it weren't published until the mid-nineteenth century. Sometimes called a "fry-up," there are many variants of this breakfast depending on location—including Northern Ireland, Wales, and Scotland, where local sausages are often added.

Drain the beans. In a large pot, combine the beans with water to generously cover. Bring to a boil, then reduce to a high simmer and cook until the beans are tender, about 1 hour. Reserving the liquid, drain the beans.

In a large saucepan, heat 2 tablespoons of the oil over medium heat. Add the onion and stir over low heat until softened, 3–4 minutes. Add the tomato sauce, 1 cup (8 fl oz/240 ml) of the reserved bean cooking water, the sugar, Worcestershire sauce, mustard powder, and beans. Season with salt to taste. Cover and simmer until the liquid is almost all gone, about 20 minutes.

In large frying pan, heat the remaining 2 tablespoons oil over medium heat. Add the bacon and fry until crisp, about 5 minutes. Set the bacon on paper towels to drain, reserving the fat and oil in the pan.

Heat the bacon fat over medium heat. Add the eggs and fry until the whites are cooked and the yolks are still runny. Season with salt.

Divide the fried eggs, bacon, and beans among four plates. Serve immediately.

Note: British-style back bacon, sometimes sold in the U.S. as "Irish bacon," is cut from the loin. If you can't find it, you can use a thick-sliced center-cut bacon or good-quality Canadian bacon.

Tofu Omelets

Preparation time: 10 minutes
Cooking time: 15 minutes
Serves: 4

1 tablespoon seedless
    tamarind pulp
1 large clove garlic, grated
2 tablespoons creamy
    peanut butter
1 tablespoon tamari
1 teaspoon chili powder
1 teaspoon sea salt, plus more
    to taste
3 tablespoons cornstarch
    (cornflour)
5 eggs, beaten
1 lb (450 g) silken tofu, cut into
    1-inch (2.5 cm) cubes
1 tablespoon minced scallion
    (spring onion)
6 tablespoons peanut
    (groundnut) oil
2 cups (150 g) shredded lettuce,
    for serving
¾ cup (80 g) bean sprouts,
    blanched, for serving

A popular Indonesian street food, *tahu telur* is an omelet stuffed with tofu and covered with a spicy peanut sauce. It is definitely worth trying. The silken tofu used for these omelets gives them a soft and creamy texture. A traditional *tahu telur* is cooked as a tall cylinder in a special metal mold, but a flat omelet, as here, is more common.

In a small bowl, soak the tamarind pulp in 2 tablespoons hot water for 5 minutes. Smash the pulp into the water with the back of a spoon. Pass through a fine-mesh sieve into another bowl and discard the solids. Stir in the garlic, peanut butter, tamari, chili, and 1 teaspoon salt and set aside.

In a separate bowl, mix together the cornstarch (cornflour) and eggs and stir until the starch is fully absorbed. Very gently stir in the tofu and scallion (spring onion) and season with salt to taste.

In a frying pan, heat the oil over medium-high heat. Carefully pour one-quarter of the tofu/egg mixture into the pan and fry on both sides until golden brown. Repeat to make 3 more omelets.

Pour the tamarind/peanut sauce over one half of each omelet and serve garnished with lettuce and bean sprouts.

Yuca Skillet Cake

Preparation time: 15 minutes
Cooking time: 45 minutes
Serves: 4

2½ lb (1.2 kg) yuca (cassava) root,
    peeled and cubed (see Note)
2½ lb (1.2 kg) hard or semi-hard
    cheese (Bolivian if you can
    find it), grated
1 egg
½ cup (4 fl oz/120 ml) milk
4 tablespoons (60 g) unsalted
    butter
Sea salt
2 tablespoons sunflower oil

Sonso de yuca is a Bolivian dish typical of the parts of the country where yuca (a starchy root also known as cassava) is easily grown, including eastern Bolivia and the department of Santa Cruz. Bolivians prepare it in three different ways: broiled (grilled), baked, and on the stovetop (as here). The result is always delicious. In addition to being a breakfast, the skillet cake can be eaten as a dessert or as a street food. (In fact it is often served molded onto a wooden skewer.) Cooked yuca has a mild and slightly nutty taste.

In a soup pot, combine the yuca (cassava) and water to generously cover and bring to a boil. Cook over medium heat until the yuca is very tender, about 30 minutes. Drain the yuca and remove the "cords" (see Note).

Transfer the yuca to a bowl and mash. Add the cheese, egg, milk, and butter. Add salt to taste (may not be needed if you use Bolivian cheese, as it's quite salty). Knead carefully until the mixture is homogeneous, soft, and a little sticky.

Grease a cast-iron skillet with the oil. Scrape the batter into the skillet and gently level the surface. Set the pan over medium-high heat and cook until the bottom is fully detached from the pan and golden brown, 8–10 minutes. Flip the cake onto a plate and then back into the pan cooked-side up. Cook until the second side is also browned, about 6 minutes.

To serve, cut into slices.

Note: The yuca root (cassava) cannot be eaten raw as it contains toxins, so it is always cooked to detoxify it. In some preparations, as this one, the raw root is grated and then squeezed to remove the bitter milky liquid that contains a lot of the toxins (though the yuca still needs to be cooked).

Yuca has a "cord," an inedible hard white fiber that runs through the center of the root. It is easier to take it out after the yuca has been cooked and softened.

Idli

 India

Preparation time: 20 minutes, plus 4 hours soaking time and 8 hours fermenting time
Cooking time: 25 minutes
Serves: 4

Scant 2 cups (350 g) converted (easy-cook) white rice, rinsed
⅔ cup (80 g) thick poha (flattened rice), rinsed
Scant 1½ cups (200 g) whole or split urad dal
¼ teaspoon fenugreek seeds
1 teaspoon coarse (rock) salt
3 tablespoons sunflower oil
Sambar (page 241), for serving

Idli are fluffy steamed savory cakes made with a batter of fermented rice and mung beans. It is a popular Indian breakfast option. The fermentation of the batter makes these cakes particularly digestible and the steaming technique makes them very light. The special molds in which they are steamed have small holes that allow uniform cooking, but in this recipe we just use individual ramekins or custard cups.

In a bowl, stir together the rice, poha, and 2 cups (16 fl oz/ 475 ml) water. Mix, cover, and let it soak for 4 hours. At the same time, in a separate small bowl, stir together the urad dal, fenugreek seeds, and ½ cup (4 fl oz/120 ml) water and soak for 4 hours.

Reserving the soaking liquid, drain the urad dal and fenugreek. Measure out ¼ cup (2 fl oz/60 ml) of the soaking water and add to a food processor along with the urad dal/ fenugreek mixture and grind to mix. Then add the rest of the soaking water and mix until you obtain a smooth paste. Pour the urad dal paste into a bowl and set aside. Clean out the processor bowl.

Drain the rice mixture. Working in batches, grind the rice in a food processor to make a smooth batter. Add all the rice batter to the urad dal paste. Add the salt and mix well.

Cover the bowl loosely and set aside at room temperature to ferment until the mixture has risen and doubled in size, 8 hours or overnight.

Bring water to a simmer in a steamer. Brush the oil on the insides of four ramekins or custard cups that are 2 inches (5 cm) across and 1½ inches (4 cm) deep. Pour the batter into the cups and set them in the steamer basket. Steam the idli until firm and cooked through, 12–15 minutes.

Place on a plate and serve steaming hot with sambar.

Mandioca Cheese Flatbread

(NF) (VT) (30) [5]   **Paraguay**

Preparation time: 10 minutes
Cooking time: 5 minutes
Serves: 6

2½ cups (400 g) cassava flour
    (see Note, page 12)
7 oz (200 g) cheese, such as
    queso paraguayo, cheddar,
    or mozzarella, shredded
1 stick plus 2 tablespoons
    (5 oz/150 g) unsalted butter
2 teaspoons sea salt
3–4 tablespoons milk
Vegetable oil, for greasing

Mbejú—a word that simply means "cake"—is a buttery, cheesy flatbread with crispy edges, typically served with a cup of coffee in Paraguay. Yuca (cassava) is a precious food for those who cannot eat gluten-containing foods, and the cuisine of Paraguay makes abundant use of this root, in the form of both tapioca starch and cassava flour. There are also versions of this flatbread in which cornmeal is added.

In a bowl, combine the cassava flour, cheese, butter, and salt and start mixing with your fingers until the mixture is crumbly. Add the milk, 1 tablespoon at a time, and mix until the crumbles look like small pebbles.
    Heat a little oil in a 12-inch (30 cm) frying pan over medium heat. Add the mixture and press with the back of a spoon or with a spatula to even the surface. Cook until golden, about 3 minutes. Flip and cook for 3 more minutes.
    To serve, cut into slices.

Sweet Potato and Carrot Fritters

(DF) (NF) (VT)   **New Zealand**

Preparation time: 30 minutes
Cooking time: 20 minutes
Serves: 4

14 oz (400 g) red kumara or sweet
    potato, peeled and grated
7 oz (200 g) carrots, grated
4 scallions (spring onions),
    finely sliced
1 teaspoon ground coriander
1 teaspoon curry powder
½ cup (80 g) potato starch
2 eggs, lightly beaten
3 tablespoons chopped fresh
    parsley, plus more for garnish
Sea salt
Vegetable oil, for frying

These crispy, golden vegetable fritters are incredibly savory. They are prepared with kumara, a New Zealand sweet potato that comes in several varieties: the red-skinned Owairaka Red has a creamy white flesh; kumara gold, sometimes sold as Toka Toka Gold, has golden skin and flesh and a sweeter flavor; and orange kumara, sometimes sold as Beauregard, has a deep-orange flesh and is even sweeter. The Beauregard is also grown in the U.S. and is usually labeled "yam."

Put the kumara and carrots in a colander and squeeze out the liquid. Transfer to a bowl and stir in the scallions (spring onions), coriander, and curry powder. Sprinkle with the potato starch and add the eggs and parsley. Season the mixture with salt to taste. Stir carefully.
    In a deep nonstick pan, heat 4 inches (10 cm) oil over medium heat to 340°F (170°C) on a deep-fry thermometer.
    Working in batches, add spoonfuls of the fritter mixture to the oil and fry until golden brown on each side, about 5 minutes. Garnish with parsley and serve hot.

Hash Browns

(DF) (NF) (VT) 5

United States

Preparation time: 1 hour
Cooking time: 30 minutes
Serves: 6

6 yellow potatoes, peeled,
    grated, and drained
1 large onion, minced
2 eggs, beaten
Sea salt and freshly ground
    black pepper
Canola (rapeseed) oil,
    for frying

This is a simple—and delicious—American breakfast dish. Though undoubtedly pan-fried potatoes had been around for a long time, they first began appearing on American restaurant menus as "hash browns" in the late nineteenth century. Since then the hash brown has been introduced around the world, especially by American fast-food chains. Here is a recipe for traditional old-school hash browns, plain and simple. Serve the potatoes with a fried egg and crispy bacon.

In a large bowl, combine the potatoes, onion, eggs, and salt and pepper to taste and stir gently to mix.
    Pour 2 inches (5 cm) oil into a large nonstick frying pan. Heat the oil over medium heat to 340°F (170°C) on a deep-fry thermometer.
    Working in batches, carefully add enough potato mixture to form a cake about 3 inches (7.5 cm) wide and ½ inch (1.25 cm) thick. Fry until browned and cooked through, about 3 minutes per side. Drain on paper towels.
    Serve hot.

Latkes

(NF) (VT)

Israel

Preparation time: 20 minutes,
    plus 15 minutes draining time
Cooking time: 15 minutes
Serves: 6

6 yellow potatoes
1 onion
2 eggs
5 tablespoons cornstarch
    (cornflour)
Sea salt and freshly ground
    black pepper
Vegetable oil, for frying
Sour cream, for serving
Rose pepper, for garnish

These potato pancakes are a Jewish recipe traditionally served for Hanukkah. They can be served with many toppings, including the classic combination of sour cream or crème fraîche, dill, and smoked salmon—and often, in the U.S., with applesauce.

Peel and grate the potatoes and set them in a colander to drain for 15 minutes. At the same time, grate the onion and set it in a sieve to drain for 15 minutes.
    In a large bowl, combine the potatoes, onion, eggs, and cornstarch (cornflour). Season with salt and pepper to taste and gently mix to combine.
    Pour 2 inches (5 cm) oil into a Dutch oven (casserole). Heat the oil to 340°F (170°C) on a deep-fry thermometer.
    Working in batches, spoon a generous tablespoon of potato mixture carefully into the oil. Fry the pancakes until golden on both sides, about 5 minutes total. Drain on paper towels. You should get about 18 latkes.
    Top with sour cream and sprinkle with rose pepper. Serve hot.

Cheese-Stuffed Potato Patties
with Peanut Sauce

**Preparation time: 20 minutes,
   plus 30 minutes chilling time
Cooking time: 45 minutes
Serves: 6**

Sea salt
5½ lb (2.5 kg) yellow potatoes,
   peeled and left whole
6 tablespoons vegetable oil
3 tablespoons achiote seeds
14 oz (400 g) your favorite
   fresh cheese or mozzarella
   cheese, diced
2 red onions, thinly diced
2 cloves garlic, chopped
2 tomatoes, seeded and diced
3 tablespoons chopped fresh
   cilantro (coriander)
1 green bell pepper, finely
   chopped
Ground cumin
Freshly ground black pepper
Generous ½ cup (250 g) peanut
   paste (see Note)
Corn oil, for frying
Fried egg and/or boiled white
   rice, for serving

These *llapingachos*, or stuffed potato patties, have melted cheese centers and are topped with a creamy peanut sauce. Achiote seeds are used to give color to the sauce and also a slightly sweet, nutty, and peppery flavor similar to nutmeg. If you can't find them, replace with 1 teaspoon paprika.

In a large pot of boiling salted water, cook the potatoes until firm-tender, about 25 minutes. Drain, transfer to a bowl, and mash.

In a small saucepan, heat 3 tablespoons of the vegetable oil with 1½ tablespoons of the achiote seeds over low heat for 1 minute. Strain the seeds out of the oil, pour the oil into the mashed potatoes, and stir carefully.

Take about ⅓-cup (2½ oz/65 g) portions of the potato mixture and roll them into balls. Place about 1 teaspoon diced cheese in the center and close the potato mixture around the cheese. Gently press to make a thick patty and place on a tray. Repeat for all the potato mixture and cheese. Transfer the tray to the fridge and chill for 30 minutes.

Meanwhile, in a saucepan, heat the remaining 3 tablespoons vegetable oil with the remaining 1½ tablespoons achiote seeds over low heat for 3 minutes. Leaving the oil in the pan, scoop out and discard the seeds. Add the red onions, garlic, tomatoes, cilantro (coriander), and bell pepper to the pan. Add 1 cup (8 fl oz/240 ml) water and season with cumin, salt, and black pepper to taste. Stir in the peanut paste and simmer until the sauce is thickened, about 5 minutes. Keep the sauce warm.

Pour 3 inches (7.5 cm) corn oil into a deep heavy-bottomed pan. Heat the oil over medium heat to 325°F (163°C) on a deep-fry thermometer.

Working in batches, add the patties and cook until golden brown on both sides, 3 minutes per side.

Serve with the vegetable/peanut sauce and fried eggs and/or boiled white rice.

Note: This is a sauce made with pure ground peanuts with no added oil, sugar, or salt.

Filled Coconut Pancakes

Thailand

Preparation time: 30 minutes
Cooking time: 50 minutes
Makes: 20–30 pancakes

For the pancake batter
¼ cup (50 g) jasmine rice
1 cup (240 ml) full-fat coconut milk
2 tablespoons (30 g) coconut
    sugar or granulated sugar
½ cup (65 g) rice flour, preferably
    Thai rice flour
3 tablespoons (35 g) tapioca
    starch or sweet rice flour
½ cup (30 g) finely shredded fresh
    coconut (grated on a regular
    box grater)
Pinch of sea salt

For the filling
Scant ⅔ cup (150 ml) full-fat
    coconut milk
1 tablespoon (15 g) coconut sugar
    or granulated sugar
4 teaspoons (15 g) rice flour,
    preferably Thai rice flour
Pinch of sea salt

For cooking and serving
Coconut oil, melted, for the pan
2 scallions (spring onions),
    chopped
2 tablespoons drained canned
    corn kernels

Kanom krok are little coconut pancakes that are one of the most popular, tasty street foods in Thailand. They can range from sweet to savory and are often served topped with scallions (spring onions) and/or corn. The Thais often eat two of these little pancakes sandwiched together into a sphere. The pancakes are traditionally cooked in a specialized pan called a *kuli paniyaram* pan, which has small cup-shaped indentations in it—very similar to a Japanese *takoyaki* pan. You can also use a Danish *æbleskiver* pancake pan.

Make the pancake batter: In a small pot, bring ¾ cup (6 fl oz/ 180 ml) water to a boil. Add the rice and simmer over low heat until very tender and the water has been totally absorbed, about 15 minutes. Add more water as necessary if the rice gets too dry. Cool slightly.

In a blender, combine the cooked rice (you should have a heaping ½ cup or 135 g), the coconut milk, sugar, rice flour, tapioca starch or sweet rice flour, shredded coconut, and salt. Mix well, starting at low speed and then higher until combined. Add ½ cup (4 fl oz/125 ml) cold water a little at a time until you get a pancake batter the consistency of heavy (whipping) cream (you may need slightly more or slightly less water, depending on the flour used).

Make the filling: In a bowl, combine the coconut milk, sugar, rice flour, and salt and whisk well.

To cook the pancakes: Heat a *takoyaki*, *kuli paniyaram*, or *æbleskiver* pan over medium-high heat. Brush the cups generously with melted coconut oil. Fill 3 or 4 of the cups each with 1–1½ tablespoons of the batter (the cups should be no more than two-thirds full). Spoon 1 teaspoon of the filling into the batter, pushing the teaspoon down into the center of the batter so the batter rises slightly up the sides of the cup. (It is important to make only 3 or 4 pancakes at a time because you don't want the batter to get too cooked before you add the filling.) Let the pancakes cook for 1–2 minutes until the edges are crispy and well browned. Cover the pan and cook for a further 2 minutes, or until the centers are almost set (smooth on top but still slightly jiggly underneath). Uncover the pan and top each pancake with either a little scallion (spring onion) or some corn kernels, cover with the lid and cook for 1 minute more. Remove from the pan with a spoon or small, thin-bladed metal spatula, and put on a serving plate. Repeat until all the batter is used up.

Serve warm.

Egg Hoppers

**Preparation time: 10 minutes,
plus 3½ hours resting time
Cooking time: 10 minutes
Serves: 6**

2¼ teaspoons (7 g) active
    dry yeast
1¼ cups (200 g) rice flour
1½ tablespoons sugar
Sea salt
1¼ cups (10 fl oz/300 ml) full-fat
    coconut milk
1 teaspoon baking soda
    (bicarbonate of soda)
2 tablespoons sunflower oil
6 eggs
Freshly ground black pepper

Appam, or hoppers, are a Sri Lankan bowl-shaped yeast bread made with a rice flour batter. They have a very mild flavor and are usually served with spice-based dressings and with vegetable stews. There are many variations that add eggs, as here, or coconut milk or molasses (treacle) to the recipe, depending on traditions and personal tastes.

In a small bowl, dissolve the yeast in ½ cup (4 fl oz/120 ml) water and let it sit for 10 minutes to rehydrate (a few little foam spots will appear over the surface).

In a large bowl, combine the rice flour, sugar, and a pinch of salt. Pour in the yeast mixture and stir carefully.

Cover the bowl with plastic wrap (cling film) and set in a warm place to rest for 2½ hours.

Pour the coconut milk and baking soda (bicarbonate of soda) into the bowl, stir carefully, cover with plastic wrap again, and let it rest for 1 more hour.

Lightly grease a hopper pan (see Note) or small (8-inch/20 cm) wok with some of the oil and heat it over high heat. Reduce the heat to medium and pour one-sixth of the batter into the pan, swirling the pan to cover the bottom and up the sides. Cook for 3 minutes, or until the pancake edges are crispy and golden. Crack an egg into the center, season with salt and pepper, cover, and cook over low heat for 3 minutes. Slide the hopper onto a plate. Repeat to make 5 more hoppers with eggs.

Note: A hopper pan—also called an *appam* pan—is a round-bottomed pan used specifically for making hoppers.

Fresh Corn Cakes

Preparation time: 15 minutes, plus 30 minutes chilling time
Cooking time: 15 minutes
Serves: 4

3½ cups (1 lb 2 oz/500 g) fresh corn kernels
4 tablespoons masarepa (precooked cornmeal)
Generous ½ cup (4.2 fl oz/125 ml) milk
1 teaspoon sea salt
2 tablespoons sugar (optional)
2 eggs
1 tablespoon (15 g) unsalted butter, plus more for the pan
Savory fillings: grated cheese, diced ham, cooked vegetables
Sweet fillings: jam, marmalade, melted chocolate

Cachapas date back to pre-Columbian times, when corn was considered sacred, a gift from the gods. Today these breakfast corn cakes are sold as street food in Venezuela (and elsewhere in Latin America). They can be plain, as here, or stuffed with fresh cheese, ham, vegetables, or a sauce. Like crêpes, they can be sweet as well as savory.

In a blender, combine the corn kernels, cornmeal, milk, salt, and sugar (if making a sweet version) and blend to a creamy sauce. Add the eggs and butter and blend until everything is perfectly mixed. Transfer the mixture to a bowl, cover with plastic wrap (cling film), and refrigerate for 30 minutes to chill.
    Heat a crêpe pan over medium heat and grease it with a little butter. Add the corn mixture, 2 large tablespoons at a time, and gently press the mixture to make it a pancake ½ inch (1.25 cm) thick. Cook it until browned on both sides, 3–5 minutes per side. Repeat to make all the corn cakes.
    Serve the corn cakes folded over a filling of choice.

Steamed Rice and Coconut Balls

Preparation time: 15 minutes
Cooking time: 30 minutes
Makes: 20

8 oz (225 g) jaggery
1 tablespoon ghee
2 teaspoons ground cardamom
7 oz (200 g) unsweetened shredded (desiccated) coconut
1 teaspoon sesame oil
Sea salt
Scant 2 cups (300 g) rice flour

In India, *pidi kozhukattai* are traditionally prepared during the festivities dedicated to the god Ganesh: They are placed In front of his statue along with red flowers and petals, handfuls of rice, and various other sweets. The sweetener in this recipe is a type of sugar common to India called jaggery. The sugar, which has not had the molasses (treacle) separated out, comes in solid, moist blocks in various shades of brown.

In a saucepan, heat 1 cup (8 fl oz/240 ml) water. Add the jaggery and let it melt over medium heat. Strain the liquid through a fine-mesh sieve and return the syrup to the same pan.
    Stir in 1 cup (8 fl oz/240 ml) water, the ghee, cardamom, coconut, sesame oil, and salt to taste. Bring to a boil. Whisking constantly, add the rice flour bit by bit. Whisk until they are no lumps. Keep cooking until it detaches from the sides of the pot.
    Transfer the mixture to a bowl and let it cool. Knead once. Divide the mixture into 20 portions and roll into balls. Press a ball gently with your knuckles to make an elongated and ridged shape.
    Set up a steamer. Arrange the pressed balls in the steamer basket and steam until they turn shiny, about 10 minutes.

Rice Balls in Coconut Milk with Poached Eggs

**Preparation time: 1 hour,
    plus 1 hour drying time
Cooking time: 40 minutes
Serves: 6**

Generous 1½ cups (250 g)
    rice flour
Scant ⅔ cup (150 g) canned
    unsweetened pumpkin purée
5 oz (150 g) fresh pandan leaves
1 oz (25 g) dried butterfly
    pea flowers
5 oz (150 g) red dragon fruit
    (pitaya), peeled
12 oz (350 g) fresh coconut, half
    grated, half cut into thin strips
6¼ cups (50 fl oz/1.5 liters)
    full-fat coconut milk
1⅓ cups (250 g) superfine (caster)
    sugar
2 teaspoons sea salt
1¾ teaspoons agar-agar
6 eggs

Served as breakfast (and also dessert) in Thailand, these very popular sweets are called *bua loi*, which translates to "floating lotus." In fact the small rice balls that float in coconut milk are about the size of lotus seeds. The dish is very simple, but making it does take a fair amount of time to color and then roll all the little rice balls.

In a small bowl, combine 6 tablespoons of the rice flour with the pumpkin to make a dough. Pinch off small quantities and roll into balls the size of peas. Set the orange balls on a large tray to dry out.

In a small saucepan, combine 1 cup (8 fl oz/240 ml) water and the pandan leaves and bring to a boil. Cook for 10 minutes. Strain out the pandan leaves, add 6 tablespoons of the rice flour, and knead to make a dough. Roll little green balls the same way as for the orange balls and set them on the tray.

In a small saucepan, combine 1 cup (8 fl oz/240 ml) water and the butterfly pea flowers and bring to a boil. Cook for 10 minutes. Strain out the flowers, add 6 tablespoons of the rice flour, and knead to make a dough. Roll little blue balls the same way as for the orange and green balls and set them on the tray.

Push the dragon fruit through a sieve to remove the seeds. Mash the dragon fruit pulp with the remaining 6 tablespoons rice flour and knead to make a dough. Roll little red balls as for all the other colored balls and add to the tray. Let all the balls dry for 1 hour.

Meanwhile, in a heavy-bottomed frying pan, toast the grated coconut until light golden, about 3 minutes.

Set up a large bowl of ice and water. Bring a large pot of water to a boil over high heat. Working in batches of a few at a time, carefully add the balls to the boiling water. As soon as they float, remove them with a skimmer and transfer to the ice bath. Scoop out of the ice bath and drain well.

Meanwhile, in a pot, combine the coconut milk, ½ cup (4 fl oz/120 ml) water, the sugar, salt, and agar-agar and bring to a boil.

When all of the rice balls have been cooked, add them to the coconut milk and simmer over medium heat for 2 minutes. Break in the eggs, 1 at a time, and simmer for 4 minutes over medium heat to poach them.

Remove from the heat. Divide among bowls and serve topped with the coconut strips and toasted grated coconut.

Grilled Plantain with Palm Sugar Sauce

 (NF) (VT) (30) [5]

Preparation time: 5 minutes
Cooking time: 20 minutes
Serves: 5

4 tablespoons (60 g) unsalted
   butter
5 green plantains or 10 saba
   bananas, peeled
Generous ¾ cup (6½ fl oz/200 ml)
   full-fat coconut milk
¼ cup (80 g) palm sugar
5 makrut lime leaves, slivered
   (see Note)
Sea salt

Pisang bakar is a traditional Indonesian dish that is quick and easy to make. In Indonesia this would be made with a saba banana, which is a very starchy banana often called a cooking banana. Saba bananas are similar to plantains, which make a perfect substitute.

Preheat a grill (barbecue) to 390°F (200°C). Or preheat a grill pan/griddle pan over medium heat.

Brush butter on the plantains or bananas and lay them on the grill grates or grill pan. Grill, turning, until charred on all sides, about 20 minutes. The charring creates caramelization that enhances the sweet flavor of the plantains. (Alternatively, in a frying pan, melt the butter over medium heat. Add the plantains and fry until golden brown on both sides, about 5 minutes.)

Set aside on a serving plate.

In a saucepan, combine 3 tablespoons water, the coconut milk, sugar, makrut lime leaves, and some salt. Bring to a boil. Once all the palm sugar has melted, remove from the heat. Strain the mixture through a sieve into a small bowl.

Drizzle some palm sugar sauce on top of the grilled plantains and serve immediately.

Note: If you can't find makrut lime leaves, which add a nice herbaceous flavor to the sauce, use some grated lime zest.

Starters

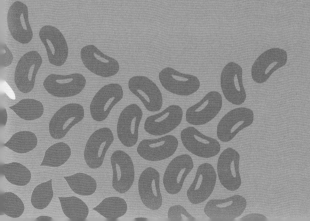

Guacamole with Homemade Tortilla Chips

Preparation time: 30 minutes
Cooking time: 30 minutes
Serves: 4

For the tortilla chips
¾ cup (6 fl oz/175 ml) sunflower oil
12 corn tortillas, store-bought
  or homemade (page 148) (see
  Note), each cut into triangles
Coarse salt

For the guacamole
2 tablespoons finely chopped
  onion
2 serrano chilies, seeded and
  very finely chopped, plus more
  for garnish
1 tablespoon minced fresh cilantro
  (coriander)
Fine sea salt
3 avocados, halved and pitted
¾ cup (135 g) finely chopped
  tomatoes, plus more
  for garnish

This much-beloved avocado dip has its origins in ancient Mexico, dating back to the time of the Aztecs. Its name in the Aztec language of Nahuatl is *ahuacamolli,* which is a combination of *ahuacatl,* meaning "avocado" (*aguacates* in Spanish), and *molli,* meaning "sauce" (*mole* in Spanish). The traditional method of preparing guacamole is in a *molcajete,* a large mortar often made of basalt—and many modern-day Mexican restaurants still do this, sometimes tableside. The secret of a good guacamole is definitely the use of perfectly ripe avocados, which should be soft, but not too soft, when you squeeze them gently.

Make the tortilla chips: Line a sheet pan with paper towels. In a frying pan, heat the oil over medium-high heat until very hot. Carefully drop a small piece of tortilla in the oil. If it sizzles, it is the right temperature.

Working in batches, carefully add a handful of tortilla wedges to the hot oil, turning them with tongs or a slotted spoon. Increase the heat to high and fry until the tortilla chips just begin to turn golden and firm, about 2 minutes. Move the chips to the paper towels using a metal slotted spoon.

Line a second sheet pan with paper towels. Reduce the heat under the frying pan to medium. Working in batches, cook the chips a second time until really crispy. Transfer the freshly fried chips to the fresh paper towels and sprinkle them with coarse salt.

Make the guacamole: In a large mortar (a *molcajete* if you have one), combine the onion, serranos, cilantro (coriander), and fine sea salt to taste. Grind with the pestle until you have a smooth paste. Scoop the avocado flesh into the mortar and grind until the mixture is still slightly chunky. Fold the tomatoes in with a fork. Add more sea salt to taste.

Serve the tortilla chips and guacamole in separate bowls, garnishing the guacamole with a little more serrano and tomato.

Note: You will get better results frying the tortilla chips if the tortillas are a bit dry and stale, so leave them out of their package overnight, exposed to air, or dry them out in the oven at 350°F (180°C/Gas Mark 4) for 5 minutes. They don't need to be crisp, just dry.

Baba Ghanoush

 Lebanon

Preparation time: 15 minutes
Cooking time: 45 minutes
Serves: 4

4 large eggplant (aubergines)
1½ tablespoons tahini
4 cloves garlic (or to taste), minced
Juice of ½ lemon
2 tablespoon extra-virgin olive oil
½ teaspoon crushed chili flakes
2 tablespoons finely chopped
   fresh parsley
Raw vegetables, such as carrot,
   cucumber, or bell pepper, cut
   into sticks for dipping
Sea salt

This Lebanese dish is often served as a sharing dish with many other small plates, or *mezze*, as they are known in Lebanon.

Position two oven racks, one in the bottom third and one in the top third of the oven, and preheat the oven to 400°F (200°C/Gas Mark 6).
   Cut a slit down the side of each eggplant (aubergine) and put them into a baking dish. Place the dish on the lower rack and roast until they are completely shrunken and soft, about 40 minutes.
   Move the baking dish to the upper rack for 5 minutes to char the skin of the eggplants. Set the eggplants aside to cool.
   When cool enough to handle, peel the eggplants (discard the skin) and put the flesh into a bowl. Mash it with a fork and stir in the tahini, garlic, and lemon juice.
   Spoon the baba ghanoush into a serving a bowl. Drizzle with the olive oil and garnish with chili flakes and parsley. Arrange the raw vegetable dippers in a cup next to the eggplant dip.

Eggplant and Yogurt Dip

Turkey

Preparation time: 10 minutes
Cooking time: 20 minutes
Serves: 4

4 Turkish orange eggplants
   (aubergines)
3 tablespoons Greek yogurt
1 clove garlic, minced
4 tablespoons extra-virgin olive
   oil, plus more for drizzling
1 teaspoon sea salt
Raw vegetables, such as radishes,
   cucumber, or bell pepper, cut
   into sticks and slices for dipping

This traditional Turkish starter combines eggplant (aubergine) with yogurt. It's best to use a thick yogurt, such as Greek yogurt, but if you don't have easy access to it, it's really simple to make your own (see Note).

Preheat an outdoor grill (barbecue) to 425°F (220°C).
   Pierce the eggplants a few times with a fork. Place them on the grill grates and cook until they are tender, about 20 minutes.
   As soon as they are cool enough to handle, scoop the eggplant flesh out of the skins into a bowl. Add the yogurt, garlic, olive oil, and salt and stir until smooth and soft. Let it cool for 10–15 minutes.
   Drizzle more olive oil over the eggplant and yogurt dip. Arrange the raw vegetable dippers in a cup next to the dip.

Note: Line a fine-mesh sieve with cheesecloth (muslin) or a coffee filter and set over a bowl. Spoon regular yogurt into the lined sieve and let it drain for 2 hours in the fridge. You should end up with about half the volume of yogurt as you started with.

Red Pepper Sauce

(DF) (NF) (VG) (VT)

Serbia

**Preparation time: 20 minutes,
plus chilling time
Cooking time: 1 hour 15 minutes
Serves: 6**

4 sweet red horn peppers
    or cubanelles
2 eggplants (aubergines),
    halved lengthwise
Coarse sea salt
4 tablespoons extra-virgin olive oil
1 onion, finely sliced
2 cloves garlic, chopped
1 dried red chili
Serbian Corn Bread (page 143),
    for serving

Ajvar is a Serbian relish/sauce. It can be served as spread for
an appetizer, or it can be served as a condiment for meat.
The ideal variety of pepper for this sauce is a *roga* pepper, aka
horn pepper (*roga* means "horn" in Serbian) or Florina pepper.
Ajvar is often prepared in fall (autumn) when the peppers are
harvested, then stored in vacuum-sealed jars to be enjoyed
in the following months.

Preheat the oven to 400°F (200°C/Gas Mark 6).

Place the peppers on a sheet pan and roast until they are
well charred, about 20 minutes. Transfer to a bowl, cover, and set
aside to steam. Gently remove the charred skin and the seeds
from the peppers, chop the flesh and set aside in a bowl.

Meanwhile, place the eggplants (aubergines) on the sheet
pan cut-side up. Sprinkle them with coarse salt and drizzle with
1 tablespoon of the oil, then roast until the center is really soft,
about 30 minutes.

When cool enough to handle, peel the eggplants, cut the
flesh into small cubes, and add to the bowl of peppers.

In a frying pan, heat the remaining 3 tablespoons oil over
medium heat. Add the onion, garlic, and dried chili pepper and
sauté until the onions soften, about 5 minutes.

Carefully stir the pepper/eggplant mixture into the frying
pan and add ½ cup (4 fl oz/120 ml) water. Simmer over low heat,
stirring frequently, until the peppers soften, about 25 minutes;
add water if the mixture dries out.

Remove from the heat and transfer to a food processor.
Pulse to coarsely chop. Refrigerate until chilled. Serve with corn
bread for spreading.

Hummus

**Preparation time: 20 minutes,
  plus overnight soaking time
Cooking time: 1 hour 5 minutes
Serves: 4**

¾ cup plus 2 tablespoons
  (6 oz/175 g) dried chickpeas,
  soaked overnight in cold water
2 cloves garlic (or to taste), peeled
⅓ cup (80 g) tahini
½ cup (4 fl oz/120 ml) fresh
  lemon juice
3 tablespoons extra-virgin olive
  oil, plus more for drizzling
½ teaspoon ground cumin
Sea salt and freshly ground
  black pepper
Raw vegetables, such as carrot,
  cucumber, or bell pepper,
  cut into thin sticks for dipping

Optional add-ins (one or both)
2 tablespoons pine nuts, toasted
2 tablespoons chopped fresh
  parsley and/or cilantro
  (coriander)

Hummus is a vital part of Middle Eastern cuisine, and here we present the Israeli version of this iconic dip. Hummus can be served any time of day, at breakfast, lunch, and dinner. Combined with raw veggies it is a healthy starter, side dish, or snack. It can bring together people with all kinds of allergies or food traditions, since it is vegan, gluten-free, dairy-free, and nut-free. For an even smoother (and some say more digestible) dish, you can peel the cooked chickpeas—a time-consuming labor of love.

Drain and rinse the chickpeas. In a small saucepan, combine the chickpeas and cold water to cover. Bring to a boil, then reduce to a high simmer and cook until soft, about 1 hour. Add hot water as necessary to keep the chickpeas submerged as they cook.

Reserving the cooking liquid, drain the chickpeas. In a food processor (or in a mortar), combine the chickpeas, garlic, tahini, lemon juice, olive oil, cumin, and salt and pepper to taste. Add at least ½ cup (4 fl oz/120 ml) of the reserved cooking liquid and process (mash) until you obtain a thick paste. Add more cooking liquid if needed.

To serve, spoon the hummus into a deep plate or a bowl. Drizzle with olive oil. If desired, sprinkle with pine nuts and/or fresh herbs. Place the vegetables dippers in a cup and serve alongside the hummus.

Liver Pâté

Preparation time: 30 minutes, plus 1 hour resting and chilling time
Cooking time: 1 hour
Serves: 4

6 oz (175 g) pork liver, chopped
3 oz (80 g) fatback (pork back fat), chopped
1 onion, finely chopped
½ cup (4 fl oz/120 ml) milk
1 egg
1 tablespoon cornstarch (cornflour) or potato starch
2 oil-packed anchovy fillets, drained and finely chopped
½ tablespoon sea salt
Freshly ground black pepper
8 oz (220 g) pickles, for serving
2 tablespoons apricot preserve, for serving

Leverpostej is a traditional pâté from Denmark, where it was introduced in the mid-nineteenth century by a Frenchman named François Louis Beauvais, who had opened a butcher store in Copenhagen. At that time pâté was considered an expensive luxury, but today it is widely available. It is usually sold in aluminum pans that can go straight into the oven to be warmed up. It is often accompanied by onions or pickles.

Preheat the oven to 300°F (150°C/Gas Mark 4).

In a bowl, combine the pork liver, fatback (pork back fat), onion, milk, egg, cornstarch (cornflour), anchovies, salt, and black pepper to taste. Mix carefully and pour the mixture into a 9 × 5-inch (23 × 13 cm) loaf pan.

Place the loaf pan in a larger pan (like a roasting pan) and pour in hot water to come 2½ inches (6 cm) up the sides of the pan. Slide into the oven and bake until the center reaches 158°F (70°C) on an instant-read thermometer, about 1 hour.

Let it rest for 20 minutes, then transfer to the fridge for 40 minutes to chill.

Serve cool with pickles and apricot preserve.

Potato Cheese Spread

Preparation time: 10 minutes
Cooking time: 40 minutes
Serves: 4

Sea salt
14 oz (400 g) yellow potatoes
7 oz (200 g) quark cheese, fromage blanc, or Camembert
Generous ¾ cup (150 g) sour cream
2 small onions, thinly sliced
Minced fresh chives
Minced fresh dill
Freshly ground black pepper

Though typical of Bavaria in southern Germany, this dish is served all around the country as well as in Austria and Switzerland as a tasty and creamy appetizer, a midafternoon snack, or a traditional Sunday side dish. In some recipes for *Kartoffelkäse*, only sour cream is used, not a combination of quark and sour cream, as here. The spread can also be seasoned with other herbs and spices, such cumin or garlic.

In a large pot of salted boiling water, cook the potatoes until tender, about 35 minutes. Drain.

When cool enough to handle, peel the potatoes, transfer to a bowl, and mash them. Add the quark and sour cream and gently combine. Stir in the onions and season generously with chives, dill, salt, and pepper. Serve.

Spicy Lima Beans
with Yogurt and Tomatoes

**Preparation time: 20 minutes,
  plus overnight soaking time
Cooking time: 1 hour 15 minutes
Serves: 4**

1 lb (450 g) dried lima beans
  (butter beans), soaked in salted
  warm water overnight, drained,
  and rinsed
4 tablespoons canola
  (rapeseed) oil
1½ teaspoons garlic powder
1 teaspoon ground cumin
1 teaspoon ground coriander
1 teaspoon ground ginger
½ tablespoon black peppercorns,
  crushed
⅓ onion, minced
Juice of ½ lemon
Sea salt
1 tomato, diced, for serving
1 jalapeño, minced, for serving
Plain yogurt, for serving

Whereas the well-known Egyptian dish *ful medames* is made with fava beans, their Eritrean neighbors have a version made with lima beans (butter beans) called *shahan ful*. It is generally served for breakfast because it can give you the energy you need for the day, and is very popular during Ramadan and Lent. Tomatoes, onions, and peppers give freshness to this dish.

In a Dutch oven (casserole), combine the soaked beans and water to cover. Bring to a boil over medium-high heat, then reduce to a simmer and cook until firm-tender, about 1 hour.

In a soup pot, heat the oil over medium heat. Add the garlic powder, cumin, coriander, ginger, and peppercorns and cook for 10 seconds. Add the onion and cook until translucent, 3–4 minutes. Add the lemon juice and beans. Toss to coat the beans with the spices. Season with salt and simmer until the beans are very soft, about 10 minutes longer. Mash the beans with a potato masher to a chunky purée.

To serve, spoon the beans onto a serving dish. Top with the tomato and jalapeño and a few spoons of yogurt.

Stewed Fava Beans

Preparation time: 30 minutes, plus overnight soaking time and 10 minutes resting time
Cooking time: 1 hour 5 minutes
Serves: 4

1⅓ cups (300 g) dried fava beans (broad beans), soaked in water overnight, drained, and rinsed
Pinch of ground cumin
Sea salt and freshly ground black pepper
1 green chili pepper, stemmed
2 cloves garlic, smashed and peeled
Juice of 1 lemon
½ scallion (spring onion), thinly sliced
½ cup (4 fl oz/120 ml) extra-virgin olive oil
2 tomatoes, peeled, seeded, and diced

Ful medames is a stew made of fava beans (broad beans), a staple food that is very popular all across the Middle East. This dish is often served as a Friday morning breakfast, the day of worship and the first day of the weekend for Muslims.

In a large pot of boiling water, cook the soaked beans until tender and soft, about 1 hour. Reserving the cooking liquid, drain the beans.

Transfer the beans to a saucepan with ½ cup (4 fl oz/120 ml) of the reserved cooking water. Bring to a simmer over medium-high heat and cook for 5 minutes. Remove from the heat, season with the cumin and salt and pepper to taste, then mash the mixture with a potato masher or with a fork.

Put the chili and garlic in a mortar and smash them. In a bowl, combine the chili/garlic mixture, lemon juice, and scallion (spring onion) and mix well. Let the sauce rest for 10 minutes.

Place the beans in a bowl and gently stir in the chili/lemon sauce and oil. Serve topped with the tomatoes.

Crispy Yuca Fritters

Dominican Republic

Preparation time: 5 minutes
Cooking time: 15 minutes
Serves: 4

1 lb 2 oz (500 g) yuca (cassava)
   root, peeled and grated
   (see Note, page 20)
2 eggs
3 tablespoons coconut sugar
1 tablespoon aniseed
Sea salt
Sunflower oil, for frying

These fried anise-flavored yuca (cassava) cakes, called *arepitas de yuca*, are a typical Dominican treat, and their main ingredient is yuca grated on the large holes of a box grater. Yuca, which is grown mainly in tropical, African, and Asian countries, is rich in complex carbohydrates and is a great and inexpensive source of energy.

Wrap the yuca (cassava) in a tea towel and squeeze to remove moisture. Transfer to a large bowl and add the eggs, sugar, aniseed, and salt to taste and mix gently until fully combined.

Line a plate with paper towels. In a large deep heavy-bottomed pot, heat 3 inches (8 cm) oil. Scoop up some of the mixture with a spoon and use a second spoon to make quenelles. Add them to the hot oil and cook until golden brown, 3–4 minutes. Drain them on the paper towels.

Serve immediately.

Yuca Fritters Stuffed with Meat and Cheese

Preparation time: 1 hour
Cooking time: 15 minutes
Serves: 6

1½ lb (680 g) yuca (cassava)
　　root, peeled and cubed
　　(see Note, page 20)
Sea salt
2 tablespoons (30 g) unsalted
　　butter
4 eggs
⅔ cup (85 g) cornmeal, or more
　　as needed
2 tablespoons extra-virgin olive oil
1 onion, cut into chunks
½ red bell pepper, cut into chunks
1 clove garlic, chopped
1 scallion (spring onion), chopped
11 oz (310 g) lean ground
　　(minced) beef
3 tablespoons passata
　　(unseasoned tomato sauce)
Freshly ground black pepper
4 oz (120 g) cheddar cheese,
　　coarsely shredded
Sunflower oil, for frying
Ground ají or chili powder,
　　for garnish

A typical Panamanian snack food, *carimañolas* are meat-stuffed pastries made with a yuca (cassava) dough. Popular throughout Latin America, the pastries can also be served for breakfast, often accompanied with *suero*, a dairy product similar to yogurt. There is also a vegetarian version that is stuffed with string cheese.

In a large pot, combine the yuca (cassava) and cold water to cover. Bring to a boil, salt the water, reduce the heat, and simmer until soft, about 20 minutes.

Drain the yuca, discard the hard central "cord," and mash it in a bowl with a fork or potato masher. Stir in the butter. Add the eggs, one at a time, stirring constantly. Add the cornmeal and work it in to form a stiff, compact, but workable dough. Add more cornmeal if needed. Cover the bowl with plastic wrap (cling film) and let cool.

In a large frying pan, heat the oil over high heat. Add the onion and bell pepper and cook until the peppers are crisp-tender, about 2 minutes. Add the garlic and scallion (spring onion) and stir for 1 minute.

Add the meat to the pan and stir for 2 minutes, then reduce the heat and simmer for 8 minutes. Pour in the tomato sauce and season with 1 teaspoon salt and black pepper to taste. Simmer for 2 minutes more. Remove from the heat and let cool.

Divide the yuca dough into 12 portions and roll each into a ball. With one finger, dig a little hole in the center of each ball and fill it with the meat mixture and 1 tablespoon cheddar. Gently seal the yuca ball and form it into an oval shape.

Pour 7 inches (18 cm) oil into a large Dutch oven (casserole) and heat to 350°F (175°C) on a deep-fry thermometer.

Working in batches, fry the *carimañolas*, turning them often, until golden brown, 3–4 minutes. Drain them on paper towels, dust with ají or chili powder, and serve.

Egyptian Falafel

**Preparation time: 30 minutes,
plus overnight soaking time
Cooking time: 20 minutes
Serves: 10**

1 lb 5 oz (600 g) dried split fava
    beans (broad beans), soaked
    in warm salted water overnight
1 red onion, quartered
2 oz (50 g) fresh parsley
2 oz (50 g) fresh cilantro
    (coriander)
2 oz (50 g) fresh dill
3 cloves garlic, peeled
1½ teaspoons ground coriander
1½ teaspoons salt
1 teaspoon ground cumin
1 cup (145 g) sesame seeds,
    toasted (optional)
Sunflower oil, for deep-frying

Egyptian falafel, *ta'ameya*, is made with fava beans (broad beans) instead of chickpeas—as in Israeli Falafel (page 48), which is the more well-known version outside the Middle East. There are some who consider the Egyptian version to be the original falafel. *Ta'ameya* can be served with tomatoes, sliced onion, and tahini sauce.

Drain the beans. Transfer to a food processor and add the onion, parsley, cilantro (coriander), dill, garlic, ground coriander, salt, and cumin. Pulse until you get a dough-like consistency.

Roll small amounts of the dough into balls. If using sesame seeds, roll the balls in the seeds to coat.

Pour 3 inches (8 cm) oil into a large deep saucepan and heat over medium heat until very hot.

Working in batches, add the falafel to the oil and fry until golden brown, about 3 minutes. Drain the falafel on paper towels.

Serve the falafel in a bowl.

Israeli Falafel

**Preparation time: 15 minutes,
plus overnight soaking and
1–2 hours chilling time
Cooking time: 20 minutes
Serves: 6**

1 lb (450 g) dried chickpeas
1 small onion, roughly chopped
3 cloves garlic, peeled
4 tablespoons chopped fresh
   parsley
1½ tablespoons chickpea
   (gram) flour
2 teaspoons ground cumin
1 teaspoon ground coriander
¼ teaspoon cayenne pepper
Pinch of ground cardamom
Sea salt and freshly ground
   black pepper
Sunflower oil, for deep-frying
Hummus (page 40), for serving

A world-famous street food, falafel was originally made with fava beans (broad beans) and in some countries, such as Egypt (page 47), it still is. However, in Israel falafel is made with chickpeas. Falafel, like any other fried food, is best served hot, freshly prepared.

In a bowl, combine the chickpeas and cold water to cover by 3 inches (7.5 cm). Let soak overnight or until doubled in size.

Drain the chickpeas and transfer to a food processor along with the onion, garlic, parsley, chickpea (gram) flour, cumin, ground coriander, cayenne, cardamom, and salt and black pepper to taste. Pulse until it's half paste, half small chunks. Pour the mixture into a bowl. Cover with plastic wrap (cling film) and refrigerate for at least 1 hour and up to 2 hours.

Pour 1½ inches (4 cm) oil into a deep heavy-bottomed pot and heat over medium heat.

With wet hands, roll small portions of the falafel mixture into balls. Be careful because the balls are delicate and there is a risk that they will stick to one another.

Working in batches, fry the falafel until they are browned, 2 to 3 minutes. It they brown too fast it means the oil is too hot. Drain the falafel on paper towels.

Serve hot with hummus on the side.

Fried Lentil Snacks

**Preparation time: 10 minutes,
    plus 6 hours soaking time
Cooking time: 10 minutes
Serves: 4**

11 oz/300 g split yellow lentils,
    soaked in cold water for 6 hours
1 onion, finely chopped
2 green chilies, finely chopped
½ bunch fresh cilantro (coriander)
    leaves, finely chopped
½ teaspoon ground turmeric
Sea salt
1½ cups (12 fl oz/355 ml)
    mustard oil
Spicy chutney, to serve

Traditionally *phulaura* are made by soaking urad dal—small black beans similar to mung beans (and often mislabeled black lentils)—overnight and then peeling them by hand. To speed up this lengthy process, this recipe uses already peeled split yellow lentils. The batter can be made ahead and stored in an airtight container in the fridge for up to 3 days. These snacks are best served hot and can be paired with a spicy chutney, but they are also great on their own.

Drain the lentils and put them in a food processor. Blend to a smooth thick paste. Add a little water if necessary. Add the onion, chilies, cilantro (coriander), turmeric, and salt to taste and blend to combine.

In a wok, heat the oil over high heat.

Working in batches, drop 1-tablespoon quantities of the batter into the hot oil and fry until golden brown, about 2 minutes. Drain on paper towels.

Serve with spicy chutney.

Shepherd's Bulz

Preparation time: 20 minutes
Cooking time: 45 minutes
Serves: 6

1 tablespoon sea salt
1¾ cups plus 2 tablespoons
  (250 g) mamaliga (polenta)
2 tablespoons (30 g) unsalted
  butter
6 (1½-inch/4 cm) cubes kashkaval,
  pecorino, or your favorite
  hard cheese

This is a traditional dish from the mountainous regions of Romania. Simple and tasty, *bulz* are balls made of *mamaliga* (polenta) and cheese, baked over an open fire or in the oven. The cheese used in Romania is kashkaval, a hard cheese made with sheep, cow, or mixed milk. A good substitute would be Italian pecorino, which, when it melts, does not ooze out of the *bulz*.

In a saucepan, bring a scant 3½ cups (27 fl oz/800 ml) water and the salt to a boil. Whisking constantly to avoid lumps, slowly pour in the mamaliga and cook until the mixture is very thick and detaches from the sides of the pan, about 25 minutes. Pour it into a bowl and let it cool enough to handle.

Preheat the oven to 400°F (200°C/Gas Mark 6). Line a sheet pan with parchment paper.

Scoop some polenta mixture, the size of an apple, and roll it into a ball. Dig a cavity into it with your finger and fill it with 1 teaspoon butter and a cube of cheese. Press firmly to close over the filling and reform into a ball. Place on the lined sheet pan. Repeat with the rest of the polenta.

Bake the balls until they are browned, 15–20 minutes.

Vegetable Pakoras with Mango Chutney

(DF) (NF) (VG) (VT) **India**

Preparation time: 40 minutes
Cooking time: 2 hours
Serves: 4

For the mango chutney
1 tablespoon sunflower oil
2 teaspoons finely minced
    fresh ginger
1 clove garlic, finely minced
1 fresh red chili, sliced
2 teaspoons nigella seeds
1 teaspoon ground coriander
½ teaspoon ground cumin
¼ teaspoon ground cardamom
¼ teaspoon ground cinnamon
¼ teaspoon ground cloves
¼ teaspoon ground turmeric
1½ cups (300 g) diced
    fresh mango
½ cup (120 g) light brown sugar
¼ teaspoon sea salt
⅔ cup (2 fl oz/70 ml) distilled
    white vinegar

For the pakora
Sea salt
2 medium yellow potatoes
2 cups (500 g) chickpea
    (gram) flour
½ cup (4 fl oz/120 ml)
    sparkling water
1 tablespoon baking soda
    (bicarbonate of soda)
Juice of ½ lemon
1 teaspoon chili powder
1 tablespoon ground coriander
5 oz (150 g) green beans,
    cut into long strips
1 onion, cut into small chunks
4 oz (120 g) spinach leaves,
    shredded
1 red bell pepper, cut into
    thin strips
1⅓ cups (200 g) drained
    canned corn
2 tablespoons garam masala
Corn oil, for deep-frying

These fritters, crunchy on the outside and tender on the inside, are easy to prepare. The batter for the fritters is spiced with garam masala: a spice blend widely used in India, typically including cinnamon, coriander, cumin, peppercorns, and cardamom. Mango chutney is an Indian classic and makes a great condiment for these snacks. Of course you can use store-bought, but this freshly made chutney is worth the extra effort.

Make the mango chutney: In a soup pot, heat the oil over medium-high heat. Add the ginger, garlic, and red chili and sauté for 1 minute. Add the nigella, ground coriander, cumin, cardamom, cinnamon, cloves, and turmeric and sauté for 1 minute. Add the mango, brown sugar, salt, and vinegar and bring to a boil, stirring. Reduce the heat to medium-low and simmer until the mango is very soft, about 1 hour. Allow the mixture to cool. Use a fork or potato masher to create a smoother chutney. Leave some small chunks of mango.

Make the pakora: In a medium pot of boiling salted water, cook the potatoes until tender, about 30 minutes. When cool enough to handle, peel the potatoes and cut into cubes.

In a large bowl, combine the chickpea (gram) flour, sparkling water, baking soda (bicarbonate of soda), lemon juice, chili powder, and ground coriander and whisk carefully until the batter is silky. Add the potato cubes, green beans, onion, spinach, bell pepper, and corn. Add the garam masala, mix thoroughly, and let it rest for 15 minutes.

Pour 3 inches (8 cm) oil into a deep frying pan and heat over medium-high heat.

Working in batches, ladle in ¼-cup (2 fl oz/60 ml) amounts of the mixture to the hot oil and fry until golden brown, about 3 minutes. Drain on paper towels and season with salt.

Serve hot or warm with the chutney.

Note: To preserve the chutney, pour it into sterilized jars. It will last in the fridge for 2 months.

Corn with Butter and Salt

Preparation time: 10 minutes
Cooking time: 20 minutes
Serves: 4

4 ears corn, husked
4 tablespoons (60 g)
  unsalted butter
Sea salt

In Peru, this very simple recipe is called *choclos con manteca y sal* (literally, "corn with butter and salt"), but it is also popular in many other countries. The corn can be boiled instead of steamed, adding a few drops of lemon juice to the cooking water to preserve the beautiful yellow color of the corn. There are also variations in which the corn is briefly oven-broiled (grilled) for 5 minutes to caramelize them.

Cook the corn in a steamer for 20 minutes. Set them, still hot, on a serving plate and place 1 tablespoon butter over each one to melt. Serve immediately. Set a pot of sea salt on the table for diners to season their own corn.

Asinan Jakarta

Preparation time: 40 minutes,
  plus 20 minutes resting time
Serves: 4

12 oz (350 g) cabbage, shredded
2 oz (50 g) alfalfa sprouts, rinsed
7 oz (200 g) cucumber, sliced
2 carrots, cut into matchsticks
4 lettuce leaves, shredded
3 oz (80 g) tofu, cubed
2 cloves garlic, sliced
3 fresh red chilies, seeded
  and thinly sliced
Generous ½ cup (80 g) roasted
  peanuts
3 tablespoons coconut sugar
1 tablespoon tamarind
  concentrate
1 teaspoon cayenne pepper
1 cup (8 fl oz/240 ml) vegetable
  stock
Sea salt, to taste

Asinan are Indonesian pickled vegetables or fruits; the name comes from the word *asin,* which means "salty" and is a reference to the salt brine used as a preservative. This type of *asinan*, called *betawi,* is made with a variety of vegetables tossed in a sweet, salty, and spicy dressing.

In a large bowl, combine all the ingredients, adding them in the order listed. Mix carefully. Let rest for 20 minutes before serving.

Catalan Roasted Vegetables

(DF) (NF) (VG) (VT)   **Spain**

Preparation time: 30 minutes
Cooking time: 50 minutes
Serves: 4

½ cup (4 fl oz/120 ml) extra-virgin
  olive oil
3 medium yellow potatoes,
  halved lengthwise
3 onions, peeled and halved
  through the equator
2 red bell peppers, cut into
  wide strips
2 small eggplants (aubergines),
  cut into slices and then
  into strips
3 tomatoes, halved through
  the equator
Juice of 1½ lemons
Sea salt and freshly ground
  black pepper

A perfect vegetarian appetizer, this Catalan dish can also be served as a side dish with meats or fish. Its name, *escalivada*, derives from the Catalan verb *escalivar*, which means "cooked in ashes," which is the traditional way the vegetables were roasted for this. Here, for convenience, the vegetables are roasted in the oven, but you can also cook them over a charcoal fire. The dish should be served at room temperature and goes perfectly with anchovy fillets and goat cheese.

Preheat the oven to 350°F (180°C/Gas Mark 4). Grease a sheet pan with 2 tablespoons of the olive oil.

Arrange the potatoes cut-side down in the pan and bake for 15 minutes.

Remove the pan from the oven and add the onions cut-side down. Return to the oven and bake for 5 more minutes.

Remove the pan from the oven and add the bell peppers and eggplants (aubergines). Sprinkle with 2 tablespoons of the oil. Return to the oven and bake for 20 minutes.

Remove the pan from the oven and add the tomatoes to the pan cut-side down. Turn the eggplants and peppers over. Return to the oven and bake until the peppers are soft and browned, 10–12 minutes longer.

In a small bowl, stir together the remaining 4 tablespoons olive oil and the lemon juice. Transfer the vegetables to a serving plate, dress with the oil/lemon juice mixture, and season to taste with salt and black pepper.

Baked Tamales with Fresh Corn

Preparation time: 45 minutes
Cooking time: 1 hour 15 minutes
Serves: 6

3¾ sticks plus 3 tablespoons
    (455 g) unsalted butter
8 large ears corn, unhusked
2 eggs
2 oz (50 g) fresh ají amarillo
    chilies, minced
4 tablespoons superfine
    (caster) sugar
4 tablespoons raisins
½ teaspoon ground aniseed
Sea salt
14 oz (400 g) Bolivian melting
    cheese, sliced, plus 12 cubes
    (1 inch/2.5 cm)

Bolivian baked tamales, called *humintas al horno*, are typically served with a cup of coffee or tea as a snack, though they could also be an appetizer or main course. Unlike Mexican tamales, the dough here is made with fresh corn kernels and the *humintas* are wrapped in fresh corn husks. They are served with a piece of cheese-topped corn bread made with the same dough as used in the stuffing.

In a saucepan, melt 3¾ sticks (15 oz/360 g) of the butter over low heat. Let cool slightly.

Husk the corn and set aside 12 of the largest leaves. Cut the kernels off the cobs and measure out a scant 7 cups (1 kg) of the corn (save any remainder for another use). In a large pot of boiling water, cook the corn until very tender, about 25 minutes.

Drain the corn, very finely chop, and place in a large bowl. Add the eggs and cooled melted butter and stir.

In a frying pan, heat 1 tablespoon of the butter. Add the ají amarillo and cook until softened, 3–4 minutes. Add the chilies to the corn along with the sugar, raisins, aniseed, and salt to taste and mix vigorously until the dough seems spongy.

Preheat the oven to 350°F (180°C/Gas Mark 4). Use 1 tablespoon of the butter to grease a 12-inch (25 cm) square baking dish.

Spread three-quarters of the dough into the greased baking dish and place the cheese slices on top. Bake until golden brown, about 30 minutes. Leave the oven on.

Meanwhile, grease a baking pan with the remaining 1 tablespoon butter. Fill each corn husk with 2 tablespoons of the remaining dough and place a cheese cube in each one. Fold the leaf over and seal the edges. Place the packets in the prepared baking pan and bake until the corn husks change color from light green to gold, about 30 minutes.

Cut the corn bread into squares. Serve a square of corn bread with 1 or 2 humintas.

Steamed Banana Packets

 Malaysia

Preparation time: 20 minutes, plus 30 minutes soaking time
Cooking time: 20 minutes
Serves: 4

3 medium bananas, sliced crosswise
3 tablespoons superfine (caster) sugar
2 tablespoons full-fat coconut milk
3 tablespoons cornstarch (cornflour)
4 banana leaf squares (12 × 12 inches/30 × 30 cm), soaked in warm water for 5 minutes
2 tablespoons grated fresh coconut, for serving

These steamed banana packets, known as *lepat pisang*, are made by wrapping and folding banana leaves around a banana filling. In Malaysia there are different types of *lepat*, made from yuca (cassava) or corn in addition to the more common banana.

In a food processor, combine the bananas, sugar, coconut milk, and cornstarch (cornflour) and process until the mixture is thick and soft.

Place the banana leaves on a work surface and fill each one with ½ cup (120 g) of the banana mixture. Wrap the leaves into packets.

Set up a steamer and steam the packets until firm, about 20 minutes.

Serve warm, topped with the grated coconut.

Fried Green Plantains

 Costa Rica

Preparation time: 10 minutes
Cooking time: 1 hour
Serves: 4

4 green plantains, peeled and halved lengthwise
Sunflower oil, for frying
Ground chili powder
Sea salt

Fried green plantains are known in Costa Rica as *patacónes* or in other Latin American countries as *tostones*. Plantains can be cooked at various stages during their ripening process, starting with the very starchy and firm green plantains. As they ripen, they get softer and sweeter, and their skin turns from green to yellow to black. Though much sweeter than green, the sweet plantains, called *maduros*, are not as sweet as bananas. These fritters are best served with a dip, such as guacamole (page 36), or a sweet-and-sour dipping sauce.

In a large pot, combine the plantains with water to cover. Bring to a boil and cook until the plantains are soft, about 40 minutes. Remove the pot from the heat and let the plantains cool in the cooking liquid.

Pour 3 inches (8 cm) oil into a Dutch oven (casserole) and heat over high heat.

Drain the plantains, cut them into thick slices, and carefully flatten them with a meat mallet, trying not to smash them completely apart.

Season the slices with chili powder and salt and add to the hot oil. Fry the plantain slices until golden and crispy on both sides, about 3 minutes. Drain on paper towels.

Serve hot.

Stuffed Shiitake Mushrooms

**Preparation time: 20 minutes,
plus 30 minutes draining time**
Cooking time: 10 minutes
Serves: 4

1½ oz (40 g) tofu
8 large fresh shiitake mushrooms
3 oz (80 g) ground (minced) beef
1 scallion (spring onion), chopped
2 cloves garlic, chopped
3 tablespoons sesame oil
2 tablespoons tamari
1 tablespoon cider vinegar
1 tablespoon cane sugar
Sea salt and freshly ground
    black pepper
4 tablespoons rice flour
Generous ¾ cup (7 fl oz/205 ml)
    rice bran oil
2 eggs

In Korea these stuffed mushrooms belong to a category called *banchan*, which are small dishes that are served as appetizers or condiments at pretty much every Korean meal. *Pyogo jeon*, as these mushrooms are called, are very popular during Korean holidays, in particular at Chuseok (the harvest festival) and on Seollal (Korean New Year).

To remove excess liquid from the tofu, set the tofu in a sieve set over a bowl and let drain for 30 minutes.

Remove the mushroom stems and set aside. Carve a light star or cross or flower on the surface of the mushroom cap with a knife. Reserve the scraps from carving and dice them with the stems. Put them in a bowl.

Finely dice the tofu and add to the bowl, along with the beef, scallion (spring onion), garlic, sesame oil, tamari, vinegar, sugar, and salt and pepper to taste. Knead until all the ingredients are fully combined.

Place the mushrooms stemmed-side up on a plate. Sprinkle 2 tablespoons of the rice flour over the mushrooms and fill the cavities with the tofu/beef stuffing. Sprinkle with the remaining 2 tablespoons flour.

In a frying pan, heat the oil over medium heat.

Meanwhile, break the eggs into a bowl and beat them. Once the oil is hot, take the mushroom caps, one at a time, and dip the stuffed side into the eggs. Add them to the hot oil and fry for 2 minutes. Flip them over and fry on the second side until the meat is well browned, 1–2 minutes.

Serve hot.

Dolmades

Preparation time: 20 minutes
Cooking time: 50 minutes
Serves: 4

24 jarred grape (vine) leaves,
    rinsed, plus more for lining
    the pot
3 tablespoons extra-virgin olive oil
½ cup (100 g) basmati rice
1 clove garlic, minced
3½ oz (100 g) ground
    (minced) veal
1 tablespoon minced fresh mint
1 tablespoon minced fresh thyme
1 tablespoon minced fresh dill
1 tablespoon minced fresh parsley
½ onion, minced
Sea salt and freshly ground
    black pepper
1 tablespoon (15 g) unsalted
    butter, melted
Generous 1 cup (17 fl oz/500 ml)
    vegetable stock, hot,
    plus more as needed

Dolmades are stuffed grape (vine) leaves and are typically part of the Greek collection of appetizers called *mezedes*. Also known as dolmas, a version of these stuffed leaves can be found all over Turkey, the Balkans, and Armenia, as well as other parts of the Mediterranean. Food wrapped in grape leaves is a tradition that dates to the ancient Greeks. Dolmades can be stuffed simply with seasoned rice or can include meat, as here.

In a large pot, bring 4 cups (32 fl oz/950 ml) water to a boil over medium heat. Reduce the heat to low and add the grape (vine) leaves. Simmer for 5 minutes, then drain well and spread them out on a cloth.

In a large frying pan, heat the oil over medium heat. Add the rice and garlic and cook until the rice is toasted, about 3 minutes. Add the veal and cook, breaking the meat up with a spoon, until browned, about 10 minutes. Add the herbs and onion and season to taste with salt and pepper. Cook until the meat is lightly browned and the juices have evaporated, about 10 minutes. Let the mixture cool slightly.

Place a grape leaf on a work surface with the vein-side up and the stem facing you. Put 1 tablespoon of the stuffing in the center of each leaf, roll the bottom up and over the filling, then fold in the sides and continue rolling up the leaf to form a tight cylindrical roll. Repeat to fill the remaining grape leaves.

Put some grape leaves on the bottom of a 10-inch (25 cm) wide pot and pack the rolls in tightly, stacking them on a second row if necessary. Pour the melted butter and vegetable stock over the rolls until they are fully covered. Cover with a lid and cook over low heat until the stock has been fully absorbed and the rice is tender, about 40 minutes.

Place the dolmades on a serving dish and let them cool for 5 minutes before serving.

Rice-Stuffed Zucchini

 (DF) (NF) (VG) (VT)

Egypt

Preparation time: 30 minutes
Cooking time: 30 minutes
Serves: 4

1½ tablespoons sunflower oil
2 onions—1 chopped, 1 thickly
   sliced
½ cup (4 fl oz/120 ml) passata
   (unseasoned tomato sauce)
½ teaspoon ground cinnamon
¼ teaspoon ground allspice
Sea salt and freshly ground
   black pepper
1¼ cups (250 g) short-grain
   white rice
½ oz (10 g) fresh parsley, chopped
½ oz (10 g) fresh cilantro
   (coriander), chopped
½ oz (10 g) fresh dill, chopped
8 zucchini (courgettes)
5 cups (40 fl oz/1.2 liters)
   vegetable stock or water

Mahshi are vegetables that are hollowed out and filled with a rice stuffing. In Egypt, the typical vegetables for stuffing include zucchini (courgettes), eggplants (aubergines), or small bell peppers. *Mahshi* take some time to make, but in North Africa cooking is often a communal activity, and time-consuming tasks such as this are the perfect opportunity for talking to one another and strengthening relationships.

In a frying pan, heat 1 tablespoon of the oil over medium heat. Add the chopped onion and cook until beginning to soften, about 3 minutes. Add the tomato sauce, cinnamon, allspice, and salt and pepper to taste and simmer for 3 minutes to infuse.

Add the rice, parsley, cilantro (coriander), and dill. Mix well and set aside.

With an apple corer, remove the center of the zucchini. Leave only a thin outer shell. Stuff each zucchini with the rice, using a teaspoon. Don't overstuff them; leave about ½ inch (1.25 cm) unstuffed to allow the rice to expand when cooked.

Pour the remaining ½ tablespoon oil into an 8-inch (20 cm) nonstick pot. Cover the bottom of the pot with the sliced onion (this protects the zucchini from burning if the water evaporates). Arrange the stuffed zucchini on top of the onions lying flat.

Add the stock and bring to a boil. Reduce the heat to very low, cover, and simmer until the rice is cooked, about 20 minutes.

To serve, arrange the zucchini on a serving dish. (Discard the onion slices.)

Rice Cakes with Vegetables and Coconut Sauce

Preparation time: 1 hour,
   plus overnight soaking time
Cooking time: 1 hour
Serves: 6

For the rice cakes
3 cups (600 g) short-grain white
   rice, soaked in water overnight
   and drained
6 banana leaf squares
   (10 × 10 inches/25 × 25 cm)

For the chili paste
2 tablespoons crushed chili flakes
1 tablespoon chopped fresh
   ginger
2¾ oz (70 g) fresh turmeric,
   chopped
3 cloves garlic, chopped
1 red onion, chopped
2 large carrots, cut into chunks

For the vegetables and
   coconut sauce
5 tablespoons rice bran oil, plus
   more for shallow-frying
4 (2-inch/5 cm) squares tempeh
4 (2-inch/5 cm) squares tofu
4¼ cups (34 fl oz/1 liter) full-fat
   coconut milk
2 oz (50 g) dried shrimp, ground
6 oz (175 g) long beans, cut into
   2-inch (5 cm) lengths
6 oz (175 g) cabbage, shredded
Sea salt

For assembly
Rice bran oil
6 tablespoons unsweetened
   shredded (desiccated) coconut
Pinch of sugar
6 hard-boiled eggs,
   halved lengthwise

Lontong are Indonesian rice cakes boiled in banana leaves. They can be cooked in coconut soup. Because their flavor is so neutral, they are often served with heavily spiced sauces, vegetables, or soup.

Make the rice cake: Divide the rice among the banana leaves, placing it in the middle of each leaf. Wrap up the rice (like wrapping a present). In a large pot of simmering water, cook the packets of rice over medium heat until tender, about 1 hour. Remove from the pot and let the rice cool. Open the parcels, divide the rice into portions, about 3½ oz (100 g), and shape into cubes.

Make the chili paste: In a bowl, soak the chili flakes in ½ cup (4 fl oz/120 ml) water for 1 hour. Transfer the chili flakes and soaking water to a small saucepan. Bring to a boil over medium heat and boil for 10 minutes. Remove from the heat. Transfer to a blender and add the ginger, turmeric, garlic, red onion, and carrots and process to a paste.

Prepare the vegetables and sauce: Pour 1 inch (2.5 cm) rice bran oil into a frying pan and heat over medium heat. Add the tempeh and tofu and fry until golden brown, about 5 minutes. Remove from the pan and set aside.

   In a bowl, combine the coconut milk and 4 cups (32 fl oz/ 950 ml) warm water.

   In a wok, heat the 5 tablespoons rice bran oil over low heat. Add the dried shrimp and chili paste and stir carefully for 3 minutes. Pour in the coconut milk mixture and bring to a boil over medium heat. Add the long beans and cabbage and simmer until softened, about 30 minutes.

   Stir in the tofu and tempeh and season with salt and sugar.

Assemble the dish: In a frying pan, heat a skim of rice bran oil over high heat. Add the coconut and sugar and sauté until golden, 3–4 minutes.

   Arrange the rice cubes on a serving plate. Top with the vegetables and coconut sauce. Add the eggs and sprinkle with golden coconut.

Rice Balls with Salmon and Umeboshi

Preparation time: 20 minutes
Cooking time: 40 minutes
Makes: 40 rice balls

2¼ lb (1 kg) salmon fillet
1 tablespoon sake
1 tablespoon tamari
2 teaspoons superfine
   (caster)sugar
½ teaspoon grated fresh ginger
1 cup (200 g) sushi rice
2½ cups (20 fl oz/590 ml)
   boiling water
4 tablespoons rice vinegar
2 tablespoons granulated sugar
Sea salt
4 umeboshi, pitted and chopped
4 large sheets nori, cut into strips
   1 × 3½ inches (3 × 9 cm)
4 tablespoons black sesame
   seeds, for sprinkling

In the name of this dish, *sake onigiri*, the word *sake* actually refers to the salmon in the rice balls, not the rice wine—though coincidentally the recipe also has rice wine in it. When buying *sake* (the rice wine), be sure to buy a premium product, as the cheaper versions sometimes contain gluten. Typically onigiri is pyramid-shaped, with a strip of nori seaweed wrapped around the bottom.

Preheat the oven to 400°F (200°C/Gas Mark 6).

Arrange the salmon in a baking pan and roast until just cooked through, about 20 minutes.

Break the fish into small pieces with a rubber spatula. Transfer to a bowl and add the sake, tamari, superfine (caster) sugar, and ginger and set aside.

Rinse the rice and drain it well. In a saucepan, combine the rice and boiling water. Cook over medium heat until the rice is tender and all the liquid is absorbed, about 20 minutes. Spread the rice out in a bowl.

Meanwhile, in a separate saucepan, combine the vinegar, granulated sugar, and 2 teaspoons salt and heat over medium heat until the sugar has dissolved.

Sprinkle the vinegar mixture over the bowl of rice and gently toss until all rice lumps break. Allow the rice to cool down. Occasionally flip it and stir the rice to speed the cooling process.

With wet hands to prevent the rice from sticking, roll 3 tablespoons of rice into a ball. Create a little cavity in the middle and fill it will a teaspoon of umeboshi or salmon. Top with a bit of rice. Reshape the rice into a pyramid shape. Wrap a strip of seaweed across the bottom and up the sides of the onigiri, pressing it lightly into the rice to adhere. Repeat until all the rice and fillings have been used.

To serve, place the onigiri on a plate. Sprinkle the sesame seeds on top. Serve immediately so the seaweed remains crisp.

Stuffed Rice Pancakes

Preparation time: 30 minutes, plus 10 minutes soaking time and 30 minutes resting time
Cooking time: 15 minutes
Serves: 4

1 oz (32 g) dried wood ear mushrooms
11 oz (300 g) ground (minced) pork
Sea salt and freshly ground black pepper
1¼ cups (200 g) rice flour, plus 2 tablespoons for dusting
1⅔ cups (200 g) tapioca starch
1 onion, finely chopped
1 tablespoon sunflower oil, plus more for frying
Fish sauce, for dipping

Called *banh cuon*, this tasty Vietnamese dish is made from sheets of steamed rice rolled around a filling of meat and mushrooms. The traditional recipe calls for wood ear mushrooms, so called because they look like little ears attached to the sides of the trees they grow on. They are widely used in Asian cuisine, especially Chinese. They have a delicate woodsy aroma and a pleasantly rubbery texture.

In a small bowl, soak the wood ears in warm water to cover for 10 minutes. Drain and chop.

Season the pork with salt and pepper.

In a large bowl, stir together the rice flour, tapioca starch, and 4 cups (32 fl oz/950 ml) warm water. Stir carefully and let the batter rest for 30 minutes.

Heat a large frying pan over medium-low heat. Add the pork and wood ears and cook, stirring constantly to break the meat into small pieces, about 5 minutes. Add the onion and stir for 2 more minutes. Transfer the mixture to a large bowl.

Spoon off the clear liquid at the top of the rice batter and replace it with the same amount of fresh water. Add 1 teaspoon salt and the 1 tablespoon sunflower oil and stir well.

Heat a 10-inch (25 cm) nonstick frying pan over low heat and lightly grease the bottom with a little oil. Pour in a small ladle of batter and swirl the pan to fully coat the bottom. Cover and cook for 1 minute. Flip the pancake onto a greased work surface or a tray lined with parchment paper and let it cool for 1 minute. Place 1 tablespoonful of the meat filling in the center of the pancake. Fold up the bottom and fold in the sides, then roll up. Repeat with the remaining batter and filling.

Serve with a little bowl of fish sauce for dipping.

Shanghai Spring Rolls

Preparation time: 40 minutes
Cooking time: 20 minutes
Serves: 6

9 oz (250 g) ground (minced) pork
2 eggs
1 can (8 oz/225 g) water chest-
    nuts, drained and chopped
1 can (8 oz/225 g) bamboo shoots,
    drained and chopped
2 cloves garlic, chopped
2 scallions (spring onions),
    coarsely chopped
3 tablespoons grated fresh ginger
Sea salt and freshly ground
    black pepper
24 rice wrappers
Peanut (groundnut) oil,
    for deep-frying
Chiu chow chili sauce,
    for dipping

A traditional dish typically served for Chinese New Year, these deep-fried spring rolls are filled with a meat mixture. You can assemble and freeze the spring rolls ahead to be fried later. After filling and rolling, spread them out on a parchment-lined sheet pan and freeze solid. Then transfer to a freezer bag and keep frozen for up to 3 months. When you need them, take them out of the freezer and fry straight from frozen.

In a bowl, combine the pork, 1 of the eggs, the water chestnuts, bamboo shoots, garlic, scallions (spring onions), and ginger. Season with salt and pepper and stir gently to combine.

Working with one wrapper at a time (keep the other wrappers covered), lightly brush a wrapper with water, then place 1 tablespoon of the filling crosswise just below the center of the wrapper. Fold the bottom up and over the filling, then fold the sides of the wrapper in to the center. Keep rolling until the spring roll is a small neat cylinder. Beat the remaining egg, brush the top corner of the wrapper, and gently press the edge against the spring roll to seal.

Pour 3 inches (8 cm) oil into a Dutch oven (casserole) or deep-fryer and heat the oil to 350°F (180°C) on a deep-fry thermometer.

Working in batches of a few at a time, fry the rolls until golden brown, about 5 minutes. Drain on paper towels.

Serve with the chili sauce for dipping.

Summer Rolls

Vietnam

Preparation time: 45 minutes
Cooking time: 10 minutes
Serves: 6

Sea salt
8 oz (225 g) shrimp (prawns)
3 oz (80 g) dried rice noodles
1 tablespoon cane sugar
Juice of 1 lemon
5 tablespoons fish sauce
1 fresh red chili pepper,
    thinly sliced
1 clove garlic, minced
1⅓ cups (5 oz/150 g) bean
    sprouts, rinsed
2 handfuls of fresh mint leaves,
    chopped
1 cucumber, cut into thin sticks
6 lettuce leaves, shredded
1 carrot, very finely slivered
18 Vietnamese round spring
    roll wrappers

One of the most popular dishes in Vietnam, summer rolls are a national dish. Fresh and light, these rice-paper rolls are called *goi cuon*, which means "spring roll." Unlike Chinese spring rolls or Filipino *lumpia*, these are not fried and are served at room temperature, accompanied with a sweet and spicy sauce.

Bring a large saucepan of salted water to a boil. Add the shrimp (prawns) and cook until they just turn pink, about 2 minutes. Drain, then peel and devein them.

In a separate saucepan of boiling water, cook the noodles until softened, about 5 minutes. Drain well.

In a small bowl, stir together the sugar, 3 tablespoons water, the lemon juice, fish sauce, chili pepper, and garlic.

In a medium bowl, combine the bean sprouts, mint, cucumber, and lettuce and mix well.

In a shallow bowl of water, working with one wrapper at a time, soften a spring roll wrapper and lay on a tea towel to absorb excess moisture. Lay some bean sprout mixture, slivered carrots, shrimp, and noodles across the bottom third of the wrapper. Fold the bottom of the wrapper up and over the filling, fold the sides in, and roll up like a cigar.

Serve the spring rolls with the sauce for dipping.

White Cornmeal Polenta

South Africa

Preparation time: 5 minutes
Cooking time: 15 minutes
Serves: 4

1 teaspoon sea salt
Generous 3 cups (500 g)
   white cornmeal

Ugali, as this dish is often known in South Africa, can be served as part of a shared selection of starters or as a side dish for stews. Although its name varies from country to country, you will find a version of this in all sub-Saharan African countries as well as in the Caribbean. It's a preparation similar to African fufu and is generally consumed by rolling it into balls that are then dipped in sauces and side dishes based on meat, fish, vegetables, or peanuts. Before the introduction of corn, *ugali* was prepared with other cereal grains such as sorghum or millet.

In a pot, bring 2 cups (16 fl oz/475 ml) water to a boil over high heat. Add the salt and reduce the heat to low. Slowly pour in the cornmeal while whisking. You may have to use a sieve to get rid of possible lumps.

Continue stirring over low heat until it thickens, about 10 minutes. Pour the mixture into a bowl and let sit for 10 minutes, or until cool enough to handle but still warm.

To serve, shape the mixture into balls the size of tennis balls using hands or two spoons.

Bean and Corn Tostadas

Mexico

Preparation time: 15 minutes
Cooking time: 30 minutes
Serves: 4

2 medium zucchini (courgettes),
   sliced
2 small onions, sliced
2 tablespoons sunflower oil,
   plus 2 cups (16 fl oz/500 ml)
   for frying
Sea salt and freshly ground
   black pepper
2 ears corn, unhusked
4 corn tortillas, store-bought
   or homemade (page 148)
½ cup (75 g) canned spicy frijoles
2 lettuce leaves, chopped
3 oz (80 g) Cotija or Parmesan
   cheese, grated

Crispy fried tortillas topped with vegetables and cheese or meat, tostadas are typical Mexican street food. The toppings for these tostadas include grilled (barbecued) zucchini (courgettes) and onions, and a sprinkling of grated cheese.

Preheat the broiler (grill).

Spread the zucchini (courgettes) and onions on a sheet pan. Drizzle with 2 tablespoons of the oil and season with salt and pepper. Broil (grill) them on both sides until golden brown, about 6 minutes.

Broil the unhusked corn, turning them frequently to brown but not burn, about 10 minutes. When cool enough to handle, husk the corn and cut the kernels off the cobs.

In a frying pan, heat the 2 cups (16 fl oz/500 ml) oil over medium heat. Add the tortillas one at a time and fry until golden and browned, about 2 minutes. Drain on paper towels.

Spread 2 tablespoons of beans on each tortilla, top with lettuce, the zucchini and onions, and corn kernels. Sprinkle each with cheese and serve.

Chilaquiles

Preparation time: 30 minutes
Cooking time: 45 minutes
Serves: 4

8 tomatillos, husked, rinsed,
   and halved
1 serrano pepper, chopped
1½ white onions—1 halved,
   ½ finely chopped
2 cloves garlic, peeled
1 fresh bay leaf
Pinch of dried thyme
Pinch of dried oregano
Sea salt
5 tablespoons vegetable stock
1 tablespoon corn oil, plus more
   for frying
12 corn tortillas, store-bought
   or homemade (page 148),
   cut into wedges
4 eggs
4 tablespoons Mexican crema
   or crème fraîche
2½ oz (65 g) hard cheese, grated
3½ oz (100 g) queso fresco or feta
   cheese, crumbled
Rose pepper, for garnish

Chilaquiles is a Mexican dish designed to make good use of leftover corn tortillas (which can go stale really quickly). The tortillas are cut into chips and fried and then served with a sauce, either a red sauce or a green sauce (as here). The distinctive flavor in the salsa verde comes from tomatillos, small tart fruits that are typically green but can also be green-purple. If you can't find fresh tomatillos, you can used canned instead.

In a saucepan, combine the tomatillos, serrano pepper, 2 onion halves, garlic, and 1½ cups (12 fl oz/355 ml) water. Bring to a boil over high heat. Reduce the heat to a simmer and cook until the tomatillos have collapsed, about 20 minutes.

Transfer the mixture to a food processor and blend for 3 minutes. Add the bay leaf, thyme, oregano, 1 teaspoon salt, and the stock and blend again until the mixture is homogeneous and smooth.

Pour the sauce into a large pot and bring to a boil over medium-high heat. Cook, stirring occasionally, until thickened, about 15 minutes. Cover the salsa verde and keep over low heat.

Pour 3 inches (8 cm) oil into a Dutch oven (casserole) and heat over medium-high heat. Add the tortilla wedges to the pan, moving and turning them so they don't stick together, and cook until they are crispy and golden brown, about 5 minutes. Drain them on paper towels.

In a frying pan, heat 1 teaspoon oil over medium heat. Crack the eggs into the pan and fry gently until the whites are set but the yolks are still runny, about 3 minutes. Take out the fried eggs with a skimmer and set on a paper towel.

Divide the tortillas among plates, top with the fried eggs and drizzle the green sauce and crema on top. Sprinkle the cheeses and rose pepper on top and serve immediately.

Layered Potato, Tuna, and Avocado Cake

Preparation time: 30 minutes, plus 30 minutes soaking time and 1 hour chilling time
Cooking time: 30 minutes
Serves: 6

2 onions, sliced
2½ lb (1.2 kg) yellow potatoes
4 eggs
4 ají amarillo chilies, seeded and chopped
Juice of 3 limes
Sea salt
1 lb 2 oz (500 g) tuna in oil, drained and chopped
3 avocados, sliced
Fresh lemon juice
10–12 black olives, for garnish
2 tablespoons olive oil

A traditional Peruvian dish, this potato and tuna layered cake is a native of Lima, hence its name, *causa limeña*. It is prepared with South American *papas amarillas* (yellow potatoes) and the very spicy yellow chili, ají amarillo. These Peruvian ingredients may be hard to find, so you can replace them with another type of yellow-fleshed potato and another variety of hot pepper. It is served cold, and shredded cooked chicken breast can be substituted for the tuna.

Soak the onions in cold water for 30 minutes. Drain and chop.

In a large pot of boiling water, cook the potatoes until tender, about 30 minutes. While still warm, peel them and mash them in a bowl.

Meanwhile, place the eggs in a saucepan and cover them with cold water. Bring to a boil over medium heat and boil for 9 minutes. Drain and cool them under cold running water. Peel and slice them.

To the mashed potatoes in the bowl, add half of the chilies and stir to combine. Then add the lime juice, season with salt, and stir carefully to combine.

In a separate bowl, gently combine the remaining chilies, chopped onions, and tuna. In a medium bowl, very gently toss the avocado slices with some lemon juice.

Using half of the potato mixture, spread it into a 14-inch (35 cm) round layer on a serving plate. Top with all of the tuna mixture and half the avocado slices. Top with the remaining potato mixture. Garnish the top with the olives, the remaining avocado slices, and the egg slices. Drizzle with the oil. Refrigerate until well chilled, at least 1 hour.

Meat-Stuffed Potato Croquettes

(DF) (NF)

Peru

Preparation time: 40 minutes
Cooking time: 45 minutes
Serves: 4

2¼ lb (1.2 kg) yellow potatoes
4 eggs
Sunflower oil, for frying
1 onion, chopped
1 clove garlic, chopped
Freshly ground black pepper
Ground cumin
11 oz (300 g) chopped raw beef
Sea salt
12 black olives, pitted
Rice flour, for dredging

Papas rellenas (which translates as "stuffed potatoes") are fried potato croquettes popular all across Latin America. In Peru this recipe gained popularity in the late nineteenth century during the War of the Pacific (a war between Peru, Bolivia, and Chile over control of the Atacama desert). The story goes that Peruvian soldiers in the Andes needed to store food for a long time as it was difficult to get supplies. Putting meat inside a potato and then frying it allowed the rations to be stored longer. When the war was over, the dish also spread among the civilian population. In Peru, this is often served with *leche de tigre*—a spicy sauce of onion, cilantro (coriander), and chili.

In a large pot of boiling water, cook the potatoes until tender, about 30 minutes. Drain them, then peel and mash.

Meanwhile, in a saucepan, combine 3 of the eggs and water to cover and bring to a boil over medium heat. Boil for 9 minutes, then drain and cool under cold running water. Peel them and cut into dice.

In a frying pan, heat 2 tablespoons sunflower oil over medium heat. Add the onion and garlic and cook until beginning to brown, about 3 minutes. Season to taste with pepper and cumin. Add the meat, reduce the heat, and cook until the meat releases juices, 5–6 minutes. Season with salt. Gently stir in the olives and diced cooked eggs and remove from the heat.

Take about 2 ounces (60 g) of the mashed potato and roll it with your hands to make a ball. Dig a small cavity and fill it with about 1 ounce (30 g) of meat and close up the hole, reforming into a ball.

Pour 4 inches (12 cm) sunflower oil into a Dutch oven (casserole) and heat over medium heat to 320°F (160°C) on a deep-fry thermometer.

Set up a shallow bowl of rice flour and in a second bowl, lightly beat the remaining egg. Dredge the potato balls in the rice flour, shaking off the excess, then quickly dip them into the beaten egg. Working in batches, add to the hot oil and cook until golden all over, about 5 minutes.

Serve hot.

Tartiflette

**Preparation time: 30 minutes,
  plus 15 minutes resting time
Cooking time: 50 minutes
Serves: 4**

Sea salt
2¼ lb (1 kg) yellow potatoes
3½ tablespoons (50 g) unsalted
  butter, plus more for greasing
1 onion, sliced
3 tablespoons dry white wine
Freshly ground black pepper
4 oz (120 g) fatback (pork back
  fat), cut into thin slices
12 oz (350 g) Reblochon cheese,
  trimmed of rind
4½ tablespoons heavy
  (whipping) cream

Tartiflette is a very tasty full-flavored winter dish that is traditionally made with Reblochon, a French pressed cheese made from raw cow's milk. It is said that the recipe was invented in the Alpine region of Haute-Savoie in eastern France to promote the Reblochon cheese that is made there. The base of the tartiflette can be made ahead and frozen, then the cheese can be added just before serving, when reheating.

In a large pot of boiling salted water, cook the potatoes until firm-tender, about 20 minutes. Drain, then peel and slice them.

Meanwhile, in a frying pan, heat the butter over very low heat. Add the onion and cook until softened, about 10 minutes. Add the wine and simmer until well reduced, about 15 minutes longer. Season to taste with salt and pepper.

In a pot, combine the simmered onion, the sliced potatoes, and all but 4 slices of the fatback (pork back fat). Gently simmer until the fatback is softened and is rendering its fat, about 8 minutes. Let it rest for 15 minutes.

In a metal bowl set over a pan of simmering water, melt together the cheese and cream.

Preheat the oven to 450°F (230°C/Gas Mark 8).

Grease an 8-inch (20 cm) round ceramic baking dish with butter. Place the 4 reserved fatback slices into the dish so that they cross each other in the middle and hang over the dish's edges. Add the potato mixture, then pour in the melted cheese. Fold the fatback slices in toward the center. Transfer the dish to the oven and bake until the surface is golden brown, about 15 minutes.

Serve warm.

Potatoes in Spicy Cheese Sauce

 Peru

Preparation time: 15 minutes
Cooking time: 20 minutes
Serves: 4

4 eggs
8 medium yellow potatoes,
   peeled and thickly sliced
5 oz (150 g) tortilla chips
2 cloves garlic, peeled
8 oz (225 g) ricotta cheese
2 ají amarillo chilies, halved
   lengthwise and seeded
Juice of 1 lemon
4 tablespoons corn oil
Sea salt
Lettuce leaves, thinly sliced,
   for garnish
8 black olives, for garnish

A traditional Peruvian recipe, *papa a la huancaína* gets its name from the city of Huancayo in the central highland region of Junín, where potatoes are among the most important crops. One of the main ingredients in the dish is the ají amarillo—a fiery Peruvian yellow chili—which gives the accompanying sauce a nice kick.

Place the eggs in a saucepan and cover them with cold water. Bring to a boil over medium heat and boil for 9 minutes. Drain and cool them under cold running water. Peel the eggs and cut into wedges.
     Meanwhile, in another saucepan, combine the potatoes and water to cover. Bring to a boil, then reduce the heat and cook until softened, about 15 minutes.
     In a food processor, combine the tortilla chips, garlic, ricotta, chilies, lemon juice, oil, and salt to taste and pulse until the mixture is smooth and creamy.
     Drain the potatoes and arrange on a serving plate. Top with the creamy sauce and the boiled eggs. Garnish with lettuce and olives.

Poutine

 Canada

Preparation time: 10 minutes
Cooking time: 20 minutes
Serves: 4

4½ tablespoons (65 g) very cold
   butter, cut into small pieces
3 tablespoons rice flour
1 tablespoon minced fresh herbs,
   such as rosemary, thyme,
   or your favorite
1⅔ cups (13 fl oz/375 ml) beef
   stock, hot
12 oz (350 g) yellow potatoes,
   peeled and cut lengthwise
   into wedges
Vegetable oil, for frying
4½ oz (130 g) cheese curds
Sea salt

Poutine is a wonderful dish from Quebec in eastern Canada. It is fried potatoes (typically French fries) topped with cheese curds and smothered in gravy. Cheese curds are a regional specialty; they're the curds formed in the process of cheesemaking, but instead of pressing them into a form to make a wheel of aged cheese, for example, they're simply left in random chunks. They can be white or yellow, and flavor- and texture-wise they are not dissimilar to mozzarella, which works as a substitute here.

In a small nonstick saucepan, melt the butter over very low heat (don't let it get too hot). Stir in the rice flour and herbs and whisk until the mixture is homogeneous. Whisking constantly, add the hot stock and whisk until the gravy is thickened and has no lumps, 3–4 minutes.
     Pour 2 inches (6 cm) oil into a large deep frying pan and heat over medium-high heat. Add the potatoes and fry until golden brown and crispy, 6–7 minutes. Drain them on paper towels.
     Divide the fries among plates, top with the cheese curds, season with salt, and pour the gravy over the top.

Spanish Tortilla

Preparation time: 20 minutes
Cooking time: 40 minutes
Serves: 4

½ cup (4 fl oz/120 ml) extra-virgin
  olive oil, plus more for greasing
1 lb 2 oz (500 g) yellow potatoes,
  peeled and diced
7 oz (200 g) onions, sliced
7 eggs
2 teaspoons salt

Tortilla de patatas is one of the most common dishes in Spain, where it can be found as an appetizer in every bar or tapas restaurant. Potatoes, which are a New World vegetable, were brought back to Europe in the sixteenth century by the Spanish conquistadors, who were introduced to them by the Inca in Peru. The first document that mentions cooking eggs and potatoes together in a cake (*tortilla*) dates to 1817 in Navarre in northern Spain: *Tortillas* were described as a frugal meal devised by poor farmers who had eggs and potatoes and not much else. The recipe today is very similar to an Italian frittata and it can be served hot or cold.

In a large frying pan, heat the oil over medium-high heat. Add the potatoes and stir for a few minutes. Add the onions, cover, and cook, stirring two or three times, until they soften, about 20 minutes. Drain off the excess oil and let the vegetables cool down.

In a large bowl, combine the eggs and salt and beat with a fork, then pour them over the vegetables and toss to combine.

Oil a 10-inch (25 cm) frying pan. Pour the egg mixture into the pan and cook over low heat for 10 minutes. Flip the tortilla by inverting a large plate over the pan as if you were putting on a lid, turn the pan upside down so that the tortilla falls onto the plate, then slide the tortilla from the plate back into the pan. Cook until the center is firm but still soft and the bottom is browned, 5–6 minutes more.

Serve hot or warm.

Greens and Cheese Corn Pie

Preparation time: 30 minutes
Cooking time: 1 hour 20 minutes
Serves: 6

2½ lb (1.2 kg) leeks, thinly sliced
    and well rinsed
4 tablespoons grated Parmesan
    cheese
2 eggs
2 leaves fresh mint, chopped
Sea salt and freshly ground
    black pepper
5 cups (600 g) finely ground
    cornmeal
2 cups (16 fl oz/475 ml)
    extra-virgin olive oil, plus
    more for greasing
3 tablespoons milk
1 tablespoon (15 g) unsalted butter

Petë misri is definitely one of the most special dishes in Albanian cuisine. It's a kind of pie with a cornmeal crust filled with various things, such as cheese or cottage cheese, yogurt, milk, eggs, and vegetables such as spinach, nettles, pumpkin, onion, or tomatoes.

In a large pot, combine the leeks and ½ cup (4 fl oz/120 ml) water, cover, and steam until they soften, about 20 minutes. Drain off any remaining liquid and stir in the Parmesan, eggs, mint, and salt and pepper to taste. Mix carefully and simmer until thickened, 10 minutes longer.

In a saucepan, bring 4 cups (32 fl oz/950 ml) water to a boil. Pour in a scant 3 cups (345 g) of the cornmeal, the oil, and 1 tablespoon salt. Stir and simmer over low heat until it forms a thick dough, about 15 minutes.

Preheat the oven to 350°F (180°C/Gas Mark 4). Grease a 12-inch (25 cm) round baking dish.

Scrape the corn dough into the baking dish and press it over the bottom and halfway up the sides of the baking dish. Pour the leek mixture into the crust. Place the remaining generous 2 cups (255 g) cornmeal into a sieve and sift it all over the top of the leek mixture. Drizzle on the milk to moisten the cornmeal. Dot with the butter.

Transfer to the oven and baked until nicely browned on top, about 30 minutes.

Cut into wedges and serve hot.

Deviled Eggs

United States

Preparation time: 15 minutes
Cooking time: 10 minutes
Serves: 4

4 eggs
2 tablespoons mayonnaise
1 tablespoon Dijon mustard
1 teaspoon fresh lemon juice
Sea salt and freshly ground
    black pepper
Paprika, for garnish

The quintessential potluck or picnic appetizer, deviled eggs are stuffed hard-boiled eggs whose name "deviled" is an eighteenth-century term that indicated a dish was spicy, usually from mustard or pepper. The basic deviled egg formula is presented here, but it's an easy dish to personalize with your own twists.

Place the eggs in a saucepan and cover them with cold water. Bring to a boil over medium heat and boil for 9 minutes. Drain and cool them under cold running water. Peel the eggs and halve them lengthwise.

Scoop the egg yolks into a bowl and arrange the egg whites on a large plate. Mash the yolks with a fork and combine with the mayonnaise, mustard, lemon juice, and salt and pepper to taste. Stir gently until the mixture is smooth.

Spoon the yolk mixture into the egg whites (or get fancy and use a piping bag). Sprinkle paprika on top and serve.

Souvlaki

Greece

Preparation time: 30 minutes,
    plus 1 hour marinating time
Cooking time: 10 minutes
Serves: 6

⅔ cup (5 fl oz/150 ml) extra-virgin
    olive oil
Juice of ½ lemon
6 tablespoons Dijon mustard
½ oz (15 g) oregano sprigs
Sea salt and freshly ground
    black pepper
1¾ lb (800 g) pork shoulder, cut
    into 1⅓-inch (3.5 cm) cubes
Tzatziki, store-bought or home-
    made (page 321), for serving

Souvlaki is popular Greek street food that you can find in every corner of the country. In addition to eating it as a snack, it can be a take-out dinner, a lunch, and even a late brunch. The word *souvlaki* means "skewer," and in Athens souvlaki are called *kalamaki,* the local word for skewer (though it literally means "straw"). Lamb, pork (as here), or chicken are all used.

In a large bowl, combine the oil, lemon juice, mustard, oregano, 1 teaspoon salt, and a pinch of pepper. Add the pork, cover with plastic wrap (cling film), and refrigerate for 1 hour.

Heat a grill pan (griddle pan) over high heat.

Thread the pork onto six 6-inch (15 cm) skewers and grill them, turning them over to brown all sides, about 12 minutes.

Serve hot with the tzatziki on the side.

Steamed Tamales

Mexico

Preparation time: 1 hour,
plus 1 hour soaking time
Cooking time: 2 hours
30 minutes
Serves: 4

13–14 dried corn husks
8 oz (225 g) fresh tomatillos,
    husked and rinsed
8 oz (225 g) pork loin
2 cloves garlic, peeled
1 bay leaf
1 tablespoon sea salt,
    plus more to taste
1 guajillo chili, soaked in water
    for 15 minutes, halved
    lengthwise and seeded
1 ancho chili, soaked in water
    for 15 minutes, halved
    lengthwise, and seeded
Pinch of ground cumin
Freshly ground black pepper
6 oz (175 g) lard
1¼ (150 g) masa harina (instant
    corn masa flour)
½ teaspoon baking powder

Mexican tamales are a corn dough encasing a sweet or savory filling, then wrapped in corn husks and steamed. Their origin dates back to the Aztecs and Maya who used these little packets as an easily transportable food, and in fact their name comes from the Nahuatl word *tamalii*, which means "wrapped food."

In a bowl of warm water, soak the corn husks for 1 hour.

In a large pot of boiling water, blanch the tomatillos for 1 minute. Drain, then peel and scoop out the seeds with a teaspoon.

In a pot, combine the pork, 1 clove of the garlic, the bay leaf, salt, and water to cover. Bring to a boil, then reduce to simmer and cook over low heat until the meat is tender, about 40 minutes. Add water if necessary to keep the meat covered as it cooks. Reserving the broth, drain the pork and set aside.

In a food processor, combine the tomatillos, rehydrated chilies, and the remaining clove of garlic and process to a sauce. Shred the meat with your fingers and put it into a saucepan, add the tomatillo/chili sauce, cumin, and 1 cup of the reserved broth and season to taste with black pepper. Bring to a simmer over low heat and cook until the mixture is lightly thickened, about 20 minutes.

In a bowl, with an electric mixer, beat the lard until light and fluffy, about 5 minutes. In a separate bowl, combine the masa harina, baking powder, and a generous ¾ cup (200 ml) broth, stirring until a soft dough is formed. Add the soft dough to the lard, a little bit at a time, beating until the dough is puffy and sticky, about 12 minutes.

Drain the corn husks. Cut one or two of the husks into thin strips to be used as ties. Place a husk on a work surface. With wet hands, spread the middle of the leaf with 2 tablespoons of the dough and top with 1 tablespoon of the meat mixture. Fold the sides in and then fold the ends over. Wrap like a present with a leaf strip, being careful not to wrap too tightly as the tamales will puff up slightly as they steam.

In a large steamer, pack the tamales in and cook for 1½ hours, or until the filling is no longer sticking to the corn husks. Serve.

Kofte Kebabs with Tahini Sauce

**Preparation time: 20 minutes,
   plus 3 hours marinating time
Cooking time: 5 minutes
Serves: 6**

For the kofte
8 oz (225 g) ground (minced) beef
8 oz (225 g) ground (minced) lamb
1 onion, finely chopped
1 clove garlic, finely minced
4 tablespoons finely chopped
   fresh parsley
1 egg
1 tablespoon (15 g) unsalted
   butter, melted
1 tablespoon ground allspice
Sea salt and freshly ground
   black pepper

For the tahini dip
Generous ½ cup (4.2 fl oz/125 ml)
   distilled white vinegar
Generous ¾ cup (200 g) tahini
2 tablespoons minced garlic
1 tablespoon dried parsley,
   plus more for garnish
1 teaspoon sea salt
½ teaspoon cayenne pepper,
plus more for garnish
Freshly ground black pepper
1 tablespoon extra-virgin olive oil

Kofte, sometimes spelled kofta, are cigar-shaped meat kebabs. A very popular dish throughout the Middle East, kofte kebabs are usually made with a mixture of beef and lamb, sometimes seasoned with mint and cilantro (coriander). These spicy meatballs can also be served with tzatziki (page 321). Once cooked, you can store the kofte in an airtight container in the fridge for up to 3 days.

Prepare the kofte: In a large bowl, mix the beef, lamb, onion, garlic, parsley, egg, melted butter, allspice, and salt and pepper to taste. Cover and marinate in the fridge for at least 3 hours.

Make the tahini dip: In a bowl, whisk together the vinegar and tahini to a thick, clumpy paste. Add ½ cup (4 fl oz/120 ml) water and mix until smooth. Add the garlic, parsley, salt, cayenne, and black pepper to taste. Set aside. When ready to serve, sprinkle with the olive oil and garnish with some more cayenne or parsley.

Cook the kofte: Preheat the broiler (grill) to medium-high heat. Set an oven rack 4 inches (10 cm) from the heat source.
   Oil a wire rack and set it in a sheet pan. With your hands, roll the meat mixture into elongated rolls the size and shape of a thumb and place on the oiled rack.
   Grill the kofte until cooked through, about 5 minutes, turning them over halfway through.
   Serve with the tahini dip.

Dried Beef, Rice, and Eggs
with Fried Plantains

Preparation time: 30 minutes
Cooking time: 2 hours
Serves: 6

3½ oz (100 g) charque (salted
    dried beef), cut into chunks
    and well rinsed 2–3 times
⅓ cup plus 1 tablespoon
    (3½ fl oz/90 ml) olive oil
2 onions, chopped
1 teaspoon achiote seeds or
    1 teaspoon annatto extract
2 tomatoes, diced
4 cloves garlic, chopped
1 cup (200 g) long-grain white rice
Ground cumin
Sea salt and freshly ground
    black pepper
3 plantains, peeled and cut into
    ¼-inch (5 mm) slices lengthwise
6 eggs

Majadito is one of the most beloved traditional dishes of Bolivia,
dating back to the time of the Spanish conquest. Its name comes
from the word *majau*, which means "beaten" or "pounded,"
a reference to the fact that traditionally the dried beef (*charque*)
is pounded in a mortar before using. *Majadito* is usually
accompanied by fried plantains and can be prepared with dried
beef (as here) as well as salted dried chicken (*majau de pollo*)
or duck (*majau de pato*).

In a large saucepan, combine the dried beef and 2¾ cups
(20 fl oz/600 ml) water and bring to a boil. Reduce to a simmer,
cover, and cook until tender, about 1 hour. Reserving the broth,
drain the meat.

In a frying pan, heat 2 tablespoons of the oil over medium
heat. Add the onions and achiote seeds and cook until the onions
are translucent, 4–5 minutes. Add the tomatoes and garlic and
cook until the tomatoes release their liquid, about 5 minutes
longer. Add the meat, reserved meat broth, 2 cups (16 fl oz/
475 ml) water, and the rice. Season to taste with cumin, salt, and
pepper. Cover and simmer, stirring occasionally, until the rice
is tender, about 15 minutes.

In a frying pan, heat 2 tablespoons of the oil over medium
heat. Add the plantains and cook until they become soft and
lightly browned, about 5 minutes per side. Drain on paper towels
and set aside.

Meanwhile, in a 5-inch (12 cm) frying pan, heat ½ tablespoon
of the oil over medium heat. Crack in an egg and fry gently
until the white is set but the yolk is still runny, about 4 minutes.
Take out the fried egg with a skimmer and set on a paper towel.
Repeat with the remaining oil and eggs.

Serve each portion of rice and beef with a fried egg and
some fried plantain slices.

Pandan Chicken

**Preparation time: 25 minutes,
    plus 2 hours marinating time**
Cooking time: 10 minutes
Serves: 4

For the marinade
4 pandan leaves, cut into
    short pieces
2 tablespoons minced garlic
2 tablespoons minced fresh ginger
3 tablespoons oyster sauce
1 tablespoon fish sauce
1 tablespoon tamari
1 tablespoon red wine vinegar
1 tablespoon light brown sugar
2 teaspoons ground coriander
1 teaspoon ground white pepper
1 teaspoon sesame oil

For the chicken
1 lb 2 oz (500 g) boneless,
    skinless chicken breast
12 pandan leaves
Sunflower oil, for deep-frying
2 tablespoons tamari
1 tablespoon light brown sugar
Sea salt
½ tablespoon white sesame
    seeds, toasted

These chicken wraps are originally from Bangkok but can now be found in Thai restaurants everywhere. The pandan leaves that the chicken pieces are wrapped in before frying give the meat a delicious aroma and keep it juicy and moist. Pandan is a plant that grows throughout Southeast Asia and its leaves are used to make desserts, to flavor jasmine rice, or as a delicate green food coloring. The leaves have a vanilla-like aroma.

Make the marinade: In a small saucepan, bring 3 tablespoons water to a boil over high heat. Remove from the heat, add the cut-up pandan, and let steep for a few minutes. Transfer to a food processor and purée, then push through a fine-mesh sieve set over a bowl to extract the juice.

To the pandan juice in the bowl, add the garlic, ginger, oyster sauce, fish sauce, tamari, vinegar, brown sugar, ground coriander, white pepper, and sesame oil.

Prepare the chicken: Cut the chicken into 12 chunks about 1½ inches (4 cm). Add to the marinade and toss to coat. Cover and marinate in the fridge for 2 hours.

Set up a steamer.

Wrap each chunk of chicken in a pandan leaf (it will not enclose it; it's just there to flavor the chicken). Secure the leaf with a wooden toothpick (cocktail stick). Add the chicken wraps to the steamer and cook for 10 minutes.

Line a plate with paper towels. Pour 5 inches (12 cm) oil into a wok and heat to 320°F (160°C) on a deep-fry thermometer.

Deep-fry the wrapped chicken until the visible parts of the chicken have turned golden brown, about 4 minutes. Drain on the paper towels.

In a small saucepan, combine the tamari, 1 tablespoon water, the brown sugar, and a little salt and heat until the sugar has dissolved. Pour into a little bowl. Add the sesame seeds.

To serve, place the pandan chicken on a serving plate. Place the bowl with the dipping sauce beside it and serve warm.

Soups

Ginseng Chicken Soup

**Preparation time: 20 minutes,
    plus 2 hours soaking time
Cooking time: 50 minutes
Serves: 4**

⅔ cup (120 g) sweet (glutinous)
    rice
1 teaspoon ginseng powder
4 cloves garlic, peeled
5 dried jujubes (Korean dates)
1 whole chicken (3½ lb/1.6 kg),
    giblets removed
Sea salt and freshly ground
    black pepper
1 tablespoon sliced scallion (spring
    onion), for garnish (optional)

Samgyetang is a traditional Korean chicken soup that is popular during the hottest days of summer (because it is believed that one should fight the heat with hot foods).

In a bowl, combine the rice with water to cover well and let soak for 2 hours.

Drain the rice, return to the bowl, and add the ginseng, garlic, and jujubes (Korean dates) and mix well. Stuff the rice mixture into the cavity of the chicken. Close off the cavity of the chicken by crossing the ends of the drumsticks together and tying them with kitchen twine.

Fill a large pot with 8½ cups (68 fl oz/2 liters) water and put the chicken in the pot. Bring to a boil over high heat and cook for 20 minutes. Reduce the heat to medium and cook until the rice stuffing is tender and the chicken is cooked through, 30 minutes longer.

Transfer the whole chicken and the broth to a serving bowl and let people serve themselves portions of the broth, chicken and rice. In a small bowl, make a mixture of salt and black pepper and set on the table for people to season their own soups. If desired, garnish with scallion (spring onion).

Chicken Soup with Potatoes and Poached Eggs

**Preparation time: 15 minutes
Cooking time: 40 minutes
Serves: 4**

6⅓ cups (50 fl oz/1.5 liters)
    chicken stock
1½ onions, chopped
4 tablespoons chopped scallions
    (spring onions)
3 cloves garlic, chopped
4 yellow potatoes, peeled and
    cut into small cubes
Sea salt and freshly ground
    black pepper
1 cup (8 fl oz/240 ml) milk
1 egg yolk, beaten
4 eggs
6 tablespoons chopped fresh
    cilantro (coriander)

Pisca andina, one of the most popular dishes in the Venezuelan Andes, is traditionally served in clay bowls. A variation mixes the egg directly into the soup, making it creamier.

In a soup pot, bring 4 cups (32 fl oz/950 ml) of the chicken stock to a boil over high heat. Stir in the onions, scallions (spring onion), garlic, potatoes, and salt and pepper to taste. Reduce the heat to a simmer and cook until the potatoes are tender, about 20 minutes.

Pour in the milk and the beaten yolk and stir for 2 minutes, then remove from the heat.

In a small wide pan, bring the remaining 2⅓ cups (19 fl oz/550 ml) stock to a simmer. Crack in the eggs, 2 at a time, and poach until the whites are set and the yolks are runny, about 4 minutes. (Discard the stock.)

Divide the soup among soup bowls and top each with a poached egg. Sprinkle with the cilantro (coriander).

Chicken and Potato Soup

Preparation time: 30 minutes
Cooking time: 1 hour
Serves: 4

4 tablespoons sunflower oil
1 onion, chopped
1 clove garlic, chopped
2¼ lb (1 kg) boneless, skinless
    chicken breast, cut into chunks
4½ lb (2 kg) yellow potatoes,
    peeled and cut into chunks
2 ears corn, husked and cut cross-
    wise into 1-inch (2.5 cm) slices
Sea salt and freshly ground
    black pepper
1 cup (8 fl oz/240 ml) heavy
    (whipping) cream
2 avocados, sliced
Fresh lemon juice

Ajiaco is a thick and creamy chicken soup that is very popular in Colombia. The traditional recipe calls for several different types of potato native to Colombia, including the small yellow *papa criolla* and the *papa pastusa* with its mottled red and yellow skin. But you can just use whatever yellow-fleshed potato you have available. The soup is traditionally scented with guasca leaves, which are common in Colombia but can be hard to find elsewhere. If you happen to find them, simmer them in the broth along with the potatoes and corn.

In a soup pot, heat the oil over medium heat. Add the onion and garlic and sauté over medium heat until the onion is translucent, about 2 minutes. Add the chicken and stir until golden brown, about 10 minutes.

Add the potatoes, corn, and water to cover by 2 inches (5 cm). Bring to a simmer and cook over low heat until the potatoes are tender, about 45 minutes, adding more water if the water level falls below the vegetables.

Season to taste with salt and black pepper. Gently stir in the cream.

In a medium bowl, dress the avocado slices with some lemon juice.

Divide the soup among soup bowls and garnish with the avocado.

Spicy Rice Vermicelli Soup

**Preparation time: 25 minutes,
    plus 10 minutes soaking time**
Cooking time: 45 minutes
Serves: 6

For the curry paste
12 dried Thai red chilies
1 teaspoon sea salt
15 cloves garlic, peeled
2 tablespoons thinly sliced
    lemongrass
4 shallots, cut into chunks
1 tablespoon sliced fresh galangal
Grated zest of 1 makrut lime
4 teaspoons freshly ground
    white pepper
1 teaspoon ground cumin
1 teaspoon ground coriander

For the soup
2 lb (900 g) bone-in, skin-on
    chicken parts
5 teaspoons (25 g) minced
    fresh galangal
2 teaspoons sea salt
1 lb (450 g) dried rice vermicelli
    noodles
2 tablespoons sunflower oil
3 cloves garlic, minced
1 can (8 oz/225 g) whole bamboo
    shoots, drained
1 can (14 fl oz/410 ml) full-fat
    coconut milk

For serving
2 carrots, cut into matchsticks
¼ small head cabbage (6 oz/
    175 g), thinly shredded
1 fresh or brined banana flower,
    sliced (optional)
A few fresh cilantro (coriander)
    leaves
A few fresh mint leaves (optional)
2 limes, cut into wedges

Khao poon is a traditional Laotian noodle soup that also goes by the name *lao laksa*, a soup that is part of Peranakan cuisine. Peranakans are descendants of settlers from the southern provinces of China who immigrated to Penang, Malacca, Singapore, and Indonesia between the fifteenth and seventeenth centuries. As is common with immigrant cuisines, the original Chinese recipe has taken on different characteristics and names, depending on where the immigrants settled and the local ingredients available to them.

Make the curry paste: Soak the chilies in water for 10 minutes. Drain and slice the chilies and transfer to a mortar. Pound them with the salt until a smooth paste is formed, about 5 minutes. Add the garlic, lemongrass, shallots, galangal, and lime zest. Pound for 10 minutes. Add the white pepper, cumin, and ground coriander and continue to pound until it becomes a homogeneous paste. (Alternatively, make the paste in a blender.) Set the curry paste aside.

Make the soup: In a large pot, combine the chicken, 8½ cups (68 fl oz/2 liters) water, the galangal, and 1 teaspoon of the salt. Bring to a boil, then reduce to a simmer and cook over low heat until the chicken is cooked through, about 30 minutes.

Meanwhile, in a pot of boiling water, cook the noodles until tender, about 5 minutes. Drain and rinse under cold running water, then drain well.

Pull the chicken pieces out of the broth and when cool enough to handle, pull the meat off the bones (discard the skin and bones) and shred it into small pieces. Set the chicken and broth aside.

In a soup pot, heat the oil over medium heat. Add the garlic and cook for 1 minute. Add 8 tablespoons of the curry paste and stir for a few minutes.

Add the shredded chicken, bamboo shoots, coconut milk, 6 cups (48 fl oz/1.4 liters) of the chicken broth (or more to taste), and the remaining 1 teaspoon salt. Bring to a boil and cook for 5 minutes to heat through.

To serve: Divide the noodles among six bowls. Ladle the soup on top. Garnish with carrots, cabbage, banana flower (if using), cilantro (coriander), and mint (if using). Serve with lime wedges for squeezing.

Cock-a-Leekie

Preparation time: 40 minutes
Cooking time: 1 hour 45 minutes
Serves: 4

1 whole chicken (3 lb/1.3 kg),
    cut into serving pieces
10 leeks, cut into ¾-inch (2 cm)
    chunks and well rinsed
Scant ¾ cup (130 g) long-grain
    white rice
4 carrots, grated
1 stalk celery, chopped
16 pitted prunes
Sea salt and crushed black
    peppercorns

Cock-a-leekie is an old Scottish soup made with leeks, a rich chicken broth, barley or rice, and prunes (perhaps surprising to some, but traditional). It is often labeled the "Scottish national soup," but it may have been born in France as a chicken and onion soup; when it arrived in Scotland, the onions replaced the leeks. The leek-based version of the soup has been known since the end of the sixteenth century, though it didn't get the name cock-a-leekie until about two centuries later. There are many variations on the soup: Some have bacon, others are made with vegetable broth.

In a large deep pot, combine the chicken, half of the leeks, and water to cover. Bring to a boil, then reduce the heat to low, cover, and simmer until the thighs are cooked through, about 1 hour 15 minutes.

Remove the chicken pieces from the broth and when cool enough to handle, pull the meat off the bones (discard the skin and bones). Pour the broth into a bowl, cover, and set aside to cool.

Strain the broth through a fine-mesh sieve into a pot (discard the solids). Add the remaining leeks, the rice, carrots, celery, and prunes. Set over medium heat and bring to a boil. Reduce to a simmer and cook, uncovered, until the rice is tender, about 30 minutes. Season to taste with salt and pepper. Add the chicken meat to the soup and very gently reheat (take care to not overcook it).

Serve in deep plates or soup bowls.

Chicken Soup with Dumplings

Preparation time: 30 minutes
Cooking time: 3 hours 10 minutes
Serves: 4

1 whole chicken (3½ lb/1.6 kg)
2 carrots, each cut into sticks
9 oz (250 g) peeled celeriac, chopped
1½ cups (120 g) chopped fresh parsley, plus parsley leaves for garnish
Sea salt
2 eggs
1 teaspoon extra-virgin olive oil
3 tablespoons corn flour
½ tablespoon cornstarch (cornflour)

Supa de pui cu galuste de gris is a traditional Romanian soup perfect for cold weather and filled with comforting flavors and textures. Traditionally semolina is used to make the dumplings (the name of the soup translates as "chicken soup with semolina dumplings"), but this version of the recipe uses cornstarch (cornflour). And to get the richest broth for the soup, a whole bone-in chicken is used.

In a large deep pot, combine the whole chicken, carrots, celeriac, chopped parsley, and 4½ quarts (4.25 liters) cold water. Set it over low heat and bring it to a boil very slowly, skimming the foam from the surface with a skimmer. Season with salt, cover, and simmer until the chicken is cooked through and falling off the bone, about 3 hours.

Pull out the chicken and set aside for other uses. Strain the broth through a fine-mesh sieve. Reserve the carrots for garnish and discard the rest of the solids.

Pour the broth into a clean pot and heat over low heat.

Meanwhile, in a medium bowl, beat the eggs with a fork. Beat in the oil and 1 teaspoon salt. Beating constantly, sprinkle in the corn flour and cornstarch (cornflour) until the mixture is thick but soft. Be prepared to cook the dumplings right away, because if this mixture sits it will stiffen.

Dip a teaspoon into the hot broth to make it hot, then use the hot teaspoon to spoon out dumplings from the egg dough. Drop the dumplings into the simmering broth one by one as you spoon them. When all the dumplings are in, cover the pot, and simmer until the dumplings double in size, about 5 minutes.

Serve the clear broth, some dumplings, and some of the reserved carrot sticks in soup bowls. Garnish with parsley leaves.

Turkey and Rice Soup

Preparation time: 45 minutes
Cooking time: 2 hours
30 minutes
Serves: 6

For the turkey and broth
1 whole turkey or turkey parts
 (5½ lb/2.5 kg)
1 stalk celery, chopped
1 leek, thinly sliced and well rinsed
Sea salt

For the soup
4 tablespoons olive oil
1 clove garlic, chopped
1 onion, chopped
2 teaspoons crushed dried chilies
Sea salt and freshly ground
 black pepper
4 teaspoons ground coriander
2¼ cups (300 g) green peas
3 carrots, diced
2¾ cups (450 g) canned corn
 kernels
1 red bell pepper, cut into strips
1⅔ cups (300 g) long-grain
 white rice

In Peru they call this dish *aguadito de pavo* and it is a dish that is often prepared in the days following Christmas to use up turkey leftovers—both the meat and the carcass, which is used to make the broth. Instead of dried chilies you can use Peruvian fresh or canned ají amarillo or ají panca, which you can find online or in stores that specialize in South American ingredients. The recipe can also be prepared with chicken instead of turkey.

Cook the turkey and broth: In a large pot, combine the whole turkey, celery, leek, and 5 quarts (5 liters) salted water. Bring to a boil, then reduce to a simmer and cook until the turkey is cooked through, about 2 hours.

Pull the turkey from the broth. When cool enough to handle, pull the meat off the bones (discard the skin and bones) and shred the meat. Strain the broth and set aside.

Make the soup: In a soup pot, heat the oil over medium heat. Add the garlic, onion, and dried chilies and sauté until the onion is translucent, about 5 minutes. Season to taste with salt and black pepper. Add the ground coriander, peas, carrots, corn, and bell pepper and simmer for 5 minutes.

Add the broth and bring to a boil. Add the rice and reserved turkey meat and simmer until the rice is tender, about 20 minutes. Serve hot.

Beef Rib Soup

Malaysia

Preparation time: 10 minutes
Cooking time: 2 hours
Serves: 4

For the spice paste
1 tablespoon coriander seeds
1 tablespoon cumin seeds
1 tablespoon fennel seeds
1 teaspoon black peppercorns
1 tablespoon ground star anise
1 tablespoon ground cloves
1 tablespoon ground cinnamon
2 teaspoons grated fresh ginger
1 tablespoon minced garlic

For the soup
4 tablespoons sunflower oil
1 tablespoon chopped shallot
2 teaspoons (10 g) grated fresh
  galangal
5 teaspoons (10 g) ground
  turmeric
2½ tablespoons (20 g) kurma
  powder (see Note)
Sea salt and freshly ground
  white pepper
1¾ lb (800 g) beef short ribs,
  cut into chunks
6 cups (48 fl oz/1.4 liters) beef
  bone broth
4 bay leaves
Scant ¾ cup (70 g) chopped
  celery
⅔ cup chopped (100 g)
  yellow potatoes
Generous ½ cup (70 g)
  chopped carrots
3 tablespoons chopped fresh
  parsley, for garnish

Sup tulang is a very rich and aromatic beef soup flavored with spices and vegetables. The traditional recipe is made with beef or mutton bone marrow but here we are using beef ribs because they give the soup a nice texture and a lighter taste.

Make the spice paste: In a dry nonstick frying pan, toast the coriander seeds, cumin seeds, fennel seeds, and peppercorns until fragrant. Put them in a mortar and pestle and grind them. Add the star anise, cloves, cinnamon, ginger, and garlic. Grind into a paste.

Make the soup: In a soup pot, heat the oil over low heat. Add the spice paste, shallot, galangal, turmeric, kurma powder, and salt and white pepper to taste. Add the meat to the pot and stir. Add the bone broth and bay leaves and simmer until the meat is tender, 1 hour to 1 hour 30 minutes.

Add the celery, potatoes, and carrots and simmer until the potatoes are firm-tender, about 25 minutes.

Serve in soup bowls and garnish with parsley.

Note: Kurma powder is a specific blend of spices (called a masala) used to make the category of Indian dishes called kurma, korma, or qorma. This well-known curry is typically made by marinating meat or vegetables in a mildly spiced yogurt, cream, or coconut milk sauce.

Beef Pho

Preparation time: 30 minutes
Cooking time: 3 hours
Serves: 6

2½ lb (1.2 kg) beef bones
1 lb 2 oz (500 g) beef sirloin
  (rump)
2 large onions—1 chopped,
  1 halved
2 sprigs parsley, chopped
2 tablespoons chopped peeled
  fresh ginger
1 star anise
8 black peppercorns
2 teaspoons fine sea salt
3 tablespoons chopped fresh
  herbs, such as cilantro
  (coriander), mint, or Thai basil
1 lb 2 oz (500 g) dried rice
  vermicelli noodles
2 fresh chili peppers, seeded
  and sliced
Coarse sea salt

Pho is a traditional Vietnamese noodle, beef, and vegetable soup that has become popular all over the world. In Vietnam, you can choose various cuts of beef for the recipe: brisket, shin, stewing beef, tendons, or tripe. Pho can be served topped with various fresh garnishes such as chilies, scallions (spring onions), onions, and bean sprouts, and is accompanied by lime wedges or sauces such as Sriracha or fish sauce.

In a large pot, combine the beef bones, beef, 2 quarts (1.9 liters) water, the onions, parsley, ginger, star anise, and peppercorns. Bring to a boil over high heat, then reduce to a simmer and cook for 2 hours, skimming any foam from the surface with a skimmer. Add the fine sea salt and simmer for 1 hour longer.

Pull out the meat and bones. Discard the bones and cut the meat into very thin slices. Strain the broth into a clean pot (discard the solids) and stir in half of the chopped herbs.

In a saucepan of boiling salted water, cook the noodles until tender, about 5 minutes. Drain well.

Add the sliced meat to the broth and reheat. Add the noodles and chilies and sprinkle some coarse salt over the meat. Serve hot, garnished with the remaining herbs.

Soups

100

Beef Bone Soup

Korea

**Preparation time: 1 hour,
    plus 30 minutes soaking time
    and overnight chilling time
Cooking time: 7 hours 30 minutes
Serves: 6**

3¼ lb (1.5 kg) beef shin bones
2½ lb (1.2 kg) Korean-style short
    ribs (flanken cut)
1 onion, peeled
1 Korean radish, peeled
2 tablespoons sesame oil
1 tablespoon sea salt
1 teaspoon freshly ground
    black pepper

A very popular soup from Seoul called *seolleongtang*, this is usually served during Korea's cold winters. The long cooking time extracts all the flavor from the beef bones. The soup is silky and clear and is usually eaten with rice (which can be cooked directly in the soup) or with various side dishes.

In two separate bowls of cold water, soak the beef bones and short ribs for 30 minutes. Drain and rinse.

In a large pot, combine 3 quarts (2.8 liters) water, the bones, and ribs. Bring to a boil over high heat and boil for 15 minutes. Drain the meat and rinse.

In a clean large pot, add the bones, ribs, onion, radish, and 8½ cups (68 fl oz/2 liters) water. Bring to a boil, then reduce the heat and simmer for 3 hours 30 minutes.

Remove the meat and radish from the broth and put them in a bowl (discard the bones and onion). Strain the broth into a bowl.

Transfer the meat to a clean pot and add the broth to cover. Bring to a boil, then reduce to a simmer, cover, and cook for 1 hour. Let the soup cool down, then cover with plastic wrap and refrigerate overnight.

Thinly slice the rib meat and cut the radish into slices. Season with the sesame oil. Remove the fat layer from the surface of the broth and reheat, then season with the salt and black pepper. Serve in individual bowls with 3 tablespoons of meat.

Veal Soup

Preparation time: 30 minutes
Cooking time: 1 hour 45 minutes
Serves: 4

Sea salt
1 cup (200 g) short-grain
   white rice
2 tablespoons lard
1 onion, finely chopped
9 oz (250 g) boneless veal, cubed
1½ cups (200 g) green peas
1 carrot, chopped
½ leek, chopped and well rinsed
1 cup (100 g) chopped celery
3 green peppercorns
4 oz (120 g) fresh horseradish root,
   peeled and grated
1 teaspoon paprika
½ teaspoon dried marjoram
1 bay leaf
5 cups (40 fl oz/1.2 liters) veal
   or beef stock
4 tablespoons (60 g) unsalted
   butter, melted
2 eggs, beaten
½ cup (95 g) sour cream
Chopped fresh parsley,
   for garnish

Popular and nutritious, *teleća čorba* can be found in casual restaurants all across the Balkans, where it is prepared in a variety of ways, but all include veal, vegetables, and fresh horseradish. The dish is finished with lots of chopped parsley and enriched with egg yolks and sour cream beaten together. Alternatively, it can be flavored with a little lemon juice.

In a saucepan, bring 4 cups (32 fl oz/950 ml) salted water to a boil. Add the rice and cook until tender, about 18 minutes. Drain well in a sieve, then run it under cold running water to cool. Set aside.

In a soup pot, heat the lard over medium heat. Add the onion and cook until lightly browned, about 3 minutes. Add the meat and brown on all sides, about 5 minutes per side. Stir in the peas, carrot, leek, celery, green peppercorns, and horseradish. Add the paprika and marjoram and season to taste with salt. Add the bay leaf and stock. Bring to a boil, then reduce to a simmer and cook until the meat is cooked through, about 1 hour 15 minutes.

Pour the melted butter into the soup and simmer gently for 5 minutes. Discard the bay leaf. Add the drained rice and remove the soup from the heat. Whisk the eggs into the hot soup and stir in the sour cream. Serve hot, garnished with parsley.

Beet Borscht

Preparation time: 30 minutes
Cooking time: 1 hour 20 minutes
Serves: 4

1 lb (455 g) beef strip steak
(sirloin), cut into chunks
(2 inches/5 cm)
5 black peppercorns
2 bay leaves
1 onion, chopped
11 oz (300 g) red beets (see Note),
peeled and diced
1 white turnip, diced
1⅓ cups (200 g) diced peeled
celeriac
Scant 3 cups (200 g) sliced
cabbage
2 carrots, diced
1 tablespoon sugar
3 tablespoons red wine vinegar
Sea salt
1 tablespoon tomato paste
(purée), dissolved in a little
warm water
4 tablespoons Greek yogurt,
for serving
½ tablespoon chopped fresh
parsley, for serving

Borscht is one of the most beloved dishes of Ukraine and
Russia, as well as other countries in Eastern Europe. There
are many variations on the theme, with different vegetables—
usually hardy winter vegetables—taking center stage, but
the distinguishing feature of a Ukrainian borscht is red beets,
which give the soup its characteristic flavor and beautiful
burgundy color.

In a soup pot, combine the beef, peppercorns, bay leaves, and
4 cups (32 fl oz/950 ml) cold water. Bring to a boil over medium-
high heat, then reduce to a simmer and cook until reduced by
one-third, about 45 minutes.

Discard the bay leaves. Add the onion, beets, turnip, celeriac,
cabbage, carrots, sugar, vinegar, and salt to taste. Cover and
simmer until the vegetables are soft, about 30 minutes.

Remove the meat chunks and divide them among soup
bowls. Stir the tomato paste (purée) mixture into the soup and
simmer for 5 minutes over high heat.

Pour the vegetables and broth over the meat. Top each
serving with 1 tablespoon yogurt and some chopped parsley.

Note: If the beets come with their greens, cut them off and rinse
well. Cut them into shreds and add to the soup, then boil until
tender, about 3 minutes.

Split Pea Soup

(DF) (NF)   **The Netherlands**

Preparation time: 30 minutes
Cooking time: 1 hour 50 minutes
Serves: 4

6¼ cups (50 fl oz/1.5 liters)
    beef stock
1 lb (450 g) dried split peas
5 oz (150 g) sliced bacon,
    cut into squares
5 oz (150 g) pork shoulder chops
5 oz (150 g) ham hock meat
1 bay leaf
1 leek, sliced and well rinsed
1 cup (150 g) diced peeled celeriac
1 carrot, diced
1 stalk celery, finely chopped
1 onion, chopped
1 baking potato, peeled and diced
1 smoked sausage (3 oz/85 g),
    sliced
Sea salt and freshly ground black
    pepper

A soup made with split peas, vegetables, and several meats, Dutch *snert* or *erwtensoep* is so thick that a spoon can stand upright in it. It is traditionally served on New Year's Eve, but is also prepared throughout the cold-weather months, served with slices of *rookworst*, a Dutch smoked sausage. Please ensure the sausage you use contains no gluten.

In a soup pot, combine the beef stock, split peas, bacon, shoulder chops, ham hock, and bay leaf. Bring to a boil over medium heat, then reduce to a simmer and cook until the chops are cooked through, about 1 hour, stirring occasionally.

   Remove the meats from the soup and cut them off the bones and into small pieces. Return the meat to the soup. Add the leek, celeriac, carrot, celery, onion, and potato and cook at a low simmer until the vegetables are tender, about 40 minutes.

   Add the sausage to the soup, then season to taste with salt and pepper. Simmer the soup for 10 minutes longer to develop the flavors. Discard the bay leaf and serve.

Note: The soup can also be served the next day, when it will be thicker and even more savory.

Yellow Pea and Pork Soup

**Preparation time: 30 minutes,
  plus 24 hours marinating time
Cooking time: 2 hours 20 minutes
Serves: 4**

1 lb 2 oz (500 g) pork shoulder, cut
  into 1-inch (2.5 cm) cubes
Sea salt
4 sprigs thyme
2 sprigs parsley
1 bay leaf
2 leeks, well rinsed—1 quartered,
  1 diced
2 onions—1 left whole (but peeled),
  1 diced
2 carrots—1 left whole, 1 diced
11 oz (300 g) dried whole
  yellow peas
1 lb 2 oz (500 g) pork sausages
11 oz (300 g) yellow potatoes,
  peeled and diced
Freshly ground black pepper

In the countries of Northern Europe, pea soup is very popular. This recipe is similar to Dutch *erwtensoep* or *snert* (see opposite), but here the pea soup and meats are cooked and served separately. For centuries, peas have been used in Danish cooking because they can be dried and stored for use throughout the winter. Traditionally, dishes were made with whole dried peas, but these days many recipes call for dried split peas, which take less time to cook. Please ensure the sausages you use contain no gluten.

Season the pork with salt, cover, and refrigerate for 24 hours.

Rinse the pork and place it in a soup pot. Add 8½ cups (68 fl oz/2 liters) water, 1 sprig of the thyme, 1 sprig of the parsley, the bay leaf, the leek quarters, whole onion, and whole carrot. Bring to a boil, then reduce to a simmer and cook until the pork is cooked through, about 1 hour 30 minutes.

Meanwhile, in a saucepan of boiling water, cook the peas until really soft, about 1 hour. Drain the peas and set aside.

Add the sausage to the simmering pork and cook for 10 minutes. Remove the pork and sausages and when cool enough to handle, slice them and set aside.

Fish out the thyme, parsley, and bay leaf and discard. In a food processor (or with a hand blender), blend the soup and return to the pot. Add the potatoes, diced onion, diced leek, and diced carrot and boil until the potatoes are firm-tender, about 15 minutes. Add the yellow peas and boil until all the ingredients are well combined, about 20 minutes. Season to taste with salt and black pepper.

Reheat the meat and sausages before serving with the soup.

Pea and Ham Soup

 NF

Preparation time: 20 minutes, plus 10 minutes resting time
Cooking time: 3 hours 30 minutes
Serves: 6

2 tablespoons (30 g) unsalted butter
2 large carrots, chopped
2 onions, chopped
1 stalk celery, chopped
2 cloves garlic, smashed and peeled
6 oz (175 g) dried green split peas
1 lb (450 g) pork hocks
8½ cups (68 fl oz/2 liters) ham bone stock
Sea salt and freshly ground black pepper
¼ lb (110 g) cured pork leg, sliced, for garnish

This is a typical English soup, which usually makes an appearance on Christmas holiday tables. It is a winter dish and for this reason is traditionally made with dried peas and not fresh.

In a soup pot, heat 1½ tablespoons (25 g) of the butter over medium heat. Add the carrots, onions, celery, and garlic and cook until the onions are soft, 5–6 minutes. Add the peas, pork hocks, and stock and season to taste with salt and pepper. Reduce the heat, cover, and simmer until the meat is very soft, about 3 hours. Remove the pot from the heat and let it rest for 10 minutes.

Remove the pork hocks from the pot and place them on a plate to cool down. When cool enough to handle, pull the meat off the bones and chop the meat.

In a pan over medium-high heat, melt the remaining 1 teaspoon (5 g) butter, then add the chopped meat and cook until crispy, about 3 minutes.

In a food processor (or with a hand blender), blend the pea mixture until it is creamy and smooth and return to the pot. Heat it over medium heat for 2 minutes, stir in the meat, and simmer for 10 minutes longer to blend the flavors. Serve hot, garnished with the sliced cured pork.

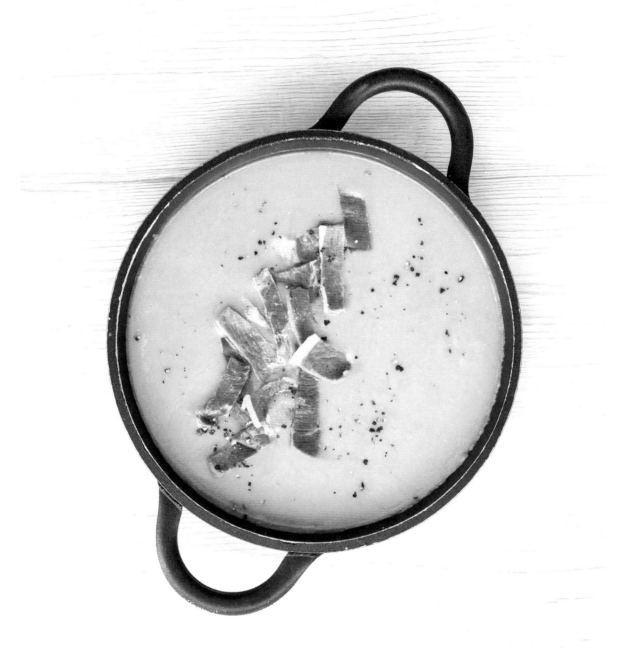

Pozole

Preparation time: 45 minutes
Cooking time: 3 hours 30 minutes
Serves: 4

2¼ lb (1 kg) pork shoulder, cut
    into chunks
1 tablespoon sea salt
4 cloves garlic, peeled
½ oz (15 g) fresh cilantro
    (coriander), plus more
    for garnish
1 lb 2 oz (500 g) tomatillos,
    husked and rinsed
3 serrano peppers
1 can (29 oz/822 g) hominy,
    drained

For garnish
4 lettuce leaves, thinly sliced
4 radishes, thinly sliced
½ red onion, finely chopped
Lime wedges, for squeezing

Called pozole, this Mexican soup gets its name from the Nahuatl word *pozilli*, which means "foam," a reference to what happens when the corn for the soup is prepared. The corn—a large white heirloom variety called *cacahuazintle*—is first soaked and/or cooked in an alkaline solution to loosen its skin, then it is peeled. The soup is served in individual bowls and toppings are placed in the center of the table so everyone can garnish their soup to taste.

In a large pot, combine the pork, 2 quarts (1.9 liters) water, and the salt and bring to a boil over high heat. Add 2 of the garlic cloves and the cilantro (coriander), then reduce the heat and simmer until the meat is cooked through, about 2 hours, skimming the foam from the surface with a skimmer. Discard the garlic.

Meanwhile, in a saucepan, combine the tomatillos and 4 cups (32 fl oz/950 ml) water and bring to a boil over medium heat. Cook until reduced by half, about 20 minutes, then remove from the heat.

Preheat a grill pan (griddle pan) over high heat. Add the serrano peppers and cook, turning, until the skin is charred on all sides. Place the chilies in a bowl, cover, and let them steam for 10 minutes. Peel the serranos and remove the stems and seeds.

In a blender, combine the tomatillos and cooking water, the serranos, and the remaining 2 garlic cloves and blend until the mixture is homogeneous and smooth. Pour the sauce into the pot with the meat and add the hominy. Cover and simmer over low heat for 1 hour, until the pork is very tender.

Spoon the pozole into soup bowls and set out the garnishes for people to add to their soups.

Cabbage Soup

Preparation time: 40 minutes, plus 2 hours resting time
Cooking time: 1 hour 40 minutes
Serves: 4

2¼ lb (1 kg) baby back (loin) pork ribs, cut into pieces
1 lb 2 oz (500 g) smoked cured ham (gammon), cubed
2 onions—1 whole, 1 diced
4 carrots—1 whole, 3 diced
10 black peppercorns
2 bay leaves
1½ sticks (6 oz/175 g) unsalted butter
2 tomatoes, diced
3 yellow potatoes, cubed
1½ oz (40 g) dried porcini, soaked in warm water and rinsed well
1 lb 5 oz (600 g) sauerkraut, store-bought or homemade (page 235)
Scant ⅓ cup (120 g) millet
Sea salt
Fresh parsley, for garnish
Fresh dill, for garnish

The main feature of this traditional Russian soup called *shchi* is the tartness from the sauerkraut, but some versions of the soup are made with fresh cabbage. There are also regional variations in which the pork is replaced by poultry or a combination of beef and pork. This type of soup is even better if made the day before; but if that is not possible it should rest for at least 2 hours, as suggested below.

In a large pot, combine the ribs, ham (gammon), whole onion, whole carrot, peppercorns, bay leaves, and 3 quarts (3 liters) cold water. Bring to a boil over medium heat, then reduce to a simmer and cook until the ribs are cooked, about 1 hour, skimming any foam from the surface so the broth remains clear.

Remove the meat from the broth and when cool enough to handle, cut it into pieces (discard the bones) and return the meat to the broth. Discard the bay leaves.

In a frying pan, heat 8 tablespoons (115 g) of the butter over low heat. Add the diced onion, diced carrots, and tomatoes and cook until the tomatoes start to be really soft, about 7 minutes.

Add the sautéed vegetables to the broth along with the potatoes and mushrooms and simmer until the potatoes are tender, about 20 minutes.

Meanwhile, in a saucepan, heat the sauerkraut with the remaining 4 tablespoons (60 g) butter for 15 minutes.

Add the stewed sauerkraut to the soup along with the millet. Season to taste with salt and simmer until the millet is cooked, about 10 minutes longer. Remove from the heat and let it rest for 2 hours before serving.

Reheat before serving. Serve garnished with parsley and dill.

Three-Meat Soup

Colombia

Preparation time: 1 hour
Cooking time: 3 hours
Serves: 6

1 lb (450 g) boneless, skinless chicken (see Note)
1 lb 5 oz (600 g) beef short ribs with fat
1 lb 2 oz (500 g) baby back (loin) pork ribs
1 medium carrot, sliced
1 yellow onion, halved
1 stalk celery, cut into 2-inch (5 cm) chunks
Sea salt and freshly ground black pepper
2 ears corn, husked and each quartered crosswise
1 plantain, peeled
½ lb (220 g) yuca (cassava) root, peeled (see Note, page 20)
2½ lb (1.2 kg) red potatoes, peeled and cut into chunks
1 lb 2 oz (500 g) pumpkin or other winter squash, peeled and cut into chunks
1 leek, sliced and well rinsed
1 fresh red chili pepper, chopped
1 sprig parsley, chopped
1 tablespoon fresh cilantro (coriander) leaves, chopped
Ground cumin
Juice of ½ lemon

Sancocho is a thick soup made with root vegetables and meat, and is one of the most popular and traditional dishes in Colombia. There are numerous versions, including this one, *sancocho trifásico*, made with three different meats, yuca (cassava), plantain, potatoes, vegetables, and herbs. Each region also has its own traditional condiments for its *sancocho*. In Colombia, this would traditionally be made with a stewing hen, but that is pretty difficult to come by in today's markets.

In a large pot, combine the chicken, beef, pork loin, and 4 quarts (4 liters) cold water. Bring to a boil over medium heat, skimming the foam from the surface with a skimmer. Add the carrot, onion, and celery and season to taste with salt and black pepper. Reduce the heat and simmer until the meats are tender, about 1 hour 30 minutes.

Add the corn and simmer for 30 minutes.

Cut the plantain and yuca (cassava) crosswise into rounds 1 inch (2.5 cm) thick. Add to the soup and simmer for 20 minutes.

Add the potatoes, pumpkin, and leek to the soup and simmer for 30 minutes more.

Stir in the chili, parsley, cilantro (coriander), and cumin to taste and cook for 5 minutes. Stir in the lemon juice and serve.

Note: For the best flavor, use a good proportion of dark to light meat (or all dark meat if you prefer).

Okra Soup

Preparation time: 20 minutes
Cooking time: 1 hour
Serves: 4

Generous 1¾ cups (350 g)
    long-grain white rice
Sea salt
9 oz (250 g) boneless goat leg,
    cubed
1 clove garlic, minced
½ onion, finely chopped
Scant 2 tablespoons grated
    fresh ginger
2 teaspoons chili powder
1½ teaspoons freshly ground
    black pepper
3 cups (24 fl oz/710 ml) chicken
    stock
6 oz (175 g) fresh okra—half
    chopped, half grated
⅓ cup plus 1 tablespoon
    (3½ fl oz/90 ml) palm oil
3½ oz (100 g) dried crayfish
1 bay leaf
2 plum tomatoes, chopped
1 fresh habanero pepper, crushed
4 oz (115 g) lump crabmeat
2 salmon steaks (3 oz/85 g each),
    skinned and chopped
4 oz (115 g) spinach

Many West African countries have their version of a soup or stew centered on okra (or *okro* as it is called in Ghana). Some of them are more stew-y than soup-y and are served with eggs. This Ghanaian okra soup is made with a combination of goat meat and seafood. The okra can be steamed before being added to the soup (which will make it more viscous) or can be incorporated raw.

In a saucepan, bring 4 cups (32 fl oz/950 ml) water to a boil. Add rice and 2 teaspoons salt. Cook until the rice is tender, about 20 minutes, stirring once halfway through and adding more water if it evaporates before the rice is tender. With a little of the water left in the pan, remove from the heat, cover and let it rest for 10 minutes.

In a saucepan, toss the meat with the garlic, salt, half of the onion, the ginger, chili powder, and black pepper. Add enough stock to cover the meat. Cook over medium heat until tender, about 15 minutes. Strain the broth into a bowl. Set the meat and broth aside.

In a bowl, soak the chopped okra in water for 10 minutes. Drain and set aside.

In a soup pot, heat the palm oil over high heat. Add the remaining onion and sauté until almost translucent, about 3 minutes. Add the crayfish, bay leaf, and meat and cook for a few minutes. Add the tomatoes and habanero and cook until the tomatoes are reduced to a coarse purée, about 12 minutes.

Add enough broth to cover all the ingredients and bring to a boil. Add the chopped okra, crab, and salmon. Reduce the heat and simmer for 5 minutes. Add the grated okra and spinach and simmer until the spinach wilts.

To serve, divide the rice among shallow bowls. Pour the okra soup on top.

Shrimp, Corn, and Vegetable Soup

Preparation time: 1 hour
Cooking time: 1 hour 15 minutes
Serves: 6

11 oz (300 g) pumpkin or other
    winter squash, seeded and cut
    into big chunks (leave the skin
    on if it's edible)
2½ lb (1.2 kg) white potatoes,
    scrubbed
4 tablespoons sunflower oil
2 fresh ají amarillo chilies, seeded,
    deveined, and chopped
4 cloves garlic, chopped
3 onions, chopped
1 teaspoon ground cumin
Freshly ground black pepper
¾ cup (6 fl oz/180 ml)
    vegetable stock
4 ears corn, husked and sliced
    crosswise
8 caiguas or 3 English cucumbers,
    sliced
9 oz (250 g) cooked or canned
    cannellini beans
½ cup (4 fl oz/120 ml) milk
11 oz (300 g) ricotta cheese
1 cup (250 g) cushuro (optional)
2½ lb (1.2 kg) shrimp (prawns),
    peeled and deveined
Sea salt

Chupe is a delicious soup made with shrimp (prawns), corn, and vegetables. Spicy and savory, it's a favorite dish in Latin America. The soup includes some native Peruvian ingredients, such as *caigua*, a sort of hollow cucumber (which is sometimes cooked stuffed), and *cushuro* (aka *murmunta*), a type of bead-shaped alga that grows in lakes in the Andes. Both are difficult to find outside of Peru, so use regular cucumber in place of the *caigua* and simply omit the *cushuro*.

In a saucepan of boiling water, cook the pumpkin until tender, about 30 minutes. Drain well.

Meanwhile, in a separate pan of boiling water, cook the potatoes until tender, about 30 minutes. Drain and when cool enough to handle, peel and cut into cubes.

In a soup pot, heat the oil over medium heat. Add the chilies, garlic, onions, cumin, and black pepper to taste and cook until the onions are translucent, about 5 minutes. Add the pumpkin and stir constantly for 5 minutes, to mash the pumpkin and combine.

Stir in the stock, corn, caiguas or cucumbers, and beans. Simmer for 10 minutes. Add the milk, ricotta, potatoes, and cushuro (if using). Simmer for 20 minutes. Add the shrimp (prawns) and bring to a boil for 4 minutes.

Serve hot.

Spanish Seafood Soup

Preparation time: 1 hour, plus 20 minutes soaking time
Cooking time: 1 hour
Serves: 4

1 lb 5 oz (600 g) clams, well scrubbed
½ cup (4 fl oz/120 ml) extra-virgin olive oil
6 cloves garlic, chopped
2 onions, chopped
1 fresh chili pepper, seeded and sliced
4 oz (115 g) unsliced ham (in one piece), diced
2¼ lb (1 kg) tomatoes, peeled, seeded, chopped, and drained
Generous ¾ cup (100 g) almond meal (ground almonds)
1 teaspoon (0.7 g) saffron
4 bay leaves
1 sprig thyme
1 sprig rosemary
1 cup (8 fl oz/240 ml) dry white wine
4 lemons—1 juiced, 3 cut into slices
Sea salt and freshly ground black pepper
14 oz (400 g) squid (calamari), cleaned, bodies cut into rings and tentacles left whole
12 scallops
6 large shrimp (prawns), peeled and deveined

From the Spanish region of Catalonia, a *zarzuela* is a typical "fisherman's" soup, meaning that it can include a multitude of different fish and shellfish, depending on the catch of the day or the whim of the cook. *Zarzuela* means "operetta," a theatrical style that mixes songs with spoken words, just as the seafood is mixed together here. In this *zarzuela de mariscos*, a favorite in Barcelona, it's just shellfish (*mariscos*) and no finfish. The broth is scented with paprika and saffron, which also make it a very colorful dish, and is thickened with almond meal (ground almonds). This soup is perfect with a glass of crisp white wine.

In a bowl of cold water, let the clam soak for 20 minutes to purge them of sand. Drain well.

In a soup pot, heat the oil over low heat. Add the garlic, onions, and chili pepper and cook until the onions are golden, about 5 minutes. Add the ham and stir for 2 minutes. Add the tomatoes and simmer for 10 minutes more.

Stir in the almond meal (ground almonds), saffron, bay leaves, thyme, and rosemary. Sprinkle with the wine and lemon juice, then season to taste with salt and black pepper. Simmer for 5 minutes. Add 2 cups (16 fl oz/475 ml) water and bring to a boil, then reduce to a simmer, cover, and cook until the sauce is thickened and creamy, about 15 minutes.

Add all the clams to the saucepan, cover, and cook until the clams open (discard any that don't), about 5 minutes.

Add the squid (calamari), scallops, and shrimp (prawns). Cover and simmer over low heat until the squid rings are cooked, about 10 minutes. Season with salt and pepper. Serve with lemon slices.

Brazilian Seafood Soup

**Preparation time: 45 minutes,
plus 1 hour marinating time
Cooking time: 40 minutes
Serves: 4**

½ cup (4 fl oz/ 120 ml) full-fat
   coconut milk
¾ cup plus 2 tablespoons
   (7 fl oz/200 ml) palm oil
Juice of 2 lemons
1¾ lb (800 g) cod fillets
2 white onions, thinly sliced
2 cloves garlic, minced
4 tomatoes, seeded and
   thinly sliced
2 red bell peppers, diced
½ oz (15 g) fresh cilantro
   (coriander)
1 dried chili pepper, chopped
Sea salt and freshly ground
   black pepper
12 red shrimp (prawns), peeled
   and deveined

This soup is called *moqueca*, a term that refers to any type of slow-cooked stew, but that is usually associated with *moqueca de peixe* ("fish" in Portuguese). This recipe is typical of Bahia, a coastal state north of Rio, that adds shrimp (prawns) to the fish fillets. Other versions, such as the *moqueca capixaba*, use only white-fleshed fish and coconut milk. Traditionally all *moquecas* should be cooked in black clay pots.

In a small bowl, stir together the coconut milk, palm oil, and lemon juice. In a large bowl, combine the cod, onions, garlic, tomatoes, bell peppers, cilantro (coriander), and chili. Pour in the coconut mixture, cover, and marinate at room temperature for 1 hour.

Transfer the fish mixture to a cast-iron Dutch oven (casserole). Bring to a boil over medium heat, season to taste with salt and black pepper, then reduce the heat to low and simmer, stirring occasionally, until the cod is tender, about 35 minutes.

Add the shrimp (prawns) to the simmering soup, cover, and cook until the shrimp are opaque throughout, about 5 minutes more. Serve hot.

Salmon Soup

**Preparation time: 40 minutes
Cooking time: 30 minutes
Serves: 4**

4½ tablespoons (65 g) butter
1 leek, sliced and well rinsed
5 cups (40 fl oz/1.2 liters) fish stock
1 lb (450 g) salmon fillet, skinned
   (skin reserved) and cut into
   large chunks
1 lb 2 oz (500 g) yellow potatoes,
   peeled and cubed
1 large carrot, sliced
1 tablespoon finely chopped fresh
   dill, plus more for garnish
1 cup (8 fl oz/240 ml) heavy
   (whipping) cream
Sea salt and freshly ground
   black pepper

Lohikeitto is a fresh tasting dill-flecked salmon soup from Finland. The potatoes give the soup a nice heft, and a generous amount of cream makes the dish lovely and rich. If you can find them, use Finnish potatoes in the soup.

In a soup pot, melt the butter over medium heat. Add the leek and cook until softened, about 10 minutes.

Meanwhile, in a saucepan, combine the fish stock and reserved salmon skin. Bring to a boil, then reduce to a gentle simmer and cook over low heat for 10 minutes to extract the flavor.

Strain the broth and add it to the pot with the leek. Add the potatoes, carrot, and dill. Cook until the potatoes are tender, about 10 minutes.

Add the salmon chunks and cream to the soup and gently simmer until the salmon is just barely cooked through, about 10 minutes. Season to taste with salt and pepper and garnish with a little more chopped dill.

New England Clam Chowder

**Preparation time: 20 minutes,
   plus 1 hour soaking time
Cooking time: 35 minutes
Serves: 4**

8–10 littleneck clams (14 oz/
   400 g), well scrubbed, soaked
   for 1 hour in cold water,
   and drained
4 oz (120 g) bacon (streaky),
   cut crosswise into 1-inch
   (2.5 cm) pieces
1 onion, chopped
1 clove garlic, chopped
2 stalks celery, chopped
2 yellow potatoes, peeled
   and cubed
1 cup (8 fl oz/240 ml) chicken
   stock
Freshly ground white pepper
Dried thyme
Scant 2 cups (15.2 fl oz/450 ml)
   heavy (whipping) cream
1 tablespoon cornstarch
   (cornflour)
2 sprigs thyme, leaves picked,
   for garnish

Tracing the origins of a recipe is notoriously difficult, but there's a good chance this famous creamy fish and potato stew has its roots in the dishes of the early French and Scottish settlers in Nova Scotia: The French fish soup *chaudière* and the Scottish smoked haddock and potato dish called Cullen skink are both very similar to New England clam chowder. There are many variations of American chowder, including the popular Manhattan Clam Chowder, which is made with a tomato-y broth and no cream. However, much of New England considers the Manhattan version an abomination, to the point that in 1939 the state of Maine considered outlawing the use of tomatoes in clam chowder (the proposal was not approved).

In a pot, combine the clams with cold water to cover. Cover, bring to a boil over high heat, and cook until the clams open (discard any that do not). Scoop out the clams. Strain the cooking liquid and set aside. Pull the clam meats out of the shells.

In a soup pot, cook the bacon over medium heat until crisp, 6–7 minutes. Transfer the bacon to paper towels to drain. Keep the bacon fat in the pot.

Add the onion, garlic, and celery to the bacon fat in the pot and cook until softened, about 5 minutes. Add the potatoes, stock, reserved clam cooking liquid, and white pepper and dried thyme to taste. Bring to a boil, then reduce the heat and simmer until the potatoes are tender, about 12 minutes.

In a bowl, combine a scant 1 cup (7.5 fl oz/225 ml) cream and the cornstarch (cornflour) and mix carefully. Pour the mixture into the soup and simmer, stirring constantly, for 2 minutes to thicken.

Add the clam meats and the remaining scant 1 cup (7.5 fl oz/ 225 ml) cream and simmer for 2 more minutes. Serve hot in bowls with the bacon and fresh thyme sprinkled on top.

Snapper in Turmeric and Lemongrass Broth

Preparation time: 20 minutes
Cooking time: 1 hour
Serves: 4

1 whole snapper (3 lb/1.5 kg),
   filleted (reserve the head
   and bones)
6 tablespoons palm oil
3 cloves garlic, sliced
7 oz (200 g) dried rice noodles
2 stalks lemongrass
5 makrut lime leaves (see
   Note, page 33)
2 small fresh red chili peppers,
   seeded and thinly
   sliced lengthwise
½ teaspoon ground coriander
½ teaspoon ground cumin
¼ teaspoon ground turmeric
1 teaspoon sea salt
2 teaspoons minced fresh cilantro
   (coriander), for garnish

For *laksa*, a spicy noodle soup from Malaysia, snapper and rice noodles are cooked in a simple Asian-style fish broth flavored with lemongrass, makrut lime leaves, and turmeric.

In a soup pot, combine 5 cups (40 fl oz/1.2 liters) water and the reserved fish head and bones. Bring to a boil, then reduce to a simmer and cook for 30 minutes. Strain the broth and set aside. When cool enough to handle, pick the meat off the head (discard the bones).

Cut the snapper fillets into small pieces and combine with the head meat.

In a small saucepan, heat the oil over medium-high heat. Add the garlic and fry until golden, about 2 minutes. Strain the garlic oil in a sieve set over a bowl (discard the oil). Fish the garlic out of the sieve and set aside on paper towels to drain.

In a pan of simmering water, cook the rice noodles for 10 minutes, then drain and rinse under cold running water.

In a soup pot, combine 4¼ cups (34 fl oz/1 liter) fish broth, the lemongrass, makrut lime leaves, chili peppers, ground coriander, cumin, turmeric, and salt. Bring to a boil, then reduce to a simmer and cook for 5 minutes.

Add the snapper and simmer until the fish is no longer translucent, about 3 minutes. It should be slightly undercooked as it will continue to cook from the residual heat of the hot broth as you get ready to serve.

To serve, divide the noodles among four bowls. Carefully place some fish on top. Pour the broth over it and garnish with fried garlic slices and cilantro (coriander).

Persian Legume Soup

Preparation time 25 minutes, plus overnight soaking time
Cooking time: 1 hour
Serves: 4

¾ cup (150 g) dried peeled fava beans (broad beans)
Scant ¾ cup (100 g) dried mung beans
2 tablespoons olive oil
1 large onion, thinly sliced lengthwise
½ cup (50 g) minced scallions (spring onions)
1 clove garlic, minced
2 teaspoons ground turmeric
1 teaspoon ground cumin
1 teaspoon freshly ground black pepper
½ cup (100 g) green lentils
6 cups (48 fl oz/1.5 liters) vegetable stock or water
1 tablespoon sea salt
2 teaspoons ground coriander
5 tablespoons (15 g) dried mint
5 oz (150 g) kashk or Greek feta cheese, grated, for serving

This Persian bean soup, called *ash,* is topped with *kashk,* a Middle Eastern dairy product that is made by draining a fermented milk (like yogurt) until it's firm enough to be shaped into chunks or balls. It tastes somewhat like feta cheese, which can be used as a substitute.

In a bowl, soak the fava beans (broad beans) and mung beans in cold water overnight. Drain the beans and set aside.

In a soup pot, heat the olive oil over low heat. Add the onion, scallions (spring onions), and garlic and stir-fry gently until the onion is translucent, about 5 minutes. Add the turmeric, cumin, and black pepper and stir for 2 minutes over low heat.

Add the lentils, fava beans, and mung beans. Add the vegetable stock to cover and stir in the salt. Simmer over low heat until the fava beans are tender, about 50 minutes, stirring every 15 minutes. The soup should be creamy and quite thick.

Stir in the ground coriander and mint. Remove from the heat and let stand for 10 minutes.

Serve hot topped with kashk or feta cheese.

Tortilla Soup

Preparation time: 30 minutes
Cooking time: 40 minutes
Serves: 4

Sunflower oil, for frying
¼ lb (110 g) corn tortillas,
    store-bought or homemade
    (page 148), cut into strips
    ½ inch (1.25 cm) wide
2 tablespoons olive oil
1 yellow onion, finely chopped
2 serrano peppers, seeded
    and finely chopped, plus more
    for garnish
1 clove garlic, chopped
1¾ lb (800 g) tomatoes, cubed
2 tablespoons chopped fresh
    cilantro (coriander) leaves,
    plus more for garnish
2 tablespoons chopped fresh
    epazote or wild fennel
1 tablespoon dried oregano
Sea salt and freshly ground
    black pepper
6 cups (48 fl oz/1.4 liters)
    chicken stock
2 avocados, cubed
9 oz (250 g) soft goat cheese
4 tablespoons Mexican crema
    or sour cream (optional)

Sopa azteca—a Mexican soup also popular in the American Southwest—is a chili-tomato broth with strips of fried tortilla, chunks of avocado, and soft fresh cheese. The soup often has cooked chicken added to it. Making fresh tortilla strips is ideal, but to save time you can use high-quality tortilla chips.

Pour 3 inches (7.5 cm) sunflower oil into a large Dutch oven (casserole) and heat over medium heat to 325°F (160°C) on a deep-fry thermometer or until the oil makes bubbles around a test strip of tortilla.

Working in batches, add the tortilla strips to the hot oil and fry, stirring frequently, until golden, about 4 minutes. Drain on paper towels.

In a soup pot, heat the olive oil over high heat. Add the onion and serranos and cook until the onion is translucent, 3–4 minutes. Add the garlic, tomatoes, cilantro (coriander), epazote or wild fennel, and oregano and simmer until the liquid is reduced by half, about 15 minutes. Season to taste with salt and black pepper.

Add the stock, bring to a boil over high heat, then reduce the heat to low and simmer for 10 minutes more.

Divide the tortilla strips among shallow bowls and pour the soup over them. Top with avocado cubes and little quenelles of cheese (or place small amounts with a teaspoon). If desired, add 1 tablespoon crema to each bowl. Garnish with a little more cilantro and serrano pepper.

Miso Soba Soup

Preparation time: 10 minutes
Cooking time: 15 minutes
Serves: 4

3 oz (80 g) soba noodles
2 tablespoons sesame oil
4 tablespoons canola
   (rapeseed) oil
2 cloves garlic, minced
1 teaspoon grated fresh ginger
3 scallions (spring onions),
   chopped
½ head broccoli, chopped
2 carrots, cut into matchsticks
4 Tuscan kale (cavolo nero)
   leaves, stemmed and
   midribs discarded
7 oz (200 g) shelled edamame
4 tablespoons white miso
Sesame seeds, for garnish

This simple noodle soup gets its umami flavor from the miso, a fermented soybean paste that comes in several forms, the most common being white (used here) and red. The vegetables we've added are simply suggestions; just use whatever vegetables you have on hand. When buying soba noodles, read the label to be certain that they are 100% buckwheat flour, as many brands add some wheat flour to the noodle dough to give them more structure.

In a pot of boiling water, cook the soba noodles until al dente, about 2 minutes. Drain and rinse and set aside.

In the same pot, heat the sesame oil over low heat. Return the noodles to the pot and toss to coat with the oil. Remove from the heat.

In a soup pot, heat the canola (rapeseed) oil over low heat. Add the garlic, ginger, and scallions (spring onions) and sauté until fragrant, about 4 minutes. Add 6 cups (48 fl oz/1.4 liters) water and bring to a boil. Add the broccoli, carrots, kale (cavolo nero), and edamame and simmer for 3 minutes.

In a small bowl, blend the miso with a spoonful of hot water from the soup pot, then stir the miso into the soup.

To serve, divide the noodles among four bowls. Pour the soup over the noodles and sprinkle sesame seeds on top.

Minestrone

Italy

Preparation time: 40 minutes
Cooking time: 45 minutes
Serves: 6

1 carrot, diced
5 oz (150 g) leeks, white part
 only, sliced and well rinsed
½ cup (50 g) diced celery
1 zucchini (courgette), diced
7 oz (200 g) pumpkin or other
 winter squash, peeled
 and diced
10 oz (280 g) fresh cranberry
 beans (borlotti beans)
11 oz (300 g) yellow potatoes,
 peeled and diced
12 oz (350 g) tomatoes, diced
6 oz (170 g) green beans,
 cut into short pieces
1½ cups (200 g) green peas
1½ cups (105 g) shredded
 cabbage
2¼ cups (80 g) shredded spinach
3–4 leaves fresh basil, slivered
3 tablespoons extra-virgin olive oil
1 tablespoon sea salt

Minestrone is a versatile soup that can be eaten both hot and cold. It can be served with corn croutons, rice, or quinoa. The vegetables in it change according to the season (or what's available in the fridge). And of course, every family has their own personal version. The soup can be served with chunks of vegetables (as here) or blended with an immersion blender to make a vegetable cream soup.

In a soup pot, combine 9 cups (72 fl oz/2.1 liters) water, the carrot, leek whites, celery, zucchini (courgette), pumpkin, beans, potatoes, tomatoes, green beans, peas, cabbage, spinach, and basil. Bring to a boil, then reduce to a simmer and cook until the potatoes are firm-tender, about 45 minutes.
    Add the oil and salt. Serve hot in winter or cold in the summer.

Variation: You can also make the soup by sautéing the vegetables first. In a soup pot, heat the oil over low heat. Add the carrots, leeks, and celery and cook until crisp-tender, about 5 minutes. Then add all the other vegetables, and finally the water. Boil until the vegetables are softened, about 40 minutes. Add the oil and salt as above.

Black Bean Soup

Preparation time: 30 minutes
Cooking time: 1 hour 30 minutes
Serves: 6

1 lb (450 g) dried black beans,
    soaked overnight in cold water,
    drained, and rinsed
Generous 3 cups (25 fl oz/750 ml)
    vegetable stock
6 eggs
2 tablespoons extra-virgin olive oil
2 onions, finely chopped
1 clove garlic, finely chopped
2 tablespoons chopped fresh
    cilantro (coriander)
2 teaspoons curry powder
Sea salt and freshly ground
    black pepper
1 avocado, sliced, for serving

Costa Rican *sopa negra*, or "black soup," gets its name from the color of the beans used to make it. It is a popular and time-honored dish, made with humble but tasty ingredients. The soup can be served with hot corn tortillas or boiled rice to make this protein-rich soup a main meal.

In a large soup pot, combine the beans and stock. Bring to a boil, then reduce the heat, cover, and gently simmer until softened, about 1 hour 30 minutes.

Meanwhile, place the eggs in a saucepan and cover them with cold water. Bring to a boil over medium heat and boil for 9 minutes. Drain and cool them under cold running water. Peel the eggs, cut into wedges, and set aside.

In a frying pan, heat the oil over medium heat. Add the onions, garlic, cilantro (coriander), and curry powder and cook until the onions are softened, about 4 minutes. Remove from the heat.

Measure out half of the beans and purée in a blender or food processor, then return to the pot. Add the sautéed vegetables. Season to taste with salt and pepper.

Divide the soup among six bowls and top each serving with egg wedges and avocado slices.

Bean Sprout Soup

Korea

**Preparation time: 30 minutes,
plus 1 hour soaking time
Cooking time: 30 minutes
Serves: 4**

10 cups (80 fl oz/2.4 liters) dashi
(see Note)
1 lb 2 oz (500 g) soybean sprouts,
rinsed
2 tablespoons chopped scallion
(spring onion)
1 teaspoon minced garlic
Sea salt

More than just a soup, Korean *kongnamul guk* is a powerhouse
of nutrients that is often made if someone isn't feeling well.
The soup is made with a clear and light dashi (broth) flavored
with anchovies and seaweed. You can make your own (see
Note), but store-bought dashi powders and granules are
easily available.

In a soup pot, bring the dashi to a boil. Add the soybean sprouts
and boil until softened, 3–4 minutes. Add the scallion (spring
onion), garlic, and salt to taste. Boil for 1–2 minutes to infuse the
broth with flavor. Serve hot or chilled.

Note: To make dashi, in a large pot, combine ½ oz (20 g) kombu
(dried kelp) and 3 quarts (3 liters) water and soak for at least
1 hour. Rinse 3 oz (85 g) dried anchovies under running water.
Add the anchovies to the pot with the water and kombu
(for a really clear stock, you can tie the anchovies in muslin
bags first). Bring to a boil and cook for 10 minutes. Remove
the kombu and let the anchovies boil for another 10 minutes.
Strain the dashi through a fine-mesh sieve.

Gazpacho

Spain

**Preparation time: 15 minutes,
plus 5 hours chilling time
Serves: 4**

1 lb 5 oz (600 g) tomatoes, halved
7 oz (200 g) cucumber, peeled
and sliced
7 oz (200 g) red bell pepper,
cut into squares
9 oz (250 g) green bell pepper,
cut into squares
1 red onion, sliced
1 clove garlic, sliced
5 tablespoons extra-virgin olive oil
2 tablespoons distilled white
vinegar
Sea salt and freshly ground
black pepper

This summer soup was born in Andalusia, the southern region
of Spain where it was originally a refreshing snack for field
laborers. Gazpacho is now famous all over the world and has
numerous variations. Some people like to enhance the refreshing
nature of this cold soup by adding some ice cubes to it.

In a food processor, combine the tomatoes, cucumber, bell
peppers, onion, garlic, and oil and pulse to obtain a creamy,
thick mixture.
    Pass the mixture through a sieve set over a bowl (discard the
skins and seeds). Return the mixture to the processor and add
the vinegar and salt and black pepper to taste and blend again.
    Pour the soup into a large bowl and refrigerate for 5 hours
before serving.

Lettuce Soup

(NF) (VT)

Romania

Preparation time: 30 minutes, plus 5 minutes resting time
Cooking time: 1 hour 15 minutes
Serves: 4

3 lb 5 oz (1.5 kg) lettuce, cut into strips
1 onion, chopped
Generous ½ cup (70 g) chopped carrot
1 tablespoon extra-virgin olive oil
3 eggs
Sea salt
4 cloves garlic, finely chopped
1⅔ cups (320 g) sour cream
½ cup (4 fl oz/120 ml) milk

In Romania there are regular soups called *supa* and then there is a category of soup called *ciorba,* which are sour soups. This *ciorba* is made with lettuce and is typically vegetarian, though there are versions, especially popular in Transylvania, that add smoked sausage or crispy bacon. In Romania, instead of milk they would use sheep whey. The soup should be served hot and can be accompanied by polenta, cheese, and fresh chili.

In a soup pot, bring 4 cups (32 fl oz/950 ml) water to a boil. Add the lettuce, onion, and carrot. Reduce the heat to a simmer and cook, uncovered, until the carrots are really soft, about 1 hour.

Meanwhile, in an 8-inch (20 cm) frying pan, heat the oil over medium heat. In a bowl, beat 2 of the eggs with some salt. Pour the eggs into the pan and cook the egg cake for 2 minutes, then flip and cook the second side for 2 minutes. Remove the egg cake from the pan. When it is cool enough to handle, cut it into squares.

Add the egg squares to the soup pot along with the garlic and simmer for 15 minutes.

Meanwhile, in a bowl, beat the remaining egg with the sour cream and the milk.

Remove the pot from the heat and let it rest for 5 minutes. Stirring constantly, pour the sour cream mixture into the soup. Season with salt.

Peanut Soup with Bananas

Preparation time: 30 minutes
Cooking time: 45 minutes
Serves: 4

1 cup (250 g) peanut butter
2 tablespoons honey
3½ cups (28 fl oz/839 ml)
    boiling water
4 tablespoons peanut
    (groundnut) oil
2 onions, chopped
2 cloves garlic, chopped
1 tablespoon chopped fresh
    ginger
1 Madame Jeanette chili,
    finely sliced
Sea salt
2 tablespoons chopped fresh
    cilantro (coriander),
    plus more for garnish
2 tablespoons ground turmeric
1 tablespoon ground cumin
1 tablespoon mustard seeds
1 teaspoon ground cloves
1½ teaspoons ground cinnamon,
    plus more for garnish
2¼ cups (18 fl oz/530 ml) full-fat
    coconut milk
2 large green bananas,
    sliced crosswise
Juice of 1 lemon

Pinda bravoe is a simple and spicy Surinamese peanut soup that brings some tropical heat to the table to beat the cold winter. The main ingredient is peanut butter (*pinda* means "peanut" in Dutch), and in Suriname it would be a spicy peanut butter made with Madame Jeanette chilies, which have about the same heat level as habaneros.

In a heatproof medium bowl, combine the peanut butter, honey, and boiling water and whisk until smooth. Set aside.

In a soup pot, heat 2 tablespoons of the oil over low heat. Add the onions, garlic, ginger, chili, and salt to taste and cook until the onions are lightly browned, about 10 minutes.

Add the cilantro (coriander), turmeric, cumin, mustard seeds, cloves, and 1 teaspoon of the cinnamon and stir for 5 minutes to develop the flavors. Add the coconut milk and peanut butter mixture, cover, and simmer, stirring occasionally, until the sauce is thickened and creamy, about 30 minutes.

Meanwhile, toss the banana slices with the lemon juice.

In a frying pan, heat the remaining 2 tablespoons oil over medium-high heat. Add the bananas and cook for 1 minute on each side. Sprinkle with the remaining ½ teaspoon cinnamon and salt to taste and gently toss.

Divide the soup among soup bowls. Garnish with the bananas and some more cinnamon and chopped cilantro.

Roasted Potato Soup

Preparation time: 30 minutes
Cooking time: 1 hour 45 minutes
Serves: 4

6 medium white potatoes,
    well scrubbed
3 tablespoons extra-virgin olive oil
Sea salt
1 stick (4 oz/115 g) unsalted butter
3 onions, chopped
1 clove garlic, chopped
1 tablespoon mustard powder
6½ cups (52 fl oz/1.5 liters)
    chicken stock
8 slices (rashers) smoked bacon
    (streaky)
4 tablespoons grated Parmesan
    cheese

Velvety soups are very popular in Belgium: creamy and warm preparations, ideal for the winter months. This simple recipe is easy to tweak: It can be vegetarian or seafood based, seasoned with different herbs and spices, or enriched with crème fraîche. Unlike many potato soups, where the potatoes are boiled, the roasting here adds another texture dimension.

Preheat the oven to 350°F (180°C/Gas Mark 4). Line a sheet pan with parchment paper.

Arrange the potatoes on the lined pan. Rub with the olive oil and sprinkle with salt. Transfer to the oven and bake until fork-tender, about 1 hour 30 minutes.

Remove the potatoes from the oven. When cool enough to handle, halve them lengthwise, peel the potatoes, and place the flesh in a bowl to cool.

In a soup pot, melt the butter over medium-low heat. Add the onions and cook until the onions are translucent, about 2 minutes. Add the garlic, mustard powder, potato flesh, and stock and stir to combine. Bring to a boil and cook until the potatoes break down into a creamy mixture, about 15 minutes.

Meanwhile, in a frying pan, cook the bacon over medium-high heat until crispy and golden, about 7 minutes. Cut 4 of the slices into little pieces.

Blend the soup with a hand blender and stir in the Parmesan. Divide the soup among four bowls and sprinkle with the bacon bits. Top each with a whole slice of bacon.

Wild Mushroom Soup

Preparation time: 30 minutes
Cooking time: 40 minutes
Serves: 4

1½ sticks (6 oz/170 g) unsalted
  butter
11 oz (300 g) fresh morel
  mushrooms, brushed clean
  and diced
7 oz (200 g) onions, diced
1 stalk celery (40 g), diced
4¼ cups (34 fl oz/1 liter) chicken
  stock
1 cup (8 fl oz/240 ml) heavy
  (whipping) cream
Fresh chives
Dried thyme
Sea salt and freshly ground
  black pepper
Fresh parsley leaves,
  for garnish

In Finland, it's a national pastime to forage for wild berries and mushrooms, including the false morel (*Gyromitra esculenta*). The false morel is a weird and wrinkly (some would say ugly) wild mushroom that is toxic if eaten raw, but there are those who know exactly how to prepare them to make them safe. To get the same delicious flavors without any of the danger, this soup is made with regular morels. And if you live in an area where they grow wild, you can get into the spirit of this Finnish soup and forage for them.

In a frying pan, heat 5 tablespoons (70 g) of the butter over medium heat. Add the mushrooms and sauté until they are lightly browned, about 5 minutes. Add the onions, reduce the heat, and cook until the onions are mostly softened, about 10 minutes longer.

In a soup pot, melt 3½ tablespoons (50 g) of the butter over medium heat. Add the celery and cook, stirring, until softened, about 10 minutes. Add the stock, cover, and simmer until the liquid is reduced by half, about 15 minutes.

Add the mushroom/onion mixture and gently stir to combine. Add the cream and the remaining 3½ tablespoons (50 g) butter. Season with chives, thyme, and salt and pepper to taste. Blend with a hand blender until the soup is creamy and smooth.

Serve warm, garnished with some parsley leaves.

Gundruk Soup

(DF) (NF) (VG) (VT)   **Nepal**

**Preparation time: 20 minutes,
    plus 10 minutes soaking time
Cooking time: 15 minutes
Serves: 4**

7 oz (200 g) gundruk
4 tablespoons mustard oil
1 tablespoon chopped seeded
    green chili
1 teaspoon chopped garlic
Scant ½ cup (65 g) chopped
    onions
2 tablespoons diced tomatoes
2 tablespoons ground cumin
1 tablespoon ground turmeric
Sea salt
3 tablespoons plus 2 teaspoons
    rice starch
Freshly ground black pepper
2 tablespoons chopped fresh
    cilantro (coriander), for garnish

This Nepalese soup is made with *gundruk*. These are fermented and dried leafy vegetables, which can include mustard greens, radish greens, and cauliflower leaves. The leaves are harvested in late fall (autumn) and placed in clay pots, where they are left to ferment. Once fermented, the leaves are dried in the sun so that they can be stored and used throughout the year. *Gundruk* has a very distinctive smell and a pungent flavor.

Soak the gundruk for 10 minutes in a bowl of cold water.
    Meanwhile, in a medium-large soup pot, heat the mustard oil over low heat. Add the chili and garlic and warm until the garlic starts bubbling in the oil, 2–3 minutes. Add the onions and cook until translucent, about 4 minutes.
    Drain and squeeze the gundruk. Add it to the pot and cook for 2 minutes. Add the tomatoes, cumin, turmeric, and 1 teaspoon salt. Add water to cover (about 4¼ cups/1 liter). Bring to a boil, then reduce to a simmer and cook for 15 minutes. Add the rice starch to thicken the soup. Season with salt and pepper taste.
    Divide among bowls or deep plates and serve garnished with cilantro (coriander).

Butternut Squash Soup

(NF)   **United States**

**Preparation time: 30 minutes
Cooking time: 50 minutes
Serves: 4**

2 tablespoons (30 g) unsalted
    butter
1 onion, chopped
1 carrot, chopped
3 medium yellow potatoes, cubed
1 butternut squash (5½ lb/2.5 kg),
    peeled, seeded, and cubed
6⅓ cups (50 fl oz/1.5 liters)
    chicken stock
Sea salt and freshly ground
    black pepper

Butternut is a winter vegetable in a category that Americans call "squash," a word derived from the Narragansett word *askutasquash*, which means "raw or uncooked." The Narragansett are northeastern Native Americans who introduced the early colonists to these vegetables. Since then, winter squash (which includes pumpkin) has become a staple of North American cooking. The butternut squash, with its dense and sweet orange flesh, is a fairly recent variety developed in the 1940s in Massachusetts.

In a soup pot, melt the butter over medium heat. Add the onion, carrot, potatoes, and squash and cook until light brown, about 5 minutes.
    Cover the vegetables with the stock and bring to a boil. Reduce to a simmer, season to taste with salt and pepper, cover, and cook until the vegetables are soft, about 45 minutes.
    Remove from the heat and purée with a hand blender until smooth. Serve hot.

Bread and Wraps

Brazilian Cheese Bread

(NF) (VT)

Brazil

Preparation time: 20 minutes
Cooking time: 20 minutes
Makes: 30–35 rolls

4¼ cups (500 g) tapioca starch
1½ cups (12.5 fl oz/375 ml) milk
6 tablespoons grapeseed oil
2 teaspoons sea salt
2 large eggs
3¼ cups (11 oz/300 g) grated
   Parmesan cheese
4⅔ cups (14 oz/400 g) shredded
   mozzarella cheese

Pão de queijo is a traditional Brazilian bread made from the starch of the yuca (cassava) root. The bread, which comes from the Brazilian states of Minas Gerais and Goiás, was originally made with nothing but the starch. But by the mid-twentieth century the bread had evolved to include milk and cheese and today it can be prepared with either sweet tapioca starch (*polvilho doce*) or sour tapioca starch (*polvilho azedo*). The shape of the bread can also vary, from round rolls (as here) to flat discs.

Position an oven rack in the center of the oven and preheat the oven to 400°F (200°C/Gas Mark 6). Line a sheet pan with parchment paper.

Place the tapioca starch in a heatproof bowl. In a saucepan, combine the milk, 4 tablespoons cold water, the oil, and salt. Bring to a boil over medium-high heat. Pour the boiling milk mixture into the tapioca starch and mix until fully incorporated.

Beat in the eggs, one at a time, mixing well until fully incorporated. Mix in the Parmesan, a little at a time, until fully incorporated. Stir in the mozzarella, a little at a time, until fully incorporated. The dough will be very sticky; if it is too sticky to handle, add a little more tapioca starch.

Wet your hands in cold water. Scoop some dough out with a spoon (about 1½ oz/40 g) and roll the dough between your hands into a ball the size of a golf ball. Place the balls on the lined sheet pan.

Transfer the sheet pan to the oven and bake until the rolls are golden and puffy, about 20 minutes. Serve warm.

Paraguayan Cheese Bread

Paraguay

Preparation time: 30 minutes
Cooking time: 30 minutes
Makes: 15 rolls

7 oz (200 g) Paraguayan cheese
 or white cheddar cheese,
 finely crumbled
7 oz (200 g) mozzarella cheese,
 shredded
7 oz (200 g) pecorino cheese,
 shredded
4 oz (120 g) blue cheese,
 crumbled
3½ cups (500 g) cassava flour
 (see Note, page 12)
1 teaspoon sea salt
1½ sticks (6 oz/175 g) butter,
 at room temperature
1 egg
1 cup (8 fl oz/240 ml) milk

A favorite Paraguayan snack, *chipa* are small, light round cheesy breads made with cassava flour. Being meatless, they are often prepared for Lent. In Paraguay there are at least 70 different variations of *chipa*, each with its own particular characteristics and ingredients.

Preheat the oven to 425°F (220°C/Gas Mark 7). Line a sheet pan with parchment paper.
 In a bowl, toss together the four types of cheese. Measure out ½ cup (60 g) of the cheese mixture and set aside.
 Add the cassava flour, salt, butter, egg, and milk and knead with your hands until a cohesive dough forms.
 Divide the dough into 15 equal portions and roll each one into a ball, then gently flatten and arrange them on the lined pan. Top each small bread with a generous teaspoon of the reserved cheese mixture.
 Bake until golden brown, about 30 minutes. Serve hot.

Cassava Bread

Guyana

Preparation time: 30 minutes,
 plus 45 minutes rising time
Cooking time: 40 minutes
Makes: 1 loaf

2 tablespoons maple syrup
¾ oz (20 g) fresh cake yeast
Generous ½ cup (80 g) cassava
 flour (see Note, page 12)
1⅓ cups (175 g) arrowroot starch
5 tablespoons (75 g) cold
 unsalted butter, grated
4 eggs, beaten
4 tablespoons coconut flour

Quinches is a delicious, slightly sweet bread from Guyana. In addition to cassava, the bread is made with arrowroot starch (often labeled "arrowroot flour" or "arrowroot powder"), which is extracted from the root of *Maranta arundinacea*, a tropical tuber that resembles yuca (cassava) in appearance.

In a small bowl, combine the maple syrup, ½ cup (4 fl oz/120 ml) warm water, and the yeast. Let the mixture froth for 15 minutes, or until it doubles.
 In a large bowl, mix the cassava flour, arrowroot starch, and grated butter with a fork until crumbs form. Add the eggs and the yeast mixture, then mix in the coconut flour. Let the dough rest for about 5 minutes.
 Line a 14 × 7-inch (36 × 18 cm) loaf pan with parchment paper. Place the dough in the lined pan, cover loosely, and let it rise until doubled, about 45 minutes.
 Preheat the oven to 350°F (180°C/Gas Mark 4).
 Bake until light golden, 30–40 minutes. Remove the bread from the pan and cool on a rack before serving.

Rice Bread

 Liberia

Preparation time: 20 minutes
Cooking time: 55 minutes
Makes: 1 loaf

1 tablespoon (15 g) unsalted
  butter, plus more for greasing
2½ cups (400 g) rice flour, plus
  more for the pan
12 very ripe plantains or bananas
1 egg
¾ cup plus 2 tablespoons (175 g)
  superfine (caster) sugar
1¼ cups (10 fl oz/300 ml) corn oil
2 teaspoons baking soda
  (bicarbonate of soda)
1 tablespoon grated fresh ginger
¾ teaspoon sea salt

Rice is a staple of Liberian cuisine and is widely used both as a grain and as flour. This traditional rice bread from Liberia is similar to banana bread, but uses plantains instead. It is delicious fresh out of the oven and stays moist for up to a week.

Preheat the oven to 345°F (175°C/Gas Mark 4). Grease and flour a 9 × 13-inch (23 × 33 cm) baking pan.

In a bowl, mash the plantains by hand. Add the egg, sugar, and oil. With an electric mixer, beat on low speed for 1 minute. Add 1 cup (8 fl oz/240 ml) water, the rice flour, butter, baking soda (bicarbonate of soda), ginger, and salt. Beat on high speed for 3 minutes or until well mixed. Scrape the batter into the prepared pan.

Bake until the sides of the bread pull away from the sides of the pan, about 55 minutes.

Serbian Corn Bread

 Serbia

Preparation time: 10 minutes
Cooking time: 40 minutes
Makes: 1 loaf

2 sticks (8 oz/240 g) unsalted
  butter, melted, or 1 cup
  (8 fl oz/240 ml) sunflower oil,
  plus more for greasing
Scant 3 cups (500 g) cornmeal
3 eggs, beaten
¾ cup plus 2 tablespoons (250 g)
  Greek yogurt
1 tablespoon sea salt
1 cup (8 fl oz/240 ml) milk

Projara is a Serbian corn bread that has its origins in peasant cooking, being made with just cornmeal and water and not much else. Today's versions are enriched with eggs, yogurt, and/or milk. This corn bread is usually served with sauerkraut or *pavlaka*, a dairy product similar to sour cream but with a more delicate flavor.

Preheat the oven to 375°F (190°C/Gas Mark 5). Grease a 9 × 13-inch (23 × 33 cm) baking pan with butter or oil.

In a bowl, mix together the cornmeal with the butter or oil, eggs, yogurt, and salt. Knead for 5 minutes, then add the milk and mix again for at least 5 minutes. Scrape the mixture into the prepared pan.

Bake until a skewer inserted in the center comes out clean, about 30 minutes. Remove the pan from the oven and cut the bread into squares without removing from the pan. Return the pan to the oven and bake until the edges of the squares are crisp, about 10 minutes longer.

Creole Corn Bread

Preparation time: 20 minutes
Cooking time: 50 minutes
Makes: 1 loaf

Generous 1 cup (200 g) long-grain
    white rice
Butter, for greasing
½ cup (65 g) yellow cornmeal,
    plus more for the pan
1 small onion, chopped
½ tablespoon seeded and
    sliced jalapeños
2 teaspoons sea salt
Pinch of baking soda
    (bicarbonate of soda)
1 egg
½ cup (4 fl oz/120 ml) milk
4 tablespoons canola
    (rapeseed) oil
1¾ cups (220 g) canned
    creamed-style corn
    (about half a 14¾ oz/418 g can)
9 oz (250 g) cheddar cheese,
    grated

Corn bread is a favorite across all the American South, and in New Orleans it gets a delicious upgrade with traditional Creole and Cajun flavors. This recipe uses cooked rice in addition to cornmeal and canned creamed corn for extra richness, and is flecked with jalapeños.

In a pot of boiling water, cook the rice until tender, about 14 minutes. Drain well.

Preheat the oven to 350°F (180°C/Gas Mark 4). Grease a 10-inch (25 cm) round cake pan with butter and sprinkle with cornmeal.

In a large bowl, stir together the cooked rice, cornmeal, onion, jalapeños, salt, and baking soda (bicarbonate of soda).

In a separate bowl, beat together the egg, milk, and oil. Stir in the creamed corn. Add the mixture to the rice and stir gently to combine. Stir in the cheddar. Scrape the batter into the prepared pan.

Bake until the top is crisp and golden brown, about 30 minutes. Serve warm.

Turkish Corn Bread

Preparation time: 10 minutes,
    plus 15 minutes resting time
Cooking time: 45 minutes
Makes: 1 loaf

½ cup (4 fl oz/120 ml) extra-virgin
    olive oil, plus more for greasing
3½ cups (500 g) cornmeal
2 teaspoons baking powder
1 teaspoon sea salt
2 tablespoons Greek yogurt
3 cups plus 3 tablespoons
    (25 fl oz/750 ml) very hot
    water (see Note)

Misir ekmeği, a corn bread typical of the Black Sea region, is usually served with butter, cheese, or preserves.

Preheat the oven to 350°F (180°C/Gas Mark 4). Oil a 14 × 7-inch (35 × 18 cm) loaf pan.

In a large bowl, mix together the cornmeal, olive oil, baking powder, and salt and stir well for 10 seconds. Stir in the yogurt and very hot water and knead the dough, using a spatula at first, then your hands when the dough has cooled a little. Knead for 5 minutes to obtain a firm dough. Cover with a damp cloth and let it rest for 15 minutes at room temperature.

Transfer the dough to the prepared pan. Bake until golden brown, 40–45 minutes. Let it cool in the pan before slicing.

Note: The water needs to be very hot 160°F (70°C), to achieve a crusty bread.

Arepas

Preparation time: 15 minutes
Cooking time: 40 minutes
Makes: 8 arepas

1½ cups (300 g) masarepa
   (precooked cornmeal)
1 teaspoon sea salt
4 tablespoons sunflower oil

Arepas are little round breads found in much of Latin America, but especially Colombia and Venezuela. They are made with *masarepa*, a precooked cornmeal. Arepas were traditionally cooked in a hinged pan held over the fire, but there are modern electric grills (similar to a sandwich press) with indentations for making several arepas at once. However, they can also be made on the stovetop.

In a bowl, combine the masarepa and salt, then add 1 cup (8 fl oz/240 ml) water and knead well. Add the oil and work again to obtain a nice dough, adding some water, little by little, if needed, to create a cohesive dough.

Divide the dough into 8 equal portions and roll each out into a compact ball (arepita). Flatten the balls into discs at least ½ inch (1.25 cm) thick.

Preheat a large cast-iron skillet or other heavy-bottomed nonstick frying pan over high heat. Working in batches if necessary, cook the arepas until golden on both sides, about 4 minutes per side.

Pork Gorditas

**Preparation time: 1 hour, plus
30 minutes cooling time
Cooking time: 1 hour 30 minutes
Makes: 6 gorditas**

6 oz (175 g) pork shoulder,
  cut into chunks
1 clove garlic, peeled
1 bay leaf
2 tablespoons sea salt
2 tablespoons extra-virgin olive oil
½ yellow bell pepper, diced
½ small yellow onion, chopped
½–1 green chili, sliced, with seeds
Generous 1¾ cups (225 g) masa
  harina
6 oz (175 g) Oaxaca cheese or
  low-moisture mozzarella
  cheese (see Note), grated
Freshly ground black pepper

A *gordita* is a small stuffed corn cake (made with the same flour used to make tortillas) whose name means "chubby." This plump street food is filled with various ingredients, including meat, vegetables, and cheese, and is often accompanied by different sauces. *Gorditas* can be cooked on red-hot griddles or fried in oil. They are quite substantial and can easily make a satisfying lunch.

In a large pot, combine the pork, garlic, bay leaf, 1 tablespoon of the salt, and water to cover. Bring to a boil over medium heat, then reduce to a simmer and cook until the pork is tender, about 45 minutes. Remove the meat from the broth and let it cool for 30 minutes. Strain the broth and set aside. When the pork is cool enough to handle, break up the chunks using two forks.

In a saucepan, heat the oil over medium heat. Add the bell pepper, onion, and chili and cook until crisp-tender, about 5 minutes. Stir in the meat. Pour 6 tablespoons (3 fl oz/90 ml) of the reserved broth into the pan and bring to a boil over high heat, then reduce the heat to low and cook until the liquid is almost completely evaporated, about 5 minutes. Season to taste with ½ tablespoon of the salt and keep warm.

In a large bowl, mix together the masa harina and the remaining ½ tablespoon salt. Add water, little by little, and start kneading, adding more water until the dough is soft and compact.

Divide the dough into 6 equal portions and roll into a ball. Flatten each ball with the palm of your hand into a disc ¼ inch (6 mm) thick. (You may find it easier to flatten the dough to the desired thickness by placing a ball between two large sheets of plastic wrap/cling film and pressing down on the ball with something flat like the base of a heavy pan.)

Preheat a cast-iron skillet or other heavy-bottomed frying pan over medium-high heat. Working in batches, add the dough discs and cook until both sides are lightly browned, about 2 minutes per side. Remove from the pan and while still hot, make a tiny slit through the side of the disc into the center to make a pocket for the stuffing.

Stuff each gordita with ¼ cup (30 g) cheese. Return the gorditas to the pan (which is off the heat) and let the cheese melt from the residual heat in the pan. Add 1–2 tablespoons meat mixture to the cheese, season with pepper, and serve.

Note: If you are using very fresh mozzarella, drain it in a sieve for about 15 minutes to get rid of excess moisture and pat dry with paper towels.

Corn Tortillas

Preparation time: 10 minutes
Cooking time: 1 hour 15 minutes
Makes: 18 tortillas

Generous 2¾ cups (350 g)
   masa harina
1 teaspoon sea salt
Sunflower oil, for the tortilla
   press (optional)

Tortillas are an iconic food of Mexican cuisine that are traditionally cooked on a special clay plate called a *comal*. They can be made with freshly ground white corn, but more conveniently are made with a corn flour called masa harina. The corn used to make masa harina is first cooked in an alkaline solution to soften the tough hulls (see Beef and Bean Burritos, page 150, for the actual process), then dried and ground.

In a bowl, combine the masa harina, salt, and 2 cups (16 fl oz/ 475 ml) water and mix until a soft dough forms, adding more water, if necessary.

Preheat a griddle, a cast-iron skillet, or other heavy-bottomed nonstick frying pan over high heat.

Making one tortilla at a time (and keeping the rest of the dough covered), grab a piece of dough (about 3 tablespoons/ 45 g) and roll into a ball a little smaller than a golf ball. Grease a tortilla press (see Note) with a little oil or use two sheets of plastic wrap (cling film). Place the dough ball on the press (between the plastic if using) and press to 5–6 inches (13–15 cm) across.

Add the tortilla to the griddle and cook for 2–3 minutes. Flip and cook on the second side for 1–2 minutes more. Wrap loosely in a clean tea towel to keep warm.

Serve right away if possible.

Note: The best way to make perfectly round tortillas is to use a tortilla press, but a good substitute is to place a ball of dough between two sheets of parchment paper or plastic wrap and press down on the ball with something flat, like a cutting board or the bottom of a pie plate (if you use a glass pie plate you can also monitor the size of the tortilla as you press).

Chicken Fajitas

Preparation time: 20 minutes, plus 1 hour 30 minutes marinating time and 10 minutes resting time
Cooking time: 20 minutes
Makes: 4 fajitas

½ cup (4 fl oz/120 ml) extra-virgin olive oil
Juice of 2 limes
1 teaspoon ground cumin
Sea salt and freshly ground black pepper
14 oz (400 g) boneless, skinless chicken breast
2 red bell peppers, cut into strips
½ onion, thickly sliced
4 corn tortillas, store-bought or homemade (page 148)

For serving
Guacamole, store-bought or homemade (page 36)
Enchilada sauce
Pico de gallo

The word *fajita* means "little strip" and is a reference to the strips the meat is cut into. Classic fajitas are made with strips of skirt steak (bavette), but this Tex-Mex dish has been adapted to other types of grilled meat. The simplest of fajitas is just grilled meat and bell peppers wrapped in a tortilla, but they can be dressed up with all sorts of things, such as cheese, guacamole (see page 36), enchilada sauce, or pico de gallo. Once cooked, the fajitas should be eaten immediately, but the chicken can be marinated a day ahead.

Pour ⅓ cup plus 1 tablespoon (3½ fl oz/90 ml) of the oil into a large bowl and stir in the lime juice, cumin, and salt and black pepper to taste. Add the chicken and marinate in the fridge for 1 hour 30 minutes.

In a large frying pan, heat the remaining 1 tablespoon oil over medium heat. Add the chicken and cook for 3 minutes each side. Reduce the heat to low and cook until lightly browned, 5 minutes more on each side. Remove the chicken from the pan and let it rest for 10 minutes, then slice the meat into strips.

In the same frying pan, cook the peppers and onion over medium heat until softened, 4–5 minutes. Add the chicken strips and stir to combine.

Using tongs, warm the tortillas over an open flame or on a really hot griddle. Bring the warmed tortillas, chicken mixture, and condiments to the table for diners to assemble their own.

Beef and Bean Burritos

Preparation time: 40 minutes,
plus 8 hours soaking time
Cooking time: 2 hours
Makes: 8 burritos

For the masa
11 oz (300 g) dried field corn
(see Notes)
1 tablespoon calcium hydroxide
(see Notes)
1 teaspoon sea salt
5 tablespoons (40 g) masa harina

For the filling
3½ oz (100 g) dried red beans,
soaked in water overnight,
drained, and rinsed
1 head of garlic, cut in half
widthwise
1 onion, cut into wedges
2 bay leaves
½ cup (4 fl oz/120 ml) sunflower oil
3 onions, finely chopped
1 lb (450 g) lean ground (minced)
beef
2 cloves garlic, minced
1 tablespoon ground cumin
1 tablespoon dried oregano
Sea salt and freshly ground
black pepper

For assembly
½ cup (80 g) minced onion
1 cup (75 g) shredded lettuce
½ cup (90 g) diced seeded
tomatoes
1 cup (115 g) grated cheddar
cheese

Originally from the northern parts of Mexico (and specifically the city of Juárez), the burrito is now well established in American cooking as well. A classic burrito is made with a flour tortilla, but corn tortillas have been around as a wrapper in Mexico for thousands of years. So here, freshly made corn tortillas are stuffed and wrapped for a satisfying snack or even dinner.

Make the masa: In a bowl of water, rinse the field corn and remove anything that is not corn.

In a stainless steel pot, combine 2 quarts (2 liters) water and stir in the calcium hydroxide until well combined. Add the corn and bring to a boil. Reduce to a simmer and cook, stirring occasionally, until the skins of the kernels come off easily, about 30 minutes. Remove from the heat, cover, and let soak at room temperature for 8 hours or overnight so the calcium hydroxide can do its work.

Drain the corn into a sieve. Under cold running water, rub the corn between your hands to remove the skins from the kernels. Continue until the water starts to run clear.

Transfer the drained and peeled corn to a food processor. Add the salt and ½ cup (4 fl oz/120 ml) water. Process for at least 5 minutes to mix thoroughly, scraping the sides of the bowl if necessary. Add a little bit more water if it is not combining well. Add the masa harina to make the dough dryer and easier to handle.

Divide the masa into 8 equal portions, roll into balls, and set aside, loosely covered.

Make the filling: In a pot, combine the beans, head of garlic, onion wedges, bay leaves, and cold water to cover. Bring to a boil over medium heat, then reduce to a simmer and cook until tender, about 45 minutes. Reserving the cooking liquid, drain the beans and set both aside. Discard the garlic, onion, and bay leaves.

In a frying pan, heat 4 tablespoons of the oil over medium heat. Add two-thirds of the chopped onions and all the beef and stir until almost cooked, about 15 minutes. Add the garlic, cumin, oregano, and salt and pepper to taste. Stir until the liquid in the pan has evaporated and the filling mixture is fairly dry, about 15 minutes. Set aside.

In a separate frying pan, heat the remaining 4 tablespoons oil over medium heat. Add the remaining chopped onions and stir until translucent, about 3 minutes. Reduce the heat to low, add the beans and ½ cup (4 fl oz/120 ml) of the bean cooking liquid. Mash some of the beans with a fork, to get a rather coarse purée. Season generously with salt and stir constantly until well mixed, about 5 minutes. Set aside.

Make the tortillas: One at a time, place a ball of masa between two sheets of parchment paper and use a rolling pin to roll tortillas about 10 inches (25 cm) in diameter.

Heat a large cast-iron skillet or other heavy-bottomed frying pan over medium-high heat. Slip a tortilla into the hot skillet. Flip after 10 seconds. Continue cooking until brown spots appear on both sides, about 2 minutes per side. Repeat for all the tortillas.

Assemble the burritos: Place a tortilla on a plate. Top with ingredients in this order: 2 tablespoons meat, 2 tablespoons beans, 1 tablespoon onion, 2 tablespoons lettuce, 1 tablespoon tomato, and 1 tablespoon cheddar. Fold the bottom edge of the tortilla up and over the filling, fold in the sides, then roll up the whole thing.

Notes: Field corn is corn with a very high starch content (and a very low sugar content). It is commonly grown for animal feed or to be turned into cornmeal and corn flour. Outside the U.S., it is commonly called maize (as opposed to sweetcorn).

Calcium hydroxide (also known as pickling lime or slaked lime) is an alkaline substance used here to soften the tough hulls of the field corn. You can buy it online, in Asian markets, or where canning supplies are sold. Unprotected exposure can cause chemical burns so take extreme care when using and do not allow to come into contact with skin.

Beef Tacos

**Preparation time: 1 hour, plus
30 minutes soaking time
and 30 minutes chilling time
Cooking time: 1 hour 5 minutes
Makes: 12–16 tacos**

For the adobo sauce
5 ancho chilies
4 dried guajillo chilies
2 cloves garlic, peeled
2 teaspoons sea salt
½ teaspoon ground cumin
½ teaspoon dried oregano
Pinch of sugar
Freshly ground black pepper
3 tablespoons distilled
    white vinegar

For the filling
1 tablespoon vegetable oil
1 onion, chopped
1 lb 2 oz (500 g) ground
    (minced) beef
1 clove garlic, minced
2 chipotle chilies, finely chopped
2–4 teaspoons chili powder
1 teaspoon sea salt

For assembly
12–16 corn tortillas, store-bought
    or homemade (page 148)
Vegetable oil, for brushing
½ cup (120 g) guacamole,
    store-bought or homemade
    (page 36)
⅓ cup (60 g) diced tomatoes

There are many, many different type of tacos, not just those from the taco's homeland of Mexico, but also from the U.S., since the taco is among the main dishes of Tex-Mex cuisine. The tortillas for the tacos can be simply warmed over a flame or on a griddle, or, as here, coated with some oil and briefly toasted in the oven.

Make the adobo sauce: Stem the chilies and shake out most (but not all) of the seeds. Set a cast-iron skillet over high heat and toast the chilies until they start to turn brown, about 15 seconds. Transfer the chilies to a bowl and add hot water to cover. Use a small plate to keep them fully submerged. Let them soak for 30 minutes.

Reserving the soaking water, drain the chilies. Put them in a mortar or food processor. Add the garlic, salt, cumin, oregano, sugar, black pepper to taste, and the vinegar. Mash with the pestle or in the food processor until you reach a soft paste, adding soaking water if necessary. Transfer the sauce to an airtight container and refrigerate until chilled.

Make the filling: In a medium saucepan, heat the oil over medium heat. Add the onion and sauté until it turns translucent, about 2 minutes. Add the beef and garlic and cook, breaking the meat up with a spoon, until the meat is lightly browned, about 12 minutes.

Add the adobo sauce, chipotles, chili powder, salt, and water to cover by 1 inch (2.5 cm). Simmer over medium-low heat until the liquid is completely evaporated, about 35 minutes.

Assemble the tacos: Preheat the oven to 375°F (190°C/Gas Mark 5).

Lightly brush the corn tortillas with oil, set them on a sheet pan, and transfer to the oven. Bake until lightly browned but still flexible, about 12 minutes.

To serve, fill the tortillas with the meat mixture. Top with a dollop of guacamole and some diced tomatoes.

Injera

Preparation time: 3–4 days
Cooking time: 40 minutes
Makes: 12 injera

2 cups (320 g) teff flour

Injera, typical of Eritrean and Ethiopian cuisine, is a large, spongy crêpe-like flatbread made from a fermented batter made with teff flour. (Teff is a grain from a type of grass native to eastern Africa.) The bread is used to scoop up dishes like stew, and is usually served with the stew spooned right on top of the bread, which acts as a kind of edible plate. The pleasantly sour taste of the bread goes well with the strong and spicy flavors of African cuisine.

In a bowl, mix together the teff flour and 3 cups (24 fl oz/710 ml) water and stir to thoroughly combine. The mixture should be a smooth, loose batter, so add more water if necessary. Cover loosely with a cloth or plastic wrap (cling film). Set aside at room temperature to ferment for 3 days.

On the third day, there will be liquid that has risen above the level of the batter. Carefully pour off this liquid.

In a small saucepan, bring 1 cup (8 fl oz/240 ml) water to a boil. Add ½ cup (120 g) dough to the boiling water and stir until the mixture has thickened, about 3 minutes. Let it cool.

Mix the cooked dough into the rest of the batter. Whisk until fully incorporated. Add water if necessary. The batter should have the consistency of a crêpe batter.

Heat a 10-inch (25 cm) round griddle pan (or frying pan) over medium heat. Starting at the outside of the pan, drizzle one ladle (½ cup/120 ml) of batter in a spiral moving in toward the center until you've covered the surface with a thin layer. Cook until you see bubbles popping on the surface. Once the first side is cooked, place a lid over the pan and steam-cook until the upper side is also cooked. The bread doesn't need to be flipped. Repeat until the batter is used up, to make about 12 injera.

Farinata

**Preparation time: 10 minutes,
   plus 5 hours resting time**
Cooking time: 1 hour 10 minutes
Makes: 4 farinata

2½ cups (300 g) chickpea
   (gram) flour
2 tablespoons extra-virgin olive
   oil, plus more for the pans
1½ teaspoons sea salt
Fresh rosemary, to garnish

Farinata is a thin cake made with a chickpea (gram) flour batter, usually cooked in a wood-fired oven. Originally from Genoa in Liguria (in the northeast of Italy), this humble family-style dish is also common on the tables of the neighboring regions of Tuscany and Emilia-Romagna.

In a bowl, combine the chickpea (gram) flour and 2 cups (16 fl oz/475 ml) water and mix it thoroughly until smooth and lump free. Cover the bowl with plastic wrap (cling film) and let it rest for at least 5 hours or up to overnight, stirring occasionally.

Position two oven racks, one in the upper third and the other in the bottom third of the oven. Preheat the oven to 480°F (250°C/Gas Mark 9). Grease four 8-inch (20 cm) round cake pans with some oil.

Skim off any foam from the surface of the chickpea batter with a skimmer. Gently stir in the oil and salt. Divide the batter evenly between the prepared pans.

Transfer two of the pans to the lower rack and bake for 20 minutes. Move them to the upper rack and continue baking until a golden crust forms on top, about 15 minutes.

Remove the first two pans from the oven and bake the second two pans.

Garnish the farinata with rosemary and cut into wedges to serve, either hot or cold.

Corn Roti

Preparation time: 15 minutes
Cooking time: 25 minutes
Makes: 4 flatbreads

2 cups (120 g) yellow corn flour,
    plus more for rolling out
½ teaspoon sea salt
Pinch of ground red chilies
1 teaspoon ajwain (carom) seeds
    or caraway seeds
Handful of dried fenugreek
    leaves, finely chopped
1½ tablespoons ghee, plus more
    for serving
½ cup (4 fl oz/120 ml) hot
    (100°F/40°C) water

Makki ki roti is an unleavened flatbread made from corn flour (*makki* means "corn"). *Roti* simply means "bread" and in most cases it's a reference to an unleavened wheat flour bread. But there are numerous other rotis, including this corn version and *jowar ki roti* (see Sorghum Roti, below). To make the dough easier to roll out (it tends to crumble), knead it several times to make it flexible, and wet your hands with a little water.

In a bowl, mix the corn flour, salt, ground chilies, ajwain, fenugreek leaves, and ghee. Add the hot water, little by little, while kneading by hand.

Divide the dough into 4 equal portions and roll into balls. Sprinkle some corn flour over them and roll out into 4 flat rounds about 10 inches (25 cm) across.

Heat a nonstick frying pan over medium heat. Working with one at a time, cook the rotis for about 3 minutes on either side, until well browned.

To serve, place on a plate and top with some ghee.

Sorghum Roti

Preparation time: 10 minutes
Cooking time: 50 minutes
Makes: 6 flatbreads

1¼ cups (175 g) sorghum flour,
    plus more for rolling out
2 teaspoons sea salt
¾ cup (6 fl oz/180 ml) hot water

Jowar ki roti is a bread made with sorghum (*jowar*), a cereal grass whose seeds are ground into a flour. Also known as *jola o jondhalaa*, this unleavened Indian flatbread is great on its own or as a wrapper for other foods.

In a bowl, combine the sorghum flour and salt and mix. Add ½ cup (4 fl oz/120 ml) of the hot water while mixing with a spoon. When absorbed, add the remaining ¼ cup (2 fl oz/60 ml) hot water while stirring. Knead the dough very well with your hands. Cover and set aside to cool to room temperature.

Divide the dough into 6 equal portions and roll into balls. Dust a work surface with sorghum flour. Flatten each ball out, adding sorghum flour to prevent it from sticking. Press lightly while rotating the roti around to make discs about ½ inch (1.25 cm) thick and 8 inches (20 cm) across.

Heat a nonstick frying pan over medium heat. Place a roti in the pan and sprinkle some water on the top. Cook until golden on both sides, about 4 minutes per side. Serve warm.

Cassava Flatbread

(DF) (NF) (VG) (VT) 5   **Cuba**

**Preparation time: 10 minutes,
    plus 3 hours chilling time
Cooking time: 30 minutes
Makes: 6 flatbreads**

2 yuca (cassava) roots (10 oz/
    300 g each), peeled and finely
    grated (see Note, page 20)
2 teaspoons sea salt

Casabe is a peasant-style bread whose name derives from the Arawakan word for cassava. The Arawak are a large group of indigenous people that stretch from South America up through the Caribbean, including Cuba. In Cuba this bread is eaten as a side dish or with butter or oil, garlic, parsley, and cheese.

Place the grated yuca (cassava) in a tea towel and squeeze over the sink to remove as much liquid as possible. Transfer to a bowl, sprinkle with the salt, and mix well to incorporate. Refrigerate, uncovered, for at least 3 hours.

Work the dough with your fingers to break up clumps.

Heat a 6-inch (14 cm) nonstick frying pan over low heat. Place one-sixth of the mixture into the pan and use a spatula to spread it over the whole bottom of the pan. Cook until golden and crispy on both sides, about 2 minutes per side. Repeat until you have cooked all the flatbreads.

Cheese Pupusas

(NF) (VT) 5   **El Salvador**

**Preparation time: 5 minutes,
    plus 20 minutes resting time
Cooking time: 30 minutes
Makes: 12 pupusas**

Generous 2¾ cups (350 g)
    masa harina
1½ teaspoons sea salt
11 oz (300 g) cheddar cheese
    or mozzarella, crumbled
    or pulled into shreds
Sunflower oil, for frying

These round griddle cakes from El Salvador, known as pupusas, are very simple to prepare at home. They are typically served with a relish called *curtido:* a tart mixture of fermented cabbage, onions, and carrots.

In a bowl, combine the masa harina and salt. Stir in 2 cups (16 fl oz/475 ml) warm water and mix and knead until the mixture is soft and elastic. Form the dough into a ball, wrap with a damp cloth, and set aside for 20 minutes.

Take a small piece of dough and roll it with your hands until it doesn't show any bubbles, then flatten it into a round cake. Fill the center with 2 heaping tablespoons cheese and pull the dough around the cheese to seal the edges and form a ball again. Press the ball gently into a disc about 1 inch (2.5 cm) thick, making sure not to expose any of the cheese.

Pour 3 inches (7.5 cm) oil into a deep frying pan. Working in batches of 2–3, fry the pupusas until golden on each side, 5–6 minutes total.

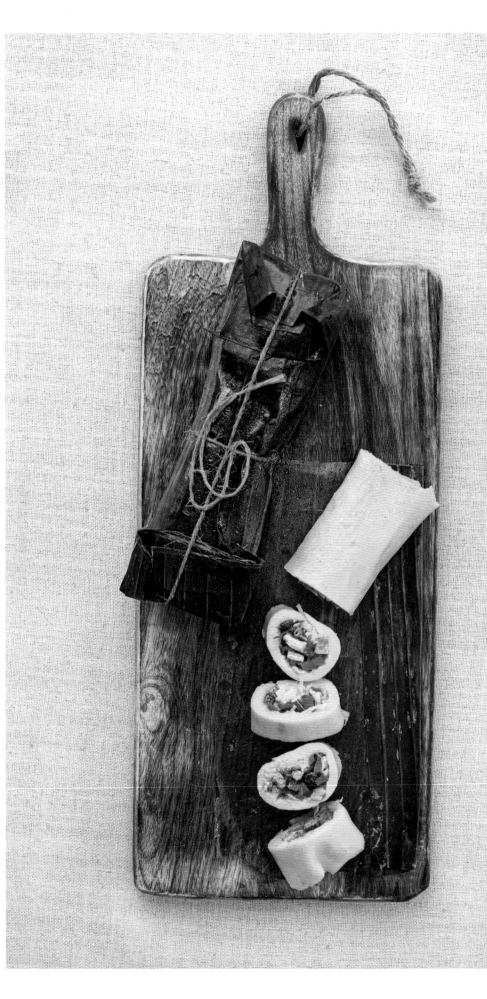

Hallacas

Preparation time: 1 hour
Cooking time: 1 hour 40 minutes
Makes: 12 hallacas

11 oz (300 g) pork shoulder,
    cut into small cubes
1 lb 2 oz (500 g) lean beef,
    cut into small cubes
1 lb 2 oz (500 g) boneless,
    skinless chicken breast,
    cut into small cubes
3 tablespoons sunflower oil
1 lb 5 oz (600 g) onions,
    minced, plus 2 small onions,
    cut into thin rings
3 cloves garlic, chopped
2 leeks, chopped and well rinsed
11 oz (300 g) red bell peppers,
    cut into strips
2 tablespoons capers, drained
1 lb 5 oz (600 g) tomatoes,
    seeded and chopped
4 tablespoons Marsala wine
Generous 1 cup (175 g) masarepa
    (precooked cornmeal)
Sea salt
3 tablespoons extra-virgin olive oil
2 teaspoons annatto powder
24 squares banana leaf
    (12 × 12 inches/30 × 30 cm)
3½ oz (100 g) black olives, pitted
4 tablespoons golden raisins
    (sultanas)
Freshly ground black pepper

Hallacas are Venezuelan-style tamales that some consider a national dish. They represent much about Venezuelan cuisine, a melting pot of indigenous foods and European influences. *Hallacas* have more elaborate fillings than a typical tamale, which makes them more celebratory and a tradition at Christmas. The tamales can be assembled ahead and refrigerated until ready to cook and serve.

In three separate saucepans of boiling water, simmer the individual meats until half-cooked, about 10 minutes. Drain.

In a saucepan, heat the sunflower oil over medium heat. Add the minced onions, garlic, and leeks and cook until the onions turn translucent, about 5 minutes. Add the bell peppers, capers, and all the meats and cook until the meats start to brown, about 20 minutes. Add the tomatoes and Marsala.

In a bowl, knead the masarepa with 1 teaspoon salt and 1⅔ cups (400 ml) warm water to form a soft dough. Cover and set aside.

In a small bowl, combine the olive oil and annatto powder.

Take a square of banana leaf, set it ridged side up and with the ridges running horizontally, and use your hands to rub it with the olive oil/annatto mix. (You also want oil on your hands to keep the dough from sticking.) Take a 1½-ounce (40 g) piece of dough and place it in the center of the leaf, and flatten it with your fingers into a round about 5 inches (12 cm) across. Put 2 tablespoons of the stew on the dough, then add a few black olives, some raisins, onion rings, and a sprinkling of black pepper. Starting with a side of the leaf close to you, lift it and the opposite side up to meet in the middle above the filling; this will push the cornmeal together to enclose the filling. Fold the edges down all the way, then fold the two open ends of the package under. Set this package diagonally in the middle of a second square of banana leaf and double-wrap the hallaca. Tie the hallaca with kitchen twine—like wrapping a package, with twine going in both directions. Repeat to make the remaining hallacas.

Bring a large pot of water to a boil. Add the packets and cook until the dough is firm, about 1 hour. Add more water, if necessary, to keep the hallacas covered. Using tongs, pull the hallacas out of the water and serve.

Dosa

Preparation time: 20 minutes, plus 6 hours soaking time and 6 hours fermenting time
Cooking time: 30 minutes
Makes: 8 dosa

2 cups (400 g) basmati rice
1¼ cups (175 g) white lentils (split urad dal) or red lentils
¾ teaspoon fenugreek seeds
1 teaspoon sea salt
4 tablespoons sunflower oil

Dosa are a very popular street food in India, though lots of home cooks make them, too. They are great as a snack or for breakfast, or as a side dish for main courses such as curry. Dosa are made by lightly fermenting a batter of lentils and rice. The "lentils" in question are actually a type of black mung bean, called urad dal, that when split and peeled are white. The split urad dal are often labeled "white lentils."

In a bowl, combine the rice and lentils. Wash under cold running water. Add the fenugreek seeds. Cover with water and mix. Cover the bowl and set aside to soak for 6 hours.

Drain the rice/lentil/fenugreek mixture and transfer to a food processor. Process the mixture, adding water as needed, until you get a smooth paste.

Transfer to a bowl, add the salt, and stir in water until the mixture has the consistency of a thick crêpe batter. Set the batter aside in a warm and dark place to ferment until it has doubled in volume, about 6 hours. The fermentation time may be shorter or longer depending on the ambient temperature—whether it's summer or winter, for example.

When the batter has doubled its volume, it is ready to make dosa. Stir the batter.

Heat a large frying pan over medium heat until it's hot. Grease the pan with ½ tablespoon oil. Reduce the heat to medium-low. Add 6 tablespoons (3 fl oz/90 ml) of the batter to the middle of the pan and swirl the pan with a circular motion to create a dosa 6–8 inches (15–20 cm) in diameter. When the top surface looks cooked, flip the dosa and let it cook on the other side for 1 more minute. Repeat until the batter is used up, to make about 8 dosa, using more oil to grease the pan for each dosa.

Uttapam

**Preparation time: 30 minutes,
plus 6 hours soaking time
and 6 hours fermenting time
Cooking time: 30 minutes
Makes: 8 uttapam**

Scant 2 cups (350 g) basmati rice
Scant 1½ cups (200 g) white lentils
 (split urad dal) or red lentils
¾ teaspoon fenugreek seeds
1 teaspoon sea salt
2 tablespoons sunflower oil,
 plus 2 tablespoons for drizzling
½ potato or ½ onion
2 onions, finely chopped
10 teaspoons crushed chili flakes
4 tomatoes, finely chopped
4 green chilies, finely chopped

Made with a slightly thicker fermented batter than dosa (see opposite), *uttapam* is a substantial vegetable-topped pancake from southern India. It is served accompanied by sambar (page 241) and various chutneys, as well as chopped fresh tomatoes, onions, and chilies. For a convenient shortcut, look for one of the already fermented instant *uttapam* mixes, available in specialty stores and online.

In a bowl, combine the rice and lentils. Wash under cold running water. Add the fenugreek seeds. Cover with water and mix. Cover the bowl and set aside to soak for 6 hours.

Drain the rice/lentil/fenugreek mixture and transfer to a food processor. Process the mixture, adding water as needed, until you get a smooth paste.

Transfer to a bowl, add the salt, and stir in water until the mixture has the consistency of a thick pancake batter. (It should have a texture similar to lightly whipped cream.) Set the batter aside in a warm and dark place to ferment until it has doubled in volume, about 6 hours. The fermentation time may be shorter or longer depending on the ambient temperature—whether it's summer or winter, for example.

When the batter has doubled the volume, it's ready to make uttapam. Stir the batter.

In an 8-inch (20 cm) nonstick frying pan, heat a few drops of oil over medium heat. Spread the oil with the help of the halved potato or onion. Pour a scant ladle (½ cup/120 ml) of the batter into the pan. Spread the batter over the pan so that it looks like a thick pancake. Sprinkle one-eighth of the onions, chili flakes, tomatoes, and green chilies on top. Gently press them into the batter with a spatula. Drizzle some oil around the edges. Cover and cook until the bottom is lightly golden and the top is looking dry, 2–3 minutes. Flip and cook for 1 more minute. Repeat to make 7 more uttapam.

Slice and serve hot.

Stuffed Rice Crêpes

(DF)

Preparation time: 20 minutes, plus 1 hour chilling time
Cooking time: 30 minutes
Makes: 6 crêpes

Scant 2 cups (300 g) rice flour
3 tablespoons cornstarch (cornflour)
1 tablespoon ground turmeric
1 teaspoon cane sugar
2 teaspoons sea salt
1 can (13 fl oz/375 ml) full-fat coconut milk
1½ cups (12 fl oz/355 ml) iced water
24 shrimp (prawns), peeled and deveined
1 tablespoon sesame oil
1⅓ cups (150 g) alfalfa sprouts, rinsed

Bánh xèo are made with rice flour and coconut milk. They are filled with ground (minced) meat or fish and are typically served with nuoc cham, a dipping sauce made with fish sauce, lime juice, and chilies. The filling for these crêpes varies throughout Vietnam, from liver and hoisin sauce, to prawns and beansprouts, as in this recipe here.

In a large bowl, combine the rice flour, cornstarch (cornflour), turmeric, sugar, and salt and mix well. Pour in the coconut milk and iced water and stir to thoroughly combine. Cover with plastic wrap (cling film), and refrigerate for at least 1 hour.

Heat an 8-inch (20 cm) nonstick frying pan over high heat. Add the shrimp (prawns) and sear for 30 seconds on each side. Remove from the pan and set aside.

Add a little of the sesame oil to the same pan and quickly pour about one ladle (½ cup/120 ml) of the batter into the pan, tilting the pan so the batter forms a nice round crêpe. Cook until golden brown on the bottom, 4–5 minutes. Place 4 shrimp and a few alfalfa sprouts on one side of the crêpe and fold over.

Repeat with the remaining sesame oil, batter, shrimp, and alfalfa sprouts to make 6 filled crêpes. Serve immediately.

Egg-Topped Buckwheat Galettes with Ham and Cheese

**Preparation time: 10 minutes,
    plus 1 hour resting time
Cooking time: 50 minutes
Makes: 6 galettes**

1 cup (8 fl oz/240 ml) milk
1 teaspoon distilled white vinegar
2 tablespoons extra-virgin olive oil
Sea salt
8 eggs
1 cup plus 1 tablespoon (130 g)
    buckwheat flour
Butter cubes, for greasing the pan
4 oz (120 g) sliced ham, cut into
    large pieces
6 oz (170 g) Gruyère cheese,
    grated
Freshly ground black pepper

Galette bretonne is a traditional dish from Brittany in the northwest corner of France. It is a savory crêpe made with buckwheat flour and traditionally served with ham, Gruyère, and a cooked egg in the middle. The recipe is also excellent with other types of semi-aged cheeses.

In a large bowl, stir together the milk, vinegar, oil, 2 teaspoons salt, and 2 of the eggs. While whisking gently, slowly pour in the buckwheat flour, mixing to avoid lumps. Cover the bowl with plastic wrap (cling film), transfer to the fridge, and let the batter rest for 1 hour.

Heat a heavy-bottomed frying pan over low heat. Stab a butter cube with a fork and use it to evenly grease the pan. Pour one ladle (½ cup/120 ml) of the batter into the pan and tilt the pan to spread the batter over the bottom. Cook until the edges of the crêpe lift up, 4–5 minutes. Flip the crêpe and crack 1 egg into the center. Sprinkle with one-sixth of the ham and one-quarter of the Gruyère. Season with salt and pepper. Increase the heat to medium, cover, and let the crêpe cook for 3 minutes, or until the egg white is perfectly cooked and the yolk is still runny. Fold the sides of the crêpe in toward the center a bit to make a square, leaving the egg in the center exposed.

Repeat to make 5 more galettes. Serve hot.

Tapioca Pancakes

Brazil

Preparation time: 15 minutes
Cooking time: 10 minutes
Makes: 10 pancakes

1⅔ cups (200 g) tapioca starch
1 teaspoon sea salt
Butter, for serving

Called *tapioca* in Brazil, these crêpe-like pancakes are named for their main ingredient, tapioca starch. The pancakes are a very popular street food and can be served with a variety of sweet and savory fillings, such as cheese, coconut, or chocolate. The simplest version is one topped with a little butter. For a cheese-filled version, the crêpe is cooked on one side, flipped, and topped with cheese on one half. The crêpe is then folded over the cheese.

In a bowl, stir together the tapioca starch and salt. Stir in about 1½ cups (300 ml) cold water, little by little, until a batter is formed. When the batter starts to form small clumps, push through a fine-mesh sieve into a bowl.

Heat a heavy-bottomed (preferably nonstick) frying pan over medium heat. Pour in a ladle (½ cup/120 ml) of the batter in a thin layer and cook for 30 seconds. Slide the pancake onto a plate and flip the pancake back into the pan cooked-side up. Cook the pancake for 30 seconds more. Continue until all the batter is used up to make about 10 pancakes.

Serve with a little butter on the side.

Deep-Fried Peanut Crackers

Preparation time: 10 minutes
Cooking time: 30 minutes
Makes: about 20 crackers

3 cloves garlic, sliced
2 candlenuts or macadamia nuts
3 makrut lime leaves (see Note, page 33)
½ teaspoon ground coriander
¼ teaspoon galangal powder
1 teaspoon sea salt
1 small egg
¾ cup (6 fl oz/175 ml) full-fat coconut milk (see Note)
5 tablespoons rice flour
4 tablespoons tapioca starch
Scant ⅔ cup (90 g) unsalted roasted peanuts
Vegetable oil, for deep-frying

Rempeyek, often shortened to *peyek,* are spiced deep-fried crackers from Java. They can be flavored with shrimp (prawns) or dried anchovies, but by far the most popular version is *rempeyek kacang,* which is made with *kacang,* or peanuts. The crackers can be served as a side dish alongside *pecel,* a Javanese vegetable salad with peanut sauce, but mostly they're simply a great snack.

In a mortar, crush and mix the garlic, candlenuts or macadamia nuts, and lime leaves with a pestle. Still mashing, add the ground coriander, galangal powder, and salt until it becomes a smooth paste. (Alternatively, do this in a food processor.)

Crack the egg into a bowl. While beating it with a fork, add the coconut milk, ¼ cup (2 fl oz/60 ml) water, half of the rice flour, and half of the tapioca starch. When the flour and liquid are fully combined, add the rest of the flour and starch, mixing until you have a nice smooth batter. Mix in the spice paste and whisk until there are no lumps in the batter. Stir in the peanuts.

Pour 3 inches (7.5 cm) of the vegetable oil into a wok and heat over medium–high heat.

Once the oil is hot, scoop up a tablespoon of batter and drop it onto the wall of the wok, above the oil. With a different spoon, scoop up some of the hot oil and pour it over the batter on the wall of the wok. The batter will start to fry. Once the batter looks set, gently push it off the wall into the hot oil to fry it further. Once the cracker turns golden brown, remove it with a spider strainer. Put it on a plate with paper towels to drain.

Let the crackers cool down a bit before serving. Let them cool completely before storing in an airtight container.

Note: Make sure to shake the can of coconut well before measuring out what you need, as the fat has usually risen to the top of the can and separated from the rest of the liquid.

Chickpea Papadum

**Preparation time: 20 minutes,
    plus 2 hours dehydrating time
Cooking time: 10 minutes
Makes: 12 papadum**

2 cups (250 g) chickpea (gram)
    flour
1 teaspoon ground cumin
1 teaspoon sea salt
Canola oil, for frying, plus more
    for kneading

Indian papadum are large thin crackers made with legume flour, and sometimes rice flour or tapioca starch. The most common type of papadum is made with urad dal (black lentils) but they can also be made with chickpea (gram) flour, as here. The crackers are first formed and then dehydrated for storage (traditionally in India they are sun-dried). The dried crackers are then deep-fried as needed.

Preheat the oven to 175°F (80°C). Line a sheet pan with parchment paper.

In a bowl, stir together the chickpea (gram) flour, cumin, and salt. Add ⅔ cup (5 fl oz/150 ml) water to form a dough, then coat your hands with a little oil and knead until the dough is thick and smooth, 5–7 minutes.

Roll the dough into a log. Cut the log into 12 equal slices. Roll each portion into a very thin disc. Arrange the papadum on the lined sheet pan. Place them in the oven to dry for 2 hours. Store the papadum in an airtight container in a cool dry place.

Pour 2 inches (5 cm) oil into a large deep frying pan. Heat the oil over medium-high heat to 300°F (150°C). Working very quickly, slip one dried papadum into the hot oil and fry for 15 seconds, then flip them and fry the other side. Drain on paper towels.

Black Lentil Papadum

**Preparation time: 20 minutes,
plus 2 hours dehydrating time
Cooking time: 10 minutes
Makes: 12 papadum**

2 cups (250 g) urad flour
    (see Note)
2 teaspoons sea salt
1 teaspoon ground cumin
1 teaspoon paprika, plus more
    for dusting
Juice of 1 clove garlic, squeezed
Canola oil, for frying, plus more
    for kneading

Papadum are crispy flatbreads popular in Bangladesh, India, Nepal, Sri Lanka, Rajasthan, and Kerala. They are commonly made with urad flour (see Note) seasoned with spices such as paprika and cumin.

Preheat the oven to 175°F (80°C). Line a sheet pan with parchment paper.

In a bowl, stir together the urad flour, salt, cumin, paprika, and garlic juice. Add a generous ¾ cup (200 ml) water to form a dough. Knead the dough (coat your hands with a little oil as needed) for at least 5 minutes or until the dough is thick and resilient (add more water a little at a time if necessary).

Roll the dough into a log. Cut the log into 12 equal slices. Lightly oil a work surface. Oil each slice of dough by placing it on the oiled work surface, then flipping it to oil the other side. Roll each portion into a very thin disc. Arrange them on the lined sheet pan. Sprinkle with paprika and transfer to the oven to dehydrate for at least 2 hours. Store in an airtight container in a cool dry place.

Pour 2 inches (5 cm) oil into a large deep skillet. Heat the oil over medium-high heat to 300°F (150°C). Working with one at a time, carefully slip a papadum into the hot oil and fry for 15 seconds per side, or until the surface makes blisters. Drain on paper towels.

Note: Urad flour is made from split and peeled urad dal, also called black lentil or black gram, though they are actually black mung beans. Once the skins are removed, the beans are white, as is flour made from them.

Rice and Noodles

Crispy Saffron Rice

Iran

Preparation time: 15 minutes
Cooking time: 1 hour
Serves: 6–8

2 cups (400 g) basmati rice
1 tablespoon sea salt
½ teaspoon saffron threads,
    plus more for sprinkling
5 tablespoons Greek yogurt
3 tablespoons olive oil

There are four basic methods for preparing Persian rice: *kateh*, *damy*, *chelow*, and *polo*. *Kateh* is steamed rice with salt and oil or butter. *Damy* is slow-steamed rice mixed with beans or grains. *Chelow* is parboiled rice seasoned and slow-steamed to form a *tahdig* (a crispy, crunchy crust at the bottom of the pot). *Polo* is a variant of *chelow*, to which meat, fruit, and/or vegetables have been added. This recipe is a version of *chelow* with a yogurt and saffron *tahdig*.

Wash the rice in a bowl. Drain in a sieve and repeat the process until the water runs clear.

Fill a 3-quart (3-liter) stockpot with water to come 2 inches (5 cm) from the top. Bring to a boil over medium heat. Add the salt and the rice. Gently stir as you bring it to a boil again. Check a grain of rice after 5 minutes. It should be soft around the edges but firm (not crunchy) in the center. If not there yet, give it another minute or two. Reserving the cooking liquid, drain the rice and rinse in a sieve under cold running water.

In a small bowl, soak the saffron in 2 tablespoons of the rice cooking liquid for 5 minutes.

In a medium bowl, stir together the yogurt and the saffron and its soaking liquid, then add 1 cup (150 g) of the cooled rinsed parboiled rice and stir again.

In a Dutch oven (casserole), heat the oil over medium-high heat until it starts to sizzle. Pour the yogurt mixture onto the bottom of the pan, then add the rest of the rinsed rice, shaping it up as a pyramid. Sprinkle some extra saffron on top.

Set the pan on a heat diffuser (if you have one, but it's optional). Wrap the bottom of the lid with a tea towel (to really trap the steam) and secure the ends of the towel on the top of the lid (to keep them away from the flame). Cover the pan and steam over medium-low heat until the rice is tender and the tahdig is lightly golden, about 50 minutes. Carefully check the tahdig by lifting it with a fork.

To serve, invert a large serving dish over the pan as if you were putting on a lid and carefully flip them over together to turn out the tahdig onto the dish.

Flattened Rice Fried with Turmeric, Chili, Onion, and Mustard Seeds

 India

Preparation time: 15 minutes
Cooking time: 30 minutes
Serves: 4

3½ cups (400 g) poha
   (flattened rice)
1 teaspoon sugar
1 teaspoon sea salt
5 tablespoons peanuts
4 tablespoons sunflower oil
1½ teaspoons cumin seeds
2 teaspoons mustard seeds
½ teaspoons asafoetida
   (hing) powder (see Note)
2 onions, finely chopped
2 sprigs curry leaves
2 green chilies, chopped
1 yellow potato, cubed
½ teaspoon ground turmeric
4 tablespoons chopped fresh
   cilantro (coriander), for serving
Juice of 1 lemon, for serving
4 tablespoons grated fresh
   coconut, for serving

Poha are rice grains that have been parboiled and then flattened into flakes and dried. The flakes absorb water easily and can be eaten uncooked. *Poha* can also be cooked and eaten like a porridge (with water or milk, salt, and sugar) or fried with oil, nuts, raisins, and spices. This recipe uses peanuts, green chili, and mustard seeds and is typical of the state of Maharashtra in western India.

Rinse the poha, drain, and let soften in the liquid left from the rinsing. When soft, add the sugar and salt. Run your fingers through the poha to break up any clumps and incorporate the sugar and salt.

In a nonstick frying pan, toast the peanuts. Set aside.

In the same nonstick frying pan, toast the cumin and mustard seeds over low heat. When they start to pop, add the asafoetida, onions, curry leaves, and chilies. Sauté until the onions start to change color, about 2 minutes. Add the potato and sauté for 10 minutes. Add ½ cup (4 fl oz/120 ml) water, cover, and cook until the potato is beginning to soften, about 10 minutes.

Add the turmeric and prepared poha and mix well. Cover the pan and cook until the potato is soft, about 3 minutes.

To serve, divide among four plates and sprinkle with cilantro (coriander), lemon juice, and grated coconut.

Note: Asafoetida (hing) is a pungent spice that is frequently used in Indian and Middle Eastern cooking.

Dill Rice with Fava Beans

Preparation time: 15 minutes, plus 20 minutes soaking time
Cooking time: 1 hour 30 minutes
Serves: 4

2 cups (400 g) basmati rice
Sea salt
Canola (rapeseed) or
    sunflower oil
14 oz (400 g) fresh fava beans
    (broad beans), blanched
    and peeled
3 cloves garlic, minced
Freshly ground black pepper
2 tablespoons Greek yogurt
1 teaspoon saffron (6 or 7 threads)
1 oz (30 g) fresh dill, chopped,
    plus more for garnish
3 tablespoons advieh polo
    (see Note)
2 tablespoons (30 g) unsalted
    butter, melted

Baghali polo is a dish of fava beans (*baghali*) and rice (*polo*). As with many Persian rice dishes, the bottom of the rice develops a *tahdig*, a deliciously crunchy layer. The dish is often served with lamb, which is nicely complemented by the dill in the rice. A good trick for chopping fresh dill without it forming wet little clumps is to spread it out between two sheets of parchment paper and let it dry overnight. The herb will then be much easier to chop.

Wash the rice in a bowl. Drain in a sieve and repeat until the water runs clear.

Fill a 3-quart (3-liter) stockpot with water to come 2 inches (5 cm) from the top. Bring to a boil over medium heat. Add salt and the rice. Gently stir as you bring it to a boil again. Check a grain of rice after 5 minutes. It should be soft around the edges but firm (not crunchy) in the center. If not there yet, give it another minute or two. Reserving the cooking liquid, drain the rice and rinse in a sieve under cold running water.

In a frying pan, heat some oil over low heat. Add the fava beans (broad beans) and garlic and cook until lightly crispy, about 6 minutes. Season with salt and black pepper to taste.

In a small bowl, soak the saffron in 2 tablespoons of the rice cooking liquid for 5 minutes.

In a medium bowl, stir together the yogurt and the saffron and its soaking liquid, then add 1 cup (150 g) of the cooled rinsed parboiled rice and stir again.

Moisten the bottom of a 10-inch (25 cm) Dutch oven (casserole) 6 inches (15 cm) deep with a little water. Add 3 tablespoons oil and stir so that the oil is evenly spread over the water. Spread the yogurt/rice mixture over the bottom. Top with half the dill, a 1-inch (2.5 cm) layer of plain rice, and 2 teaspoons advieh. Add a ½-inch (1.25 cm) layer of fava beans and the remaining dill. Continue layering, ending with rice and advieh sprinkled on top. Poke some holes down through the layers with the handle of a wooden spoon until you reach the yogurt layer.

Cover and cook over high heat for 10 minutes. Wrap the bottom of the lid with a tea towel (to really trap the steam) and secure the ends of the towel on the top of the lid (to keep them away from the flame). Cover and cook over medium-low heat for 1 hour. Halfway through, pour the melted butter over the rice. Garnish with some more dill and serve hot.

Note: *Advieh* means "spice" and *polo* means "rice," so *advieh polo* is a Persian mixture typically used to season rice dishes. It commonly includes turmeric, cinnamon, cardamom, cloves, rose petals or rose buds, cumin, and ginger.

Rice and Beans

(DF) (NF) (VG) (VT) 5

Costa Rica

Preparation time: 15 minutes
Cooking time: 30 minutes
Serves: 4

3 tablespoons corn oil
1 onion, finely chopped
1½ cups (300 g) basmati rice
1⅓ cups (350 g) canned red beans
1 clove garlic, chopped
Sea salt and freshly ground
    black pepper

Gallo pinto means "spotted rooster" in Spanish and it is thought that the name is a reference to the spots of color from the black or red beans cooked with the rice. The rice and beans can be stored in the fridge for 1–2 days in an airtight container.

In a large pot, heat 2 tablespoons of the oil over medium heat. Add the onion and 6 tablespoons water and gently simmer over low heat for 5 minutes. Add the rice and stir for 5 minutes.

Add half the beans and 1⅓ cups (325 ml) water. Cover and simmer over very low heat until the rice is tender, about 20 minutes.

In a bowl, stir the remaining beans with the garlic, remaining 1 tablespoon oil, and salt and pepper to taste.

Remove the rice from the heat and stir it with a fork to separate the grains. Add the bean/garlic mixture and stir again. Serve immediately.

Risi e Bisi

Italy

Preparation time: 15 minutes
Cooking time: 1 hour 35 minutes
Serves: 4

4¼ cups (34 fl oz/1 liter) vegetable stock, warmed
2¼ lb (1 kg) fresh peas in the pod, peas shelled and pods reserved
4 tablespoons extra-virgin olive oil
5 tablespoons (70 g) unsalted butter
1 scallion (spring onion), cut into thin rings
2 tablespoons chopped fresh parsley
2 oz (50 g) pancetta, chopped
11 oz (300 g) Vialone Nano short-grain rice or other risotto rice
Sea salt and freshly ground black pepper
Generous ½ cup (50 g) grated Parmesan cheese

Risi e bisi, born in Veneto, in the north of Italy, is one of the most famous and beloved dishes in Italian cuisine. Halfway between a soup and a rustic risotto, the dish—whose name means "rice and peas"—is best enjoyed in the spring, when tender and sweet peas come into season.

In a soup pot, bring 3 cups (24 fl oz/710 ml) of the stock to a boil over medium heat. Add the pea pods and let them cook for 1 hour. Transfer the liquid and pods to a blender and purée. Pour the purée into a sieve set over a bowl and press with a spoon (discard the solids). Reserve the pea pod liquid.

In a soup pot, heat the oil and 2½ tablespoons (35 g) of the butter over medium heat. Add the scallion (spring onion), parsley, and bacon and sauté for 1 minute. Add the peas and remaining 1 cup (8 fl oz/240 ml) stock and cook over low heat for 10 minutes. Add the reserved pea pod liquid, the rice, and salt and black pepper to taste. Stir over medium heat until the rice is tender, about 20 minutes. Remove from the heat and stir in the remaining 2½ tablespoons (35 g) butter and the Parmesan. Stir gently for 2 minutes and serve immediately.

Rice and Lentils

India

Preparation time: 10 minutes, plus 30 minutes soaking time
Cooking time: 50 minutes
Serves: 6

⅔ cup (130 g) basmati rice, rinsed, soaked in water for 30 minutes, and drained
Scant 1 cup (175 g) red lentils, rinsed, soaked in water for 30 minutes, and drained
2 tablespoons ghee
1 tablespoon cumin seeds
½ teaspoon sea salt
1 teaspoon ground turmeric
1 teaspoon asafoetida (hing) powder (see Note, page 175)

Khichri is beloved in India because of its comforting texture and delicate flavors. Northern Indians regularly have *khichri* for dinner, but specifically Saturday night dinner: Legend has it that eating *khichri* on Saturday night brings luck and money. The name of the dish comes from the Sanskrit *khicca,* which means a dish of rice and legumes.

In a large pot, combine the rice, lentils, and 2 quarts (2 liters) water. Bring to a boil over medium heat, then reduce to a simmer and cook until the water is fully absorbed and the rice and lentils are very soft, about 45 minutes.

In a small saucepan, heat the ghee over medium heat. Add the cumin seeds and toast for 3–4 minutes. Add to the rice and lentils, then add the salt and stir. Finally, gently stir in the turmeric and asafoetida and serve.

Biryani

**Preparation time: 20 minutes,
    plus 30 minutes soaking time
Cooking time: 25 minutes
Serves: 4**

3 tablespoons ghee
2-inch (5 cm) cinnamon stick
2 Indian bay leaves
6 black peppercorns
5 whole cloves
2 star anise
8 green cardamom pods
1½ teaspoons caraway seeds
4 blades of mace
6 cloves garlic, peeled
1 inch (2.5 cm) fresh ginger
2½ tablespoons chopped fresh
    cilantro (coriander) leaves
2½ tablespoons chopped fresh
    mint leaves
1¾ cups (350 g) basmati rice,
    rinsed, soaked in water for
    30 minutes, and drained
30 saffron threads
Juice of ½ lemon
1 teaspoon sea salt

With its origins in Persian cuisine, biryani is a spiced rice dish that has spread throughout South Asia. There are numerous regional variations, and in India each household may have their own version. The dish is often served with various proteins (beef, chicken, lamb, fish, or shrimp), sauces, or hard-boiled eggs.

In a saucepan, heat the ghee. Add the cinnamon, bay leaves, black peppercorns, cloves, star anise, cardamom, caraway seeds, and mace. Sauté until fragrant, about 2 minutes.

In a mortar, mash the garlic and ginger to a paste. Add the paste, cilantro (coriander), and mint to the saucepan and cook until the garlic fragrance comes out.

Stir in the soaked rice, saffron strands, 3½ cups (28 fl oz/ 830 ml) water, the lemon juice, and salt.

Bring to a boil, lower the heat to a simmer, cover tightly, and cook the rice until tender, about 20 minutes. Remove from the heat, uncover, and gently fluff up the rice with a fork. Cover and let it sit for 10 minutes. Serve hot.

Fried Rice with Mutton

(DF) (NF)

Preparation time: 15 minutes
Cooking time: 30 minutes
Serves: 4

2 cups (400 g) basmati or
  jasmine rice
2 tablespoons sunflower oil
4 onions, cut into rings
4 cloves garlic, minced
11 oz (300 g) carrots, cut into
  matchsticks
11 oz (300 g) green cabbage,
  shredded
2 medium-small red bell peppers,
  cut into strips
14 oz (400 g) boiled mutton or
  cooked leg of lamb, shredded
Sea salt and freshly ground
  black pepper

Budaatai khuurga is a simple and traditional Mongolian mutton dish that was designed to give energy and help the people resist cold winters. Originally made with sheep fat, these days it's made with oil; and because mutton can be hard to come by, you can substitute lamb. The vegetables, too, can be changed to your preference, but they must always be cut into strips.

Wash and drain the rice. In a saucepan, combine the rice and 3 cups (24 fl oz/710 ml) water. Bring to a boil and cook until the water has been absorbed and the rice is tender, about 20 minutes.

In a saucepan, heat the oil over medium heat. Add the onions and garlic and cook until the onions are translucent, about 3 minutes. Add the carrots, cabbage, and bell peppers and stir-fry until the peppers start to become tender, about 4 minutes. Add the meat and stir-fry to heat through. Season with salt and black pepper to taste. Stir in the rice and serve.

Rice with Potatoes, Meat, and Eggs

Preparation time: 45 minutes
Cooking time: 1 hour
Serves: 4

Sea salt
4 medium yellow potatoes,
    peeled and sliced
5 tablespoons sunflower oil
1 lb 5 oz (600 g) beef top round
    (topside), sliced into 4 steaks
Freshly ground black pepper
2 tablespoons chopped fresh
    parsley
2 cloves garlic, chopped
1½ cups (7 oz/200 g) cornmeal
2 onions, diced
2 tomatoes, diced
1 tablespoon extra-virgin olive oil
⅔ cup (120 g) short-grain white
    rice, rinsed
4 eggs

Silpancho, a Bolivian dish typical of the city of Cochabamba, is a hearty meal of rice, potatoes, and meat, topped with a fried egg. It is also a pleasing combination of textures, from the crunchy fried cornmeal-crusted beef and the tender potatoes and rice to the creamy and rich egg. Finish with a dusting of fragrant cumin and a splash of lemon juice. The dish can be made with pounded beef, as here, or with very thin patties of ground (minced) beef.

In pot of simmering salted water, cook the potatoes until tender, about 10 minutes. Drain well.

In a large frying pan, heat 2 tablespoons of the sunflower oil over medium heat. Add the potatoes and cook until golden, about 10 minutes.

Meanwhile, sprinkle the meat with salt, black pepper, the parsley, and half the garlic. Place the meat on a cutting board, sprinkle the surface with the cornmeal, and pound with the flat side of a meat tenderizer until it's thin.

In a large frying pan, heat 2 tablespoons of the sunflower oil over medium heat. Add the beef and cook until lightly browned, about 2 minutes per side.

In a medium bowl, toss together half the onions, all the tomatoes, the olive oil, and salt to taste.

In a large dry saucepan, toast the rice over medium heat, stirring constantly, until it's dry. Add the remaining garlic and stir until golden. Add the remaining onions and 1½ cups (12 fl oz/ 355 ml) hot water. Simmer until the water has evaporated and the rice is tender, about 15 minutes.

In a frying pan, heat the remaining 1 tablespoon sunflower oil over medium heat. Crack in the eggs and fry to your preferred level of doneness.

Serve the steaks with the rice and the golden potatoes. Top the meat with the fried egg and the onion salad.

Bibimbap

(DF) (NF)

**Preparation time: 30 minutes,
    plus 30 minutes resting time
Cooking time: 40 minutes
Serves: 6**

Sea salt
Handful of spinach
1 lb (450 g) lean ground
    (minced) beef
3 cloves garlic, chopped
2 tablespoons tamari
2 tablespoons sugar
2¼ cups (450 g) short-grain rice,
    rinsed under cold running
    water until the water is clear
6 tablespoons sesame oil
1½ cups (175 g) bean sprouts,
    rinsed
11 oz (300 g) carrots, cut into
    matchsticks
1 lb (450 g) zucchini (courgettes),
    cut into thin sticks
6 eggs
2 tablespoons sesame seeds,
    for garnish
4 tablespoons gochujang
    (Korean chili paste)

An ancient Korean dish, *bibimbap* means "all-mixed," and appropriately is a mixture of ingredients stirred into rice. It is often served in a hot *dolsot*, which is a carved stone bowl. The ingredients are arranged in separate piles on top of the rice so that the neighboring colors complement each other and it is said that each has a symbolic meaning: the dark ones represent the North and the kidneys; the red the South and the heart; the green the East and the liver; the white the West and the lungs; and the yellow is the center and the stomach. The bowl will arrive at the table perfectly arranged, and then the diner mixes all the ingredients together, *bibimbap* style, before eating.

In a pot of boiling salted water, blanch the spinach for 30 seconds. Drain and cut into strips. Set aside.

In a bowl, gently mix together the beef, one-third of the garlic, the tamari, and sugar and let it rest for 30 minutes.

Meanwhile, in a heavy 4-quart (4-liter) pot, bring 3¾ cups (30 fl oz/900 ml) water to a boil. Add the rice and simmer, uncovered, without stirring, until the surface looks dry, 5–6 minutes. Cover the pot and simmer over very low heat until the water is fully absorbed, about 15 minutes more. Remove from the heat, cover, and let it rest for 5 minutes. Fluff the rice with a fork and set aside.

In a large frying pan, heat 2 tablespoons of the oil over high heat. Add the meat, season with 1 teaspoon salt, and cook, stirring constantly, until browned, about 5 minutes. Remove the meat from the pan and set aside.

In the same pan, toast one-third of the garlic over medium heat. Stir in the spinach and cook for 30 seconds. Remove from the pan and set aside.

In the same pan, heat 2 tablespoons of the oil over medium heat. Add the remaining garlic, the bean sprouts, carrots, and zucchini (courgettes). Season with salt and cook for 1 minute.

In a separate large frying pan, heat the remaining 2 tablespoons oil over medium-high heat. Fry the eggs until the whites are fully cooked and the yolks are still creamy.

Divide the rice among bowls, then arrange the meat, spinach mixture, and carrot/zucchini/sprout mixture in separate piles. Top each bowl with a fried egg. Sprinkle with sesame seeds and dollop with gochujang or serve on the side. Mix all just before eating.

Cook-Up Rice

Preparation time: 30 minutes, plus overnight soaking time and 1 hour resting time
Cooking time: 1 hour
Serves: 4

1¼ cups (200 g) dried black-eyed peas (beans), soaked in water overnight
2 onions—1 halved, 1 chopped
4 cloves garlic, peeled—2 whole, 2 chopped
1 Scotch bonnet pepper, seeded
3 scallions (spring onions)—1 whole, 2 finely chopped
1 teaspoon sea salt
1 whole chicken (3¼ lb/1.5 kg), cut into serving pieces
1 lb (450 g) beef rump, cut into small cubes
2 cups (16 fl oz/475 ml) beef or chicken stock
Scant 2 cups (350 g) long-grain white rice
1 bay leaf
1 tablespoon sunflower oil
10 sprigs thyme
1 wiri wiri chili or chile de árbol, seeded and minced
1 can (13.5 oz/400 ml) full-fat coconut milk

This dish is usually served for Sunday lunches in Guyana. It's a rustic rice dish made with beef, pork, or chicken, and is frequently served with a piece of fried fish on top. Its origin dates back to the arrival of African slaves in Guyana who prepared it with the less noble cuts of meat and with inexpensive and available ingredients such as peas and beans. The ideal rice for this dish is parboiled rice, which can withstand long cooking.

Drain the black-eyed peas (beans) and place in a soup pot with fresh water to cover. Bring to a boil over medium heat, then reduce to a simmer and cook over low heat until softened, about 10 minutes. Drain.

In a food processor, combine the onion halves, whole garlic cloves, Scotch bonnet, whole scallion (spring onion), and salt and process to a paste. Rub the chicken pieces with the mixture and let it rest at room temperature for at least 1 hour.

In a saucepan, combine the beef with water to cover and cook over medium heat until the liquid is reduced by half, about 30 minutes. Drain.

Meanwhile, in another saucepan, bring the stock to a boil. Add the rice, chopped scallions, and bay leaf and stir thoroughly. Cover, reduce the heat to a simmer, and cook until the rice is tender, about 20 minutes.

In a Dutch oven (casserole), heat the oil over medium heat. Add the chicken and cook for 5 minutes each side. Add the chopped onion, chopped garlic, thyme, wiri wiri chili, beef, and coconut milk and stir for 5 minutes. Add the black-eyed peas to the rice and simmer for 2 minutes. Discard the bay leaf.

Serve the meat mixture hot with the rice.

Cajun Dirty Rice

 United States

Preparation time: 20 minutes
Cooking time: 1 hour
Serves: 4

9 oz (250 g) hot or mild pork
    sausage, casings removed
9 oz (250 g) lean ground
    (minced) beef
9 oz (250 g) chicken livers, minced
1 red bell pepper, chopped
1 onion, chopped
1 stalk celery, minced
2 tablespoons minced scallions
    (spring onions)
2 cloves garlic, minced
1⅓ cups (250 g) long-grain
    white rice
½ cup (4 fl oz/120 ml) beef stock
½ cup (4 fl oz/120 ml) chicken
    stock
1 tablespoon Worcestershire sauce
1 bay leaf
Sea salt and freshly ground
    black pepper
Cajun seasoning
1 tablespoon chopped fresh
    parsley

Cajun dirty rice is a typical and traditional New Orleans and Louisiana dish, made with chopped chicken livers, which gives the rice its particular flavor and a "dirty" color. Every family has its own spin on the dish, though of course they all have chicken livers. The ideal rice to use is long-grain white rice, but you can also use wild pecan rice (an aromatic rice from Louisiana) or brown rice—though the cooking times will be longer if you use a whole-grain rice. For a fresh flavor, top the dish with more chopped parsley. Please ensure the sausage you use contains no gluten.

In a large saucepan, crumble in the sausage and beef and add the livers. Brown over medium-high heat. Drain all but a couple of tablespoons of fat from the pan. Add the bell pepper, onion, and celery and stir until the vegetables soften, about 5 minutes. Add the scallions (spring onions), garlic, and rice and stir gently until it toasts.

Add both stocks, the Worcestershire sauce, and bay leaf. Season with salt, black pepper, and Cajun seasoning to taste. Cover and simmer over low heat until the rice is tender, about 25 minutes.

Remove from the heat and stir in the parsley. Discard the bay leaf before serving.

Paella Valenciana

(DF) (NF)

Spain

**Preparation time: 30 minutes,
plus 5 minutes resting time
Cooking time: 50 minutes
Serves: 4**

5 tablespoons extra-virgin olive oil
1 lb 2 oz (500 g) rabbit meat,
    cubed
1 lb 2 oz (500 g) boneless, skinless
    chicken thighs, cubed
1 tomato, peeled and diced
7 oz (200 g) green beans, diced
1⅓ cups (200 g) drained canned
    lima beans (butter beans)
    or white beans
2½ cups (500 g) short-grain white
    rice
6⅓ cups (50 fl oz/1.5 liters)
    vegetable stock
1 sprig rosemary
Sea salt
1 teaspoon saffron threads,
    steeped in 2 tablespoons water

Paella is a classic Spanish dish from Valencia and it takes its name from a *paella*, which is the shallow round pan it is cooked in. Paella was born as a dish of the poor, the recipe customized according to whatever was available. The key ingredients in a paella are very good rice and saffron. It is really important not to mix the rice after adding the broth because the rice layer at the bottom of the pan will toast, giving the dish its characteristic delicious flavor and crust.

In a paella pan or a large cast-iron skillet, heat the oil over low heat. Add the rabbit and chicken and cook until golden brown, about 10 minutes.

Add the tomato, green beans, and lima beans (butter beans) to the pan and cook over low heat until the tomato releases its liquid, about 10 minutes.

Add the rice and let it toast. Add the stock and rosemary sprig and bring to a boil over high heat. Remove the rosemary sprig and add salt to taste and the saffron liquid. Take care not to mix the rice. After about 10 minutes, reduce the heat and cook for 10 minutes more. Once the broth has been absorbed, remove from the heat, cover, and let sit for 5 minutes before serving.

Hainanese Chicken Rice

Preparation time: 20 minutes
Cooking time: 35 minutes
Serves: 4

For the chicken
1 whole chicken (3½ lb/1.8 kg)
1 teaspoon kosher (flaked) salt
Sea salt
6 slices fresh ginger
2 scallions (spring onions),
    cut into 1-inch (2.5 cm) lengths
1 tablespoon sesame oil

For the rice
3 tablespoons canola (rapeseed)
    or sunflower oil
4 slices fresh ginger
2 cloves garlic, minced
Scant 2 cups (350 g) long-grain
    white rice, rinsed and soaked
    for 10 minutes
½ tablespoon sesame oil
1 tablespoon sea salt

For the chili sauce
1 tablespoon fresh lime juice
2 teaspoons sugar
4 cloves garlic, peeled
4 slices fresh ginger
4 tablespoons Sriracha sauce

To finish
3 tablespoons canola (rapeseed)
    or sunflower oil
½ tablespoon grated fresh ginger
2 cloves garlic, minced
½ teaspoon sea salt
1 teaspoon rice vinegar or
    distilled white vinegar
2 cucumbers, thinly sliced,
    for serving
½ oz (10 g) fresh cilantro
    (coriander), minced

This recipe is named for the Chinese island of Hainan, just off the coast of Vietnam. When Chinese immigrants from Hainan brought the dish to Malaysia it was transformed into the dish we know today and it is considered one of Malaysia's national dishes—although it is widespread throughout Southeast Asia. It is eaten everywhere, every day, and can be bought as street food from street vendors.

Cook the chicken: Rub the chicken all over with the kosher salt, getting rid of any loose skin, and let sit for 5 minutes. Rinse well, both inside and outside. Season the chicken all over with sea salt, including the cavity. Stuff the chicken with the ginger slices and scallions (spring onions).

Place the chicken in a large stockpot and add cold water to cover the chicken by 1 inch (2.5 cm). Bring to a boil over high heat, then reduce to a simmer and cook until done, about 30 minutes. To check if the chicken is done, stick a chopstick into the flesh under the thigh. If the juices run clear, it is done. Reserving the broth, transfer the chicken to a bowl of ice and water to cool off. Discard the ginger and scallions. When cool, pat the chicken dry with paper towels, rub the sesame oil all over it, and set aside.

Meanwhile, make the rice: In a wok, heat the canola (rapeseed) oil over medium-high heat. Add the ginger and garlic and fry until fragrant. Add the rice and stir for 1 minute. Add the sesame oil and mix well. Take 2 cups (16 fl oz/475 ml) of broth from poaching the chicken and pour over the rice. Add the sea salt and bring to a boil. Reduce the heat to low, cover, and cook for 15 minutes. Remove from the heat, cover, and let stand for 10 minutes.

Make the chili sauce: In a blender, combine the lime juice, 2 tablespoons of broth from the chicken, the sugar, garlic, ginger, and Sriracha sauce and blend until smooth.

To finish: In a small saucepan, heat the canola oil over medium-high heat until it starts smoking. Turn the heat off. Immediately, add the ginger and garlic and let them sizzle a few seconds. When it settles, stir in the salt and vinegar.

To serve, heat up the rest of the broth. For each serving, pack some rice into the bottom of a bowl and invert the domed rice onto a plate. Place the cucumber slices next to it. Slice the chicken and place it next to the rice. Divide the chili sauce into four little cups and place one on each plate. Pour the broth into soup bowls and garnish with cilantro (coriander). Serve all together.

Rice and Chicken Stew

(DF) (NF)   **Brazil**

**Preparation time: 30 minutes,
   plus 1 hour marinating time
Cooking time: 1 hour 15 minutes
Serves: 4**

4 bone-in, skin-on chicken thighs
   (about 5¼ oz/150 g each)
Juice of ½ lime
1 clove garlic, minced
1 tablespoon sea salt
Freshly ground black pepper
2 tablespoons extra-virgin olive oil
1 onion, diced
1 tablespoon tomato paste (purée)
1 teaspoon ground turmeric
Ground cumin
2 cups (16 fl oz/475 ml) chicken
   stock
¾ cup (150 g) short-grain white
   rice, well rinsed
1½ cups (200 g) frozen green peas
   (no need to thaw)
Scant 1½ cups (200 g) frozen corn
   kernels (no need to thaw)
2 tablespoons chopped fresh
   parsley, for garnish

Galinhada is a Brazilian dish that comes from the areas of Goiás and Minas Gerais. Its name derives from *galinha*, which means "chicken." There are numerous Brazilian variations of this stew: The most common includes hearts of palm and *pequi*, a small native fruit. The short-grain rice must first be washed to remove some of its starch.

In a large bowl, toss the chicken thighs with the lime juice, garlic, salt, and black pepper to taste. Marinate for 1 hour in the fridge.

In a Dutch oven (casserole), heat the oil over low heat. Increase the heat to medium, add the chicken thighs, and brown them on all sides, about 10 minutes. Add the onion, tomato paste (purée), turmeric, and cumin to taste and cook until the onion is softened, about 10 minutes.

Pour in the stock and simmer over low heat for 30 minutes.

Add the rice and cook for 15 minutes, Add the peas and corn and cook until the peas are soft but there is still some liquid on the bottom, about 10 minutes more. Add water if it gets too dry.

Garnish with the parsley and serve.

Barberry Rice with Saffron Chicken

Preparation time: 15 minutes
Cooking time: 2 hours 30 minutes
Serves: 4

4 bone-in, skinless chicken thighs or skin-on drumsticks (about 6 oz/175 g each)
1 teaspoon ground turmeric
2 onions—1 halved, 1 thinly sliced
Sea salt and freshly ground black pepper
1¾ cups (350 g) basmati rice
2 tablespoons olive oil
2 tablespoon tomato paste (purée)
2 oz (50 g) dried barberries
2 pinches of saffron threads
2 tablespoons fresh lemon juice
2 tablespoons sliced almonds or pistachios
Greek yogurt, for serving
Shredded fresh mint, for serving

Zereshk polo morgh is an Iranian classic made with barberries (*zereshk*), steamed rice (*polo*), and chicken (*morgh*). If you can't find dried barberries, which have a tart flavor similar to cranberries, you can use fresh or dried rosehips, cut into two or three pieces. This dish is commonly served with yogurt and fresh mint on the side.

In a large Dutch oven (casserole), combine the chicken, turmeric, onion halves, and 3 cups (24 fl oz/710 ml) cold water and season with salt and pepper. Bring to a boil over medium-high heat. Skim off the foam with a slotted spoon. Reduce the heat to medium-low, cover, and cook until the meat is tender and the liquid is reduced by half, about 1 hour, turning the chicken halfway through the cooking time.

Wash the rice in a bowl. Drain in a sieve and repeat the process until the water runs clear.

Fill a 3-quart (3-liter) soup pot with water to come 2 inches (5 cm) from the top. Bring to a boil over medium heat. Add salt and the rice. Gently stir as you bring it to a boil again. Check a grain of rice after 12 minutes. It should be soft around the edges but firm (not crunchy) in the center. If not there yet, give it another minute or two. Drain the rice and rinse in a sieve under cold running water.

In a medium frying pan, heat the oil over medium heat. Add the thinly sliced onion and sauté until golden, about 5 minutes. Add the tomato paste (purée) and cook briefly. Transfer the onion/tomato mixture to a bowl and set aside.

In the same frying pan, add the barberries and a pinch of saffron and cook over low heat for a few minutes.

When the chicken is done, discard the onion halves. Sprinkle the remaining pinch of saffron over the chicken, rubbing it in with the back of a spoon. Add the onion/tomato mixture, lemon juice, and barberries. Bring to a boil over medium heat. Reduce the heat to medium-low, cover, and cook until all the ingredients are well combined and the meat is really tender, about 40 minutes, turning the chicken halfway through the cooking time. Reduce the sauce until the oil starts to rise to the surface.

To serve, spread one-third of the rice on the serving plate and top with one-third of the sauce. Continue alternating layers of rice and sauce until all is used. Garnish with the sliced almonds. Serve the chicken on a separate plate. Set out bowls of yogurt and mint so that everyone can add their own toppings to taste.

Jollof Rice

Preparation time: 30 minutes
Cooking time: 1 hour 30 minutes
Serves: 8

3½ cups (700 g) basmati or other
    long-grain rice
Sea salt
6 tomatoes, chopped
12 oz (340 g) tomato paste (purée)
2 Scotch bonnet or habanero
    peppers, seeded and
    finely chopped
4 cloves garlic, chopped
½ sweet onion, finely chopped
1½ teaspoons finely chopped fresh
    ginger
3½ oz (100 g) smoked bacon,
    minced
Generous ¾ cup (200 ml) palm oil
    or peanut (groundnut) oil
1 lb (450 g) shrimp (prawns),
    peeled and deveined
7 oz (200 g) cooked chicken
    breast, chopped
¼ lb (115 g) ham, cut into 1-inch
    (2.5 cm) chunks
1 cup (150 g) finely chopped red
    bell peppers
¾ cup (100 g) chopped carrots
¾ cup (100 g) green peas
¾ cup (100 g) corn kernels, fresh
    or frozen
1 cup (100 g) chopped green beans
2 bay leaves
1 tablespoon paprika
6 sprigs thyme
2 cups (16 fl oz/475 ml) chicken
    stock
Minced fresh parsley, for garnish

This famous and ancient West African dish is so popular that it has its own day: World Jollof Rice Day is celebrated every year on August 22. Though the dish is especially loved in Liberia, there are other countries that claim the authorship of the recipe, most notably Ghana and Nigeria. It is certainly a dish to share with friends and family, especially on holidays.

Wash the rice in a bowl. Drain in a sieve and repeat until the water runs clear.

Fill a 3-quart (3-liter) soup pot with water to come 2 inches (5 cm) from the top. Bring to a boil over medium heat. Add salt and the rice. Gently stir as you bring it to a boil again. Check a grain of rice after 12 minutes. It should be soft around the edges but firm (not crunchy) in the center. If not there yet, give it another minute or two. Drain the rice and rinse in a sieve under cold running water.

In a food processor, combine the tomatoes, tomato paste (purée), chilies, garlic, onion, and ginger and process to a paste.

In a large Dutch oven (casserole), heat the tomato/chili paste until it bubbles and thickens, then set the pot aside.

In a large frying pan, sauté the bacon until lightly crisp. Leaving the fat in the pan, remove the bacon from the pan and set aside.

Pour ¼ cup (60 ml) of the oil into the frying pan with the bacon fat. Set the pan over medium-high heat and add the shrimp (prawns), chicken, and ham and cook until slightly browned, about 5 minutes. Remove the meats from the frying pan and set aside.

Return the Dutch oven to the heat and add the remaining generous ½ cup (140 ml) oil to the tomato/chili paste. Heat over medium-high heat, then add the bell peppers, carrots, peas, corn, and green beans and reduce to medium heat. Simmer for 5 minutes. Stir in the bay leaves, paprika, and thyme.

Add the chicken/shrimp/ham mixture and the bacon to the Dutch oven. Cover and simmer over low heat until the ingredients are well combined and the meats are very tender, about 20 minutes.

Lift the meat and shrimp from the sauce with a slotted spoon. Stir the parboiled rice into the sauce. Mix well. Stir in 1 cup (8 fl oz/240 ml) of the chicken stock. Cover with foil, reduce the heat to medium, and cook until the rice is almost tender, about 20 minutes.

Add the remaining 1 cup (8 fl oz/240 ml) stock and cook over low heat until the liquid is reduced, about 15 minutes. Discard the bay leaves.

To serve, spoon the rice on plates and top with the meat and shrimp. Garnish with minced parsley.

Creole Jambalaya

Preparation time: 30 minutes
Cooking time: 40 minutes
Serves: 4

14 oz (400 g) shrimp (prawns),
    peeled and deveined
2 tablespoons extra-virgin olive oil
1 onion, chopped
1 clove garlic, chopped
2 red bell peppers, diced
1 bay leaf
3 andouille sausages, casings
    removed, crumbled
½ fresh chili pepper, chopped
Fresh thyme leaves
Sea salt and freshly ground
    black pepper
4 tomatoes, peeled, seeded,
    and diced
4 cups (32 fl oz/950 ml) hot water
1⅔ cups (300 g) long-grain
    white rice
Chopped fresh parsley,
    for garnish

Jambalaya is a rice dish from Louisiana with Spanish, French, and West African influences, the embodiment of the state's melting pot history. This dish is in fact very similar to Spanish paella (see Paella Valenciana, page 188), though it does not include saffron. The original jambalaya was actually a dish created in Cajun country, in the bayous of southwestern Louisiana. It got adopted and adapted by the "city folk" in New Orleans who made a tamer, less rustic version of the dish. They also added tomatoes, which is why today the main difference between the two version is its color: Creole is red and Cajun is brown. Please ensure the sausages you use contain no gluten.

In a large pot of boiling water, cook the shrimp (prawns) for 2 minutes. Drain and lay out on paper towels.

In a Dutch oven (casserole), heat the oil over low heat. Add the onion and garlic and cook for 5 minutes.

Add the bell peppers and bay leaf and stir for 2 minutes. Stir in the sausage meat and sprinkle with the chili, thyme, and salt and black pepper to taste. Increase the heat to medium-high heat and cook until the sausage is lightly browned, about 5 minutes more.

Add the tomatoes, shrimp, and hot water and cook at a high simmer for 5 minutes. Thoroughly stir in the rice, reduce to a low simmer, cover, and cook until the rice is tender, about 20 minutes. Discard the bay leaf.

Garnish with parsley and serve hot.

Coconut Milk Rice

**Preparation time: 30 minutes,
    plus 15 minutes soaking time
Cooking time: 30 minutes
Serves: 4**

1¾ cups (350 g) jasmine or
    basmati rice
¾ cup (6 fl oz/175 ml) full-fat
    coconut milk
Sea salt
3 pandan leaves, tied together
5 oz (150 g) dried anchovies
Sunflower oil, for frying and
    deep-frying
1 teaspoon shrimp paste
4 shallots, peeled and quartered
1 clove garlic, peeled
10 dried chilies, seeded
1-inch (2.5 cm) chunk of seedless
    tamarind pulp
½ red onion, sliced into rings,
    rings separated
1 tablespoon sugar
4 small fresh fish, such as sardines
    or smelt, gutted and deboned
1 small cucumber, sliced,
    for serving
2 hard-boiled eggs, peeled
    and halved, for serving

Nasi lemak is the national dish of Malaysia, where it is frequently consumed for breakfast. The base of the dish is a generous portion of fragrant rice cooked in coconut milk with aromatic pandan leaves. The rice is then accompanied by many small side dishes including spicy sauces, peanuts, vegetables, hard-boiled or fried egg, fried chicken or fish, or curry. In Malaysia, *nasi lemak* is very spicy, but in neighboring countries it tends more toward the sweet and sour.

Rinse the rice until the water runs clear. Drain well and transfer to a large saucepan. Add the coconut milk, salt to taste, and 1½ cups (12 fl oz/350 ml) water. Add the pandan leaves and bring to a simmer over medium heat. Stir gently, then cover and cook over low heat until tender, about 15 minutes, stirring two or three times to keep the rice from sticking.

Rinse the dried anchovies and pat dry. In a frying pan heat 3 tablespoons oil over low heat. Add the anchovies and fry until they turn light brown, about 3 minutes. Set the fried anchovies aside.

In a mortar or food processor, mash together the shrimp paste, shallots, garlic, and chilies.

In a small bowl, soak the tamarind pulp in water for 15 minutes, squeezing the tamarind with your fingers to loosen it up and extract the flavor. Strain the mixture through a sieve set over a bowl (discard the solids). Set the tamarind juice aside.

In a frying pan, heat 3 tablespoons oil over medium heat. Add the shallot/chili paste and fry until fragrant. Add the onion rings, toasted anchovies, tamarind juice, sugar, and a pinch of salt. Simmer over low heat until thickened, about 4 minutes. Set the spicy anchovy/tamarind mixture aside.

Pour 2 inches (5 cm) oil into a deep frying pan and heat over high heat. Season the fresh fish with salt. Deep-fry the fish until the skin is crisp and golden. Drain on paper towels.

To serve, divide the rice among four plates and top each serving with some of the spicy anchovy/tamarind mixture. Top with a fried fish, cucumber slices, and half a hard-boiled egg.

Fried Rice with Shrimp and Egg

Preparation time: 10 minutes
Cooking time: 40 minutes
Serves: 4

2¼ cups (400 g) long-grain
  white rice
2 teaspoons sea salt
4 tablespoons sunflower oil
10 shallots, minced
4 eggs, lightly beaten
3 cloves garlic, peeled
1 fresh red chili, halved
1 teaspoon shrimp paste
4 tablespoons tamari
1 teaspoon sugar
1 scallion (spring onion), chopped
8 oz (225 g) cabbage, shredded
1 tomato, sliced, for serving
1 cucumber, sliced, for serving

Nasi goreng is traditionally made with cooked rice from the day before. As with many leftover rice dishes, the rice is seasoned and fried to reheat it and give it more interest. You can change up the vegetables and also enhance with some protein, such as strips of chicken or beef. Assuming you might not have any leftover, cooking rice from scratch is included here.

In a saucepan, bring 4 cups (32 fl oz/950 ml) water to a boil. Add the rice and salt. Reduce to a simmer, cover, and cook until tender, about 20 minutes. Stir once every 10 minutes and check if the rice is cooked. If not, give it some more time and water if needed. Let it rest for 10 minutes.

In a large frying pan, heat 2 tablespoons of the oil over medium heat. Add half of the shallots and cook until crisp, about 5 minutes. Set aside.

In a wok, heat the remaining 2 tablespoons oil over medium-high heat. Pour the eggs into the wok and scramble them. Remove them from the wok and set aside. Reserve the oil in the wok.

In a food processor, combine the remaining shallots, the garlic, chili, and shrimp paste and process to a paste.

Heat the reserved oil in the wok over medium heat. Fry the paste for 2 minutes. Add the cooked rice, tamari, and sugar. Sauté over high heat for 7 minutes. Add the scallion (spring onion) and cabbage and sauté for 2 minutes.

To serve, divide the rice among four plates and top with the scrambled eggs and fried shallots. Place a few slices of tomato and cucumber on the side.

Fish and Rice

(DF) (NF)

Preparation time: 30 minutes
Cooking time: 1 hour 45 minutes
Serves: 4

2 tablespoons chopped fresh
    parsley
2 shallots, minced
4 cloves garlic, chopped
4 fresh chilies, chopped
Sea salt
4 whole firm-fleshed fish,
    such as snapper, sea bream,
    or bass (about 1 lb/450 g each),
    heads removed, cleaned,
    gutted, and boned
4 tablespoons sunflower oil
1 onion, chopped
1 tablespoon nététou powder
    (see Note, page 239)
2 small (2 oz/50 g) guedge
    (see Note, page 239)
1 tablespoon yete (see Note,
    page 239), if available
4 tablespoons tomato paste
    (purée)
2 cups (18 oz/500 g) canned
    peeled plum tomatoes
Freshly ground black pepper
4 bay leaves
2 carrots, cut into chunks
2 sweet potatoes, peeled
    and cut into chunks
1 large eggplant (aubergine),
    thickly sliced crosswise
    into rounds
¼ small head cabbage,
    cut into wedges
1 (7 oz/210 g) yuca (cassava)
    root, peeled and cut into chunks
    (see Note, page 20)
6 okra pods
2½ cups (450 g) broken rice
    (see Note), washed
1 lime, cut into wedges,
    for serving

Thieboudienne Is the French spelling of the Wolof words *thiebu djen*, which literally mean "rice and fish." In other West African countries the dish is also known as *riz au gras* and Jollof rice. Oral Senegalese history tells us that this recipe was adapted to its current form in the nineteenth century by a cook named Penda Mbaye. She lived in the Senegalese city of Saint-Louis at the time, which in the 1800s was culturally important in West Africa. One day she decided to add mashed tomatoes to the dish. It was an instant hit. From there, the recipe spread throughout the region.

In a mortar, pound together the parsley, shallots, 2 garlic cloves, 2 chilies, and 2 teaspoons salt. This is your fish stuffing.

Make 3 deep diagonal cuts on both sides of each fish. Push the stuffing mixture into each cut.

In a large frying pan, heat the oil over medium heat. Add the fish and fry for 7 minutes on each side. Remove from the pan and set aside.

In the same pan, sauté the onion and remaining garlic and chilies over medium heat until golden brown, about 5 minutes. Set aside.

In a food processor, combine the nététou, guedge, and yete and pulse until finely ground.

Transfer the nététou mixture and onion mixture to a large pot. Add the tomato paste (purée), peeled tomatoes, and salt and black pepper to taste. Simmer for 5 minutes over medium heat. Add the bay leaves and 1 cup (8 fl oz/240 ml) water. Reduce the heat to low, cover, and simmer for 15 minutes.

Add the carrots, sweet potatoes, eggplant (aubergine), cabbage, and yuca (cassava) to the pot. Cover and simmer until the vegetables are firm-tender, about 30 minutes. Scoop out the vegetable chunks and set aside.

Add 4 cups (32 fl oz/950 ml) water to the pot and the okra. Bring to a simmer and cook for 5 minutes. Remove the okra. Add the rice. Ensure there is enough liquid to cover the rice and if not, add some. Cook uncovered, stirring occasionally, until tender, about 25 minutes.

Return the vegetables and fried fish to the pot. Cook for 5 minutes to heat through.

To serve, scoop some the rice onto plates and arrange the vegetables and fish on top. Place some lime wedges on the side.

Note: Broken rice can be bought online or found in Southeast Asian and African stores.

Salmon Sushi Rolls

Preparation time: 20 minutes
Cooking time: 20 minutes
Serves: 6

1 cup (200 g) short-grain
    or sushi rice
3 tablespoons rice vinegar
1 tablespoon sugar
1 teaspoon sea salt
5 sheets nori (seaweed)
9 oz (250 g) sushi-grade salmon
    fillet (see Note)
Tamari, for dipping

For sushi, rice is seasoned with a vinegar, sugar, and salt mixture called *su*. There are various styles of sushi, including the type that is rolled up in seaweed, which is called *makizushi* or *maki* for short. The recipe here is for a simple salmon *maki*, but you could add other ingredients such as cucumber or avocado, or replace the salmon with tuna. The rolls here are made with a special bamboo rolling mat called a *sudare* or *makisu*, but you could also use parchment paper.

Rinse the rice three times in cold water and drain. In a saucepan, combine the rice and 2 cups (16 fl oz/480 ml) water. Bring to a boil for 3 minutes, then reduce to a simmer and cook until the water has been absorbed, about 20 minutes. Transfer the rice to a wide shallow bowl and spread it out.

Meanwhile, in another saucepan, combine the vinegar, sugar, and salt and heat over medium heat until the sugar has dissolved.

Sprinkle the vinegar mixture over the rice and then mix well but gently. Continue until all the rice clumps have been broken up. Let cool completely.

Set a sheet of nori shiny-side down on a bamboo sushi mat. Dampen your hands with cold water to prevent sticking. Spread a layer of rice a scant ½ inch (1 cm) thick over the surface.

Cut the salmon into strips a scant ½ inch (1 cm) thick. Arrange the salmon strips in a line across the center of the rice.

Holding the edge of the mat closest to you, lift and roll away from you and continue rolling into a log, pressing gently when you reach the salmon to make sure it stays in place instead of being pushed forward. As you roll, use the mat to keep the log uniform and compact.

Repeat to make the remaining rolls.

Dip a knife into water or rice vinegar to prevent sticking and cut each roll into 6 neat rounds about 1⅓ inches (3 cm) each.

To serve, line the pieces up on serving plates. Provide each person with a small bowl of tamari for dipping.

Note: When buying raw fish for sushi, food safety experts recommend that the fish be frozen before using to kill any possible parasites.

Chinese Soybean Sauce with Rice Noodles and Vegetables

(DF) (NF) (VG) (VT)

China

Preparation time: 30 minutes, plus 15 minutes resting time
Cooking time: 25 minutes
Serves: 6

½ cup (4 fl oz/120 ml) sunflower oil
5 shallots, finely chopped
5 cloves garlic, finely chopped
2 inches (5 cm) fresh ginger, peeled and chopped
Scant ¾ cup (175 g) fermented black beans, soaked in warm water for 30 minutes and drained
7 oz (200 g) yellow soybean paste
3½ oz (100 g) black bean chili paste
5 tablespoons sugar
14 oz (400 g) dried rice noodles
3½ oz (100 g) napa cabbage (Chinese leaf), thinly sliced (optional)
1 large carrot, diced (optional)
1 stalk celery, cut into sticks (optional)

Chinese soybean sauce is usually served with noodles, but it also goes well with fried chicken, shrimp, or white rice. Once prepared, the sauce can be stored in the fridge for 2 weeks and when serving, it should be softened with a little hot water. When you buy soybean paste, check the label to make sure it's made with just soybeans and not wheat.

In a wok, heat the oil over very low heat. Add the shallots, garlic, and ginger and cook for 8 minutes, stirring constantly.

In a blender, combine the fermented black beans, soybean paste, and black bean chili paste and process until smooth. Add the mixture to the wok along with the sugar and simmer over low heat, stirring occasionally, until all the ingredients are incorporated, 4–5 minutes. Remove from the heat and let it rest for 15 minutes.

In a saucepan, bring 4 cups (32 fl oz/950 ml) water to a boil. Add the noodles and boil for 2–3 minutes, then drain and cool them under running water.

Add the noodles to the wok along with 1 cup (8 fl oz/240 ml) warm water and cook over medium heat, stirring constantly, for 3–4 minutes to coat and heat through. (Alternatively, reheat the sauce on its own and serve the sauce as a topping for the noodles.)

Divide the noodles among six bowls. If desired, top with napa cabbage (Chinese leaf), carrot, and celery.

Rice and Noodles

200

Sesame Chicken Soba Noodles

 Japan

Preparation time: 15 minutes
Cooking time: 20 minutes
Serves: 4

⅔ cup (80 g) plus 1 tablespoon
    white sesame seeds
3 tablespoons tamari
3 tablespoons rice vinegar
1 tablespoon honey
1 teaspoon finely grated
    fresh ginger
3 tablespoons sesame oil
9½ oz (270 g) soba noodles
    (see Note)
3½ tablespoons (40 g) black
    sesame seeds
7 oz (200 g) boneless, skinless
    chicken breast, thinly sliced
4 scallions (spring onions),
    finely sliced
1 tablespoon thinly sliced beni
    shōga (pickled ginger)

Soba means "buckwheat," and the noodles made from this grain are high in protein and fiber and are especially nutritious. The noodles have a nutty and earthy flavor, so it's best to keep the flavors in the rest of the dish simple. This sesame chicken recipe is a great example.

In a dry nonstick frying pan, toast 1 tablespoon of the white sesame seeds until golden. Cool them for a minute, then mash them with a mortar and pestle.

In a bowl, combine the mashed sesame seeds, tamari, vinegar, honey, ginger, and 2 tablespoons of the sesame oil. Set the dressing aside.

Preheat the oven to 400°F (200°C/Gas Mark 6).

Set up a large bowl of ice and water. In a large pot of boiling water, cook the soba noodles until al dente. Drain the noodles and transfer to the ice bath to stop them from cooking further. Soak the noodles until they're ice cold.

In a shallow bowl, stir together the black sesame seeds and the remaining ⅔ cup (80 g) white sesame seeds and spread out. Dip each piece of chicken in the sesame seeds and place in an 11 × 7-inch (28 × 18 cm) baking pan. Bake in the oven until the chicken is cooked through, about 5 minutes.

To serve, drain the noodles. In a wok, heat the remaining 1 tablespoon sesame oil over low heat. Add the noodles, the reserved dressing, the scallions (spring onions), and pickled ginger and stir-fry for 3 minutes to heat through.

To serve, divide the noodles among four plates. Place the chicken on top. Serve immediately.

Note: Make sure the soba are made with 100% buckwheat flour.

Shrimp Pad Thai

Preparation time: 30 minutes
Cooking time: 15 minutes
Serves: 6

4 tablespoons rice bran oil
1 cup (175 g) roasted peanuts
6 cloves garlic, minced
14 oz (400 g) dried rice noodles,
    cooked according to the packet
    directions and drained
5 tablespoons tamarind paste
4 tablespoons fish paste
2 tablespoon tamari
2 handfuls of fresh cilantro
    (coriander) leaves, chopped
2 handfuls of chives, chopped
2 cups (225 g) bean sprouts,
    rinsed
11 oz (300 g) black tiger prawns,
    peeled and deveined
2 limes, cut into wedges,
    for serving

This is one of the most traditional and well-known dishes from Thailand. One of the most popular versions is one with shrimp, as here; chicken is another good choice. For a vegetarian pad Thai, omit the fish paste and replace the shrimp with tofu or scrambled eggs. Pad Thai is best served as soon as it is ready.

In a wok, heat 2 tablespoons of the oil over medium heat. Add the peanuts and toast, stirring constantly, for 3–4 minutes. Drain the peanuts on paper towels and pour the oil out of the wok.

Set the wok back over medium heat and heat the remaining 2 tablespoons oil. Add the garlic and sauté, stirring constantly, until it begins to sizzle, about 2 minutes. Stir in the noodles and stir-fry, stirring constantly, for 2 minutes more.

Add the tamarind paste, fish paste, 1 tablespoon of the tamari, half the cilantro (coriander), and half the chives. Add 4 tablespoons water and 1½ cups (175 g) of the bean sprouts, bring to a boil over high heat, and cook, stirring constantly, for 3–4 minutes. Transfer to a large bowl.

Add the prawns and remaining 1 tablespoon tamari to the hot wok and gently stir over medium-high heat for 1 minute. Add the noodles and two-thirds of the toasted peanuts and cook for 1 minute more to combine and heat through. Top off with the remaining toasted peanuts, cilantro, chives and bean sprouts.

Serve hot, with lime wedges for squeezing.

Stir-Fried Noodles with Shrimp and Vegetables

(DF) (NF)

Preparation time: 30 minutes
Cooking time: 35 minutes
Serves: 4

2 tablespoons extra-virgin olive oil
1 white onion, thinly sliced
2 cloves garlic, thinly sliced
1 carrot, thinly sliced
2 stalks celery, chopped
½ head cabbage, thinly sliced
1 teaspoon freshly ground
    black pepper
4 tablespoons tamari
1 lb 2 oz (500 g) dried rice
    noodles, soaked for 20 minutes
    in water and drained
¾ lb (350 g) shrimp (prawns),
    peeled and deveined

Pancit, which means either "noodles" or "convenient food," is a beloved Filipino dish. The noodles in the dish, and actually noodles in general, are considered auspicious of a long life and good health. For this reason the noodles must be long and uncut in order not to compromise that symbolism. This dish can also be prepared with golden bihon, noodles made of cornstarch.

In a large saucepan, heat 1 tablespoon of the oil over medium heat. Add the onion and garlic and sauté until they start to get gold, about 3 minutes. Add the carrot, celery, cabbage, black pepper, 2 tablespoons of the tamari, and ½ cup (4 fl oz/120 ml) water. Stir and cook over medium heat until the vegetables are tender, about 15 minutes.

Add the rice noodles, ½ cup (4 fl oz/120 ml) water, and the remaining 1 tablespoon oil and remaining 2 tablespoons tamari. Simmer over medium-high heat, stirring, until everything is well combined, about 5 minutes.

Add the shrimp (prawns), cover, and simmer until the shrimp are fully cooked, about 10 minutes more, adding more water if needed. Serve hot.

Shiritaki Noodle Stir-Fry with Mushrooms

(DF) (NF) (VG) (VT) (30)

Japan

Preparation time: 10 minutes
Cooking time: 20 minutes
Serves: 4

2 teaspoons tamari
2 teaspoons rice vinegar
2 small fresh red chilies,
    seeded and sliced
14 oz (400 g) dried shirataki
    noodles
2 teaspoons sesame oil
14 oz (400 g) enoki mushrooms,
    bottoms trimmed off
2 scallions (spring onions),
    coarsely chopped
1 teaspoon shichimi tōgarashi
    (Japanese 7-spice blend)

Shirataki noodles are made from the starch of the konjac root. The extracted starch is mixed with an alkaline solution to form a gel, which is extruded in thin strands into boiling water. You can buy cooked and softened shirataki or you can buy the dried form, which is what we are using here.

In a bowl, stir together the tamari, vinegar, and chilies. Set aside.

In a pot of boiling water, cook the shirataki for 3 minutes. Drain thoroughly.

In a frying pan, heat the sesame oil over medium heat. Add the shirataki noodles and stir-fry for 1 minute. Add the enoki mushrooms and cook for 5 minutes to soften. Add the scallions (spring onions) and the tamari mixture and cook for 7 minutes.

To serve, divide among four plates. Sprinkle the shichimi tōgarashi on top. Serve immediately.

Rice and Noodles

204

Salads

Cucumber Sesame Salad

(DF) (NF) (VG) (VT)

China

Preparation time: 15 minutes, plus 35 minutes resting time
Serves: 4

2 cucumbers, cut into noodles or thin lengthwise slices
Salt
2 tablespoons sesame oil
2 tablespoons vegetable oil
Juice of ½ lemon
2 tablespoons vegetable stock
1 tablespoon rice miso
2 tablespoons black sesame seeds
Handful of fresh mint leaves, chopped
Mint sprigs, to garnish

This light and refreshing salad comes from the Yunnan region of China. Although cucumber skin has some important phytonutrients, you may want to peel it first if it is waxed or not organic. Salting the sliced cucumber and letting it rest for 30 minutes makes the salad less watery.

In a colander, toss the cucumber noodles with some salt and set aside in the sink for 30 minutes to drain. Rinse well.

In a small bowl, whisk together the sesame oil, vegetable oil, lemon juice, stock, and miso. Stir in the sesame seeds.

Place the rinsed cucumber in a large bowl, add the dressing and the mint leaves, and mix with a wooden spoon. Let it rest for 5 minutes before serving. Garnish with sprigs of mint.

Vegetable and Tuna Salad

Spain

Preparation time: 15 minutes, plus 1 hour resting time
Cooking time: 20 minutes
Serves: 4

Sea salt
5 medium yellow potatoes
1 green bell pepper, diced
1 red bell pepper, cut into squares
1 onion, thinly sliced
2 large tomatoes, seeded, chopped
2¾ oz (70 g) pitted green olives, halved
4 tablespoons extra-virgin olive oil
Juice of 1 lemon or 2 tablespoons red wine vinegar
6 oz (175 g) canned tuna packed in olive oil, drained and broken into chunks

A cold salad from Andalusia—the southernmost region of Spain—*pipirrana* can be enriched with eggs or tuna or other fish. Each city has its own version of this dish, in terms of both ingredients and preparation. Sometimes instead of being presented as a salad, the vegetables are mashed to a puree, or even turned into a cold soup.

In a large pot of boiling salted water, cook the potatoes until firm-tender, about 20 minutes. Drain and when cool enough to handle, peel and cut into 1-inch (2.5 cm) cubes.

Put the potatoes into a large bowl. Add both bell peppers, the onion, tomatoes, and olives. Add the oil, lemon juice, and salt to taste and gently toss.

Add the tuna and mix carefully. Cover and refrigerate for 1 hour to rest and cool before serving.

Variation: Replace the tuna with 6 hard-boiled eggs, cut in half. Or include both the tuna and the eggs.

Raw Fish Salad

 DF NF

Peru

**Preparation time: 15 minutes,
plus 30 minutes chilling time
Cooking time: 30 minutes
Serves: 4**

Sea salt
4 medium white potatoes
2¼ lb (1 kg) sea bass fillets,
 cut into thin slices
3 fresh ají amarillo chilies,
 seeded and sliced
¾ cup (150 g) ají amarillo paste
Scant 2 cups (450 ml) fresh
 lemon juice
4 ice cubes
4 tablespoons chopped fresh
 cilantro (coriander), for garnish

This Peruvian salad made with raw fish is called *tiradito*. Though similar to ceviche, for a *tiradito* the fish is cut into sashimi shapes, served with a chilled spicy/sour sauce, and accompanied with pieces of boiled potato. In some versions it is also served with white corn.

In a pot of boiling salted water, cook the potatoes until firm-tender, about 25 minutes. Drain. When cool enough to handle, peel and cut into chunks.

Lay the fish slices on a plate and refrigerate for 15 minutes.

In a bowl, combine the sliced amarillos, amarillo paste, lemon juice, and ice cubes. Season with salt and mix carefully. Chill the sauce for 15 minutes in the fridge.

To serve, pour the sauce over the fish. Garnish with the cilantro (coriander) leaves and serve with the potatoes.

Greek Salad

NF VT

Greece

**Preparation time: 20 minutes,
plus 15 minutes resting time
Serves: 4**

1 cucumber, peeled and sliced
 crosswise into rounds ½ inch
 (1.25 cm) thick
1 green bell pepper, cut into
 strips ½ inch (1.25 cm) wide
1 red onion, sliced
4 tomatoes on the vine,
 cut into wedges
Sea salt
1 tablespoon distilled white
 vinegar
32 Greek black olives, pitted
6 tablespoons extra-virgin olive oil
Fresh oregano leaves
6 oz (175 g) Greek feta cheese,
 cubed

Called *horiatiki* (which translates to "village salad"), this simple salad is a staple dish in most Greek homes, and has been adopted by countries around the world. As the tomatoes are very much the star of the show, this salad will be at its absolute best when locally grown tomatoes are in season.

In a large bowl, combine the cucumber, bell pepper, and onion. Working over the bowl to catch the juices, cut the tomatoes into wedges. Add salt to taste and the vinegar and carefully toss. Add the olives, olive oil, and oregano to taste and stir again. Add the feta and mix one more time.

Let the salad rest for 15 minutes before serving.

Fava Bean Salad

Preparation time: 25 minutes
Cooking time: 40 minutes
Serves: 4

Sea salt
2 ears corn, unhusked
1 lb 5 oz (600 g) fresh fava beans
    (broad beans), podded
1 carrot, diced
1 tomato, seeded and diced
7 oz (200 g) queso fresco or
    feta cheese, diced
11 oz (300 g) green olives, pitted
    and chopped
Chopped fresh parsley
4 tablespoons extra-virgin olive oil
1 onion, diced
½ fresh rocoto chili, diced
    or chopped
1 tablespoon red wine vinegar
Juice of ½ lemon
Freshly ground black pepper
4 lettuce leaves, for serving

More than a salad, this large and savory salad belongs to the gastronomic heritage of the city of Arequipa, in southern Peru, where, on the second Sunday of February, El Día del Solterito de Queso is celebrated. The celebration falls just before Valentine's Day and is dedicated to *solteritos*, or bachelors. The thinking is that if bachelors eat this hearty dish, they will be satisfied but won't gain weight.

In a large pot of boiling salted water, cook the unhusked corn for 30 minutes. Drain and when cool enough to handle, husk the ears and cut them crosswise into discs.

Meanwhile, in a large pot of boiling salted water, blanch the fava beans (broad beans) for 20 seconds. Drain the beans under cold running water until cool enough to handle, then remove the skins.

Bring a pot of salted water to a boil. Add the peeled fava beans and carrot, reduce the heat to low, and simmer for 3 minutes. Set up a bowl of ice and water. Drain the vegetables and transfer them to the ice bath to stop cooking. Drain again.

In a large bowl, combine the fava beans, carrot, corn, tomato, queso fresco, olives, and parsley to taste. Dress with 2 tablespoons of the oil and gently toss.

In a frying pan, heat the remaining 2 tablespoons oil over medium heat. Add the onion, rocoto chili, and vinegar and season with salt and black pepper. Cook until browned, about 5 minutes. Stir in the lemon juice.

Add the sautéed onion/chili mixture to the bowl of vegetables and mix thoroughly.

To serve, place a lettuce leaf on each plate and spoon the salad into the leaf.

Salade Niçoise

Preparation time: 20 minutes
Cooking time: 15 minutes
Serves: 4

Sea salt
2 medium white potatoes, peeled
    and cut into small cubes
8 oz (225 g) green beans
2 large tomatoes, seeded
    and diced
1 red onion, sliced
1 small red bell pepper,
    thinly sliced
3 leaves lettuce, cut into
    small pieces
4 oz (120 g) pitted green
    or black olives
3 tablespoons extra-virgin olive oil
2 tablespoons red wine vinegar
Freshly ground black pepper
5 oil-packed anchovy fillets
4 oz (120 g) oil-packed canned
    tuna, drained and divided
    into chunks
2 eggs, hard-boiled, peeled,
    and quartered lengthwise

This traditional dish is from the south of France, in particular the city of Nice (Niçoise means "from Nice"), from which it takes its Mediterranean flavors. The original recipe included only a few ingredients (tomato, anchovies, oil, and salt), but over time it has expanded and today includes potatoes, green beans, tuna, and eggs. The anchovies called for are oil-packed fillets, but you could use salt-packed if necessary, though you will have to desalt them and remove the backbones.

In a pot of boiling salted water, cook the potatoes until tender, about 10 minutes. Drain well and set aside to cool.

Meanwhile, set up a bowl of ice and water. In another pot of boiling salted water, cook the beans until crisp-tender, about 6 minutes. Drain and transfer to the ice bath to stop the cooking. Cut the beans into short pieces.

In a large serving bowl, combine the potatoes, green beans, tomatoes, onion, bell pepper, lettuce, and olives. Add the oil and vinegar, season with salt and black pepper, and mix thoroughly.

Garnish with the anchovy fillets, tuna, and egg quarters. Serve immediately. (The salad can be prepared several hours in advance and refrigerated in an airtight container. Do not dress it with oil and vinegar until ready to serve.)

Gado-Gado

(DF) (VT)

Indonesia

Preparation time: 20 minutes
Cooking time: 20 minutes
Serves: 6

½ cup plus 1 tablespoon (4½ fl oz/
135 ml) toasted sesame oil
1½ lb (700 g) green cabbage,
cored and thinly sliced
7 oz (200 g) cauliflower
(about ½ medium head),
separated into florets
2¼ cups (9 oz/250 g) bean
sprouts, rinsed
4 carrots, peeled and cut
into chunks
Handful of green beans,
trimmed and sliced crosswise
1⅓ cups (7 oz/200 g) salted
peanuts
Juice of 1 lemon
2 cloves garlic, mashed
2 shallots, finely chopped
3 eggs, hard-boiled, peeled,
and quartered

The name of this Indonesian side dish comes from the verb *menggado*, which literally means "mix up" but also means "eat without rice." Gado-gado (which translates as "mix-mix") is a tasty mixture of vegetables and peanut sauce, and is usually served with meat.

In a Dutch oven (casserole), heat 5 tablespoons of the sesame oil over medium-high heat. Carefully add the cabbage, cauliflower, bean sprouts, carrots, and green beans and cook, stirring occasionally, until browned, about 5 minutes. Remove the vegetables from the pan and let them cool in a serving dish.

In a medium frying pan, heat the remaining 4 tablespoons sesame oil over high heat. Add the peanuts and stir-fry until golden brown, about 5 minutes. Scoop the peanuts out of the pan (reserving the oil in the pan) and into a food processor. Add the lemon juice to the food processor and process to a soft and smooth paste.

Add the garlic and shallots to the oil in the frying pan and heat over medium heat for 5 minutes. Stir into the peanut paste.

Top the vegetables with the egg quarters and serve with the peanut sauce on the side.

Tomato and Onion Salad

(DF) (NF) (VT) (30)

Tanzania

Preparation time: 20 minutes
Serves: 4

4 tablespoons extra-virgin olive oil
2 tablespoons chopped fresh basil
2 tablespoons chopped fresh
parsley
½ bunch fresh cilantro (coriander),
chopped
2 cloves garlic, minced
Juice of 1 lime
1 tablespoon honey
Sea salt and freshly ground
black pepper
½ large red onion, sliced
1 cucumber, diced
1 jalapeño, seeded and sliced
4 tomatoes, diced

The original Swahili name for this recipe, *kachumbari*, actually comes from the Hindi verb *kachumar* ("to mix"), as Indian food traditions are one of many that have influenced the cuisines of Africa. The salad is a very popular dish in Tanzania and the Great Lakes region of Africa, which includes Kenya, Rwanda, Uganda, Burundi, and the southern African countries of Malawi and Congo.

In a small bowl, whisk together the oil, basil, parsley, cilantro (coriander), and half of the garlic. Stir in the lime juice, honey, and salt and pepper to taste.

In a large bowl, combine the onion, cucumber, jalapeño, tomatoes, and remaining garlic. Pour in the herb dressing and mix well. Let the salad rest for 10 minutes before serving.

Spicy Mango Salad

Preparation time: 30 minutes
Serves: 4

2 tablespoons dried shrimp,
    chopped
4 mangoes, cut into matchsticks
1 red onion, thinly sliced
1 fresh red chili, chopped
    (with seeds for more heat)
¼ cup (40 g) unsalted roasted
    peanuts, roughly chopped
Juice of 1 lime
2 tablespoons fish sauce
2 tablespoons raw sugar
Fresh cilantro (coriander) leaves,
    for garnish

Kerabu mangga is a Malaysian classic. The salad has a lot of contrasting textures and flavors, including the satisfying umami flavors of fish sauce and dried shrimp. It's easy to adjust to your tolerance for spice by leaving the chili seeds out and/or using less of the chili itself for a tamer version.

In a bowl of water, soak the shrimp in cold water for 3 minutes. Drain well.

In a serving bowl, combine the shrimp, mangoes, onion, chili, and peanuts.

In a small bowl, mix together the lime juice, fish sauce, and sugar.

Pour the dressing over the salad and toss. Serve garnished with cilantro (coriander) leaves.

Green Papaya Salad

Preparation time: 30 minutes
Cooking time: 15 minutes
Serves: 6

Sea salt
¾ lb (340 g) green beans,
    cut into 1-inch (2.5 cm) pieces
2 tablespoons tamarind paste
4 red chili peppers
Generous ¾ cup (2¾ oz/70 g)
    dried shrimp
3 green papayas, peeled, seeded,
    and cut into matchsticks
3 cloves garlic, finely minced
4 tablespoons palm sugar
Juice of 1 lime
3 tablespoons fish sauce
Generous ½ cup (80 g) salted
    roasted peanuts
8 cherry tomatoes, quartered

Som tum Thai is a savory and fresh salad that is a balance of spicy, salty, sour, and sweet. Green, or unripe, papaya is firm-crisp, and not at all sweet—the sweetness (and softness) develops as the fruit matures. This classic version of green papaya salad is enriched with dried shrimp and peanuts.

Set up a bowl of ice and water. In a small pot of boiling salted water, cook the beans until crisp-tender, about 8 minutes. Drain and transfer to the ice bath to stop the cooking. Drain well.

In a small bowl, stir 2 tablespoons water into the tamarind paste to loosen it up.

Put the chilies, dried shrimp, papaya, and garlic in a large bowl. Add the tamarind mixture, palm sugar, lime juice, and fish sauce and stir to extract and combine all the flavors from the ingredients. Stir in the peanuts.

Add the tomatoes and green beans and stir gently for 2 minutes and serve.

Layered Herring Salad

Preparation time: 30 minutes, plus 6 hours chilling time
Cooking time: 1 hour 10 minutes
Serves: 6

1 lb 5 oz (600 g) beets, well scrubbed
14 oz (400 g) potatoes, well scrubbed
12 oz (350 g) carrots, well scrubbed
5 eggs
2 cups (440 g) mayonnaise
2 red onions, finely chopped
6 pickled herring fillets in oil (see Note), finely chopped
Freshly ground black pepper
Chopped fresh parsley

Russian herring salad, known as *shuba* or *seledka pod shuboy,* translates to "herring under a fur coat," a reference to the mayonnaise dressing that completely covers the salad. The fur coat in question can be a white fur coat (from just mayonnaise), but if it has beets, it's a red fur coat. The layered salad of pickled herring, eggs, beets, carrots, and potatoes is best assembled and chilled at least 6 hours before serving so it will firm up and can be sliced to display the layers. Even better is to make this salad the day before.

Bring a large pot of water to a boil. Add the beets and cook over medium heat for 25 minutes. Add the potatoes and simmer for 20 minutes. Add the carrots and let simmer until all the vegetables are soft, about 20 minutes longer. Take care that the water doesn't evaporate; add some if necessary.

Drain the vegetables. When cool enough to handle (but still warm), peel the vegetables. Mince the carrots and the beets separately and chop the potatoes.

Place the eggs in a saucepan and cover them with cold water. Bring to a boil over medium heat and boil for 9 minutes. Drain and cool under cold running water. Peel and finely chop them.

Place a 6-inch (15 cm) ring mold on a serving plate and pour in all the potatoes, covering the ring bottom. Spread the potatoes with one-third of the mayonnaise. Spread half of the beets in a thin layer over the potatoes, then half of the carrots and half of the onions. Arrange the pickled herring on top and spread with another one-third of the mayonnaise to cover. Layer the remaining onion and carrots and sprinkle with the eggs to finish. Season with pepper. Fully cover with the rest of the mayonnaise and the remaining beets.

Refrigerate for at least 6 hours or overnight, then carefully remove the ring and garnish with chopped parsley. Cut into wedges to show the salad layers.

Note: Eastern European pickled herring typically comes packed in oil. Seek it out if possible for this dish. If it's difficult to find, you can substitute pickled mackerel.

Salad with Tuna and Eggs

Preparation time: 30 minutes, plus 15 minutes steaming time and 10 minutes cooling time
Cooking time: 40 minutes
Serves 4

4 tomatoes
2 red bell peppers
2 jalapeños
2 sweet onions
1 teaspoon caraway seeds
½ teaspoon coriander seeds
½ cup (4 fl oz/120 ml) extra-virgin olive oil
1 tablespoon sherry vinegar
1 clove garlic, finely minced
Sea salt and freshly ground black pepper
5 oz (150 g) tuna fillet, cubed
4 eggs, hard-boiled, peeled, and cut into wedges
10 green olives, pitted and halved, for garnish
¼ bunch fresh parsley or cilantro (coriander), chopped

Mechouia salad, or *slata mechouia*, translates loosely as "roasted vegetable salad." In Tunisia, this salad is served as a cold appetizer, either on its own (as here), with bread, or as a sandwich filling. Eggs and tuna are added for protein and to make the dish more substantial.

Position an oven rack in the upper third of the oven and preheat the oven to 475°F (240°C/Gas Mark 8).

Arrange the tomatoes, bell peppers, jalapeño, and onions on a sheet pan. Transfer to the oven and roast, turning them frequently, until they look charred and soft, about 30 minutes. Transfer them to a large bowl, cover the bowl with plastic wrap (cling film), and let them steam in their own heat for 15 minutes.

Peel the vegetables, chop them in big chunks, and place in a bowl.

In a small dry frying pan, toast the caraway and coriander seeds until fragrant, 4–5 minutes. Tip out of the pan to stop the cooking and grind them in a mortar.

Sprinkle the toasted seeds over the vegetables. Sprinkle in 6 tablespoons of the olive oil, the vinegar, garlic, and salt and pepper to taste. Toss well.

In a medium frying pan, heat the remaining 2 tablespoons oil over medium heat. Add the tuna and brown for 5 minutes, stirring frequently. Remove from the heat and let it cool for 10 minutes.

To serve, put the salad on a large serving dish. Garnish with the egg quarters, tuna cubes, olives, and parsley.

Salad with Cod

(DF)

Spain

**Preparation time: 30 minutes,
  plus 2 days soaking time**
Cooking time: 3 minutes
Serves: 4

12 oz (350 g) salt cod
4 tablespoons extra-virgin olive
  oil, plus more for the pan
3 cloves garlic, peeled
Scant ½ cup (100 g)
  roasted almonds
Scant ½ cup (65 g) roasted
  hazelnuts
3 salt-packed anchovies, rinsed
  to remove salt and filleted
5 ñora peppers, seeded
1 fresh chili pepper
Red wine vinegar
Sea salt
11 oz (300 g) canned oil-packed
  tuna, drained and flaked
2 Belgian endive (chicory),
  trimmed and chopped
4 oz (120 g) unpitted olives

From Catalonia, a region in the northeast corner of Spain, *xató de Sitges* is a cod salad named for the city of Sitges and dressed with a chili-based sauce called *xató*, similar to a romesco sauce. The salad originally was served during Carnival, before Lent, but since the end of the nineteenth century, ritual Lenten meals called *xatonades* have been dedicated to the dish. Arbequina olives (small, dark brown, aromatic olives from Catalonia) are usually used to make this salad.

Soak the salt cod in cold water for 2 days, changing the water every 8 hours. Drain well and pull into shreds.

In a medium frying pan, heat a little oil over low heat. Add the garlic cloves and cook until lightly browned, about 3 minutes.

In a mortar, pound the garlic, almonds, hazelnuts, anchovies, ñoras, and chili pepper until a paste is formed. Add the vinegar and salt to taste and pound again, then add the olive oil and continue to pound until it becomes a smooth and emulsified sauce.

In a bowl, combine the tuna, salt cod, and endive (chicory). Add the olives and sauce.

Mix everything gently and serve.

Salt Cod and White Bean Salad

(DF) (NF)

Spain

**Preparation time: 20 minutes,
  plus 2 days soaking time**
Serves: 4

1 lb (450 g) salt cod
1 can (15 oz/440 g) white beans,
  rinsed and drained
2 tomatoes, seeded and chopped
2 onions, chopped
1 red bell pepper, chopped
20 unpitted black olives
Extra-virgin olive oil, for dressing
Sea salt
4 eggs, hard-boiled, peeled, and
  quartered

This traditional cold Catalonian summer dish, *empedrat,* gets its name from its appearance, as the word *pedres* means "pebbles." The salad has a substantial amount of protein from not only the fish and eggs, but also the beans. Other legumes, such as chickpeas or lentils, can also be used.

In a bowl of water, soak the salt cod for 2 days, changing the water every 8 hours. Drain and pull into shreds.

In a large bowl, combine the beans, tomatoes, onions, bell pepper, and olives. Dress the ingredients with some oil and season with salt. Add the eggs. Serve at room temperature. (The salad can be prepared 2 days in advance and refrigerated.)

Olivier Salad

(DF) (NF)

Russia

Preparation time: 35 minutes, plus 30 minutes cooling time
Cooking time: 40 minutes
Serves: 8

1 lb (450 g) boneless, skinless
　chicken breast
Sea salt
4 potatoes, peeled and cut into
　½-inch (1.25 cm) cubes
4 carrots, peeled and cut into
　½-inch (1.25 cm) cubes
6 eggs
1 onion, diced
1 cucumber, peeled and diced
¾ cup (100 g) green peas, boiled
　and drained
1 tablespoon superfine (caster)
　sugar, or more to taste
Freshly ground black pepper
Fresh dill
¾ cup plus 2 tablespoons (200 g)
　mayonnaise

Olivier salad, named for Lucien Olivier, a nineteenth-century Belgian chef in Moscow, is traditional to the cuisines of Russia and the post-Soviet countries. Also known as Russian Salad, it is served in most Russian restaurants, and most families have a big bowl of it on the table for Christmas, Easter, and other important celebrations. The salad is very easy to put together, but take particular care to cut all the ingredients to the same size.

In a saucepan of boiling water, cook the chicken until tender, about 30 minutes. Drain well. When cool enough to handle, cut into ½-inch (1.25 cm) cubes.

Meanwhile, in a separate saucepan of boiling salted water, cook the potatoes and carrots until tender, 20–25 minutes. Drain and set aside to cool for 30 minutes.

In a small saucepan of boiling water, cook the eggs for 9 minutes. Run under cold water and when cool enough to handle, peel and cut into ½-inch (1.25 cm) cubes.

In a large bowl, combine the chicken, potatoes, carrots, eggs, onion, cucumber, and peas. Season to taste with the sugar, salt, pepper, and dill and stir carefully. Add the mayonnaise and stir again.

Cobb Salad

Preparation time: 30 minutes
Cooking time: 30 minutes
Serves: 4

6 tablespoons extra-virgin olive oil
4 tablespoons red wine vinegar
2 tablespoons Dijon mustard
Sea salt and freshly ground
    black pepper
4 lettuce leaves, cut into thin strips
Small bunch of watercress
    (2¾ oz/70 g), washed and
    well drained
½ lb (225 g) bacon, diced
¾ lb (340 g) boneless, skinless
    chicken breast
4 eggs, hard-boiled, peeled,
    and sliced
8 cherry tomatoes, halved
2 white onions, thinly sliced
2 avocados, sliced
5 oz (150 g) Roquefort or
    cheddar, diced

This classic American salad is named for its inventor, Bob Cobb, the owner of the Brown Derby restaurant in Los Angeles, California. Apparently, late one night in 1937, he was hungry and rummaged in the restaurant's fridge and assembled leftovers there into a salad. There are some sources that claim the salad was invented by a chef. Either way, it's a delicious and satisfying version of a chopped salad.

Preheat a grill (barbecue).
    In a little bowl, whisk together 4 tablespoons of the oil, the vinegar, mustard, and salt and pepper to taste.
    In a large bowl, toss together the lettuce and watercress. Spread this mixture over a large serving plate and dress it with half of the vinaigrette.
    In a large frying pan, cook the bacon over medium-high heat until it is crispy and golden brown, 5–8 minutes. Remove from the pan and set aside.
    Brush the chicken with the remaining 2 tablespoons oil and season it with salt and pepper. Set on the grill grates and grill until it is fully cooked, at least 10 minutes on each side. Slice the chicken across the grain.
    Arrange the sliced eggs on one side of the serving plate. Arranging them in separate rows, place the bacon, tomatoes, onions, avocado, chicken, and cheese on the other side. Pour the remaining vinaigrette over the tomatoes and onions to dress them and serve. The salad is presented in all its glory and then tossed together just before serving.

Vegetables and Legumes

Ratatouille

(DF) (VG) (VT)   **France**

Preparation time: 10 minutes
Cooking time: 35 minutes
Serves: 4

20 cherry tomatoes
3 tablespoons extra-virgin olive oil
2 red onions, chopped
1 green bell pepper, cut into
   chunks
1 red bell pepper, cut into chunks
½ stalk celery, cut into chunks
2 cloves garlic, finely minced
12 fresh basil leaves, slivered
1 sprig thyme, leaves picked
2 bay leaves
2 cups (475 ml) peanut
   (groundnut) oil, for frying
1 lb (455 g) zucchini (courgettes),
   cut into chunks
1 lb (455 g) eggplant (aubergine),
   cut into chunks
5 saffron threads, bloomed
   in a little hot water
Sea salt and freshly ground
   black pepper

This tasty side dish has its origins in the Provence region of southern France. Ratatouille is a humble home-style dish, often made with whatever vegetables are languishing in the fridge, but it is also a dish that has made it onto the menus of some of the most famous restaurants. This dish can be prepared on the stovetop or in the oven, but this stovetop method is the most common and the original.

Set a sieve over a bowl to catch the juices. Halve the cherry tomatoes and place in the sieve to drain.

In a frying pan, heat the olive oil over low heat. Add the onions and cook over low heat until they soften, about 5 minutes. Add the bell peppers, celery, garlic, basil, thyme, and bay leaves. Add the drained tomatoes. Cover and cook for 10 minutes. Add half the liquid collected from draining the tomatoes.

Meanwhile, in a deep frying pan, heat the peanut (groundnut) oil over medium heat. Add the zucchini (courgettes) and cook, stirring frequently, until golden brown, about 8 minutes. Remove and set on paper towels to drain. Add the eggplant (aubergine) to the pan and cook until soft and golden, about 7 minutes. Pat the eggplant dry with the paper towels.

Add the eggplant and zucchini to the pan with the pepper/tomato mixture. Add the saffron and season to taste with salt and black pepper. Stir for 5 minutes and serve hot.

Mashed Root Vegetables

 Sweden

Preparation time: 30 minutes
Cooking time: 20 minutes
Serves: 6

Sea salt
2 turnips, peeled and cubed
2 carrots, peeled and cubed
2¼ lb (1 kg) baking potatoes,
    peeled and cubed
4 tablespoons (60 g) unsalted
    butter
2½ cups (20 fl oz/590 ml)
    vegetable stock
2 tablespoons chopped fresh
    parsley, for garnish

A traditional Swedish side dish, this savory root purée is usually served as an accompaniment to pork or lamb and is sometimes baked along with fish. The best potatoes to use here are starchy (floury) baking potatoes as they will make the fluffiest mash.

Bring a large pot of salted water to a boil. Add the turnips and carrots, reduce to a simmer, and cook for 5 minutes. Add the potatoes and let simmer until softened, 15 minutes longer.

Drain well and transfer to a large bowl. Mash gently with the butter and season with salt to taste. Add as much stock as required to get to the consistency you prefer. Serve garnished with the parsley.

Colcannon

 Ireland

Preparation time: 15 minutes
Cooking time: 35 minutes
Serves: 4

2¼ lb (1 kg) baking potatoes,
    peeled and cubed
5 tablespoons extra-virgin olive oil
12 oz (350 g) cabbage, shredded
4½ oz (130 g) scallions
    (spring onions), minced
1 cup (240 ml) milk
Sea salt and freshly ground
    black pepper
6 tablespoons (85 g) unsalted
    butter

Colcannon is a simple side dish of mashed potatoes and shredded cabbage that you will find everywhere in Ireland, particularly during the winter when it makes a perfect marriage with Irish lamb stew. Creating a little well in the center of the colcannon to hold a knob of butter while it melts makes this dish even more irresistible.

In a large pot, combine the potatoes with water to cover by 2 inches (5 cm). Bring to a boil and cook until softened, about 10 minutes. Drain, transfer to a bowl, and mash.

In a large frying pan, warm the oil over medium heat. Add the cabbage and cook, stirring, until soft, about 15 minutes. Add the scallions (spring onions) and stir again for 3 minutes.

Pour in the milk, reduce the heat to low, and add the mashed potatoes. Season to taste with salt and pepper and cook for 5 minutes.

Scoop the mixture onto a serving plate. Make a well in the center of the potatoes and add the butter to melt from the heat.

Hasselback Potatoes

NF VT 5

Preparation time: 20 minutes
Cooking time: 45 minutes
Serves: 4

4 baking potatoes (about 9 oz/
250 g each), scrubbed and
patted dry
3 tablespoons (45 g) unsalted
butter
Coarse sea salt
1 bunch chives, minced

Hasselback potatoes were created in 1953 by a trainee chef at the Hotel Hasselbacken in Stockholm. By cutting a series of slits the length of a potato, the chef created the perfect way to integrate butter into a potato as it bakes. We should give thanks to chef Leif Elisson for coming up with such a simple, yet elegant side dish.

Preheat the oven to 350°F (180°C/Gas Mark 4). Line a sheet pan with parchment paper.

Place a potato on a cutting board with a long side facing you. With a sharp knife, make slits ¼ inch (6 mm) apart across the width of the potato and the whole length of the potato, left to right. Do not cut all the way through to the bottom as you want the potato to stay in once piece. A good trick here is to put chopsticks on either side of the potato and this will keep you from slicing too far.

Generously grease the surfaces of the potato slices with the butter. Place the potatoes on the lined sheet pan and bake until golden brown, about 45 minutes.

Season with coarse salt and strew with the chives.

Fried Potatoes with Onions and Bacon

NF 30 5

Preparation time: 10 minutes
Cooking time: 20 minutes
Serves: 4

4 tablespoons clarified butter
2¼ lb (1 kg) yellow potatoes,
peeled and thinly sliced
2 onions, thinly slices
5 oz (150 g) slab bacon, diced,
or lardons
Herbed salt (see Note)
Freshly ground black pepper

To prepare *Bratkartoffeln*, as they are called in Germany, the potatoes must be cut into very thin slices. For an even crunchier outside and softer inside, the potatoes can be first blanched before frying: Cook them whole in salted boiling water for just 5–10 minutes (just to parboil them), then peel and thinly slice. This will shorten the cooking time in the frying pan.

In a large frying pan, heat the clarified butter over medium heat. Add the potatoes, cover, and cook, stirring occasionally, until the potatoes are tender and lightly browned, about 10 minutes.

Add the onions and bacon cubes and season to taste with herbed salt and pepper. Fry, uncovered, until the potatoes are golden brown, about 10 minutes longer.

Note: Seek out a store-bought herbal salt or make one yourself, mixing sea salt with your favorite fresh herbs, such as oregano, parsley, or rosemary.

Jacket Potatoes with Cheese, Sour Cream, Scallions, and Crispy Bacon

Preparation time: 45 minutes
Cooking time: 1 hour 15 minutes
Serves: 4

8 medium baking potatoes,
 scrubbed and patted dry
2 tablespoons vegetable oil
4 oz (120 g) smoked bacon, cubed
1 tablespoon (15 g) unsalted
 butter, at room temperature
5 oz (150 g) cheddar cheese,
 grated
2 cups (195 g) sour cream
 (see Note)
1 scallion (spring onion), minced
Sea salt
2 teaspoons chopped fresh
 parsley, for garnish

A jacket potato is a typical English dish that is popular in almost all English-speaking countries, including, notably, the United States, where the dish is called Twice-Baked Potatoes or sometimes Loaded Potatoes. Baking potatoes are cooked and cut open, then the potato flesh is scooped out and mixed with cheese and other ingredients such as bacon, butter, ham, or mushrooms. The filling is popped back into its "jacket" and can then be served as is or heated in the oven.

Preheat the oven to 400°F (200°C/Gas Mark 6). Line a sheet pan with parchment paper.

Prick the potatoes all over with a fork. Rub them with the oil and place them on the lined sheet pan. Bake until they are firm-tender, about 55 minutes. Remove from the oven and let them cool for 15 minutes. (Leave the oven on.)

Meanwhile, in a frying pan, cook the bacon over medium-high heat until crispy, 7–8 minutes. Drain on a paper towel.

Cut open the potatoes lengthwise, but do not go all the way through. Scoop the potato flesh out with a spoon into a bowl, leaving enough flesh in place to create a sturdy shell ("jacket"). Place the scooped potato shells in a baking dish.

Mash the potato, then stir in the butter, half of the bacon, half of the cheddar, 1½ cups (145 g) of the sour cream, and the scallion (spring onion). Season to taste with salt and mix well. Fill the potatoes with the mixture and top with the remaining cheddar.

Return to the oven and bake until the cheese is golden brown, about 12 minutes.

Transfer the potatoes to a serving plate, top with the remaining bacon, and garnish with the parsley. Top with the remaining ½ cup (50 g) sour cream.

Note: If you would like to make a homemade sour cream, pour ⅓ cup (2.5 fl oz/75 ml) milk into a bowl. Add 1 tablespoon fresh lemon juice and stir carefully. Let it rest for 15 minutes, then stir in 1¼ cups (10 fl oz/300 ml) heavy (whipping) cream. Cover with a towel and let it rest at room temperature for at least 24 hours.

Endive Mash

Preparation time: 20 minutes
Cooking time: 45 minutes
Serves: 8

4½ lb (2 kg) yellow potatoes,
   peeled
1 cup (8 fl oz/240 ml) milk,
   warmed
11 oz (300 g) smoked bacon
   (streaky), cut into strips
2¼ lb (1 kg) Belgian endive
   (chicory), sliced
14 oz (400 g) sharp cheddar
   cheese, grated
Dijon mustard
Nutmeg
Sea salt and freshly ground
   black pepper

This warming Dutch dish is popular in the wintertime, especially around Christmas. *Stamppot*, which translates as "mash pot," has been gracing Dutch dining tables since the 1600s, and there are many versions with different vegetables (see Root Vegetable Mash, below), though it typically contains potatoes.

In a large pot, combine the potatoes with water to cover and bring to a boil. Reduce to a high simmer and cook over medium heat until softened, about 40 minutes. Drain the potatoes, transfer to a bowl, and mash with the warm milk. Stir well.

In a frying pan, cook the bacon over medium-high heat until crispy, about 5 minutes. Add the bacon and all the bacon fat to the potatoes. Stir in the endive (chicory) and cheddar. Season with mustard, nutmeg, salt, and pepper to taste.

Root Vegetable Mash

Preparation time: 15 minutes
Cooking time: 30 minutes
Serves: 8

2¼ lb (1 kg) carrots, peeled
   and cut into pieces
2¼ lb (1 kg) parsnips, peeled
   and cubed
2 tablespoons (30 g) unsalted
   butter
1 onion, chopped
1 clove garlic, chopped
2 tablespoons Dijon mustard
2 tablespoons milk
Sea salt and freshly ground
   black pepper

Unlike most other Dutch *stamppots* (see Endive Mash, above), *wortel stamppot* is not made with potatoes. It dates from a time before potatoes were readily available in Western Europe and is made with other types of root vegetables (*wortel* means "root"). It is ideal to serve with stewed meat.

In a large pot, combine the carrots, parsnips, and water to cover. Bring to a boil over medium heat, then reduce to a high simmer and cook until tender and soft, about 25 minutes. Drain the vegetables and return them to the same pot over low heat and let them fully dry.

Transfer the vegetables to a food mill set over a bowl and process to a soft purée. (Alternatively, you can use a food processor to process the vegetables but the resulting purée will not be as smooth.)

In a saucepan, heat the butter over low heat. Add the onion and garlic and cook until softened, about 5 minutes. Stir in the mustard and mix well.

Stir in the carrots/parsnip mixture, milk, and salt and pepper to taste.

Paneer with Spinach

Preparation time: 10 minutes
Cooking time: 10 minutes
Serves: 4

1 tablespoon sunflower oil
2 onions, chopped
7 oz (200 g) spinach, chopped
3½ oz (100 g) paneer, crumbled
Sea salt and freshly ground
    black pepper

This dish combines paneer (Indian fresh cheese) and spinach. It is a very popular vegetarian recipe in northern India. This dish is ideal to serve with Corn Roti (page 157) or rice. It can also be garnished with a little butter or cream or a few drops of lime juice and slivers of fresh ginger.

In a saucepan, heat the oil over medium heat. Add the onions and cook until translucent, about 3 minutes. Add the spinach and sauté until wilted, about 3 minutes. Let the onion/spinach mixture cool completely.

Transfer the cooled onion/spinach mixture to a blender. Add 1½ cups (12 fl oz/355 ml) water and blend. Pour the spinach purée back into the pan. Add the paneer and stir over medium heat until heated through. Season with salt and black pepper to taste.

Mashed Green Plantains

Preparation time: 10 minutes
Cooking time: 35 minutes
Serves: 6

6 green plantains, peeled and
    sliced
Juice of 2 limes
Sea salt
4 tablespoons olive oil
2 onions, diced
4 cloves garlic, chopped
Freshly ground black pepper

Called *fufú de plátano*, this savory Cuban mash is African in origin and was introduced to Cuba by African slaves who prepared the dish because was it inexpensive and provided a lot of energy. It can also be made with medium-ripe plantains, which will make the dish a little sweeter.

In a large pot, bring 3 cups (24 fl oz/710 ml) water to a boil. Carefully add the plantains, lime juice, and salt to taste. Reduce to a high simmer and cook over medium heat until soft in the center, about 20 minutes. Drain the plantains.

In a saucepan, heat the oil over medium heat. Add the onions and garlic and cook until the onions are translucent, about 2 minutes. Add the plantains and pepper to taste. Gently mash the mixture while cooking over medium heat until golden brown, about 10 minutes.

Remove from the heat and continue mashing the mixture until it is the consistency of a purée.

Mashed Plantains
with Kidney Beans and Onions

(DF) (VG) (VT)

Uganda

Preparation time: 15 minutes
Cooking time: 1 hour 45 minutes
Serves: 4

8 oz (225 g) dried red kidney
    beans, soaked overnight in
    warm salted water
4 plantains, peeled and cut
    into small chunks
1 onion, chopped
2 cloves garlic, smashed with
    the side of a knife
1½ cups (225 g) corn kernels
5 tablespoons full-fat
    coconut milk
1¼ cups (10 fl oz/295 ml)
    vegetable stock
Sea salt

Matoke, a variety of plantain, is a staple food in Uganda, as well as Kenya, Tanzania, and other neighboring countries. The traditional preparation requires that the fruits be peeled, wrapped in the leaves of the tree, and boiled for about 2 hours in a pot called a *sufuria*. As it cooks, the flesh of the fruit changes color and texture, from white and hard to yellowish and soft. The plantain is then mashed to form a purée that is usually served wrapped in a leaf. Here the plantains are served with kidney beans cooked in coconut milk.

Drain and rinse the beans. In a large pot, combine the beans and water to cover, bring to a boil over high heat, and cook for 3 minutes. Reduce the heat and simmer until tender, about 1 hour 15 minutes. Drain.

Meanwhile, in a separate pot, combine the plantains with water to cover and bring to a boil over medium heat. Reduce to a simmer and cook until firm-tender, about 30 minutes.

Drain the plantains, transfer to a food mill set over a bowl, and process to a soft purée. (Alternatively, you can use a food processor to process the plantains but the resulting purée will not be as smooth.)

In a saucepan, combine the cooked beans, onion, garlic, corn, coconut milk, stock, and salt to taste. Bring to a boil over medium-high heat, then reduce to simmer and cook over low heat until a creamy compote is formed, about 20 minutes.

To serve, divide the beans among plates and top with the plantain purée.

Sauerkraut

(DF) (NF) (VG) (VT) 5   **Germany**

**Preparation time: 1 hour, plus
   3 weeks fermenting time
Serves: 4**

1 lb 5 oz (600 g) head green
   cabbage
2 tablespoons sea salt

Sauerkraut may be the most iconic vegetable dish of Germany.
The word *sauerkraut*, which translates loosely as "sour cabbage,"
is made by fermenting cabbage, giving the vegetable a very
intense sweet-and-sour taste. For main dishes, sauerkraut is
paired with many different meats, though typically it's served
with sausage. But it can also be served as a side dish to
accompany grilled meats or cheese.

Pull off 3 large outer leaves from the head of cabbage. Shred
the rest of the head and place it in a large bowl. Add the salt
and lightly massage the cabbage, tossing well to coat in the salt
and juices. Cover with a towel and let it rest for 45 minutes.
   Reserving the accumulated liquid, drain the cabbage and
layer it into a sterilized 15-inch (32 cm) ceramic crock 4 inches
(10 cm) deep, tossing the cabbage well. Press down with your
hands and top with the reserved whole leaves. Pour in the
reserved liquid and top with a weight to compress the cabbage,
then cover loosely with the lid or with a towel, secured with a
rubber band. Let sit at room temperature overnight.
   The next day, the cabbage liquid should be lightly bubbling.
Replace the towel with a clean one and seal the crock again.
Set aside to ferment in a cool, dark, and ideally humid, place
for 3 weeks. Once fermented, drain the cabbage and use as
a side dish.

Yellow Curry with Tofu and Mushrooms

Preparation time: 30 minutes
Cooking time: 45 minutes
Serves: 6

Salt
4 medium potatoes, peeled
   and left whole
Peanut (groundnut) oil, for frying
   and deep-frying
⅓ cup (7 oz/200 g) yellow curry
   paste
2 inches (5 cm) fresh ginger,
   peeled and minced
2 tablespoons cane sugar
4¼ cups (34 fl oz/1 liter) full-fat
   coconut milk
4 tablespoons tamari
1 red bell pepper, diced
1 yellow bell pepper, diced
1 green bell pepper, diced
6 ears baby corn, fresh or
   canned, sliced
5 oz (150 g) mushrooms,
   roughly torn
2 onions, thinly sliced
2 tablespoons rice flour
2 tablespoons paprika
11 oz (300 g) tofu, cubed,
   for serving

Thai yellow curry is not as well known as Thai red and green curries, but is equally delicious. The lively yellow color in the Thai curry paste comes from the fresh turmeric. Serve this vegetarian curry with basmati rice to round out the meal.

In a pot of boiling salted water, cook the potatoes until firm-tender, about 25 minutes. Drain and cut into cubes. Set aside.

Meanwhile, in a pot, heat 2 tablespoons peanut (groundnut) oil over medium heat. Add the curry paste and ginger and cook for 2 minutes. Add the sugar, 1 teaspoon salt, the coconut milk, and tamari. Simmer until the mixture has reduced by half, about 20 minutes. Use a hand blender to blend the sauce.

In a frying pan, heat 2 tablespoons peanut oil over medium heat. Add all the bell peppers and the corn and cook until the peppers are lightly browned, about 5 minutes. Transfer the peppers and corn to a bowl. Add the mushrooms to the pan and sauté over medium heat until they give up their liquid and the liquid evaporates, 3–4 minutes.

Pour 6 inches (15 cm) peanut oil into a deep Dutch oven (casserole) or deep-fryer. Heat to 350°F (180°C) on a thermometer (or until a cube of bread thrown into the oil browns in 30 seconds).

In a small bowl, toss the onions slices with the rice flour and paprika. Add the onions to the hot oil and fry until golden brown and crispy, about 4 minutes.

To serve, divide the sauce among shallow bowls, add the sautéed vegetables, the tofu, and potatoes, and top with the fried onions.

Quinoa Stew with Cheese, Parsley, and Ají Amarillo

 Peru

Preparation time: 5 minutes
Cooking time: 25 minutes
Serves: 4

4 tablespoons canola
   (rapeseed) oil
1 onion, diced
1 clove garlic, chopped
1 teaspoon ají amarillo paste
Sea salt
Ground cumin
Dried oregano
Scant ⅔ cup (3½ oz/100 g)
   quinoa, rinsed
2 cups (16 fl oz/475 ml)
   vegetable stock
3½ oz (100 g) queso fresco or feta
   cheese, diced
Chopped fresh parsley, for garnish

Quinoa atamalada (which translates to "tamale-like quinoa") is a Peruvian stew made from quinoa, a grain-like seed that is high in protein and a key ingredient in Peruvian cuisine. The stew is warming because of both its temperature as well as the chili heat of ají amarillo paste, made from a very hot Peruvian yellow chili used since Incan times.

In a large pot, heat the canola (rapeseed) oil over medium heat. Add the onion and garlic and cook until the onion is translucent, about 5 minutes. Add the ají amarillo paste and season to taste with salt, cumin, and oregano.
   Add the quinoa and stock and bring to a boil. Reduce the heat and simmer until the mixture is creamy, about 20 minutes.
   Stir in the cheese. Serve warm, garnished with parsley.

Maque Choux

 United States

Preparation time: 30 minutes
Cooking time: 40 minutes
Serves: 4

9 oz (250 g) smoked bacon, diced
4 cups (1 lb 5 oz/600 g) corn
   kernels (fresh, frozen,
   or canned)
1 yellow onion, chopped
1 red bell pepper, chopped
1 jalapeño, chopped
1 tablespoon Cajun seasoning
½ cup (4 fl oz/120 ml) heavy
   (whipping) cream (or
   chicken stock for a more
   traditional version)

Maque choux is a Cajun dish from Louisiana and its origins lie somewhere in the amalgam of cultures that ended up in this area at the mouth of the Mississippi River. There were clearly French influences by way of the Cajun immigrants, and the fact that the dish centers on corn suggests a Native American influence too. This rich and spicy blend of corn and vegetables is highlighted by the smoky flavor of bacon (vegetarians can substitute smoked paprika) and Cajun spices. Some people take *maque choux* a step further by adding chicken or lobster nuggets or shrimp.

In a frying pan, cook the bacon, stirring, over medium heat until it starts becoming crisp and rendering its fat, about 10 minutes.
   Add the corn, onion, bell pepper, and jalapeño. Sprinkle with the Cajun seasoning and simmer, stirring frequently, until the corn is softened, about 25 minutes.
   Stir in the cream (or chicken stock) and simmer for 5 minutes more. Serve hot.

Okra Fish Stew with Rice

Preparation time: 20 minutes
Cooking time: 1 hour
Serves: 6

Sea salt
2¼ cups (400 g) long-grain
    white rice, rinsed
1 (1-inch/2.5 cm) piece yete
    (see Notes), rinsed
1 (1-inch/2.5 cm) piece guedge
    (see Notes), rinsed
2 lb (900 g) bass fillets
1 lb (400 g) okra, trimmed
    and sliced
2 onions, peeled and cut
    into chunks
3 cloves garlic, peeled
2 tablespoons nététou powder
    (see Notes)
Red chili powder
Freshly ground black pepper
1 diakhatou eggplant
    (see Notes), rinsed
7 oz (200 g) shrimp (prawns),
    peeled and diced
⅔ cup (5 fl oz/150 ml) palm oil
2 red bell peppers, diced

This Senegalese stew is called *soupou kanja*. Its name literally means "okra sauce" in Wolof, one of the languages spoken in Senegal. Okra has a rather sweet taste not unlike asparagus. It can be eaten fresh in salads, but it is also good steamed or stewed. It's an ideal ingredient in soups and stews as it contains a natural substance that thickens the broth.

In a large pot, bring 5 cups (40 fl oz/1.2 liters) salted water to a boil. Add the rice and cook, stirring occasionally, until tender, about 20 minutes. Drain the rice.

Meanwhile, in another large pot, bring 5 cups (40 fl oz/ 1.2 liters) water to a boil. Add the yete, guedge, and bass fillets. Simmer for 20 minutes. Remove the fish from the pot and set aside on a plate. Return the pot of broth to the stove.

Place the okra slices in a bowl with water to cover. Rub gently and rinse. Repeat twice to reduce some of the stickiness. Drain the okra, add it to the pot of broth, and bring the broth to a boil over medium heat. Reduce to a simmer and cook for 10 minutes.

Meanwhile, in a food processor, combine the onions, garlic, nététou powder, and chili powder, salt, and black pepper to taste and grind to a coarse paste. Stir the mixture into the pot and simmer for more 10 minutes.

Crumble the fish fillets and add half to the pot along with the eggplant, shrimp (prawns), and palm oil. Stir and simmer over medium heat until reduced by half, 10 minutes longer.

Finally add the remaining fish and the bell peppers. Mix gently and simmer for 10 minutes over low heat. When the oil rises to the surface it means the dish is ready.

To serve, divide the rice among shallow bowls and serve the stew on top.

Notes: *Yete* is fermented sea snails. It adds a signature briny flavor to the dish, but you could use dried shrimp (prawns).

Guedge is a fermented fish. If you can't find it, use salt cod.

Nététou powder is ground locust beans. If you can't find it, you can substitute 2 teaspoons of miso.

Diakhatou eggplant, also known as African eggplant, is a small, squat light-green eggplant about the size of a beefsteak tomato (beef tomato). You could substitute white eggplant for it.

Bhujia

(DF) (NF) (VG) (VT)

India

Preparation time: 15 minutes,
plus 15 minutes resting time
Cooking time: 45 minutes
Serves: 4

8 medium yellow potatoes
(about 4 oz/115 g each)
1½ cups (175 g) chickpea
(gram) flour
4 tablespoons sunflower oil
1 tablespoon chaat masala
(see Note)
1 tablespoon chili powder
1 teaspoon powdered asafoetida
(hing) (see Note, page 175)
1 teaspoon baking soda
(bicarbonate of soda)
1 tablespoon fresh lemon juice
Sea salt
Vegetable oil, for frying
1 teaspoon dried mint

This typical spicy Indian snack is made with chickpea (gram) flour and mashed potatoes. The first recorded production of this crunchy street food was in 1877 in the city of Bikaner in Rajasthan, a state in northwestern India. The snack is known all over India, but Bikaner claims fierce and proud credit for it and in the 2010s filed with the Indian Patent Office to register the name *Bikaneri bhujia* as the only authentic *bhujia*.

In a saucepan of boiling water, cook the potatoes until tender, about 30 minutes. When cool enough to handle, peel the potatoes, place them in a bowl, and mash.

Add the flour, sunflower oil, chaat masala, chili powder, asafoetida, baking soda (bicarbonate of soda), lemon juice, and salt to taste. Mix thoroughly and add enough water to make a thick dough. Cover the bowl with plastic wrap (cling film) and let it rest for 15 minutes.

Pour 6 inches (15 cm) vegetable oil into a deep Dutch oven (casserole) or deep-fryer. Heat the oil to 320°F (160°C).

Divide the dough into 4 portions. Put a portion of dough into an Indian sev press or a potato ricer and extrude long strands of dough into the hot oil. Fry until golden, about 6 minutes. Transfer the bhujia to paper towels to drain. Repeat until you have used all the dough.

Sprinkle evenly with the mint. Serve hot.

Note: Chaat masala is a spice mixture used for seasoning snacks. It typically includes powdered green mango, cumin, coriander, ginger, and kala namak (black salt).

Sambar

Preparation time: 30 minutes
Cooking time: 35–55 minutes,
  (or 15 minutes if using
  a pressure cooker)
Serves: 4

½ cup (60 g) tamarind
  concentrate
⅓ cup (85 ml) hot water
1½ cups (6 oz/175 g) fresh pigeon
  peas or ½ cup (2 oz/50 g) dried
  pigeon peas
½ teaspoon ground turmeric
2½ teaspoons sea salt
2 tablespoons vegetable oil
1 small eggplant (aubergine),
  chopped
2 carrots, diced
8 moringa pods (aka drumsticks),
  peeled and chopped (see Notes)
1 tomato, chopped
2 tablespoons sambar powder
  (see Notes)
2 teaspoons jaggery sugar
½ teaspoon Kashmiri chili powder
1 tablespoon ghee
¾ teaspoon mustard seeds
¼ teaspoon powdered asafoetida
  (hing) (see Note, page 175)
15 fresh curry leaves
¼ cup fresh cilantro (coriander)
  leaves, chopped, for garnish

Sambar is a South Indian vegetable stew often eaten with idli (page 21) or dosa (page 162). One of its most distinguishing features comes from sambar powder (see Notes), the spice mixture used to flavor the stew. Pigeon peas and an assortment of vegetables are cooked in a tamarind-scented broth. The vegetables can vary, but often include an Indian vegetable called a "drumstick," which is another name for the long, thin seed pod of the moringa tree (see Notes).

Soak the tamarind in the hot water for 30 minutes. Strain the liquid through a sieve into a bowl (discard the fibers). Set aside.

Place the pigeon peas in a large pot with the turmeric, 1 teaspoon of the salt, and 4¼ cups/34 fl oz/1 liter water. Bring to a boil and cook for 5 minutes, then reduce the heat and simmer for 30 minutes for fresh peas or 50 minutes for dried peas, or until the peas are soft. (Alternatively, place the pigeon peas in a pressure cooker with the turmeric, 1 teaspoon salt, and 3 cups (24 fl oz/710 ml) water. Pressure-cook on high for 5 minutes, then reduce to low pressure and cook for another 5 minutes or until soft and smooth. Quick-release the pressure.) Set aside.

In a saucepan, heat 2 teaspoons of the oil over medium heat. Add the eggplant (aubergine) and sauté for 2 minutes. Add the carrots, moringa pods, and the remeaining ½ teaspoon salt and cook for 2 more minutes. Add the tomato and cook for 1 minute. Add 3 cups (24 fl oz/710 ml) water, the sambar powder, jaggery, 4 tablespoons of the tamarind water, the pigeon peas, and the chili powder. Stir well. Let the soup simmer for 5–6 minutes over medium heat.

In a frying pan, heat the ghee over medium heat. Add the mustard seeds and cook until they crackle, about 20 seconds. Add the asafoetida and curry leaves. Stir for 1 minute or until the leaves become crispy. Add to the soup.

Serve hot, garnished with the cilantro (coriander) leaves.

Notes: If you can't find moringa pods, you can substitute 5 ounces (150 g) okra or green beans.

Sambar powder, which is usually sweeter than other spice mixtures typical of Indian cuisine, contains fenugreek, cumin, coriander seeds, chili, curry leaves, black mustard, dried red pepper, urad dal, white pepper, and cinnamon. The ingredients are roasted and then reduced to a fine powder; the mixture sometimes includes salt.

Lentil Balls

Preparation time: 10 minutes
Cooking time: 40 minutes
Serves: 4

¾ cup (150 g) red lentils
⅔ cup (80 g) millet
1 teaspoon sea salt
4 tablespoons extra-virgin olive oil
1 onion, very finely chopped
2 tablespoons tomato paste
    (tomato purée)
1 tablespoon ground cumin
Juice of ½ lemon
⅓ bunch fresh parsley, finely
    chopped
½ bunch scallions (spring onions),
    finely chopped
4 leaves curly lettuce, for serving

Mercimek köftesi, a vegetarian version of meatballs (*köfte*), is one of the most popular appetizers in Turkish cuisine. They are served as *meze* with tzatziki (page 321) or tahini sauce for dipping, or as is with lettuce leaves and a squeeze of lemon juice. The lentil mixture can be made ahead and stored in an airtight container in the fridge for up to 5 days. The mixture also freezes well—just thaw overnight in the fridge before using.

In a saucepan, combine the lentils and 2 cups (16 fl oz/475 ml) water and bring to a boil over medium heat. Cook until almost all the water has been absorbed and the lentils are tender, about 30 minutes.

Meanwhile, in a separate saucepan, combine the millet with water to cover. Bring to a boil over medium heat, then cover and simmer until softened, about 10 minutes.

Drain the millet, add to the lentils pot, and season with the salt. Cover with a lid to let the millet soak up the excess lentil cooking water.

In a frying pan, heat the olive oil over medium heat. Add the onion and stir-fry until soft, about 5 minutes. Stir in the tomato paste (tomato purée) and cook for 2 minutes. Remove from the heat and stir in the cumin.

Add the onion mixture to the lentils/millet mixture. Mix in the lemon juice, half of the parsley, and half of the scallions (spring onions).

Prepare the lentil balls by taking a tablespoon of the lentil mixture in your hands and rolling it into an oval shape. Wet your hands frequently as the mixture will make them sticky.

Line a platter with the lettuce leaves. Gently place the lentil balls on top of the leaves. Sprinkle with the remaining parsley and scallions. Keep the dish in the fridge until serving time.

Red Lentil Dal

Preparation time: 10 minutes
Cooking time: 45 minutes
Serves: 4

1 cup (200 g) red lentils
1 tablespoon sunflower oil
½ teaspoon cumin seeds
1 cinnamon stick
1 onion, finely chopped
1 green chili pepper, seeded
   and minced
4 cloves garlic, minced
1 tablespoon minced fresh ginger
¾ teaspoon sea salt
½ teaspoon ground cardamom
½ teaspoon paprika
½ teaspoon ground turmeric
1 tomato, chopped
Juice of ½ lemon

This is a quick and simple red lentil dish. As is true of many Indian dishes, the whole spices are first briefly cooked in hot oil to awaken their flavors; this cooking method is called *tadka*. Pair this nutritious lentil dish with some basmati rice.

In a saucepan, combine the lentils and 3 cups (24 fl oz/710 ml) water. Bring to a boil and cook until the lentils are very tender, about 25 minutes.

Meanwhile, in a separate saucepan, heat the oil over medium heat. Add the cumin seeds and cinnamon stick and cook for 1 minute. Add the onion, chili pepper, garlic, and ginger and sauté until the onions turn gold, about 4 minutes. Add the salt, cardamom, paprika, turmeric, and tomato. Stir frequently and cook until the tomato is soft and mushy, about 8 minutes.

Drain the lentils, add them to the onion/tomato/spice mixture, and stir to combine. Cook for 5 more minutes. Sprinkle with lemon juice to taste.

Boiled Corn with Lima Beans, Potatoes, and Fried Cheese

Preparation time: 30 minutes
Cooking time: 1 hour
Serves: 4

For the llajwa

2 large tomatoes, seeded and
    finely diced
4 tablespoons chopped fresh
    cilantro (coriander)
1 tablespoon finely minced
    red onion
1 ají rocoto or serrano chili,
    seeded (optional) and minced
1 clove garlic, minced
2 tablespoons olive oil
1 teaspoon sea salt

For the vegetables

4 ears of corn, husked and husks
    reserved
1 lb 2 oz (500 g) fresh lima beans
    (butter beans) or 1½ cups
    (180 g) dried beans (see Note)
4 medium white potatoes, peeled
4 tablespoons (60 g) unsalted
    butter
7 oz (200 g) queso fresco or feta
    cheese, cut into 4 slices

This Bolivian dish, often served in La Paz, is made with lima beans, potatoes, corn, and fried cheese. Though lima beans are well known in the United States, where they are a big part of Southern cuisine, the beans are actually originally from Peru and are called "lima" after the Peruvian city of Lima. Often called "butter beans" because of their starchy but buttery texture, this light-green or cream-colored bean has a delicate flavor. Fresh lima beans can be hard to find, while dried or canned beans are available all year round. This dish is served with *llajwa*, a Bolivian fresh salsa, similar to a pico de gallo or salsa cruda.

Make the llajwa: In a large bowl, stir together the tomatoes, cilantro (coriander), onion, chili, garlic, oil, and salt. (If you'd prefer, a smooth sauce, make this in a food processor). Refrigerate for at least for 1 hour. Serve at room temperature.

Prepare the vegetables: Layer 2 corn husks (about 3 inches/ 10 cm long) on the bottom of a large pot. Cover them with 2 inches (5 cm) hot water. Bring to a boil over high heat. Add the ears of corn to the pan, layer with more 2 husks, then add the lima beans (butter beans) and let simmer over medium heat until the beans are tender, about 30 minutes.

Add the potatoes, then more 2 corn husks, and simmer until the potatoes are firm-tender, about 30 minutes longer. Discard the corn husks.

In a large frying pan, heat the butter over high heat. Add the cheese and fry until golden, about 20 seconds per side.

To serve, place 1 ear of corn on each plate, along with lima beans, 1 potato, and a slice of fried cheese. Spoon the salsa over the top.

Note: If using dried lima beans, soak them in water for several hours or overnight.

Black Bean Stew

Preparation time: 1 hour,
  plus overnight soaking time
Cooking time: 2 hours
  40 minutes (or 2 hours
  if using a pressure cooker)
Serves: 4

6 oz (175 g) smoked pork ribs,
  cut crosswise into 2-inch
  (5 cm) lengths
1 lb (450 g) dried black beans,
  soaked in salted warm water
  overnight, undrained
1 bay leaf
9 oz (250 g) bacon, diced
3 cloves garlic, chopped
Sea salt and freshly ground
  black pepper
4 tablespoons extra-virgin olive oil
1 onion, finely chopped
3 sprigs thyme
6 oz (175 g) smoked sausages,
  sliced
1 chili pepper, sliced

Feijoada is perhaps the most famous dish of Brazil and takes its name from *feijão*, a Portuguese word meaning "bean." There are many variations of this dish, both in the type of bean used (black beans are typical of the carioca version from Rio de Janeiro) and in the meat, which can be pork or beef and of different cuts (including offal or pig's ear). Serve the stew with white rice for a complete meal. Please ensure the sausages you use contain no gluten.

In a large pot, combine the pork ribs and 6⅓ cups (50 fl oz/ 1.5 liters) water, bring to a boil, and cook for 5 minutes, then reduce the heat and simmer for 1½ hours, or until the meat is tender. (Alternatively, place the pork ribs in a pressure cooker with 4¼ cups (34 fl oz/1 liter) water. Seal and pressure-cook on low for 1 hour. Natural-release the pressure.) Reserving the cooking water, drain the pork and set aside.

In a large pot, combine the black beans, their soaking water, and the pork rib cooking water. Bring to a boil over medium heat. Add the bay leaf and cook until the beans are softened, about 40 minutes. Discard the bay leaf. Reserving the liquid, drain the beans.

In a large Dutch oven (casserole), combine the bacon, one-third of the garlic, and salt and black pepper to taste. Cook over medium heat until the bacon is browned, about 5 minutes. Remove the bacon to paper towels. Add the olive oil, the remaining garlic, the onion, and thyme and cook until the onion is browned, about 5 minutes.

Add the drained beans, sliced sausages, pork ribs, chili pepper, and salt and black pepper to taste. Add 1 cup of the reserved bean cooking liquid and simmer over low heat for 20 minutes. Add more of the bean liquid if the mixture is too dry; the consistency has to be thick but loose. Serve hot.

Andalusian Chickpea Stew

DF NF

Spain

Preparation time: 45 minutes, plus overnight soaking time and 15 minutes resting time
Cooking time: 1 hour 40 minutes
Serves: 4

1 lb 5 oz (600 g) dried chickpeas, soaked in salted warm water overnight, drained, and rinsed
1 carrot, cut into 4 chunks
4 cloves garlic, peeled—2 chopped, 2 left whole
4 tablespoons extra-virgin olive oil
12 oz (50 g) pork shoulder, cubed
Sea salt
1 chorizo or other cured beef and pork sausage, diced
1 onion, chopped
2 fresh bay leaves
½ cup (4 fl oz/120 ml) dry white wine
3 medium white potatoes, peeled and diced

Garbanzos andaluz, a rich stew typical of Andalusia in southern Spain, is made with chickpeas, pork, and chorizo—a cured Spanish beef and pork sausage seasoned with sweet and hot paprika, which give the sausage its signature bright-red color. Meatless versions of the stew, chickpeas only, can also be found in Andalusia during Lent. As with many stews, this is better if prepared the day before to let the flavors blend perfectly. Please ensure the sausage you use contains no gluten.

In a large pot, combine the soaked chickpeas, carrot, 2 whole garlic cloves, and water to cover. Bring to a boil, then reduce the heat and simmer until the chickpeas are tender, about 1½ hours, removing any foam from the surface with a skimmer.

Meanwhile, in a large frying pan, heat the oil over medium heat. Season the pork cubes with salt. Add the pork to the pan and cook until browned all over, about 8 minutes. Remove the pork to a plate and set aside. Add the chorizo to the same pan and fry it, then set aside on a separate plate.

Add the chopped garlic, onion, and bay leaves to the pan and gently cook over low heat until browned, about 10 minutes. Return the pork to the pan and pour in the wine. Simmer over medium heat for 10 minutes.

Transfer the pork mixture to the pot of chickpeas along with the potatoes. Season with salt, cover, and simmer over low heat until the potatoes are tender, about 10 minutes. Stir in the chorizo. Remove from the heat and let it rest for 15 minutes before serving.

Chickpea Stew with Poached Eggs and Tuna

(DF) (NF)

Tunisia

Preparation time: 30 minutes, plus overnight soaking time
Cooking time: 1 hour 45 minutes
Serves: 4

1 lb (450 g) dried chickpeas, soaked in salted warm water overnight, drained, and rinsed
4 cloves garlic, minced
6 tablespoons extra-virgin olive oil
1 onion, minced
2 teaspoons ground cumin
1 teaspoon sea salt, plus more to taste
Juice of 1 lemon
2 tablespoons harissa
1 teaspoon ground caraway
3 tablespoons distilled white vinegar
4 eggs, at room temperature
8 oz (225 g) canned tuna
8 black olives, for garnish

Lablabi, which at its essence is chickpea broth seasoned with spices, can be made in different forms and with different garnishes. Here we are including a lemon seasoning, poached eggs, and tuna.

In a pot, bring 4 cups (32 fl oz/950 ml) water to a boil over high heat. Add the chickpeas and half of the garlic. Cook for 15 minutes. Reduce the heat to medium, cover, and cook until the chickpeas are tender, about 1 hour. Check regularly to see if the chickpeas are still immersed in water and add a little more water if necessary. Skim any white foam off the top.

In a medium frying pan, heat 3 tablespoons of the olive oil over medium heat. Add the onion and 1 teaspoon of the cumin. Cook until the onion becomes soft, about 3 minutes. Add the remaining garlic and ½ teaspoon salt. Reduce the heat to low and cook for 15 minutes. Scrape everything out of the pan into the chickpea pot.

In a salad bowl, combine the lemon juice, harissa, caraway, the remaining 3 tablespoons olive oil, 1 teaspoon cumin, and ½ teaspoon salt. Mix well and set aside.

Set up a bowl of ice and water next to a clean cloth on a plate. In a saucepan, combine the vinegar and 3 cups (24 fl oz /710 ml) water and bring to a boil. Break each egg onto a small plate, yolk intact. Give the boiling water a whirl with a fork and slide the eggs in one at a time. The whirlpool in the water ensures that the white immediately wraps up the yolk. Poach for 4 minutes in the simmering water. Remove the eggs with a slotted spoon and place in the cold water for 3 seconds. Then transfer to the cloth to drain. Season with salt to taste.

To serve, divide the chickpeas and their broth among deep plates. Add 2 tablespoons lemon/harissa dressing to each serving, top with a poached egg and a quarter of the tuna, and garnish with the olives.

Hilbet with Berbere Sauce

(DF) (NF) (VG) (VT)

Eritrea

Preparation time: 10 minutes, plus 1 hour 30 minutes cooling time
Cooking time: 1 hour
Serves: 4

1 cup (130 g) hilbet (fava bean/broad bean flour with fenugreek)
2 onions, diced
3 cloves garlic, peeled
6 tablespoons vegetable oil
1 tablespoon berbere (see Note)
4 tomatoes, chopped, or generous ¾ cup (200 g) passata (unseasoned tomato sauce)
1 tablespoon tomato paste (tomato purée)
1 tablespoon fresh rosemary leaves
Sea salt and freshly ground black pepper
1 Injera (page 153), for serving

Hilbet is one of the main dishes eaten in Eritrea, where it's often served with injera (page 153) and a spicy tomato sauce.

Pour the hilbet into a bowl. Gradually add 1 cup (8 fl oz/240 ml) cold water, stirring constantly to make a thin smooth batter.

In a saucepan, bring 1 cup (8 fl oz/240 ml) water to a boil. Pour the batter into the water, while stirring vigorously. Bring to a boil and continue stirring. Cook it over low heat until it gets a thick as a béchamel sauce, about 15 minutes. Remove from the heat, sprinkle some drops of cold water on top, cover with a lid, and let it cool down for about 30 minutes. Refrigerate for 1 hour.

In a blender, purée the onions and garlic. Heat a medium frying pan over medium-high heat. Add the onion/garlic mixture and stir until golden brown, about 3 minutes. Add the oil and berbere and cook for 10 minutes. Add the tomato sauce and tomato paste (tomato purée). Reduce the heat to medium-low and simmer for 30 minutes. Add more water if the pan seems dry. Add the rosemary and salt and black pepper to taste and simmer for a few more minutes.

Take the hilbet from the fridge. Whip with a hand mixer until the texture is soft, fluffy, and smooth.

Place the injera on a serving plate, make a mound of hilbet on the injera and make a well in the hilbet. Pour the berbere sauce into the well.

Note: Berbere is a spice blend that can include chili, ginger, clove, coriander, ajwain (a type of caraway), and sometimes even long pepper.

Refried Red Beans with Mozzarella Cheese

**Preparation time: 30 minutes,
  plus overnight soaking time
Cooking time: 1 hour 20 minutes
Serves: 6**

1 lb 2 oz (500 g) dried red or black
  beans, soaked in water overnight, drained, and rinsed
4 tablespoons vegetable oil
Sea salt
1 small onion, minced
5 oz (150 g) hard-cured chorizo,
  crumbled
4 tablespoons (60 g) unsalted
  butter
1½ cups (135 g) shredded
  mozzarella or Oaxaca cheese
Tortilla chips, for serving

This Honduran appetizer—made from refried beans and cheese—is also an excellent side dish to complement meat dishes. It is traditionally served in an *anafre*, a small clay pot. The beans can be flavored with chilies or other spices according to your taste. Please ensure the chorizo you use contains no gluten.

In a small pot, combine the soaked beans and water to cover. Bring to a boil, then reduce to a high simmer and cook until the beans are tender, about 40 minutes. Reserving the cooking water, drain the beans.

In a saucepan, heat 2 tablespoons of the oil over medium heat. Add the drained beans and onion and cook, stirring frequently, until browned, about 5 minutes. Add 5 tablespoons of the reserved cooking water and season with salt. Transfer the bean/onion mixture to a blender and blend to a purée.

In a large frying pan, heat the remaining 2 tablespoons oil over high heat. Add the bean purée and fry it, stirring occasionally, until the mixture is toasted and browned, about 10 minutes.

In a cast-iron skillet, cook the chorizo over medium heat until it's browned, about 10 minutes. Remove half of the chorizo from the pan and set aside. Add the butter to the skillet and add the refried beans. Stir gently for 3–4 minutes to incorporate the beans and chorizo, then stir in the mozzarella. Top with the remaining chorizo. Cook over low heat, without stirring, for about 10 minutes to melt the cheese.

Serve out of the skillet with tortilla chips for scooping.

Baked White Beans with Paprika

Preparation time: 20 minutes
Cooking time: 1 hour
Serves: 4

1 lb 5 oz (600 g) fresh white
    beans, rinsed
3 onions, cut into chunks
14 oz (400 g) bone-in pork ribs,
    cut into individual ribs
1 clove garlic, chopped
5 tablespoons sunflower oil
1 tablespoon cornstarch
    (cornflour)
1 tablespoon paprika
Minced fresh parsley, to taste
Sea salt and freshly ground
    black pepper

Tavče gravče is prepared with fresh beans that are baked and served in a traditional clay pot called a *tava*. If kept in perfect condition and if used regularly, the clay pot can give a special flavor to the recipe.

In a large pot, combine the beans with water to cover. Bring to a boil and cook for 5 minutes.

Drain the beans and return to the pot with fresh water and the onions and pork. Bring to a boil, then reduce the heat to low and simmer until the beans are soft but not mushy, about 30 minutes. Check occasionally to make sure that the beans are still covered with water and add a little more water if necessary. Stir in the garlic.

Preheat the oven to 475°F (245°C/Gas Mark 9).

In a small saucepan, heat the oil over medium heat. Add the cornstarch (cornflour) and paprika and stir for 2 minutes. Stir this mixture into the beans. Season with parsley, salt, and pepper to taste.

Pour the bean mixture into a 14-inch (35 cm) ovenproof terra-cotta pot 6 inches (15 cm) deep. Bake until the surface is crusty, about 15 minutes.

Baked Gigante Beans

Preparation time: 15 minutes,
    plus overnight soaking time
Cooking time: 2 hours 30 minutes
Serves: 4

1 lb 2 oz (500 g) dried gigante
    beans, soaked in warm water
    overnight, drained, and rinsed
Sea salt
½ cup (4 fl oz/120 ml) extra-virgin
    olive oil
2 onions, finely chopped
1 clove garlic, peeled
3 tablespoons finely chopped
    celery
5 tablespoons finely chopped
    fresh parsley
1⅔ cups (14 oz/400 g) passata
    (unseasoned tomato sauce)
2 teaspoons dried oregano
Freshly ground pepper

Gigantes plaki is a traditional Greek recipe made with gigante beans. *Gigantes* means "giants" and that's indeed how these beans look. They are baked in a tomato sauce with herbs and lots of olive oil, a signature of many Greek dishes.

In a large pot, combine the drained gigantes with cold water to cover. Season the water with salt and bring to a boil. Reduce the heat to a simmer and cook the beans over low heat until softened, about 40 minutes. Drain the beans.

Meanwhile, preheat the oven to 350°F (180°C/Gas Mark 4).

Pour the oil into a 14-inch (32 cm) round baking dish 3 inches (7.5 cm) deep. Add the onions and garlic and stir to coat. Transfer the pan to the oven and bake for 20 minutes.

When the beans are cooked and drained, add them to the baking dish along with the celery, parsley, and ½ cup (4 fl oz/120 ml) hot water. Stir and add the tomato sauce, oregano, and salt and pepper to taste. Bake until the beans are soft and the sauce is thick, about 1½ hours.

Boston Baked Beans

**Preparation time: 30 minutes,
plus overnight soaking time
Cooking time: 4 hours 30 minutes
Serves: 6**

11 oz (300 g) dried navy (haricot)
   beans, soaked in cold water
   overnight, undrained
2 tablespoons light brown sugar
1 tablespoon superfine (caster)
   sugar
3 tablespoons molasses (treacle)
1 tablespoon Worcestershire sauce
½ teaspoon mustard powder
Sea salt
½ onion, chopped
1 tablespoon diced carrot
3½ oz (100 g) salt pork, diced
Freshly ground black pepper

This dish is so firmly associated with Boston that the recipe bears the name of the city, and the city is nicknamed Beantown. Introduced to beans by the Wampanoag tribe in the seventeenth century, people in Massachusetts have enjoyed slow-cooked beans in various forms ever since. Traditionally the dish was made with small white beans, which in the early twentieth century were dubbed "navy beans," as beans were the typical fare for U.S. Navy sailors. Navy (haricot) beans are cream-colored and readily absorb the stronger flavors and red-brown color in the dish.

Put the beans into a pot with their soaking water and bring to a boil over medium heat. Reduce the heat to low and cook until the beans are firm-tender, about 2 hours. Reserving the cooking liquid, drain the beans.

Preheat the oven to 325°F (165°C/Gas Mark 3).

In a saucepan, combine half of the reserved bean cooking liquid, the brown sugar, superfine (caster) sugar, molasses (treacle), Worcestershire sauce, mustard, and 1 teaspoon salt. Bring to a boil over medium heat and simmer, stirring, until reduced by half, about 5 minutes.

Spread the beans in a 12-inch (30 cm) round baking dish 3 inches (7.5 cm) deep. Sprinkle with the onion, carrot, and salt pork (do not stir in). Pour the molasses mixture over the beans.

Cover the baking dish with a lid or foil and bake for 2 hours. Uncover and bake until the liquid is absorbed but the beans are not dried out, about 30 minutes longer. Check occasionally and add some more bean cooking liquid if the beans get too dry while baking. Season the top with some black pepper.

Black-Eyed Peas and Rice with Waakye Leaves

 5

Ghana

Preparation time: 5 minutes, plus overnight soaking time
Cooking time: 1 hour 10 minutes
Serves: 4

8–10 waakye leaves (dried millet or sorghum stalks)
Generous ¾ cup (5 oz/150 g) dried black-eyed peas (beans), soaked in salted warm water overnight, drained, and rinsed
2 cups (360 g) long-grain white rice
Sea salt

Waakye, a traditional rice and bean dish from Ghana, can be served with stew on top but is also a highly regarded street food, usually sold wrapped in banana leaves. The beans and rice are cooked with "waakye leaves" (available online or in African stores), which are dried millet or sorghum stalks that add color to the dish, but are not edible.

In a soup pot, combine the waakye leaves and about 6 cups (48 fl oz/1.4 liters) water and bring to a boil over medium heat. The leaves will turn the water deep red.

Add the soaked peas (beans) to the boiling water, cover, and cook until tender, about 40 minutes.

Add the rice and salt to taste and boil until tender, about 20 minutes. Stir once and cover. Reduce the heat and cook for 5 minutes. Remove from the heat and let it rest for 5 minutes.

Discard the waakye leaves. Fluff the rice mixture with a fork and serve.

White Bean and Rice Cake

Peru

Preparation time: 15 minutes
Cooking time: 20 minutes
Serves: 6

1¾ cups (450 g) cooked or canned white beans
2 tablespoons extra-virgin olive oil
1 tablespoon (15 g) unsalted butter
2 cloves garlic, minced
2 onions, diced
3 fresh ají amarillo chilies, chopped
2¾ cups (450 g) cooked long-grain white rice
Sea salt

Tacu-tacu is a cake made with rice and beans whose name may come from the quechua word *tacuni*, which means to mix one thing with the other. This dish is a common way of using up leftover rice and/or beans from the day before. It is often served with fried eggs.

Put the beans in a food mill set over a bowl and process to a soft purée. (Alternatively, you can use a food processor to process the beans but the resulting purée will not be as smooth.)

In a large nonstick frying pan, combine the oil, butter, and garlic and heat over low heat. Add the onions and chilies and cook until browned, about 5 minutes.

Add the cooked rice and the bean purée. Season the mixture with salt and stir gently. Cook over medium-high heat, shaking the pan but not stirring, until the mixture is thick, about 10 minutes. Invert the cake onto a plate and then slide it back into the pan and cook the second side for 5 minutes longer.

Transfer the cake to a cutting board and cut into 6 portions.

Red Beans and Rice

Preparation time: 20 minutes
Cooking time: 1 hour 40 minutes
Serves: 4

11 oz (300 g) dried kidney beans,
    soaked in warm water over-
    night, drained, and rinsed
Sea salt
1½ cups (12 fl oz/355 ml)
    sunflower oil
2 cloves garlic, minced
½ large onion, diced
10 baby carrots, diced
4 small tomatoes, diced
Cayenne pepper
2 cups (16 fl oz/475 ml) full-fat
    coconut milk
Scant 1 cup (350 g) long-grain rice
1 large plantain

Wali na maharage—whose name means "rice and beans" in Swahili—is a typical daily meal for most Tanzanian families. It is nutritious, delicious, and uses local and affordable ingredients, such as coconut milk, which gives a great softness to the sauce and contrasts with the spiciness of the cayenne pepper.

In a large pot, combine the soaked beans with water to cover. Add salt to taste. Bring to a boil, then reduce the heat to medium-low and cook until the beans are firm-tender, about 45 minutes. Drain and set aside.

In a soup pot, heat 4 tablespoons of the oil over medium heat. Add the garlic and onion and cook until translucent, about 4 minutes. Add the carrots and tomatoes and cook until lightly browned, about 5 minutes. Add the drained beans and season with salt and cayenne. Pour in the coconut milk, making sure the vegetables are covered; if not, add some water. Cover and cook over low heat until the beans are soft and the sauce has thickened, about 45 minutes.

Meanwhile, in a saucepan, bring 4 cups (32 fl oz/950 ml) water to a boil. Add the rice and some salt. Cook, stirring once every 10 minutes, until almost all the water is absorbed, about 20 minutes. When there is just a little water left at the bottom of the pan, remove from the heat, cover, and let it rest for 10 minutes.

Trim the ends of the plantain. Cut crosswise into 4 pieces and peel off the skin.

In a deep frying pan, heat the remaining 1¼ cups (10 fl oz/295 ml) oil over medium heat. Add the plantain and cook for 3 minutes on each side.

To serve, divide the rice among four plates. Pour the beans over the rice and set a slice of fried plantain on top.

Fish and Shellfish

Jansson's Temptation

Preparation time: 20 minutes
Cooking time: 25 minutes
Serves: 4

2 tablespoons (30 g) unsalted
butter, plus more for greasing
8 yellow potatoes, peeled
and cut into thin French fry
(chip) shapes
2 yellow onions, thinly sliced
5 oz (150 g) oil-packed
anchovy fillets
1½ cups (12 fl oz/350 ml) heavy
(whipping) cream
1 tablespoon anchovy oil
(from a jar of anchovies)
2 tablespoons cornmeal

Jansson frestelse, as this simple potato dish is called in Swedish, is often present at a Scandinavian Christmas buffet as well as on other holidays. In Sweden this would be made with a pickled sprat (a small fish in the herring family). However anchovies are certainly easier to find, so we have used them in this recipe. The origins of this dish are not clear, but some say the dish was dubbed *Jansson frestelse* (Jansson's Temptation) after a 1928 film of the same name.

Preheat the oven to 425°F (220°C/Gas Mark 7). Butter a 13-inch (35 cm) square baking dish.
    Arrange the potatoes, onions, and anchovies in the baking dish. Pour in the cream and anchovy oil. Sprinkle with the cornmeal and dot with the butter.
    Bake until the potatoes are soft and golden brown, about 25 minutes.

Ceviche

Preparation time: 15 minutes,
    plus overnight marinating time
Serves: 4

1 cup (8 fl oz/250 ml) fresh
lemon juice
Juice of 2 limes
Sea salt and freshly ground
white pepper
8 oz (225 g) salmon fillets, sliced
⅓ inch (8 mm) thick
8 oz (225 g) sea bream fillet,
sliced ⅓ inch (8 mm) thick
8 oz (225 g) shrimp (prawns),
peeled and deveined
1 onion, cut into thin rings
11 oz (300 g) tomatoes, diced
1 ají rocoto or other red chili
pepper, diced
2 tablespoons minced fresh
cilantro (coriander)

Famous throughout the world, this raw fish dish from Peru is typically served with sweet potatoes and Andean corn. The citrus liquid used to "cook" the raw fish is called *leche de tigre* (tiger's milk) and it is often served in a separate glass to be drunk, as people think it has an aphrodisiac power.

Pour the citrus juices into a pitcher (jug) and season with salt and white pepper.
    Place all the sliced fish and shrimp (prawns) in a large glass bowl. Add the onion rings, tomatoes, chili, and cilantro (coriander). Pour the citrus juices over everything, cover the bowl with plastic wrap (cling film), and refrigerate overnight.
    Serve chilled.

Gravlax

 DF NF 5

Norway

Preparation time: 30 minutes, plus 48 hours curing time
Serves: 6

4 skin-on salmon fillets (about 7 oz/200 g each)
½ cup (4 fl oz/120 ml) aquavit or brandy
6 tablespoons superfine (caster) sugar
½ cup (100 g) sea salt
3 tablespoons freshly ground black pepper

Gravlax or *gravlaks* is a Nordic dish of cured salmon (its name translates as "buried salmon"; *grav* means "grave" and *laks* means "salmon" in Norwegian). The fish is cured in a mixture of salt, sugar, and sometimes dill. The salmon is then served thinly sliced and accompanied by mustard or whipped sour cream.

Place the salmon fillets skin-side down in a glass baking dish in a single layer. Drizzle the aquavit or brandy evenly over them.

In a small bowl, stir together the sugar, salt, and black pepper and mix well. Divide the curing mixture into 2 equal portions.

Working with one portion of curing mixture and 2 fish fillets at a time, sprinkle one-third of the mixture onto one side of the baking dish. Place 1 fillet skin-side down on the curing mixture. Sprinkle the flesh side with another one-third of the curing mixture. Lay a second fillet on top of the first, flesh-side down. Sprinkle the skin side with the remaining cure. Repeat this process with the remaining portion of cure and 2 fillets.

Cover with plastic wrap (cling film) and place something heavy on top of the salmon (like heavy pots, for example) to weight the fish down. Refrigerate the fish for 12 hours.

The next day, drain the fillets and return them to the baking dish, stacking them again, but this time with their skin sides in contact. Cover again with plastic wrap, refrigerate, and cure for another 12 hours.

Repeat the two 12-hour steps again and after 48 hours, you may cut the fillets into very thin slices and serve.

Smoked Salmon with Shrimp, Horseradish Cream, and Lemon Dressing

Preparation time: 30 minutes
Cooking time: 5 minutes
Serves: 4

20 shrimp (prawns)
4 tablespoons prepared
    horseradish
3 tablespoons sour cream
Sea salt and freshly ground
    black pepper
1 tablespoon honey
1 teaspoon finely grated peeled
    fresh ginger
Grated zest and juice of 2 lemons
6 tablespoons extra-virgin olive oil
7 oz (200 g) baby salad greens
8 slices smoked salmon (1 oz/
    30 g each)

A few simple ingredients in perfect harmony make this a beloved dish in Belgium, popular with locals and tourists alike. An important ingredient is the savory and spicy horseradish sauce that complements the smoked salmon and shrimp. The same style of horseradish sauce is found in much of central European cuisine as an accompaniment to pork dishes.

Set up a large bowl of ice and water. In a large pot of boiling water, blanch the shrimp (prawns) for 2 minutes, then transfer to the ice bath to cool down. Drain, then peel and devein.

In a small bowl, stir together the horseradish, sour cream, and salt and black pepper to taste.

In a separate bowl, whisk together the honey, ginger, lemon zest, lemon juice, and oil. Season with salt and black pepper.

Put the salad greens in a large bowl and gently toss with half the dressing.

Place the smoked salmon and shrimp on a serving plate and top with the creamy horseradish sauce and salad. Drizzle with the rest of the dressing.

Creamy Cod and Polenta

(NF)

Italy

**Preparation time: 15 minutes,
plus 24 hours soaking time
and 30 minutes cooling time
Cooking time: 1 hour 40 minutes
Serves: 6**

1 lb 5 oz (600 g) salt cod
Sea salt
Generous 2 cups (300 g) polenta
6 tablespoons extra-virgin olive oil
1 clove garlic, chopped
2 oil-packed anchovy fillets
½ cup (4 fl oz/120 ml) sparkling
    white wine, such as Prosecco
⅔ cup (5 fl oz/150 ml) milk
Freshly ground black pepper

Baccalà mantecato is a tasty Venetian antipasto made with creamy, delicate salt cod and polenta. Salt cod arrived in Venice for the first time in the fifteenth century, brought by a merchant who had been shipwrecked in the Norwegian archipelago of Lofoten, where he encountered the preserved fish. It was immediately popular and gave rise to various recipes, like this one. The dish is best eaten the day it is made, but it will hold in the fridge for about a day.

In a large bowl, combine the salt cod and cold water to cover. Soak in the fridge for 8 hours. Drain, add fresh water to cover, and soak for another 8 hours. Repeat this one more time, then peel and debone the cod and cut it into cubes.

Line a sheet pan with parchment paper.

In a saucepan, bring 6 cups (48 fl oz/1.4 liters) salted water to a boil. Whisking constantly, stream in the polenta. Reduce the heat and simmer, stirring constantly, until firm and thick, about 1 hour.

When the polenta is cooked, pour it into the lined pan and let it cool, about 30 minutes.

Preheat the oven to 425°F (200°C/Gas Mark 6).

While still in the pan, cut the polenta into 5 × 1½-inch (13 × 4 cm) rectangles. Brush the top of the polenta with 1 tablespoon of the oil. Bake for 15 minutes to make crunchy corn croutons.

In a saucepan, heat 1 tablespoon of the oil over low heat. Add the garlic and anchovy fillets and let infuse for 2 minutes. Add the cod and cook over low heat for 7 minutes.

Add the wine, increase the heat to high, and cook until the wine is evaporated. Add the milk and salt to taste. Reduce the heat to medium and cook until the milk is completely absorbed, about 15 minutes.

Pour the mixture into a food processor and process to a smooth cream. Keep processing until the mixture cools down to warm 86°F (30°C). With the machine running, slowly stream in the remaining 4 tablespoons olive oil. The mixture should be firm-soft like a mousse.

To serve, spread the cod on top of the polenta croutons and sprinkle with black pepper.

Garlic Arriero Salt Cod

**Preparation time: 30 minutes,
plus 24 hours soaking time
and 30 minutes draining time
Cooking time: 45 minutes
Serves: 4**

2¼ lb (1 kg) salt cod, cut into
  pieces
4 dried chiles de árbol
½ cup (4 fl oz/120 ml) extra-virgin
  olive oil
9 oz (250 g) yellow potatoes,
  chopped
8 cloves garlic, chopped
2¼ cups (18 fl oz/530 ml) passata
  (unseasoned tomato sauce)
2 teaspoons finely chopped fresh
  parsley, for garnish

Typical of Navarre in northern Spain, *ajoarriero de bacalao* can
be found on every traditional menu and at all saint's day feasts.
As is typical of regional cuisine, every town puts its own spin on
the dish, using different vegetables or accompaniments—though
they all start with salt cod. It is served very hot, traditionally in a
clay pot, and more hot pepper is often added at the end.

In a large bowl, combine the salt cod and cold water to cover.
Soak in the fridge for 8 hours. Drain, add fresh water to cover,
and soak for another 8 hours. Repeat this one more time.

Meanwhile, in a separate bowl, combine the chiles de árbol
and water to cover and soak for 4 hours. Drain and cut into strips.

Drain the cod and set it in a colander to drain for at least
30 minutes.

In a soup pot, heat the oil over medium heat. Add the
potatoes and garlic and cook until the potatoes are tender and
golden brown, about 20 minutes.

Add the strips of rehydrated chilies and simmer over low
heat for 15 minutes.

Add the cod and stir gently, pour in the tomato sauce, and
simmer for 10 minutes to combine the flavors. Garnish with the
parsley and serve.

Seville Cod

Preparation time: 15 minutes
Cooking time: 5 minutes
Serves: 4

Olive oil, for frying, plus more
    for the salad
1 egg
Sea salt
3¼ lb (1.5 kg) cod fillet, cut into
    2-inch (5 cm) cubes
1 head curly endive or escarole,
    chopped
Seeds of 1 pomegranate
1 clove garlic, chopped

These fried fish nuggets are popular throughout the Spanish region of Andalusia and are served as a *tapa*, a small portion ideal for an aperitif. The fish for this can be changed up: Try it with hake, salmon, or even desalted salt cod.

Pour 6 inches (15 cm) oil into a deep Dutch oven (casserole) and heat over high heat.

Crack the egg into a bowl, add a pinch of salt, and beat it with a fork. Dip the cod cubes into the egg, then add to the hot oil and fry until golden brown, 3–4 minutes.

In a bowl, toss together the endive, pomegranate seeds, and garlic. Dress with a little olive oil and season with salt to taste.

Serve the fried cod with the salad.

Fish Cakes

Preparation time: 10 minutes
Cooking time: 10 minutes
Serves: 4

7 oz (200 g) skinless cod fillet
1 egg white
2 tablespoons grated yamaimo
    (Japanese mountain yam)
1 tablespoon mirin
1½ teaspoons sugar
Sea salt
Chopped fresh parsley,
    for garnish
Lemon wedges, for squeezing

Japanese fish cakes, called *hanpen*, have a mild taste and chewy texture. They are made with white fish such as cod or pollock. Often the component of more elaborate recipes, such as *oden* (a one-pot dish of eggs, vegetables, and fish cakes in a light broth), *hanpen* can also be quickly pan-fried in a little vegetable oil and served as is.

In a food processor, blend all the ingredients until the mixture is smooth. Spread the mixture in a 6-inch (15 cm) square pan or heatproof dish at least 1¾ inches (4.5 cm) deep.

In a large pot (at least 4 inches/10 cm deep), bring water to a boil. Immerse the square pan or dish in the boiling water and cook for 8 minutes.

Using tongs, carefully remove the pan or dish from the water, pouring off any water on top of the fish cake, and let it cool. Invert the fish cake out of the pan and cut into 4 triangles. Garnish with parsley and serve with lemon wedges.

Fish Skewers

**Preparation time: 30 minutes,
plus 1 hour marinating time
Cooking time: 5 minutes
Serves: 4**

1 lb 2 oz (500 g) fillets firm-fleshed
   fish, cut into 1½-inch
   (4 cm) cubes
6 cloves garlic, minced
1 tablespoon paprika
4 tablespoons distilled
   white vinegar
Juice of 1 lemon
½ cup (4 fl oz/120 ml) sunflower
   oil, plus 1 tablespoon
   for the sauce
Sea salt and freshly ground
   black pepper
Ground cumin
1 tablespoon chopped fresh ají
   amarillo chilies or 2 teaspoons
   ají amarillo paste

For Peruvian *anticucho de pescado*, choose a firm-fleshed fish that will hold together on the outdoor grill. The recipe is also good with salmon. In Peru, the fish skewers are often served with golden corn or potatoes and lettuce.

In a bowl, combine the fish, garlic, paprika, vinegar, lemon juice, ½ cup (4 fl oz/120 ml) of the oil, and ½ teaspoon salt. Season with black pepper and cumin to taste. Marinate in the fridge for 1 hour.

Meanwhile, in a frying pan, heat the remaining 1 tablespoon oil over medium heat. Add the chilies and season with salt and black pepper. Stir-fry for 5 minutes. Set aside.

Preheat an outdoor grill (barbecue).

Reserving the marinade, skewer the fish pieces onto bamboo skewers, 4 pieces for each. Grill them, brushing with marinade, until fully cooked, 2–3 minutes on each side.

Serve with the sautéed chilies and oil.

Whole Barramundi Baked
In Banana Leaves

Preparation time: 30 minutes
Cooking time: 1 hour
Serves: 4

4 banana leaf pieces (15 × 10
    inches/40 × 25 cm), rinsed
1 whole barramundi (4½ lb/2 kg),
    cleaned and gutted
Sea salt
3 fresh red chilies, seeded
    and chopped
3 cloves garlic, chopped
4 tablespoons chopped
    fresh thyme
4 tablespoons chopped
    fresh parsley
6 tablespoons extra-virgin olive oil
Grated zest and juice of 2 lemons
1 tablespoon tamari
2 tablespoons sugar
1 scallion (spring onion), chopped
1 shallot, chopped
Freshly ground black pepper

For this dish a whole fish is wrapped in banana leaves and baked; the leaves keep the fish moist and also scent the fish at the same time. The large flexible leaves of the banana tree are used all throughout Asia to wrap food for steaming or baking and this practice has also extended to Australia. The barramundi is a fish that can live in both fresh and salt water; it is fished in the northern seas of Australia and the Indo-Pacific regions, as well as in the Persian Gulf.

Preheat the oven to 375°F (190°C/Gas Mark 5).

Bring a large pot of water to a boil. Add the banana leaves and blanch for 2 minutes, then drain and set aside on a towel.

Season the fish with salt, 1 teaspoon of the chilies, 1 teaspoon of the garlic, the thyme, and parsley, rubbing it all over the skin and in the cavity.

Place 2 banana leaves on a work surface and lay the fish over them. Sprinkle with the oil. Place the remaining leaves on top and wrap the fish thoroughly. Tie with kitchen twine. Transfer the bundle to a sheet pan and bake for 1 hour.

Meanwhile, in a bowl, stir together the lemon zest, lemon juice, tamari, sugar, scallion (spring onion), shallot, the remaining garlic and chilies, and black pepper to taste.

Unwrap the fish and place on a serving plate. Pour the sauce all over the fish and serve.

Steamed Fish Curry

Preparation time: 30 minutes
Cooking time: 30 minutes
Serves: 4

1¾ cups (350 g) jasmine rice
3 cloves garlic, chopped
1 large shallot, chopped
3 stalks lemongrass, chopped
½ inch (1.25 cm) fresh galangal,
    chopped
2 makrut lime leaves, slivered
    (see Note, page 33)
2 teaspoons crumbled
    dried chilies
1 teaspoon ground turmeric
1 teaspoon light brown sugar
2 teaspoons sea salt
1 tablespoon rice bran oil
½ teaspoon shrimp paste
1 cup (8 fl oz/240 ml) full-fat
    coconut milk
1 tablespoon granulated sugar
1 lb 5 oz (600 g) barramundi
    fillets, finely chopped
1 egg
1 tablespoon fish sauce
4 banana leaf squares
    (7 × 7 inches/18 × 18 cm),
    for serving

Amok trey is a spicy fish curry that is often eaten during Bon Om Touk, the Cambodian Water Festival that marks the end of Cambodia's rainy season. This three-day festival is a way of thanking the Mekong River for providing abundant fish and fertile land. The banana-leaf bowls in which the curry is served add flavor to the dish.

Wash the rice and soak it in water for 30 minutes.

In a saucepan, bring 3 cups (24 fl oz/710 ml) water to a boil. Add the rice and cook over high heat for 10 minutes. Reduce the heat to medium and cook until almost all the water has been absorbed, about 8 minutes. Remove the pan from the heat, cover, and let it rest for 15 minutes.

Meanwhile, in a mortar or food processor, combine the garlic, shallot, lemongrass, galangal, makrut lime leaves, chilies, turmeric, brown sugar, and 1 teaspoon of the salt and pound or process to a paste.

In a saucepan, heat the oil over medium-high heat. Add the curry paste and cook for 1 minute. Add the shrimp paste, coconut milk, granulated sugar, and remaining 1 teaspoon salt. Whisk to combine. Reduce the heat to medium and simmer for 2 minutes. Add the fish, gently folding it into the curry sauce with a silicone spatula. Let it simmer until the fish is cooked, 3–4 minutes.

In a small bowl, whisk together the egg and fish sauce, then whisk in 2 tablespoons of the curry sauce from the saucepan. Pour this back into the curry and thoroughly fold it in.

Set up a large bowl of ice and water. Bring a pot of water to a boil. Add the banana leaves and blanch for 1 minute to soften. Drain the leaves and transfer to the ice bath to stop them from cooking further. Drain and pat dry.

To make the banana-leaf bowls, lift the sides of each banana leaf square up to form a bowl and twist and secure the corners with wooden toothpicks to hold the bowl shape in place.

To serve, fluff up the rice with a fork, divide the rice among the banana-leaf bowls, and top with the fish curry.

Grilled Marinated Fish

Preparation time: 30 minutes,
   plus 30 minutes
   marinating time
Cooking time: 1 hour
Serves: 4

For the marinated fish
1 whole freshwater fish (5 lb/
   2.2 kg), cleaned, gutted, head
   removed, and butterflied
2 tablespoons extra-virgin olive oil
1 teaspoon tamarind concentrate,
   dissolved in 3 tablespoons water
1 teaspoons ground turmeric
1 teaspoon sea salt
Freshly ground black pepper

For the tomato sauce
2 tablespoons extra-virgin olive oil
2 cloves garlic, minced
2 onions, diced
2 tablespoons tomato paste
   (purée)
9 oz (250 g) cherry tomatoes,
   halved
1 teaspoon ground turmeric
1-inch (2.5 cm) piece fresh ginger,
   minced
2 teaspoons curry powder
2 sprigs parsley, finely chopped
Freshly ground black pepper
Juice of 1 lemon

For serving
3 oz (80 g) spinach
1 onion, cut into rings
11 oz (300 g) tomatoes, diced
Generous 1 cup (200 g)
   pomegranate seeds
1 lemon, cut into wedges
1 sprig parsley, finely chopped

Masgouf is the national dish of Iraq. It is a butterflied freshwater fish (usually carp) that is marinated, then cooked over a woodfire. This recipe uses the oven's broiler (grill), but if you have access to a woodfire, try it for an authentic flavor.

Prepare the fish: Rinse the fish in cold water, drain, and pat dry with paper towel.
   In a small bowl, stir together the olive oil, tamarind mixture, turmeric, salt, and black pepper to taste and mix until smooth. Rub the mixture all over both sides of the fish, using a spoon or brush. Place it in a ceramic baking dish, cover, and refrigerate for 30 minutes.

Make the tomato sauce: In a medium pot, heat the oil over medium–high heat. Add the garlic and onions and cook until they turn translucent, about 3 minutes. Add the tomato paste (purée) and cherry tomatoes and cook for 5 minutes. Stir in the turmeric, ginger, curry powder, parsley, and black pepper to taste and cook over medium heat until the tomatoes start to soften, about 7 minutes. Stir in the lemon juice and set aside.

Bake the fish: Preheat the oven to 450°F (230°C/Gas Mark 8). Place the fish in the preheated oven and bake until the flesh just barely flakes, about 35 minutes. Remove the fish and preheat the broiler (grill). Drizzle some of the tomato sauce over the fish, return to the oven, and broil (grill) for 2 minutes.

To serve: Make a bed of spinach and onion rings on a large serving plate. Lay the fish on top of the spinach and onions, arrange the tomatoes, pomegranate seeds, lemon wedges, and parsley around the fish and add the remaining tomato sauce.

Grilled Pike

Preparation time: 10 minutes
Cooking time: 25 minutes
Serves: 4

5½ tablespoons (80 g)
    unsalted butter
4 large cloves garlic, minced
1 fresh red chili, seeded and
    finely chopped
4 tablespoons apricot jam
Sea salt
4 tablespoons chopped fresh
    cilantro (coriander)
1 pike (2½ lb/1.2 kg), cleaned,
    gutted, and butterflied
2 tablespoons olive oil,
    plus more for drizzling
Freshly ground black pepper
Juice of 1 lemon
1 red onion, sliced, for garnish
1 stalk celery, sliced, for garnish

One of the food traditions that unites all South Africans is a good old *braai*, the Afrikaans word for barbecue. A whole butterflied *snoek* (pike) is grilled over a charcoal fire; it is the perfect opportunity for families to get together and chat while the fish cooks. The ideal side dish for this fish dish is a grilled sweet potato salad accompanied by more apricot jam. If you don't have a charcoal grill (barbecue), you can make this in the oven (see Note).

Light a charcoal grill (barbecue). When the coals are gently glowing, it is ready for cooking.

Meanwhile, in a saucepan, heat the butter over medium heat. Add the garlic and sauté until fragrant, about 1 minute. Stir in the chili, apricot jam, 4 tablespoons water, and salt to taste. When mixed well, reduce the heat and simmer for 5 minutes. Stir in the cilantro (coriander). Pour the mixture into a bowl.

Coat both sides of the fish with the oil. Season the flesh side with salt and black pepper. Place the fish in a hinged grilling basket and set on the grates skin-side up. Cook until it changes color from pink to white with spots of brown, about 3 minutes.

Flip the basket so the fish is skin-side down. Open the basket and brush the flesh with the spicy apricot mixture. Close the basket and cook for 10 minutes, or until done (when done, the fish's eyes will be completely white; flip the basket to check).

Flip the fish again so it is skin-side up and cook for about 2 minutes more to caramelize the sugars in the sauce.

To serve, cut off the head and discard it, then place the fish on a plate skin-side down. Sprinkle with the lemon juice, garnish with the onion and celery, and drizzle with olive oil.

Note: Position an oven rack close to the top of the oven and preheat the oven to 465°F (240°C). Lay the fish skin-side down on a sheet pan and roast for 15 minutes. Brush the flesh with the apricot mixture. Then switch on the broiler (grill) to high and broil for 5 minutes to crisp the skin.

Bouillabaisse

**Preparation time: 30 minutes,
plus 1 hour chilling time
Cooking time: 20 minutes
Serves: 6**

2¼ lb (1 kg) assorted fish fillets,
  such as monkfish, cod, John
  Dory, cut into large pieces
2¼ lb (1 kg) snapper fillets,
  cut into large pieces
1 lb 2 oz (500 g) shellfish, such
  as shrimp (prawns), peeled
  and deveined, and/or crabs,
  rinsed and cut in 4
2 tomatoes, peeled, seeded,
  and cubed
1 sprig wild fennel
1 bunch parsley
1 bunch thyme
Bay leaves
5 saffron threads, softened in
  ¼ cup (2 fl oz/60 ml) water
Strips of zest from 1 orange
Sea salt and freshly ground
  black pepper
3 tablespoons extra-virgin olive oil
½ onion, chopped
2 cloves garlic, minced
7½ cups (60 fl oz/1.75 liters) fish
  stock, homemade (see Note)
  or store-bought

Bouillabaisse is a traditional Provençal fish stew that can
be found in every restaurant in the port city of Marseille. It's
traditionally prepared by making a broth with fish bones and
trimmings, while the fish marinates with fresh herbs, saffron,
and tomatoes. Bouillabaisse looks amazing when it is served,
so it is a great dish for a lunch or dinner party. It can be even
more luxurious if octopus or lobster are added.

In a large bowl, combine the fish, shellfish, tomatoes, fennel,
parsley, thyme, bay leaves, saffron, orange zest, and salt and
pepper to taste. Refrigerate for 1 hour.

In a large Dutch oven (casserole), heat the oil over medium
heat. Add the onion and garlic and cook until the onion is
translucent, about 4 minutes. Add the seafood (and the rest of
the aromatics from the bowl) and fish stock to cover. Bring to a
boil over high heat, then reduce the heat, stir well, and simmer
until the seafood is just cooked through, about 15 minutes.

Discard the herb sprigs, bay leaf, orange zest, and wild
fennel. Serve hot.

Note: If you filleted your own fish and have trimmings, or if
you can get fish heads and bones from your fishmonger, you
can make a homemade stock. In a stockpot, combine the fish
trimmings and add double their volume of water. Salt the water,
bring to a boil, and cook for 20 minutes. Strain the stock.

Fish and Shellfish

276

Cioppino

Preparation time: 20 minutes, plus 1 hour soaking time
Cooking time: 45 minutes
Serves: 4

Sea salt
8 littleneck clams, well scrubbed
4 tablespoons extra-virgin olive oil
1 bulb fennel, chopped
1 shallot, chopped
1 clove garlic, chopped
Freshly ground black pepper
1 cup (8 fl oz/240 ml) dry
    white wine
1 can (14 oz/400 g) crushed
    tomatoes
1 bottle (8 fl oz/240 ml) clam juice
8 mussels, well scrubbed
    and debearded
9 oz (250 g) shrimp (prawns),
    peeled and deveined
9 oz (250 g) skinless halibut
    fillet, cubed
Chopped fresh parsley,
    for garnish
Lemon quarters, for squeezing

A perfect example of the American melting pot of cuisines, this seafood stew was born in California, but was created by Italian immigrants from Genoa living in San Francisco. The immigrants were fishermen who simply adapted their traditional fish stew to local ingredients, including their Pacific Ocean catch of fish and shellfish. The name of the recipe, *cioppino*, derives from the dialect word *ciuppin*, which either means a "small soup" or is a reference to the small size the ingredients were cut into for the stew. Exactly when it was created is a mystery, but it begins to show up as a published recipe in the early twentieth century.

In a bowl of salted water, soak the littleneck clams for 1 hour to purge them of sand.

In a soup pot, heat the oil over medium heat. Add the fennel and shallot and cook until the shallot is lightly browned, about 5 minutes. Add the garlic, season to taste with salt and pepper, and stir for 1 minute. Add the wine, bring to a boil, and cook until it reduces by half, about 5 minutes. Add the tomatoes, clam juice, and 1 cup (8 fl oz/240 ml) water. Simmer over low heat, stirring occasionally, until the tomatoes break down into a thick sauce, about 20 minutes.

Add the clams, cover, and cook for 5 minutes. Add the mussels, shrimp (prawns), and halibut. Cover and cook, without stirring, until the clams and the mussels have opened (discard any that remain closed), about 5 minutes longer. Season with salt and pepper.

Serve hot, garnished with parsley and with lemon wedges for squeezing.

Tuscan Seafood Stew

**Preparation time: 1 hour
30 minutes
Cooking time: 2 hours
Serves: 6**

2¼ lb (1 kg) assorted whole
   rockfish, such as scorpion
   fish, monkfish, angler fish,
   trunkfish, or red mullet,
   cleaned and gutted
14 oz (400 g) other fish, such
   as dogfish (small shark),
   mackerel, conger eel, or moray
   eel, cleaned and gutted
7 oz (200 g) shrimp (prawns)
1 bay leaf
7 oz (200 g) mussels, well
   scrubbed and debearded
½ cup (4 fl oz/120 ml) extra-virgin
   olive oil
1 onion, chopped
3 cloves garlic, diced
8 fresh sage leaves
1 lb 2 oz (500 g) octopus,
   cuttlefish, or squid, cleaned
   and cut into small chunks
4 tomatoes, peeled, seeded,
   and chopped
½ cup (4 fl oz/120 ml) red wine
2 tablespoons tomato paste
   (purée)
1 fresh chili pepper, seeded
   and diced
Sea salt and freshly ground
   black pepper

The traditional *cacciucco Livornese* is a stew that includes various fish caught in the waters off the coast of Tuscany, along with other ingredients typical of the region. The stew takes its name from the port city of Livorno. The classic recipe calls for the use of 13 species of seafood, but 6 or 7 are enough to prepare an excellent *cacciucco*.

For the rockfish, cut off the heads and cut the fish into fillets. Reserve the heads and trimmings for the fish stock. For the other fish, debone them and slice. Reserve the trimmings for the stock. Peel and devein the shrimp (prawns), saving the shells for the stock.

In a saucepan, combine all the fish trimmings and shrimp shells with 2 cups (16 fl oz/475 ml) water and bring to a boil. Add the bay leaf and simmer for 30 minutes. Strain the stock.

Place the mussels in a large pan set over high heat, cover, and heat them until the mussels have opened (discard any that remain closed), about 5 minutes. Pull the flesh out of half of them and set all aside.

In a large pot, heat the oil over medium heat. Add the onion, garlic, and sage and cook, stirring frequently, until soft and translucent, about 5 minutes. Add the octopus, cuttlefish, or squid and stir until well infused with onion flavor, 4–5 minutes. Pour in the tomatoes, reduce to low heat, and cook for 10 minutes longer.

Add all the fish to the pot, then add the red wine and let evaporate over medium-high heat. Add the tomato paste (purée), reduce the heat, and gently simmer for 15 minutes. Add ½ cup (4 fl oz/120 ml) of the fish stock, the chili, and salt and black pepper to taste. Cover and simmer for 30 minutes.

Add the shrimp (prawns) and mussels and cook over high heat for 1–2 minutes longer. Season with salt and serve.

Spicy Korean Seafood Stew

**Preparation time: 30 minutes,
plus 1 hour soaking time
Cooking time: 30 minutes
Serves: 6**

Sea salt
8 littleneck clams, well scrubbed
2 tablespoons gochugaru
(Korean chili flakes)
1 teaspoon gochujang (Korean
chili paste)
1 teaspoon doenjang (Korean
fermented soybean paste)
1 clove garlic, chopped
1 tablespoon grated fresh ginger
Pinch of freshly ground black
pepper
1 carrot, diced
1 onion, sliced
2 scallions (spring onions),
thinly sliced
9 oz (250 g) napa cabbage
(Chinese leaf), cut into strips
3½ oz (100 g) Korean radish,
cut into small cubes
2 mushrooms (your favorite),
sliced
1¾ cups (200 g) bean sprouts,
rinsed
1½ cups (24 fl oz/750 ml) iriko
dashi (anchovy broth)
2 oz (50 g) watercress
2 blue crabs, rinsed, cut in 4
9 oz (250 g) squid, cleaned
and cut into small cubes
9 oz (250 g) tilapia fillet,
cut into small cubes
8 shrimp (prawns), peeled
and deveined
Juice of ½ lemon

In Korea, this spicy fish stew is called *haemultang* and is one of the most famous dishes in that country. The assorted seafood is seasoned with Korea's famous gochujang (chili paste) and cooked in a broth with fresh vegetables, such as peppers, mushrooms, onions, and bean sprouts. It is an ideal stew for cold days because it is hearty, spicy, and full of flavor. The secret to a great result is to use a variety of seafood.

In a bowl of salted water, soak the littleneck clams for 1 hour to purge them of sand.

In a blender, combine the gochugaru, gochujang, doenjang, garlic, ginger, 1 teaspoon salt, black pepper, and 3 tablespoons water and blend to a thick paste.

In a large pot, combine the carrot, onion, scallions (spring onions), napa cabbage (Chinese leaf), radish, mushrooms, and bean sprouts. Add the anchovy broth and the seasoning paste. Top with the watercress and cook over medium–high heat for 20 minutes.

Add the clams, crabs, squid, tilapia, and shrimp (prawns) and cook until the crabs are cooked through, about 10 minutes. Stir in the lemon juice and serve hot.

Shrimp Stew

Preparation time: 40 minutes
Cooking time: 20 minutes
Serves: 4

1 red bell pepper, diced
6 tomatoes, peeled and seeded
1 onion, diced
2 cloves garlic, chopped
2 tablespoons dendê or clear
    palm oil or olive oil
1 lb 2 oz (500 g) yuca (cassava)
    root, peeled and grated
    (see Note, page 20)
1 cup (8 fl oz/250 ml) full-fat
    coconut milk
Sea salt and freshly ground
    black pepper
4 tablespoons chopped fresh
    cilantro (coriander)
1 lb 5 oz (600 g) shrimp (prawns),
    peeled and deveined
Hot red pepper sauce
Fresh parsley, for garnish

Bobó de camarão is a creamy shrimp stew typical of the state of Bahia on the east coast of Brazil. *Bobó*, as it is called in Brazil, is thickened with starchy yuca (cassava). The classic recipe calls for *dendê*, a red oil from the fruit of oil palm trees. It can be difficult to find, so in this recipe you can use regular palm oil or olive oil.

In a food processor, combine the bell pepper, half the tomatoes, half the garlic, and half the onion and process to a smooth purée, about 2 minutes.

In a saucepan, heat 1 tablespoon of the oil over medium heat. Add the pepper/tomato purée and stir well. Add the yuca (cassava), coconut milk, and ½ cup (4 fl oz/120 ml) water. Reduce the heat and whisk constantly until the mixture breaks down into a smooth purée, about 10 minutes. Season with salt and black pepper.

In a frying pan, heat the remaining 1 tablespoon oil over medium heat. Add the remaining garlic, remaining tomatoes, and remaining onion and cook until the tomatoes start to release their liquid, about 3 minutes. Add the cilantro (coriander) and the shrimp (prawns) and cook for 3 more minutes.

Transfer the shrimp mixture to the yuca purée and stir to combine. Season with hot red pepper sauce and serve garnished with parsley.

Shrimp and Grits

Preparation time: 20 minutes
Cooking time: 30 minutes
Serves: 4

2 cups (16 fl oz/475 ml) chicken
    stock
2 cups (16 fl oz/475 ml) milk
7 tablespoons (100 g) unsalted
    butter
½ tablespoon sea salt
½ tablespoon freshly ground
    black pepper
Scant 1½ cups (200 g) hominy grits
11 oz (300 g) cheddar cheese,
    grated
12 slices (rashers) smoked bacon,
    chopped
1 lb (450 g) shrimp (prawns),
    peeled and deveined
2 cloves garlic, minced
2 scallions (spring onions),
    minced, for garnish

This is a traditional breakfast dish from coastal South Carolina and Georgia that is now served any time of day. Grits are coarsely ground yellow or white corn, most commonly from hominy, which is large white field corn that has been treated with an alkaline solution to remove its skin. Sweet shrimp (prawns) are the perfect partners for the creamy comfort of grits.

In a large saucepan, bring the stock to a boil over medium heat. Add the milk, butter, salt, and pepper. Stir in the grits, cover, and simmer over low heat until thickened, about 15 minutes. Stir in the cheddar and stir until it is melted. Remove the saucepan from the heat.

In a large frying pan, crisp the bacon over medium heat. Reserving the fat in the pan, drain the bacon on paper towels

Set the frying pan over high heat. Add the shrimp (prawns) and garlic and cook in the bacon fat until the shrimp are golden brown, about 3 minutes.

Spoon the grits into shallow bowls and set the bacon and shrimp on top. Garnish with the minced scallions (spring onions) and serve.

Moules Marinière

France

Preparation time: 20 minutes
Cooking time: 15 minutes
Serves: 4

2 tablespoons extra-virgin olive oil
2 red onions, chopped
3 cloves garlic, chopped
4 tablespoons finely chopped
    fresh parsley
1 cup (8 fl oz/250 ml) white wine
Freshly ground black pepper
1 cup (240 g) heavy (whipping)
    cream
4½ lb (2 kg) mussels, well
    scrubbed and debearded

Moules marinière is a typical seafood dish from Normandy in northern France. In a recipe this simple, the freshness and quality of the mussels is key. The mussels should be shiny black and have a light and pleasant smell—and they should be alive. You can tell that a mussel is alive because the shell will be tightly closed. If any mussel shell is slightly open, rap the shell on the counter. If the mussel is alive, it will immediately close the shell. If the shell doesn't close, discard the mussel.

In a large frying pan, heat the oil over medium heat. Add the onions, garlic, and parsley and cook until the onions are translucent, about 3 minutes.

    Add the white wine and black pepper to taste and stir for 2 minutes over high heat. Add the cream and cook until reduced by half, about 5 minutes. Add the mussels, cover, and cook until the mussels open, about 5 minutes. Discard any that do not open.

    Serve immediately.

Mussels and French Fries

Preparation time: 30 minutes
Cooking time: 20 minutes
Serves: 4

Sunflower oil, for frying
2½ lb (1.2 kg) white potatoes,
    peeled and cut into
    French-fry shapes
Sea salt
4 tablespoons (60 g) unsalted
    butter
1 onion, finely chopped
1 sprig parsley, chopped
1 stalk celery with leaves,
    finely chopped
9 lb (4 kg) mussels, well scrubbed
    and debearded
1 cup (8 fl oz/250 ml) dry
    white wine
Freshly ground black pepper

Moules frites can be found in every restaurant in Belgium—it's pretty much a national dish (though of course you can also find it in neighboring France). There are numerous variations on the theme, including one in which the mussels are cooked in beer.

Pour 7 inches (20 cm) oil into a deep Dutch oven (casserole) or deep-fryer and heat the oil to 340°F (170°C) on a deep-fry thermometer.

Working in batches of a few at a time, fry the potatoes until golden, about 5 minutes. Drain them on paper towels and season with salt.

Meanwhile, in a large saucepan, heat the butter over medium heat. Add the onion, season with a little salt, and add the parsley and celery. Cook, stirring frequently, until the celery starts to soften, about 5 minutes.

Add the mussels and wine, cover, and cook over high heat until the mussels open, about 3 minutes. Discard any that do not open. Season with black pepper.

Serve the mussels hot with the French fries on the side.

Callao-Style Mussels

Preparation time: 20 minutes,
    plus 30 minutes resting time
Cooking time: 5 minutes
Serves: 6

18 mussels, well scrubbed
    and debearded
1 small onion, diced
1 fresh ají rocoto, minced
2 tomatoes, seeded and diced
2 tablespoons chopped fresh
    parsley
¼ cup (40 g) canned corn kernels
Juice of 1 lemons
1 tablespoon ground dried ají
    amarillo
2 tablespoons extra-virgin olive oil
Sea salt and freshly ground
    black pepper

The key factor in making delicious *choros a la chalaca*, as these stuffed mussels are called in Peru, is finding excellent quality mussels. The best mussels in the world are said to be found in Callao, Peru's main port city just outside the capital city of Lima, where this recipe was born. The mussels and savory filling can be prepared the day before and assembled just before serving.

In an empty saucepan, heat the mussels over high heat until they just open, about 5 minutes. Discard any that do not open. Pull open the mussel shells and discard the top shell. Set aside the bottom halves with the mussels in them. Drain off the mussel liquor and let the mussels cool.

In a bowl, stir together the onion, ají rocoto, tomatoes, parsley, corn, lemon juice, ground ají amarillo, and oil. Season with salt and black pepper. Let the salsa rest for 30 minutes.

To serve, spoon 1 tablespoon of the salsa onto each mussel.

Fish and Shellfish

Lobster Catalan

Preparation time: 30 minutes
Cooking time: 10 minutes
Serves: 4

1 red onion, sliced into rings
1 tablespoon distilled white
    vinegar
1 lobster (2¼ lb/1 kg), rinsed
    under running water
Juice of ½ lemon
½ cup (4 fl oz/120 ml) extra-virgin
    olive oil
Sea salt and freshly ground
    black pepper
9 oz (250 g) cherry tomatoes,
    halved or quartered, for serving

Lobster Catalan is originally from Catalonia, in the northwest corner of Spain, but this dish has also been adopted by the Italian island of Sardinia. It can be served as either an appetizer or a main course. For the best flavor and firmest flesh, buy a medium-size lobster.

Bring a large pot of water to a boil for the lobster.

Meanwhile, combine the onion, vinegar, and 1 cup (8 fl oz/ 240 ml) water and soak for 10 minutes.

Plunge the lobster into the boiling water. Cover the pot and cook for 10 minutes, then remove the lobster and let it drain.

Cut open the tail with scissors and remove the meat. Cut it crosswise into slices ⅓ inch (8 mm) thick. Crack open the claws and pull out the meat. Pull out the green tomalley from the head (along with any coral/roe if the lobster is a female).

In a bowl, mix together the lemon juice, oil, tomalley, coral (if available), and salt and pepper to taste. Whisk to emulsify.

Arrange the tomatoes around a serving plate. Add the sliced tail meat and the claw meat. Top with the drained onion slices and pour the sauce over everything.

Lobster Newberg

**Preparation time: 20 minutes,
plus 30 minutes marinating
time**
Cooking time: 15 minutes
Serves: 4

4 fresh lobster tails
Sea salt and freshly ground
    black pepper
½ cup (4 fl oz/120 ml) Cognac
    or other brandy
2 tablespoons canola (rapeseed)
    oil
8 tablespoons (120 g) butter
1 shallot, thinly chopped
11 oz (300 g) mushrooms, sliced
2 cups (16 fl oz/475 ml) heavy
    (whipping) cream
2 tablespoons minced
    fresh parsley

Lobster Newberg is a rich lobster dish made famous by a New York City restaurant called Delmonico's. In the late 1870s, a regular customer at the restaurant, Ben Wenberg, suggested the idea of this lobster dish to one of the owners; it was then perfected by the restaurant's chef, Charles Ranhofer. The dish was named in honor of Wenberg and was called Lobster à la Wenberg—that is until he had a falling out with the restaurant manager. The restaurant did not want to remove the popular dish from the menu, so instead they rearranged some of the letters from the name Wenberg to make Newberg.

Cut the lobster meat out of the tails, chop, and season with salt and pepper. In a large bowl, toss the lobster with the Cognac and marinate for 30 minutes. Reserving the liquid, drain the lobster.

In a large frying pan, heat 1 tablespoon of the oil and 4 tablespoons (60 g) of the butter over medium heat. Add the lobster and cook until the meat turns opaque, about 2 minutes. Remove it from the pan and place it on a plate.

Add the remaining 1 tablespoon oil and 4 tablespoons (60 g) butter to the pan. Add the shallot and mushrooms and sauté over medium heat until softened, 4–5 minutes. Stir in the reserved Cognac marinade. Pull the pan off the heat and with a long fire lighter, carefully flambé the liquid. Wait for the flames to extinguish.

Add the cream and parsley and bring to a simmer. Add the lobster and serve with buckwheat crêpes.

Crab Gratin

Preparation time: 30 minutes
Cooking time: 1 hour 20 minutes
Serves: 4

Sea salt
2 bay leaves
1 crab (about 1 lb 5 oz/600 g)
4½ tablespoons (65 g) unsalted
  butter
2 white onions, finely chopped
1 small leek, sliced
2 cloves garlic, chopped
2 tablespoons sunflower oil,
  plus more for greasing
1 teaspoon chopped dried
  chili pepper
7 oz (200 g) Parmesan cheese,
  grated
Freshly ground black pepper

In Chile this crab dish is called *chupe de centolla*. To prepare it according to the original recipe, you need to find a *centolla*, a large crab called Antarctic (Chilean) king crab. The crab has large meaty legs with a delicate flavor. Because this very special crab can be hard to find if you don't live in Chile, this gratin is made with regular crab.

In a large pot, bring 2 quarts (2 liters) water to a boil. Salt the water and add the bay leaves. Plunge the crab into the boiling water and cook for 18 minutes.

Remove the crab from the pot and reserve the cooking liquid. Cut the crabmeat out of the shells. Shred the meat with a fork. Reserve the shells.

In a saucepan, heat 1 tablespoon (15 g) of the butter over low heat. Add half the onions, the leek, and half the garlic and cook for 1 minute. Add the crab shells and stir. Pour in 2 cups (16 fl oz/475 ml) of the reserved crab cooking liquid and bring to a boil. Season with salt and simmer for 30 minutes. Strain the crab stock.

In another saucepan, heat the oil over medium heat. Add the chili pepper and remaining onions and garlic and cook until softened, about 5 minutes. Add 1 cup (8 fl oz/240 ml) of the crab stock. Bring to a boil, add the crabmeat, three-quarters of the Parmesan, and the remaining 3½ tablespoons (50 g) butter, and season with salt and black pepper. Simmer for 10 minutes. stirring constantly, to thicken.

Preheat the oven to 375°F (190°C/Gas Mark 5). Oil a 10-inch (25 cm) round baking dish.

Scrape the crab mixture into the baking dish and sprinkle the surface with the remaining Parmesan. Bake until golden brown, about 15 minutes. Serve hot.

Meat and Poultry

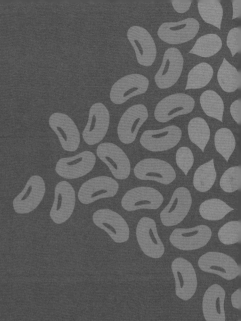

Dark Roast Beef

Venezuela

Preparation time: 20 minutes, plus overnight marinating time
Cooking time: 3 hours 45 minutes
Serves: 4

2¼ lb (1 kg) top round (topside) roast, well trimmed
Sea salt and freshly ground black pepper
2 cloves garlic, chopped
3 tablespoons Worcestershire sauce
½ cup (4 fl oz/120 ml) red wine, such as Cabernet Sauvignon or Merlot
4 tablespoons sunflower oil
4 tablespoons papelón or brown sugar
2 onions, cut into large pieces
1 teaspoon dried oregano
2 bay leaves
½ cup (4 fl oz/120 ml) Marsala wine
1 cup (8 fl oz/250 ml) beef stock (optional)

Asado negro is one of the most traditional dishes in Venezuela, and every family has its own version. Part of what gives the roast its "black" (*negro*) color and the sauce a deep, sweet flavor is the brown sugar from unrefined sugar cane juice. In Venezuela the sugar is called *papelón,* but the same idea exists elsewhere in the world as jaggery, *piloncillo, rapadura*, and *panela.* If you can't locate one of those, just use regular brown sugar. Serve the beef with white rice, fried plantains, or mashed potatoes.

Rub the beef with 1 teaspoon salt, black pepper to taste, and the garlic. Place in a resealable plastic bag (or bowl) and pour in the Worcestershire sauce and red wine. Seal the bag (or cover the bowl) and marinate overnight in the fridge.

In a Dutch oven (casserole), heat the oil over medium heat. Add the papelón or brown sugar and cook until the mixture is a dark caramel color. Reserving the marinade, drain the meat, add to the pan, increase the heat to high, and cook until it is browned on all sides, about 5 minutes.

Add the reserved marinade, the onions, oregano, bay leaves, Marsala, and salt to taste. Cover and cook over very low heat for 3 hours. Keep an eye on the liquid level and add stock as needed if the meat is getting dry.

Remove the meat from the pan and let it sit for 10 minutes before slicing.

Transfer the cooking juices and onions to a food processor and process until it changes color from a dark brown to a lighter brown and is smooth. Pour into a large saucepan and simmer over medium heat for 10 minutes to thicken. Return the meat slices to the sauce and let simmer for 15 more minutes.

Meat and Poultry

292

Roast Beef with Potatoes, Parsnips, Carrots, and Peas

(DF) (NF)

Preparation time: 30 minutes
Cooking time: 1 hour 20 minutes
Serves: 8

6 tablespoons extra-virgin olive oil
2 cloves garlic, peeled
3 tablespoons Dijon mustard
Freshly ground black pepper
4½ lb (2 kg) beef strip loin roast
1 tablespoon fresh rosemary,
    chopped
1 tablespoon chopped fresh sage
14 oz (400 g) yellow potatoes,
    peeled and cut into 1½-inch
    (4 cm) cubes
4 carrots, cut into slices ½ inch
    (4 cm) thick
9 oz (250 g) parsnip, peeled
    and cut into slices ½ inch
    (4 cm) thick
2 teaspoons sea salt
7 oz (200 g) green peas

Roast beef is a Sunday dinner classic in the UK as well as the United States, Canada, and Ireland. If you have a meat thermometer, use it to get the best results: The internal temperature should read between 120° and 125°F (48° and 52°C) for rare. Note that the temperature of the meat will rise another couple of degrees after you take it out of the oven.

Preheat the oven to 450°F (230°C/Gas Mark 8).

In a bowl, combine 4 tablespoons of the oil, the garlic, mustard, and 1 teaspoon black pepper. Add the meat to the mixture and rub it all over. Add the rosemary and sage. Transfer everything to a 9 × 13-inch (23 × 33 cm) baking pan. Roast for 10 minutes, then turn the meat over and continue to roast for 30 minutes for rare and 45 minutes for medium.

Remove from the oven and reduce the oven temperature to 400°F (200°C/Gas Mark 6).

Transfer the meat to a carving board and let it rest while you finish preparing the meal.

Strain the pan juices into a small saucepan and cook until reduced by half.

Meanwhile, in a large bowl, toss the potatoes, carrots, parsnip, and the remaining 2 tablespoons oil. Season with the salt and pepper to taste. Transfer to a large sheet pan and roast for 25 minutes.

In a saucepan of boiling water, cook the peas for 3 minutes, or until tender. Drain well

Slice the meat and set on a platter. Serve the meat with the roasted vegetables and peas, and drizzle the pan juices on top of the meat.

Salted Beef with Potatoes, Onions, Beets, Pickled Gherkins, and Herring

Preparation time: 20 minutes, plus 30 minutes soaking time
Cooking time: 1 hour
Serves: 4

4 salted herrings
Sea salt
2½ lb (1.2 kg) yellow potatoes, peeled and left whole
2 tablespoons olive oil, plus more for the eggs
1 onion, finely chopped
2¾ oz (70 g) unsliced smoked bacon, cubed (or lardons)
14 oz (400 g) corned beef, cut into 2-inch (5 cm) cubes
8 pickled gherkins, sliced
Freshly ground black pepper
7 oz (200 g) cooked beets, sliced
4 eggs

Labskaus is popular in northern Germany, and in particular in the cities of Bremen, Lübeck, and Hamburg—all prominent port cities. Historically this dish was common aboard sailing ships because the salted beef (corned beef) could last a long time, as could other salted foods, like herring. If you want, add nutmeg, pepper, coriander, or allspice to the meat mixture. And you can substitute ham for the salted herring.

In a bowl of water, soak the salted herring for 30 minutes. Drain, then debone and cut into small pieces.

In a pot of boiling salted water, cook the potatoes until firm-tender, about 25 minutes. Drain, transfer to a bowl and mash with a fork until coarsely mashed.

In a Dutch oven (casserole), heat 2 tablespoons of the oil over medium heat. Add the onion and bacon and cook until the bacon has rendered some fat, about 5 minutes. Add the corned beef, herring, potatoes, and gherkins. Season with salt and pepper to taste. Cover and cook gently for 20 minutes over low heat. Add the beets and stir gently for 1 minute to heat through.

Meanwhile, in a frying pan, heat a little oil over medium heat. Crack in the eggs and cook to your desired doneness.

Divide the meat mixture among plates and top each portion with a fried egg.

Air-Dried Cured Beef

**Preparation time: 30 minutes,
    plus 3–4 weeks curing time**
**Makes: about 1 lb (450 g)
    air-dried cured beef**

2¼ lb (1 kg) beef top round
    (topside) or flank steak,
    2 inches
    (5 cm) thick
1 cup (100 g) fine sea salt
4 tablespoons ground fenugreek
3½ tablespoons paprika
1 tablespoon ground allspice
1½ teaspoons freshly ground
    black pepper
1 teaspoon ground cumin
½ teaspoon cayenne pepper
5 cloves garlic, finely minced

Basturma is air-dried cured beef (and sometimes other meats). It is usually prepared in the fall (autumn) and cured over the winter. The meat is salted, then dried and pressed to remove moisture. Finally it's coated with *çemen*, a spicy paste of fenugreek, chili, and garlic that gives the meat its aroma and beautiful red color.

With a fork, poke the meat all over. Rub the meat with ⅔ cup (65 g) of the salt. Place the meat in a deep dish. Place a heavy item on top. Refrigerate for 3 days. Turn every day and drain the liquids that are released.

On the fourth day, wash the meat thoroughly. Soak the meat in cold water for 1 hour. Drain and dry with paper towels, then put the meat inside a cheesecloth (muslin) bag.

In a mortar, combine the fenugreek, paprika, allspice, black pepper, cumin, cayenne, garlic, and remaining ⅓ cup (35 g) sea salt. Grind into a smooth paste.

With the meat still in its cheesecloth bag, coat the meat with the paste.

Thread kitchen twine through a large needle and double it to make it very strong. Pull the thread through a portion of the cheesecloth bag at one end to make a loop from which to suspend the bag. Hang the meat in a cool dry place for 2 or 3 weeks until the skin is dry and the meat is hard.

To serve, very thinly slice the basturma and present on a serving plate.

Beef Stroganoff

Russia

Preparation time: 20 minutes
Cooking time: 35 minutes
Serves: 4

6 tablespoons (90 g) unsalted
    butter
14 oz (400 g) onions, finely sliced
1 lb (450 g) white mushrooms,
    sliced
2 tablespoons chopped
    fresh parsley
3 tablespoons olive oil
1 lb 2 oz (500 g) beef tenderloin
    (fillet), cut into small pieces
3 tablespoons vodka
Sea salt and freshly ground
    black pepper
1 tablespoon prepared English
    mustard
2 cups (16 fl oz/475 ml) sour cream

Beef stroganoff is a delicious Russian beef and mushroom stew enriched with sour cream. It is said that the name of this dish derives from Count Pavel Stroganoff, whose French chef added sour cream to a classic beef stew to make it more pleasing to the Russian aristocrat.

In a frying pan, combine 1 tablespoon (15 g) of the butter, the onions, and 3 tablespoons water and heat over medium heat. Simmer for 10 minutes, then add the mushrooms and parsley and cook for 10 minutes more.

Meanwhile, in a Dutch oven (casserole), melt the remaining 5 tablespoons (75 g) butter and the oil over medium heat. Add the meat and brown, stirring constantly, then pour in the vodka and let simmer for 10 minutes.

Season with salt and pepper. Add the mushroom/onion mixture, the mustard, and sour cream. Reduce the heat to low and cook, stirring, for 5 minutes more. Serve hot.

Chilean Beef Stew

Chile

Preparation time: 30 minutes,
    plus 5 minutes resting time
Cooking time: 55 minutes
Serves: 6

3¼ lb (1.5 kg) beef loin, cut into
    large chunks
1 onion, halved and thinly sliced
1 stalk celery, chopped
2 cloves garlic, peeled
Dried oregano
Sea salt and freshly ground
    black pepper
1 carrot, cut into matchsticks
1 red bell pepper, cut into strips
4 medium yellow potatoes, peeled
¾ cup (150 g) short-grain
    white rice
1 lb 5 oz (600 g) pumpkin, peeled
    and cut into 2-inch (5 cm) cubes
7 oz (200 g) green beans, cut into
    short pieces
2 ears corn, husked and halved
    crosswise

Cazuela de vacuno is a comforting Chilean stew. Its name comes from a cooking vessel called a *cazuela,* which roughly translated means "casserole." This stew's ingredients change with the season: In spring and summer it is prepared with green beans, peas, corn, and even tomatoes, while in the fall (autumn) and winter it's made with potatoes, carrots, chard, or spinach. It can also include rice or a special type of pumpkin called *chuchoca*.

In a large pot, combine the meat, 6 cups (48 fl oz/1.4 liters) water, the onion, celery, garlic, oregano to taste, 1 teaspoon salt, and black pepper to taste. Bring to a boil over medium heat, then reduce to a simmer and cook for 30 minutes.

Add the carrot, bell pepper, potatoes, and rice. Simmer for 15 minutes. Add the pumpkin, green beans, and corn and simmer for 10 more minutes. Season with salt. Remove from the heat and let it sit for 5 minutes before serving.

Costa Rican Beef Stew

Preparation time: 30 minutes
Cooking time: 1 hour 30 minutes
Serves: 4

Sea salt
2 lb (910 g) beef ribs, cut into
  chunks
8 oz (250 g) carrots, diced
2 ears corn, husked and halved
1 lb 5 oz (600 g) yuca (cassava)
  roots, peeled and cut into
  chunks (see Note, page 20)
1 plantain, peeled and cut into
  4 pieces
1 lb 5 oz (600 g) yellow potatoes,
  peeled and diced
1 lb 5 oz (600 g) sweet potatoes,
  peeled and diced

Despite being a dish that requires long cooking, *olla de carne* is eaten by Costa Ricans at least once a week. The stew is an example of Costa Rica's multiethnic heritage: It's a blend of an indigenous cooking style and ingredients introduced from both Europe and Africa. The dish is typically served in three containers: a serving dish containing the vegetables, a bowl with the meat and broth, and third dish for the boiled rice that usually accompanies the stew. In Colombia there is a very similar version called *sancocho*, which is made with chicken.

In a soup pot, bring 2½ quarts (2.4 liters) salted water to a boil over high heat. Add the meat, then reduce the heat and simmer for 45 minutes.

Add the carrots, corn, yuca (cassava), and plantain and cook for 15 minutes. Add the yellow potatoes and sweet potatoes, cover, and simmer over low heat for 30 minutes more.

Adjust the salt if needed and serve hot.

Ropa Vieja

Preparation time: 20 minutes
**Cooking time: 2 hours
  40 minutes**
Serves: 6

2¼ lb (1 kg) beef chuck (roast)
  or brisket
2 cloves garlic, peeled—1 left
  whole, 1 chopped
2 bay leaves
Sea salt
4 tablespoons sunflower oil
1 onion, diced
1 red bell pepper, diced
1 fresh chili, chopped
4 tablespoons dry white wine
Freshly ground black pepper
Generous ¾ cup (200 ml) passata
  (unseasoned tomato sauce)
2 cups (16 fl oz/475 ml) beef stock

Ropa vieja is one of the most famous of Cuban dishes. Its name translates to "old clothes," a reference to taking something old (like leftovers) and turning it into something new and delicious. In Cuba, the stew is traditionally accompanied by white rice and fried plantains. The recipe is well known in other neighboring Latin American countries and has also emigrated from Cuba to Miami, where the dish has a sweet note from red bell peppers.

In a large pot, bring 2 quarts (2 liters) water to a boil. Add the meat, whole garlic clove, 1 bay leaf, and 2 teaspoons salt. Reduce to a simmer and cook for 2 hours. Drain the meat and pull into shreds. Discard the garlic clove and bay leaf.

In a Dutch oven (casserole), heat the oil over medium heat. Add the onion, chopped garlic, bell pepper, and chili and cook until the onion is beginning to brown, about 5 minutes. Add the shredded meat, wine, remaining bay leaf, and black pepper to taste. Cook over high heat for 5 minutes to reduce a little. Season with salt.

Add the tomato sauce and 1 cup (8 fl oz/240 ml) of the stock. Reduce the heat and simmer for 30 minutes, adding more stock if it seems too dry. Discard the bay leaf and serve.

Meat and Banana Stew

Preparation time: 20 minutes
Cooking time: 45 minutes
Serves: 4

Sea salt
Scant 2 cups (350 g) long-grain
    white rice
3¼ lb (1.5 kg) beef top sirloin,
    cut into 1-inch (2.5 cm) cubes
2 cloves garlic, halved
2 teaspoons curry powder
1 teaspoon ground cumin
½ teaspoon freshly ground
    black pepper
¼ teaspoon ground turmeric
¼ teaspoon cayenne pepper
1 bay leaf
3 tablespoons sunflower oil
1 medium onion, diced
3 tomatoes, chopped
1 tablespoon tomato paste (purée)
2 green bananas or plantains
1½ cups (12 fl oz/355 ml) full-fat
    coconut milk

Bananas and plantains are a very important part of Tanzanian cuisine. They're used for a multitude of things: fries, cakes, chips, beer, wine, and stews, to name a few. *Ndizi na nyama*, a name that literally means "bananas and meat," is one such dish. Try it and you will see why it is so popular.

In a saucepan, bring 4 cups (32 fl oz/950 ml) salted water to a boil. Add the rice and cook for 20 minutes, stirring once halfway through. Check to see if the rice is cooked. If not, give it some more time and water if needed. Set aside, covered, when there is just a little water left at the bottom of the pan. Let it rest for 10 minutes.

Meanwhile, in a soup pot, combine the beef, ¾ cup (6 fl oz/ 180 ml) water, the garlic, curry powder, cumin, black pepper, turmeric, cayenne, and bay leaf. Bring to a simmer over medium heat, then cover, reduce the heat to low, and cook until the meat is tender, about 25 minutes. Set aside.

In a frying pan, heat the oil over medium-low heat. Add the onion and sauté for 5 minutes.

Add the sautéed onion to the meat pot, along with the tomatoes and tomato paste (purée). Mix well and let simmer for 5 minutes.

Peel the bananas and cut them into pieces the same size as the meat. Add to the stew along with the coconut milk. Bring to a simmer and stir until the bananas are tender but not mushy, about 10 minutes.

Serve the stew with the rice.

Beef and Amaranth Greens Stew

Preparation time: 20 minutes
Cooking time: 2 hours
   20 minutes
Serves: 4

6 tablespoons extra-virgin olive oil
2¼ lb (1 kg) boneless beef shank
   or knuckle, finely sliced
½ teaspoon light brown sugar
½ teaspoon ground cardamom
½ teaspoon freshly ground
   black pepper
Sea salt
3 large cloves garlic, finely
   chopped
1 onion, finely chopped
14 oz (400 g) tomatoes, seeded
   and chopped
1 green bell pepper, cut into strips
1½ fresh red cayenne chilies,
   minced
1-inch (2.5 cm) piece fresh ginger,
   finely chopped
½ teaspoon coriander seeds,
   freshly ground
½ teaspoon cumin seeds,
   freshly ground
1 cup (8 fl oz/240 ml) beef stock
1 lb 5 oz (600 g) yam or potato,
   peeled and sliced
10 oz (285 g) amaranth greens,
   stemmed and coarsely
   chopped

Shoko, a beef stew from Ghana, is traditionally prepared with amaranth greens, but they can be replaced by spinach. The slightly bitter amaranth leaves go very well with the sweetness of the sauce and the intense flavor of all the spices. In Ghana this recipe is very spicy. *Shoko* is traditionally accompanied by some kind of starch, such as yam, plantain, or rice.

In a soup pot, heat 4 tablespoons of the oil over medium heat. Season the meat with the brown sugar, cardamom, black pepper, and salt to taste. Add the beef to the pot and cook until browned, about 5 minutes. Transfer the beef to a bowl, cover, and set aside.

Add the remaining 2 tablespoons oil to the pot along with the garlic and onion. Sauté until golden brown, about 2 minutes. Reduce the heat to low and add the tomatoes and bell pepper. Cover and simmer for 5 minutes. Return the beef to the pot and add the chilies, ginger, coriander, cumin, and beef stock. Simmer for 2 hours.

Meanwhile, in a small pot of boiling water, cook the yam until tender, about 30 minutes. Drain and set aside.

In another small pot, bring 1½ cups (12 fl oz/350 ml) water to a boil. Add the amaranth, cover, and cook for 3 minutes.

Reserving the cooking liquid, drain the amaranth leaves and stir into the spiced tomato/beef sauce along with 2 tablespoons of the reserved cooking liquid. Simmer for 3 minutes.

To serve, put the yams on plates and pour the shoko on top.

Irish Beef Stew

Ireland

Preparation time: 30 minutes
Cooking time: 2 hours 35 minutes
Serves: 4

2¼ lb (1 kg) beef chuck, trimmed
    of fat, cut into 1-inch (2.5 cm)
    cubes
5 tablespoons extra-virgin olive oil
1 teaspoon paprika
Sea salt and freshly ground black
    pepper
2½ tablespoons tomato paste
    (purée)
1 clove garlic, minced
2 yellow onions, chopped
1½ cups (12 fl oz/350 ml) beef
    stock
7 oz (200 g) carrots, cut into
    rounds
1 tablespoon (15 g) unsalted butter
3 sprigs thyme, leaves picked,
    for garnish
1 tablespoon chopped fresh
    parsley, for garnish
Colcannon (optional; page 228),
    for serving

This aromatic stew is usually served with mashed potatoes or the traditional and rich colcannon (page 228). The stew can also be made with lamb, goat, or mutton, all of which have stronger flavors.

In a large bowl, toss the meat with 2 tablespoons of the oil, the paprika, 1 tablespoon salt, and black pepper to taste.

In a frying pan, heat the remaining 3 tablespoons oil over high heat. Carefully add the meat and brown it, stirring, for at least 20 minutes.

In a small bowl, stir the tomato paste (purée) into ½ cup (4 fl oz/120 ml) warm water to dissolve.

Add the tomato paste liquid, garlic, and onions to the beef and cook for 10 minutes.

Scrape the meat mixture into a large Dutch oven (casserole). Pour the stock into the frying pan and heat it over medium heat to cook off for 5 minutes, then add it to the meat. Add the carrots and butter and simmer over low heat for 2 hours, stirring the meat occasionally.

Serve hot, garnished with fresh thyme and parsley. If desired, serve with Colcannon on the side.

Beef Rendang

Preparation time: 20 minutes
Cooking time: 40 minutes
Serves: 4

6 whole cloves
½ tablespoon cumin seeds
1 teaspoon coriander seeds
2-inch (5 cm) piece fresh ginger,
    peeled and minced
½ tablespoon ground cinnamon
1 teaspoon ground turmeric
1 teaspoon grated nutmeg
1 teaspoon freshly ground
    black pepper
2 tablespoons coconut flour
2 cloves garlic, peeled
5 shallots, sliced
Juice of 2 limes
1¾ lb (795 g) lean beef, cut into
    1-inch (2.5 cm) cubes
4 tablespoons coconut oil
2 cups (16 fl oz/475 ml) full-fat
    coconut milk
Sea salt
½ cup (25 g) coconut chips

This Indonesian dish is served on special occasions in Indonesia as well as Malaysia. The spices in beef rendang were used originally as a way to help preserve meat in a tropical area. The long, slow braising makes the beef stew tender and deeply flavored. A rendang can also be made with lamb, goat, chicken, duck, or liver.

In a spice grinder, combine the cloves, cumin seeds, and coriander seeds and grind to a powder.

In a food processor, combine the spice mixture, ginger, cinnamon, turmeric, nutmeg, black pepper, coconut flour, garlic, shallots, and lime juice. Process to a thick paste. In a bowl, massage the meat with the paste.

In a large Dutch oven (casserole), heat the coconut oil over medium-high heat. Add the beef and brown for 5 minutes. Add the coconut milk and ½ cup (4 fl oz/120 ml) water, season with salt, and reduce the heat. Cover and simmer, stirring occasionally, until the liquid is fully absorbed and the meat is dark brown, about 30 minutes.

Just before serving, preheat the oven to 350°F (180°C/Gas Mark 4). Line a sheet pan with parchment paper.

Place the coconut chips on the lined sheet pan and toast them for 2 minutes.

To serve, spoon the meat onto plates and top with the toasted coconut chips.

Beef and Peanut Stew

Preparation time: 15 minutes
Cooking time: 1 hour
Serves: 4

Generous 1¾ cups (350 g)
   long-grain white rice
Sea salt
1 lb 2 oz (500 g) flat iron steak,
   cubed
2 onions—1 left whole (but peeled),
   1 chopped
6 tablespoons sunflower oil
2 tomatoes, chopped
3 cloves garlic, chopped
2 tablespoons chopped fresh
   parsley
1 teaspoon smoked paprika
½ teaspoon freshly ground
   white pepper
9 oz (250 g) sweet potatoes,
   peeled and diced
2 carrots, chopped
3 tablespoons peanut butter
1 Scotch bonnet chili, sliced

Peanut soups and stews are popular all over West Africa, where groundnuts (peanuts) are a staple crop. *Maafe*, as this dish is called in Ghana, is made with beef and is basically a one-pot meal. It is much like a curry in its balance of heat, spice, sweet, and savory. In Ghana this dish is often accompanied by fufu.

In a saucepan, bring 4 cups (32 fl oz/950 ml) water to a boil. Add the rice and salt to taste. Cook until the rice is tender, about 30 minutes, stirring once every 10 minutes; add more water if the liquid evaporates before the rice is tender. Cover, and set aside with a little of the water left in the pan and let it rest for 10 minutes.

Meanwhile, season the meat with salt. In a saucepan, bring 4 cups (32 fl oz/950 ml) water to a boil. Add the meat and the whole onion and cook until the meat is tender, about 15 minutes. Remove the meat. Strain the broth and set aside.

In a Dutch oven (casserole), heat 4 tablespoons of the oil over low heat. Add the meat and cook, stirring frequently, until lightly browned, about 8 minutes. Remove the meat from the pot and set aside.

In a medium bowl, stir together the tomatoes, half of the chopped onion, the garlic, and parsley.

Add the remaining 2 tablespoons oil to the Dutch oven and sauté the remaining chopped onion until soft, about 3 minutes. Add the tomato mixture, smoked paprika, and white pepper. Cook for about 10 minutes. Stir frequently, adding a bit of broth if the pan looks dry.

Add the sweet potatoes, carrots, peanut butter, Scotch bonnet chili, and 3 cups (24 fl oz/710 ml) of the reserved broth. Cook until the sweet potatoes are firm-tender, about 10 minutes.

Return the meat to the pot and simmer for 2 more minutes to heat through.

To serve, divide the rice among shallow bowls and spoon the stew on top.

Green Curry with Beef

Preparation time: 30 minutes
Cooking time: 30 minutes
Serves: 6

For the green curry paste
1 teaspoon coriander seeds
1 teaspoon cumin seeds
8 green Thai chili peppers,
   seeded and sliced
2 scallions (spring onions),
   chopped
Grated zest of 3 limes
4 cloves garlic, chopped
2 pieces fresh ginger (each
   2 inches/5 cm long),
   peeled and grated
2 tablespoons sea salt

For the curry
2 tablespoons sunflower oil
1 lb (450 g) beef rump,
   thinly sliced
3¼ cups (25 fl oz/750 ml) full-fat
   coconut milk
1 purple eggplant, sliced crosswise
1 cup (100 g) halved green beans
1 onion, sliced
2 tablespoons tamari
1 tablespoon sugar
1 fresh red chili, seeded and
   thinly sliced
2 cups (400 g) jasmine rice
1 tablespoon rice bran oil
1 tablespoon chopped fresh
   cilantro (coriander) leaves,
   for garnish

This is a delicious Thai coconut curry with beef and vegetables. The rich sauce is scented with a homemade spicy green curry paste. If you want to shortcut the recipe, use a high-quality store-bought green curry paste.

Make the green curry paste: In a dry frying pan, toast the coriander and cumin seeds over medium heat for 3–4 minutes. Transfer them to a mortar or food processor and add the green chilies, scallions (spring onions), lime zest, half of the garlic, half of the ginger, and the salt. Grind or process to a paste. Set the green curry paste aside.

Make the curry: In a wok, heat the sunflower oil over medium heat. Add the remaining ginger and garlic and stir-fry for 1 minute. Add the beef and brown for 5 minutes. Remove the meat from the wok and set aside.

Stir the green curry paste into the wok and add the coconut milk and 1½ cups (12 fl oz/355 ml) water. Bring to a light boil and add the eggplant, green beans, onion, tamari, and sugar. Reduce to a simmer and cook until softened, about 20 minutes. Return the beef to the wok and add the red chili.

Meanwhile, in a saucepan, bring 4 cups (32 fl oz/950 ml) water to a boil. Add the rice and rice bran oil and simmer until tender, about 18 minutes. Drain any excess liquid.

Divide the rice among plates and top with the curry. Garnish with the cilantro (coriander) leaves and serve.

Chichinga Beef Kebabs

**Preparation time: 20 minutes,
 plus overnight marinating time**
Cooking time: 4 minutes
Serves: 4

½ cup (80 g) roasted peanuts,
 ground
1 teaspoon cayenne pepper
½ teaspoon ground ginger
½ teaspoon grated nutmeg
½ teaspoon garlic powder
¼ teaspoon ground cinnamon
¼ teaspoon ground cloves
4 tablespoons canola (rapeseed)
 oil, plus more for brushing
2¼ lb (1 kg) beef rump, cut into
 2-inch (5 cm) cubes
3 bell peppers (1 green, 2 red),
 cut into 2-inch (5 cm) chunks
1 red onion, quartered
Sea salt and freshly ground
 black pepper

Chichinga, a very popular Ghanaian street food, is grilled skewered meat that has been marinated in spicy peanut mixture called *suya*. This recipe uses beef, but in Ghana goat is widely used. And for those who would prefer white meat, you can make these with chicken.

In a small bowl, stir together the ground peanuts, cayenne, ginger, nutmeg, garlic powder, cinnamon, cloves, and oil to form a smooth paste.

In a large bowl, toss the beef with the spiced peanut paste and mix well with your hands. Place in the fridge to marinate overnight.

Preheat the broiler (grill).

Skewer the bell peppers, onions, and beef, alternating them. Brush the meat with some oil and season with salt and black pepper. Lay the skewers on a sheet pan and broil (grill) for 4 minutes or until the meat is browned on all sides.

Beef Kebabs

Preparation time: 20 minutes
Cooking time: 10 minutes
Makes: 10 skewers

2½ lb (1.2 kg) lean ground
 (minced) beef
¼ cup (15 g) finely chopped fresh
 parsley, plus more for garnish
3 tomatoes—1 finely diced, 2 sliced
½ onion, finely diced
Sea salt and freshly ground
 black pepper
1 tablespoon sumac, for serving

The term kebab (or kabob) refers to chunks of meat or poultry (sometimes both) threaded on skewers and grilled. There are dozens of variations on this theme all over the Middle East, each region having its own favorite recipes. This version is from Iraq.

In a large bowl, combine the meat, parsley, diced tomato, onion, and salt and black pepper to taste. Mix with your hands. Work the meat gently, just enough to mix with the other ingredients.

Divide the meat mixture into 10 equal portions (about 4 ounces/115 g) each. Press each portion around one end of a long metal skewer, creating a cylindrical kebab about 7 inches (18 cm) long.

Prepare an outdoor grill (barbecue) to 400°F (200°C). Grill the skewers 4 minutes on each side for a medium-well kebab.

To serve, sprinkle the kebabs with sumac and plate with sliced tomatoes and parsley.

Shredded Beef with Rice and Beans

Preparation time: 40 minutes
Cooking time: 2 hours
Serves: 4

14 oz (400 g) flank steak
4 tablespoons sunflower oil
2 cloves garlic, minced
1½ cups (12 fl oz/355 ml) beef
   stock
2 teaspoons sea salt
Generous ¾ cup (150 g) long-
   grain white rice
2 onions, chopped
Scant ½ cup (340 g) canned
   black beans
Ground cumin
1 tablespoon red wine vinegar
1 tablespoon (15 g) unsalted butter
1 tomato, diced

Pabellón criollo is a traditional dish of Venezuela composed of three ingredients: shredded beef, black beans, and rice. The dish is usually plated with each component (brown, black, and white) kept separate, and is often set up like the stripes on a flag. It is said that the dish dates back to the sixteenth century, when slaves of African descent prepared it using leftover meat from their Spanish masters. One of the most popular variations is *pabellón a caballo,* which is enriched with a fried egg.

In a soup pot, combine the meat with cold water to cover. Bring to a boil, then reduce to a simmer and cook until firm-tender, about 1½ hours. Let the meat cool in the cooking liquid. When cooled, reserving the cooking liquid, drain the meat. Cut the meat into small pieces. Set both meat and cooking liquid aside.

In a saucepan, heat 3 tablespoons of the oil over medium heat. Add half the garlic and cook for 2 minutes. Add 1 cup (8 fl oz/240 ml) of the stock and bring to a boil. Stir in 1 teaspoon of the salt and the rice, and simmer over low heat until the rice is tender, about 15 minutes. Remove from the heat, cover, and let sit for 5 minutes.

Meanwhile, in a separate saucepan, heat the remaining 1 tablespoon oil over medium heat. Add the remaining garlic and half of the onion and cook, stirring often, until softened, about 5 minutes. Add the beans, cumin to taste, the vinegar, and remaining ½ cup (4 fl oz/120 ml) stock and 1 teaspoon salt. Simmer for 10 minutes over low heat.

In a third saucepan, melt the butter over medium heat. Add the remaining onion and cook until translucent, about 3 minutes. Add the tomato, ½ cup (4 fl oz/120 ml) of the meat cooking liquid, and the meat shreds. Stir gently and simmer over medium heat for 5 minutes.

To plate, place the meat, rice, and black beans in separate sections of the plate.

Beef Roulades

(NF)

Preparation time: 30 minutes
Cooking time: 1 hour
Serves: 4

4 beef or veal fillet steaks
   (7 oz/200 g each)
Sea salt
4 teaspoons sweet mustard,
   such as Dijon mustard
8 thin slices ham
16 pickled gherkins, thinly sliced
3 onions—1 minced, 2 thinly sliced
1 tablespoon (15 g) unsalted butter
½ cup (8 fl oz/120 ml) red wine
2 bay leaves
2 cups (16 fl oz/475 ml) vegetable
   stock
1 tablespoon potato starch

In addition to being traditional in Germany, *rouladen* are popular in the Upper Silesian regions of Poland and also in the Czech Republic. These rolls are usually made with beef but can also be pork, and they are stuffed with a variety of fillings, but typically include pickled gherkins. They are served with boiled or mashed potatoes.

Place the meat between two sheets of parchment or plastic wrap (cling film) and lightly pound to about ⅛ inch (3 mm) thick.

Rub each slice of meat with a pinch of salt and 1 teaspoon mustard. Place 2 slices of ham, some gherkins, and a little minced onion on each slice. Roll the meat up into a tight package and tie with kitchen twine.

In a deep frying pan, melt the butter over medium heat. Add the rolls and brown them for about 3 minutes on each side. Add the sliced onions and cook until golden, about 5 minutes. Add the wine and bay leaves, increase the heat to medium-high, and let the wine evaporate. Add the stock, cover, reduce the heat to low, and simmer until the liquid is reduced by half and the meat is tender, about 30 minutes, stirring occasionally and turning the rolls twice. Remove the rolls from the pan and keep warm.

Sprinkle the potato starch over the sauce in the pan, stir to combine, and simmer over low heat until the sauce is creamy, 6–7 minutes. Adjust the seasoning with salt, if needed.

To serve, arrange the rolls on a serving plate and pour the sauce over the rolls.

Steaks with Fried Onions, Potatoes, and Eggs

Preparation time: 10 minutes
Cooking time: 45 minutes
Serves: 4

3 tablespoons sunflower oil,
    plus more for frying
4 onions, thinly sliced
10 yellow potatoes, peeled and
    cut into French fries
Sea salt
4 filet mignons or fillet steaks
    (about 8 oz/225 g each)
Freshly ground black pepper
4 eggs

The name of this popular dish, *lomo a lo pobre*, translates to "poor man's loin." It is, however, the opposite of "poor," since it calls for the loin, a prized and tender cut of meat. There are a number of explanations for the term *a lo pobre* (some of which might simply be ironic), but one suggestion is that poor people had to stretch meat by adding other more affordable ingredients, such as potatoes and eggs.

In a frying pan, heat the 3 tablespoons oil over medium heat. Add the onions and cook until they are browned and crispy, about 4 minutes. Leaving the oil in the pan, scoop out the onions with a slotted spoon and set aside. Set the oil and pan aside for frying the eggs.

Pour 7 inches (18 cm) oil into a deep Dutch oven (casserole) and heat over high heat.

Working in batches, fry the potatoes in the hot oil until they are golden brown and crusty but still soft on the inside, about 5 minutes. Drain them on paper towels and season with salt.

Preheat a grill pan (griddle pan). Add the fillets and cook for 2–3 minutes each side for rare. Season the fillets with salt and pepper to taste.

Set the frying pan with the reserved onion oil over medium heat. Crack in the eggs and cook until the whites are firm and the yolks still runny, about 3 minutes. Season the eggs with salt.

Divide the potatoes among four plates and top with some onions, a steak, and an egg, one on top of the other.

Steak with Chimichurri Sauce

Preparation time: 15 minutes
Cooking time: 6 minutes
Serves: 4

For the chimichurri sauce
2 tablespoons fresh parsley leaves
2 teaspoons dried oregano
2 cloves garlic, peeled
2 shallots, peeled and diced
1 tablespoon minced fresh chili
  pepper
4 tablespoons extra-virgin olive oil
5 tablespoons red wine vinegar
Juice of 1 lemon

For the steaks
4 beef strip/Porterhouse (sirloin)
  steaks (about 5 oz/150 g each)

One of the most beloved Argentinian condiments, chimichurri sauce has been adopted worldwide. Here we offer it in its traditional companionship with beef steak, but it is also great with chicken or turkey, and even shrimp and vegetables. Some versions use fresh red chilies to add nice deep-red flecks to the sauce, though dried chilies will provide more heat. Chimichurri sauce can be stored for 2 days in the fridge and can be frozen.

Make the chimichurri sauce: In a food processor, combine the parsley, oregano, garlic, and shallots and pulse to just combine. Add the chili, oil, vinegar, and lemon juice and process to a smooth sauce.

Cook the steaks: Preheat a grill pan (griddle pan).
    Rub the meat with a little sauce and place on the hot pan for 3 minutes each side for rare (or more according to taste). Plate the steaks and drizzle the sauce over them.

Corn Chip Pie

Preparation time: 15 minutes
Cooking time: 40 minutes
Serves: 4

4 tablespoons canola (rapeseed)
  oil, plus more for the
  baking dish
9 oz (250 g) lean ground
  (minced) beef
½ onion, chopped
1¾ cups (300 g) canned ranch-
  style beans or pinto beans,
  drained
1¾ cups (14 fl oz/415 ml)
  enchilada sauce
9 oz (250 g) cheddar cheese,
  grated
1 lb (450 g) corn chips

This American Southwest and Midwest dish is a really tasty dinner when you don't have much time. It is a real people-pleaser and can be garnished with all sorts of things, including salsa, sour cream, onion, lettuce, and jalapeño.

Preheat the oven to 350°F (180°C/Gas Mark 4). Grease a 10-inch (25 cm) round baking dish with oil.
    In a frying pan, heat the 4 tablespoons oil over medium heat. Add the beef and onion and cook until the meat is browned, about 10 minutes. Transfer to the prepared baking dish and spread into an even layer.
    Top the meat with layers in this order: beans, enchilada sauce, cheddar, and corn chips. Transfer to the oven and bake for 30 minutes to melt the cheese and heat everything through.

Vitello Tonnato

**Preparation time: 1 hour, plus
  40 minutes cooling time**
Cooking time: 1 hour
Serves: 6

2 eggs
3 tablespoons extra-virgin olive oil
1¾ lb (800 g) veal eye of round
  (silverside), trimmed of fat
1 stalk celery, diced
1 onion, halved
1 clove garlic, peeled
1 carrot, diced
Sea salt
½ tablespoon black peppercorns
3 whole cloves
1 bay leaf
1 cup (8 fl oz/250 ml) dry white
  wine
4 anchovy fillets in oil, drained
1 tablespoon salt-packed capers,
  rinsed
3.5 oz (100 g) canned tuna in oil,
  drained
6 caper berries, for garnish
Lemon slices, for garnish

This is a typical dish from Piemonte, a region in the north of Italy. The veal is tender and tasty and the tuna sauce enriches it with umami flavor. In some versions, mayonnaise is used in the sauce instead of hard-boiled eggs (see Note), making the preparation of the dish faster. You can both cook the veal and make the tuna sauce ahead, but store them separately; they will keep for 2–3 days in airtight containers in the fridge.

Place the eggs in a saucepan and cover them with cold water. Bring to a boil over medium heat and boil for 9 minutes. Drain and cool them under cold running water. Peel the eggs and quarter them.

In a soup pot, heat the oil over medium heat. Add the veal, celery, onion, garlic, carrot, and salt to taste and cook over high heat to sear the meat all over, about 3 minutes.

Tie the peppercorns, cloves, and bay leaf in a square of cheesecloth (muslin) and add to the pot. Add the wine and 6½ cups (52 fl oz/1.5 liters) water. Bring to a low boil and cook gently until the meat registers 149°F (70°C) on a meat thermometer, about 40 minutes. Don't let it go over that temperature.

Pull out the veal and set aside. Bring the liquid in the pot to a boil and cook until the broth is reduced by half, 15–20 minutes. Reserving the broth, drain the vegetables and transfer them to a food processor. Discard the bag with the bay leaf, peppercorns, and cloves.

To the vegetables in the food processor, add 1 cup (8 fl oz/ 240 ml) of the reserved broth, the hard-boiled eggs, anchovies, capers, and tuna and process, adding more broth if necessary to obtain a creamy sauce.

Slice the meat with a sharp knife and arrange on a large serving dish. Pour the sauce in the middle of the plate and garnish with caper berries and lemon slices.

Note: For a quicker version, omit the eggs and add ⅔ cup (150 g) mayonnaise to the sauce.

Mutton and Potato Stew

Preparation time: 20 minutes
Cooking time: 1 hour
Serves: 4

1⅓ cups (245 g) long-grain white
    rice, rinsed
5 tablespoons sunflower oil
1 lb (450 g) mutton, cut into 1-inch
    (2.5 cm) cubes
1 onion, sliced
¼ head cabbage, sliced
1 green bell pepper, sliced
2 yellow potatoes, peeled
    and chopped
2 tomatoes, chopped
½ teaspoon paprika
2 bay leaves
2 cups (16 fl oz/475 ml) vegetable
    stock
Sea salt and freshly ground black
    pepper
1 clove garlic, minced
2 scallions (spring onions),
    chopped
1 bunch fresh parsley, chopped
1 cup (40 g) chopped fresh basil
½ cup (25 g) chopped fresh dill
1 cup (290 g) Greek yogurt

For hundreds of years the Kazakhs were herders of sheep, camels, and horses. This influenced their cuisine, which is heavily focused on mutton, horse meat, and milk products. *Kuurdak* (or *quwyrdaq*) is Kazakhstan's national dish and falls perfectly within that tradition, as it is made with mutton and yogurt. Sometimes sheep's liver, kidneys, heart, and lungs are also used in the stew.

In a saucepan, combine 2⅔ cups (21 fl oz/630 ml) water and the rice and bring to a boil. Reduce to a simmer and cook until tender and almost all the water has been absorbed, about 20 minutes. Cover and let it rest.

Meanwhile, in a wok, heat 2 tablespoons of the oil over medium heat. Add the mutton and sauté until browned, about 5 minutes. Add the onion, cabbage, bell pepper, potatoes, tomatoes, paprika, bay leaves, stock, and salt and black pepper to taste. Cover and bring to a boil, then reduce to a simmer and cook until the vegetables are soft and most of the water has been absorbed, about 40 minutes.

In a frying pan, heat the remaining 3 tablespoons oil over medium heat. Add the garlic and scallions (spring onions) and cook until golden, about 4 minutes. Add the parsley, basil, and dill and stir-fry for a minute. When ready to serve, stir in the yogurt.

To serve, divide the rice among plates. Spoon some of the meat mixture on top and dollop with the herbed yogurt.

Salted Lamb Ribs
with Mashed Root Vegetables

(NF)

Norway

**Preparation time: 40 minutes,
    plus 30 hours soaking time
Cooking time: 3 hours 30 minutes
Serves: 6**

5½ lb (2.5 kg) pinnekjøtt (salted
    lamb ribs)
Sea salt
4½ lb (2 kg) rutabaga (swede),
    peeled and roughly chopped
4 carrots, roughly chopped
3 yellow potatoes, peeled
    and roughly chopped
4 tablespoons heavy (whipping)
    cream
4 tablespoons light (single) cream
5 tablespoons (75 g) salted butter
Freshly ground black pepper
Lingonberry jam, for serving

This dish is typical of western and northern Norway and is mostly served for Christmas and other important festive lunches. Although lamb is now available fresh or frozen all year round, dried, salted, and smoked lamb ribs, called *pinnekjøtt*, should be used to prepare this recipe. (If you can't source salted lamb ribs, you can use fresh; the finished dish will still taste delicious, just different from the original Norwegian recipe.) Before cooking, the meat should be cut into individual chops and soaked to remove excess salt and soften the meat.

Cut the lamb into individual chops, place in a very big bowl or pan, and cover with water. Let it soak at room temperature for at least 30 hours.

Set a trivet at the bottom of a very large pot. Drain the meat and carefully place it on top of the trivet. Add enough water to cover the meat, bring to a boil, then reduce the heat to a simmer, cover, and cook over low heat for 3½ hours. Keep an eye on the water level and add water as needed if the meat is getting dry.

When there is 30 minutes cooking time left, cook the root vegetables. In a large pot, bring 8 cups (2 qt/1.9 liters) lightly salted water to a boil. Add the rutabaga (swede), carrots, and potatoes and cook until firm-tender, about 20 minutes. Drain, transfer to a bowl, and mash with a fork. Add both creams and the butter and season with salt and black pepper. Stir to combine.

Serve the lamb ribs with the mashed root vegetables and lingonberry jam.

Lamb and Vegetable Stew

 South Africa

Preparation time: 30 minutes
Cooking time: 2 hours 30 minutes
Serves: 4

½ cup (4 fl oz/120 ml) extra-virgin
  olive oil
2 onions, chopped
2¼ lb (1 kg) bone-in leg of lamb
½ inch (1.25 cm) fresh ginger,
  minced
1 clove garlic, minced
Sea salt and freshly ground
  black pepper
½ cup (4 fl oz/120 ml) white wine,
  such as Sauvignon Blanc
2¼ cups (400 g) diced fresh
  tomatoes
4 bay leaves
4 yellow potatoes, cut into chunks
2 carrots, cut into chunks
1 small zucchini (courgette)
7 oz (200 g) green beans, cut into
  1-inch (2.5 cm) lengths
Cooked rice, for serving

Potjiekos in South Africa is traditionally prepared outdoors in a *potjie*, a round cast-iron three-legged pot set over a low wood fire. In fact, the name of the dish translates as "little pot of food." The stew is slow-cooked and remains unstirred until finished. It is served with rice. The meat can be lamb, beef, or pork, and the best cuts to use are the tougher cuts that become tender after long cooking. The meat is usually cooked in a spiced alcoholic beverage such as beer, sherry, or wine, such as Edelspatz (a dessert wine) or Sauvignon Blanc.

In a large cast-iron Dutch oven (casserole), heat the oil over low heat. When hot, add the onions and cook until translucent, about 5 minutes.

Rub the lamb with the ginger, garlic, and salt and black pepper to taste. Carefully add the lamb to the pan and brown on all sides, about 5 minutes per side.

Add ½ cup (4 fl oz/120 ml) water, the wine, tomatoes, and bay leaves. Cover and gently simmer, without stirring, for 1 hour. Add the potatoes and carrots and cook until the vegetables are tender, about 30 minutes.

Add the zucchini (courgette) and green beans and gently shake the pot to check if there is enough liquid on the bottom. If not, add more water. Simmer until the vegetables are cooked through and everything is well combined, about 30 minutes. Discard the bay leaves.

Serve hot with rice on the side.

Lamb and Cabbage Stew

Preparation time: 30 minutes
Cooking time: 4 hours
Serves: 6

4½ lb (2 kg) boneless lamb, cut
    into 1½-inch (4 cm) pieces
1 large head cabbage, cut into
    2-inch (5 cm) squares
Sea salt
4 teaspoons black peppercorns

Fårikål is a traditional Norwegian lamb and cabbage stew, typically served in the fall (autumn) months, as the weather turns colder—and when the lamb is cheaper. So revered is this dish that it has its own day—Fårikål Day—celebrated on the last Thursday of September. Lamb is one of Norway's favorite meats and it is shown to wonderful advantage in this slow-cooked stew.

In a large pot, layer in the meat and cabbage, season each layer with salt, then add the peppercorns and 3 quarts (3 liters) water. Bring to a boil over high heat, then reduce the heat to low, cover, and cook until the meat is very tender and the liquid is reduced by one-third, about 4 hours, checking that the water does not dry out.

Serve the meat and cabbage hot with the broth.

Sweet and Sour Braised Lamb

Preparation time: 10 minutes
Cooking time: 2 hours 20 minutes
Serves: 4

2 tablespoons sunflower oil
2¼ lb (1 kg) lamb knuckle or other
    lamb stew meat
2 large onions, sliced
4 cloves garlic, minced
1 teaspoon grated nutmeg
½ teaspoon ground allspice
6 whole cloves
2 bay leaves
4 tablespoons tamarind
    concentrate
2 teaspoons sugar
¼ cup (2 fl oz/60 ml) red wine
    vinegar
Sea salt and freshly ground black
    pepper

South African cuisine is a melting pot of many cultures. *Denningvleis* is a great example of the mix of cultures all in one recipe. *Vleis* is the Afrikaans word for meat and *denning* comes from the Javanese word *dendeng*, which means "water buffalo." However, these days *denningvleis* is instead commonly made with lamb or mutton.

In a Dutch oven (casserole), heat the oil over medium heat. Working in batches, sauté the lamb until golden brown, about 5 minutes. Set the lamb aside.

Reduce the heat under the pan to medium-low. Add the onions and garlic and sauté until softened, about 4 minutes.

Return the lamb to the pan along with the nutmeg, allspice, cloves, bay leaves, and 2 cups (16 fl oz/475 ml) water. Bring to a boil, then reduce the heat to low, cover, and simmer until the lamb is tender, about 1 hour 45 minutes.

Stir in the tamarind, sugar, vinegar, and salt and black pepper to taste. Uncover and cook for 15 minutes more to meld the flavors.

Lamb Kebabs with Tzatziki

Preparation time: 30 minutes, plus 4 hours marinating time
Cooking time: 15 minutes
Serves: 6

For the tzatziki
1 small cucumber, chopped, lightly squeezed to remove liquid
2 cloves garlic, chopped
4 fresh mint leaves, shredded
⅔ cup (175 g) Greek yogurt
1 teaspoon sea salt
Freshly ground black pepper

For the lamb
1 lb (450 g) boneless lamb leg, cut into 1-inch (2.5 cm) cubes
Juice of 1 lemon
½ cup (4 fl oz/12 ml) extra-virgin olive oil
4 cloves garlic, chopped
1 bunch fresh oregano
Sea salt and freshly ground black pepper
24 cherry tomatoes
6 onions, cut into 1-inch (2.5 cm) squares

This is one of the most popular street foods in Greece, as well as open-air lunch or dinner on hot summer Sundays. It's juicy, tasty, and well-seasoned meat garnished with tzatziki, a garlicky/minty cucumber and yogurt sauce. The kebabs can be made with pork instead of lamb, but they should always be served with tzatziki, a refreshing note for the summer season.

Make the tzatziki: In a bowl, toss together the cucumber, garlic, and mint. Add the yogurt, salt, and a generous amount of pepper. Stir gently, cover, and refrigerate until serving time.

Prepare the lamb: In a bowl, combine the lamb, lemon juice, oil, garlic, most of the oregano, reserving a few stems, and salt and black pepper to taste. Toss to evenly coat. Cover and marinate in the fridge for 4 hours.

Reserving the marinade, drain the meat and thread the cubes onto skewers, alternating the meat with the tomatoes and onion chunks.

Preheat a grill pan (griddle pan) over medium heat.

Add the kebabs to the pan and cook until golden brown and crispy on all sides, at least 15 minutes, brushing each side with the marinade while turning them for even cooking.

Serve hot, garnished with the remaining oregano and the chilled tzatziki.

Goat Stew

Angola

**Preparation time: 20 minutes,
plus 4 hours marinating time
Cooking time: 40 minutes
Serves: 4**

1 lb (450 g) boneless leg of goat,
cut into 1-inch (2 cm) cubes
5 tablespoons extra-virgin olive oil
1 tablespoon peri-peri sauce
8 cloves garlic, peeled—4 minced,
4 left whole
1 lb (450 g) yellow potatoes,
cut into 1-inch (2 cm) cubes
1 teaspoon paprika
Sea salt
2 onions, chopped
1 red bell pepper, sliced
2 tomatoes, chopped
8 oz (225 g) chouriço sausage,
chopped
½ cup (4 fl oz/120 ml) white wine

Caldeirada de cabrito , which literally means "goat stew" in Portuguese, is an Angolan dish traditionally served on Angolan Independence Day. Because it is a former colony of Portugal, Angola's cuisine has many Portuguese influences, including the use of chouriço, the Portuguese version of chorizo. But the stew also reflects African culture in the addition of peri-peri sauce, made from a chili pepper originally from Ethiopia but cultivated in numerous African countries. Please ensure the sausage you use contains no gluten.

In a bowl, toss the goat with 2 tablespoons of the olive oil, the peri-peri, and the minced garlic. Marinate in the fridge for 4 hours.

In a Dutch oven (casserole), heat the remaining 3 tablespoons oil over medium heat. Add the goat and sauté until lightly browned, about 3 minutes. Transfer the meat to a plate and set aside.

Season the potatoes with the paprika and salt to taste and put them in the Dutch oven. Make layers in the Dutch oven with half of the following ingredients in this order: onions, bell pepper, meat, tomatoes, chouriço, and whole garlic cloves. Repeat the layering with the remaining ingredients. Pour the white wine over the layers.

Cover and cook over medium heat until the potatoes are tender, 30–35 minutes. Stir occasionally to ensure it doesn't stick to the bottom.

Serve in bowls.

Coconut-Braised Goat with Mashed Plantains

Preparation time: 1 hour,
plus 3 hours marinating
and curing time
Cooking time: 13 hours
Serves: 4

1 lb (450 g) goat thigh meat, cut
   into 1½-inch (4 cm) chunks
Juice of 3 lemons
1 tablespoon kosher (flaked) salt
3 tablespoons adobo criollo
   seasoning
½ cup (4 fl oz/120 ml) olive oil
2 white onions, sliced
½ cup (4 fl oz/120 ml) passata
   (unseasoned tomato sauce)
6 cloves garlic, peeled—5 sliced,
   1 left whole
1 teaspoon cumin seeds
½ teaspoon curry powder
2 tablespoons achiote seeds
Sea salt
Generous 3 cups (25 fl oz/750 ml)
   coconut water
1¼ cups (10 fl oz/300 ml) full-fat
   coconut milk
⅓ cup (15 g) chopped fresh
   cilantro (coriander)
2 cups (16 fl oz/475 ml) red palm
   oil, plus more for garnish
4 green plantains or green
   bananas—3 cut into 1-inch
   (2.5 cm) chunks, 1 cut into
   ¾-inch (2 cm) slices
2 fresh culantro leaves (see Note),
   chopped, for garnish

Chivo en coco, which translates as "goat in coconut milk," is typical of the arid regions of Venezuela, where the country's goats are typically raised. Serve with mashed green plantains, as here, or, for a sweeter taste, use ripe plantains.

In a bowl, toss the meat with the lemon juice and marinate for 1 hour. Drain, add the kosher (flaked) salt, and let it sweat for 1 hour. Drain again, then season with 1 tablespoon of the adobo criollo seasoning and let cure for 1 hour.

Preheat the oven to 225°F (110°C/Gas Mark ¼).

In a 9-inch (23 cm) round braising pan (2 inches/5 cm deep), heat 3 tablespoons of the olive oil over medium heat. Add the onions and sauté for 3 minutes. Add the meat and sauté, stirring frequently, until browned, 3–4 minutes. Add the tomato sauce, sliced garlic, cumin seeds, curry powder, achiote seeds, and 1 teaspoon sea salt. Add the coconut water and transfer to the oven. Cover and bake until the goat is very tender, about 12 hours.

Remove the goat from the pan and set aside on a tray. Strain the cooking liquid into a saucepan.

Bring the pan of cooking liquid to a boil over medium heat, then reduce to a simmer and cook for 10 minutes. Add the coconut milk, reduce the heat to low, season with 1 teaspoon sea salt, and simmer until the liquid is reduced by half, about 20 minutes. Strain and add to the goat to moisten the meat.

In a blender, combine the cilantro (coriander), remaining 2 tablespoons adobo criollo seasoning, 1 whole garlic clove, and the remaining 5 tablespoons olive oil and purée. Set the cilantro purée aside.

In a frying pan, heat the red palm oil over high heat. Add the plantain chunks and cook until they are pale yellow and tender, about 5 minutes. Leaving the oil in the pan, transfer the plantain to a bowl and mash with a fork.

Add the sliced plantains to the frying pan with the red palm oil and cook until crispy, 3–4 minutes. Drain them and season with salt.

Combine the mashed plantain and the cilantro purée, stirring and mashing to obtain a soft mass.

Arrange the meat on serving plates. Scoop quenelles of the plantain mash on top and garnish with the red palm oil, plantain slices, and chopped culantro.

Note: Culantro is similar to fresh cilantro (coriander) in flavor but they are not the same plant. If it's difficult to find, you can substitute cilantro.

Fried Pork with Beans, Rice, and Fresh Salsa

Preparation time: 1 hour, plus overnight soaking time
Cooking time: 2 hours 30 minutes
Serves: 4

For the beans
9 oz (250 g) dried black beans (see Note), soaked overnight in warm salted water
4 tablespoons extra-virgin olive oil
1 teaspoon finely chopped fresh cilantro (coriander), or more to taste
1 scallion (spring onion), finely chopped
2 red bell peppers, finely chopped
3 cloves garlic, minced
5 oz (150 g) chicharrón (fried pork belly), cut into pieces
1 teaspoon ground chilies
½ teaspoon sea salt
Freshly ground black pepper

For the chimichurri
2 tomatoes, peeled, seeded, and diced
1 onion, diced
2 tablespoons extra-virgin olive oil
1 tablespoon finely chopped fresh cilantro (coriander)
½ teaspoon sea salt
Juice of 2 limes

For the rice
3 tablespoons sunflower oil
1 onion, finely chopped
2 cloves garlic, minced
Scant 2 cups (400 g) long-grain white rice
2 cups (16 fl oz/475 ml) vegetable stock
Sea salt

For the pork
5 oz (150 g) boneless pork shank, cubed
1 tablespoon paprika
1 teaspoon dried thyme
1 teaspoon dried oregano
½ teaspoon sea salt
Freshly ground black pepper
3 tablespoons sunflower oil

In Costa Rica this dish is called *chifrijo*, a mash-up of the words *chicharrón* (fried pork belly) and *frijoles* (beans). The dish is served over rice and topped with a Costa Rican chimichurri, which is not like the Argentinian sauce of the same name (page 312), but more like a pico de gallo.

Make the beans: Drain the beans and place them in a pot. Add 2 tablespoons of the olive oil, the cilantro, half the scallion, half the bell peppers, 2 of the garlic cloves, and 2 cups (16 fl oz/ 475 ml) water. Simmer over low heat for 10 minutes, then cover and simmer until the beans are tender, about 2 hours. Add warm water as needed if the beans get dry.

Meanwhile, in a frying pan, heat the remaining 2 tablespoons oil over medium heat. Add the chicharrón, ground chilies, the remaining scallion, garlic, and bell pepper and sauté until the scallion and bell pepper are softened, 2–3 minutes. Season with the salt and black pepper to taste.

When the beans are tender, add the chicharrón mixture and simmer over low heat for 20 minutes.

Meanwhile, make the chimichurri: In a bowl, toss the tomatoes with the onion, olive oil, cilantro, salt, and lime juice. Cover and refrigerate for 30 minutes to marinate.

Cook the rice: In a saucepan, heat the sunflower oil over low heat. Add the onion and garlic and cook, stirring, until the onion is softened, about 5 minutes. Add the rice and toast for 3 minutes. Add the stock, season with salt to taste, and simmer until the rice is tender, about 15 minutes.

Make the pork: Season the pork with the paprika, thyme, oregano, salt, and black pepper to taste.

Preheat a frying pan over medium heat. Add the sunflower oil and the meat and brown for 5 minutes. Add ½ cup (4 fl oz/ 120 ml) water and simmer over low heat until fully cooked, about 10 minutes.

To serve, make a bed of rice and top with the beans and their sauce, the pork, and the chimichurri.

Note: To simplify the dish, you could use canned black beans instead. You'll need about 2½ cups (600 g) canned beans. Just rinse and drain them, then cook them with all the seasonings in the first step for about 10 minutes.

Asturian Beans and Sausages

Preparation time: 1 hour, plus overnight soaking time and 30 minutes resting time
Cooking time: 2 hours 30 minutes
Serves: 6

14 oz (400 g) dried fabes de la granja (see Note)
Pinch of baking soda (bicarbonate of soda)
7 oz (200 g) lacón
3½ oz (100 g) fatback (pork back fat)
1 teaspoon sea salt
5 saffron threads steeped in 2 tablespoons water
7 oz (200 g) chorizo, cubed
3½ oz (100 g) dry-cured chorizo, cubed
7 oz (200 g) morcilla, cubed

The *fabada* is the most famous dish of Asturias, a northern coastal region of Spain where the cuisine focuses prominently on beans (in the Asturian language, *fabes* means "beans") with meat, usually pork. Some of the ingredients in this recipe are not easily found outside Spain: the *morcilla*, however, can be replaced by blood sausage (black pudding) and the *lacón*, which is a cured pork shoulder, can be replaced by ham. Please ensure the chorizo and morcilla you use contain no gluten.

In a bowl, soak the beans overnight in cold water with the baking soda (bicarbonate of soda). In two separate bowls, soak the lacón and fatback (pork back fat) in cold water overnight in the fridge.

Drain the beans and place them a large pot with 1 quart (1 liter) water. Bring to a boil over high heat for 10 minutes, skimming the foam from the surface with a slotted spoon.

Drain the lacón and fatback, add to the pan with the beans, reduce the heat, cover, and cook for 2 hours. Stir the mixture and shake the pan while cooking.

Add the salt, the saffron, both chorizos, and the morcilla and cook until the chorizo is cooked, about 15 minutes Remove from the heat and let it rest for 30 minutes before serving.

Note: These large white runner beans are named for the Spanish town of La Granja, and are sometimes also labeled *fabes de Asturias*. Some brands also carry on their label the word *fabada*, to indicate that these are the beans for making this dish. You can substitute any large white beans, such as cannellini.

Smoked Sausages
with Sauerkraut-Potato Mash

 (NF)

Preparation time: 30 minutes
Cooking time: 30 minutes
Serves: 4

Sea salt
2½ lb (1.2 kg) baking potatoes,
  peeled and cubed
1 lb 5 oz (600 g) sauerkraut,
  store-bought or homemade
  (page 235), drained
4 whole cloves
1 apple, peeled and sliced
2 tablespoons milk
4 tablespoons (60 g) butter
4 smoked sausages (5 oz/
  140 g each)

Smoked sausages with *zuurkoolstamppot* (a sauerkraut and potato mash; see page 232 for more about this type of Dutch dish) is perfect comfort food for a cold winter's day. Be sure to use starchy (floury) potatoes here for a tender mash. Please ensure the sausages you use contain no gluten.

In a large pot of boiling salted water, cook the potatoes until firm-tender, about 20 minutes.

Meanwhile, in a large saucepan, combine the sauerkraut and cloves and heat over medium heat for 20 minutes (just 5 minutes if using store-bought sauerkraut). Add the apple and stir for 5 minutes. Discard the cloves.

Drain the potatoes, return to the pot, add the milk and butter, and mash to create a creamy mixture. Stir the sauerkraut into the mashed potatoes.

On a grill pan (griddle pan) or in a frying pan, heat the sausages for 5 minutes.

Divide the sauerkraut/potato mash among plates and serve with the sausages.

Fried Sausages with Vegetables,
Potatoes, and Butter Sauce

 (NF)

Preparation time: 30 minutes
Cooking time: 20 minutes
Serves: 4

1 lb (450 g) yellow potatoes,
  peeled and cut into 3-inch
  (7 cm) cubes
1 lb (450 g) carrots, cut into
  1½-inch (4 cm) cubes
1 lb (450 g) rutabaga (swede)
  or celeriac, sliced
Sea salt and freshly ground
  black pepper
1½ sticks (6 oz/180 g) unsalted
  butter, cut into chunks
2¼ lb (1 kg) pork sausages,
  casings removed

Stekte pølser, which literally translates to "fried sausages," is a simple and tasty Norwegian dish in which fried fresh sausages, usually pork, are served with root vegetables, potatoes, and sometimes a sauce. Norway boasts a huge variety of sausages and preserved meats, each with a different flavor profile depending on the region it comes from. Please ensure the sausages you use contain no gluten.

In a large pot, combine the potatoes, carrots, and rutabaga (swede) or celeriac with salted water to cover. Bring to a boil over medium heat and cook until the potatoes are soft, about 10 minutes. Drain, season with salt and black pepper, and add 1 stick (4 oz/120 g) of the butter. Cover and let the butter melt.

Meanwhile, in a frying pan, heat the remaining 4 tablespoons (60 g) butter over medium-high heat. Add the sausages and brown them for 2–3 minutes on each side.

Serve the sausages with the vegetables and butter sauce.

Braised Pork Knuckle

Preparation time: 30 minutes, plus overnight soaking time
Cooking time: 4 hours
Serves: 4

1 carrot, peeled
2 onions—1 whole (but peeled), 1 cut into rings
2 bay leaves
4 pork knuckles (12 oz/300 g each)
11 oz (300 g) dried peas, soaked in warm salted water overnight
8 tablespoons (4 oz/115 g) butter
1 cup (8 fl oz/240 ml) meat stock, hot
Sea salt and freshly ground black pepper
1 tablespoon lard
11 oz (300 g) sauerkraut, store-bought or homemade (page 235)
1½ cups (12 fl oz/350 ml) dry white wine
1 teaspoon sugar
1 tablespoon red wine vinegar

Berliner Eisbein is a traditional dish from Berlin made with pork knuckle (a cut from the shank). *Eisbein* translates to "ice bone," because the bone from this part of the pig at one time was used to make the blades of ice skates. Pork knuckle is sold brined and sometimes smoked. In addition to mashed peas and sauerkraut, this dish can be served with mashed potatoes and mustard sauce. In the southern parts of Germany, the dish is called *Schweinshaxe* ("pig knuckle") and is roasted rather than braised.

In a large pot, combine the carrot, the whole onion, 1 bay leaf, and the pork knuckles and simmer over low heat until very tender, at least 4 hours.

Meanwhile, drain the peas. In a saucepan, combine the peas with cold water to cover. Cover, bring to a boil, and cook until very tender, about 10 minutes. Drain and transfer to a food processor. Add 1 tablespoon (15 g) of the butter, the stock, 1 teaspoon salt, and black pepper to taste and pulse to combine. Transfer to a bowl and set aside.

In a frying pan, heat the remaining 7 tablespoons (105 g) butter over low heat. Add the onion rings and cook until soft, about 7 minutes. Add to the pea purée.

In a saucepan, heat the lard over low heat. Stir in the sauerkraut until well combined. Add the wine, sugar, vinegar, and salt and black pepper to taste. Simmer for 45 minutes.

Divide the sauerkraut and pea purée among four plates. Top each with a pork knuckle.

Meat and Poultry

328

Paisa Platter

Preparation time: 45 minutes
Cooking time: 2 hours 15 minutes
Serves: 4

½ cup (4 fl oz/120 ml) extra-virgin
    olive oil
3 onions, finely chopped
3 tomatoes, finely chopped
3 scallions (spring onions),
    finely chopped
1 green bell pepper, finely
    chopped
3 cloves garlic, chopped
¼ teaspoon saffron powder
4 tablespoons fresh cilantro
    (coriander) leaves
Sea salt
2½ cups (540 g) dried white
    beans, soaked overnight in
    warm salted water, undrained
12 oz (350 g) fatback (pork
    back fat)
1 lb 5 oz (600 g) pork shoulder,
    finely chopped
Sunflower oil, for frying
2 plantains, halved
4 eggs

Bandeja paisa is a hearty Colombian dish from the Paisa region in the northwestern part of the country. The translation of *bandeja* to "platter" is appropriate, since this is a generous amount of food. Cooked beans and pork are seasoned with *hogao* (a traditional Colombian spiced tomato sauce) and served with fried plantains and eggs. Often *mazamorra*, or cooked white hominy, is included.

In a saucepan, combine 4 tablespoons of the olive oil, the onions, tomatoes, scallions (spring onions), bell pepper, garlic, and saffron. Bring to a simmer over medium heat and cook for 10 minutes or until fragrant. Add 3 tablespoons of the cilantro (coriander) and a pinch of salt and simmer until softened, 5–6 minutes. Let the hogao sauce cool.

Pour the beans and their soaking water into a large pot. Add 2 tablespoons of the olive oil and bring to a boil. Reduce the heat and simmer until tender, about 1½ hours. Stir in 1 teaspoon salt and the remaining 1 tablespoon cilantro. Drain the beans, return to the pot, and keep warm. Set aside

In a large frying pan, cook the fatback (pork back fat) over medium heat for 2 minutes to render the fat. Add the pork shoulder and remaining 2 tablespoons olive oil. Cook until browned, about 5 minutes. Stir in the hogao sauce and simmer for 5 minutes. Remove from the heat and set aside.

Pour 1 inch (2.5 cm) sunflower oil into a frying pan and heat over medium-high heat. Fry the plantains until golden on both sides, then drain on paper towels. In the same pan, fry the eggs to your desired doneness.

Add the meat mixture to the beans and reheat. Serve with the plantains and eggs.

Stir-Fried Pork in Lettuce Cups

Preparation time: 20 minutes
Cooking time: 10 minutes
Serves: 4

1 tablespoon peanut
    (groundnut)oil
9 oz (250 g) lean ground
    (minced) veal
9 oz (250 g) lean ground
    (minced) pork
1 clove garlic, minced
1 tablespoon grated fresh ginger
¾ cup (200 g) canned water
    chestnuts, chopped
3 scallions (spring onions),
    chopped
4 tablespoons tamari
4 tablespoons oyster sauce
Sea salt
½ cup (55 g) bean sprouts, rinsed,
    plus more for garnish
8 lettuce leaves

Sung choi bao, a stir-fried meat and vegetable mixture served in lettuce "packages" (*bao*), is substantial enough for a main course (but if divided into smaller portions can make a nice starter course, too). The lettuce leaf acts as a bowl and is then used to roll the meat up to eat with hands.

In a large frying pan, heat the oil over medium-high heat. Add the veal and pork and cook, stirring and breaking the meat up with a spoon, until cooked and browned, about 5 minutes. Add the garlic, ginger, water chestnuts, scallions (spring onions), tamari, and oyster sauce, season with salt, and stir for 5 minutes.

Remove from the heat and stir in the bean sprouts.

To serve, arrange the lettuce leaves on plates, spoon the meat mixture into the lettuce cups, and garnish with some more bean sprouts.

Kimchi Stew with Pork

Preparation time: 30 minutes
Cooking time: 50 minutes
Serves: 4

7 large dried anchovies, heads
    and guts removed
3½ oz (100 g) Korean radish or
    daikon radish, thinly sliced
½ oz (14 g) dried kelp
1 medium white onion, sliced
5½ oz (160 g) kimchi
¼ cup (2 fl oz/60 ml) kimchi brine
3 red onions, sliced
½ lb (450 g) pork shoulder
    or pork belly, cut into 2-inch
    (5 cm) cubes
2 teaspoons sugar
2 teaspoons gochugaru
    (Korean chili flakes)
1 tablespoon gochujang
    (Korean chili paste)
1 teaspoon sea salt
1 teaspoon sesame oil
9 oz (250 g) tofu, cut into 1¼-inch
    (3 cm) pieces
Cooked short-grain white rice,
    for serving
1 scallion (spring onion), sliced on
    the diagonal, for garnish

Kimchi jjigae is a spicy stew that is often served family-style from a stone pot (*dolsot*) at the center of the table, accompanied by rice and *banchan*, the traditional Korean side dishes.

In a soup pot, combine the anchovies, radish, kelp, white onion, and 3 cups (24 fl oz/710 ml) water and boil for 20 minutes. Reduce the heat and cook for 5 more minutes. Strain the anchovy stock.

In a pot, combine the kimchi, kimchi brine, red onions, pork, sugar, gochugaru, gochujang, and salt. Add the sesame oil and anchovy stock. Cook, covered, over medium heat for 10 minutes. Arrange the tofu on top of all the other ingredients, cover, and cook for 15 minutes longer, or until the tofu is soft.

Serve with rice and garnish with the scallion (spring onion).

Bigos

                                                     Poland

Preparation time: 20 minutes
Cooking time: 1 hour 45 minutes
Serves: 4

3 tablespoons (45 g) unsalted
  butter
11 oz (300 g) unsliced bacon,
diced (or bacon lardons)
9 oz (250 g) lean ground (minced)
  pork
5 oz (150 g) kielbasa or other
  smoked sausage, sliced
1 clove garlic, minced
5 oz (150 g) onions, finely chopped
1 bay leaf
11 oz (300 g) green cabbage,
  shredded
7 oz (150 g) mushrooms, diced
Ground cumin
Sea salt
1 tomato, seeded and diced
1 teaspoon paprika
1 teaspoon dried marjoram

Bigos is a typical cold-weather Polish stew, filled with hearty meats and cabbage. Often translated as "hunter's stew," old-time recipes for *bigos* call for game meat, though more modern preparations call for various cuts of pork, veal, or beef. If you can find it, use kielbasa, a Polish smoked sausage, for an authentic flavor. Please ensure the sausage you use contains no gluten.

Preheat the oven to 375°F (190°C/Gas Mark 5).

In a 10-inch (25 cm) Dutch oven (casserole), melt the butter over medium-high heat. Add the bacon, ground (minced) pork, kielbasa, garlic, onions, and bay leaf and cook until the meat is browned, about 10 minutes.

Reduce the heat and add the cabbage and mushrooms. Season to taste with cumin and salt. Stir gently for 5 minutes, then add the tomato, paprika, and marjoram. Add enough water to cover the ingredients. Cover the pan, transfer to the oven, and bake until the cabbage is tender, about 1 hour 30 minutes.

Peameal Bacon

Preparation time: 30 minutes, plus 5 days curing time
Cooking time: 1 hour 45 minutes (baked), or 5 minutes (fried)
Serves: 4

½ cup (4 fl oz/120 ml) apple cider vinegar
1 tablespoon sugar
1 tablespoon hot pepper sauce
2 cloves garlic, minced
1 tablespoon yellow mustard seeds
3 or 4 black peppercorns, or more to taste
1 bay leaf
2 tablespoons sea salt
4–5 ice cubes
1 lb (450 g) boneless pork loin
⅔ cup (80 g) yellow cornmeal
Canola (rapeseed) oil

Canadian peameal bacon is so-named because as part of the original preservation process, the bacon was rolled in dried and ground yellow peas. These days, the bacon is coated in cornmeal instead (which replicates both the color and the crunch of the original coating). Peameal bacon is from the same cut of pork as what in the U.S. is called Canadian bacon, and in the UK is called back bacon.

In a large pot, combine 1 cup (8 fl oz/240 ml) water, the vinegar, sugar, hot sauce, garlic, mustard seeds, peppercorns, bay leaf, and salt. Bring to a boil over high heat, then reduce the heat and simmer for 5 minutes.

Remove from the heat and quick-start the cooling of the liquid by plunging the ice cubes in it. Let it cool completely.

Place the loin in a vacuum bag or into an airtight container and add the cooled brine. Vacuum-seal the bag (to 100%) or cover the container and put it into the fridge for 5 days

Open the bag or the container. Transfer the meat to a bowl and add cold water to generously cover. Soak for 10 minutes, drain, and add more water. Soak for another 10 minutes. Repeat this one more time. Drain and carefully pat dry with a towel.

Spread the cornmeal in a shallow bowl. Roll the meat in the cornmeal to completely coat.

There are a number of ways to cook the peameal bacon:

To bake the bacon: Preheat the oven to 375°F (190°C/Gas Mark 5). Set the whole uncut bacon in a 12-inch (30 cm) baking dish with the fat-side up. Cover the dish with foil and bake for 45 minutes. Remove the foil and bake until the meat is tender, about 1 hour more. Remove from the oven and let it rest for 5 minutes before slicing and serving.

To fry the bacon: Cut the bacon into thin slices. In a nonstick frying pan, heat a little oil over medium heat. Fry the slices for 2 minutes per side.

Note: You can also smoke the bacon if you omit rolling it in cornmeal. Preheat a smoker to 200°F (95°C). Add the cured pork and smoke until the center of the meat reaches 150°F (70°C), about 2 hours or more. Once done, let the meat cool down and slice it to fill sandwiches.

Pulled Pork Sandwich with Cabbage-Apple Slaw

Preparation time: 45 minutes, plus overnight brining time
Cooking time: 6 hours
Serves: 4

For the sauce
¾ cup (6 fl oz/180 ml) apple cider vinegar
1¼ cups (120 g) barbecue sauce
2 tablespoons light brown sugar
2 tablespoons Worcestershire sauce
1 tablespoon hot red pepper sauce
1 tablespoon honey
1 tablespoon fresh lemon juice
1 tablespoon dried chili flakes

For the pork
2 tablespoons light brown sugar
1 tablespoon sweet paprika
1 tablespoon ground cumin
1 teaspoon dried oregano
1 clove garlic, chopped
2 teaspoons sea salt
Sea salt and freshly ground black pepper
2½ lb (1.2 kg) skin-on boneless pork shoulder
1⅓ cups (10 fl oz/300 ml) apple cider vinegar

For the cabbage-apple slaw
⅓ cup (7 oz/200 g) Greek yogurt
4 tablespoons mayonnaise
2 teaspoons apple cider vinegar
1 teaspoon Dijon mustard
1 teaspoon chopped fresh chives
½ head cabbage, thinly shredded
1 carrot, shredded
1 Granny Smith apple, peeled and shredded

For serving
Corn bread

This dish comes originally from the American South, but it's well known all over the world. Made with a well marbled and juicy cut of pork cooked until so tender it can be pulled apart with a fork (hence the name "pulled pork"), it's traditionally cooked on the grill or in a pit barbecue. However it can also be baked in the oven, braised on the stovetop, or cooked in an electric pressure cooker. It can range from smoky and sweet to hot and tangy, depending on the region and on the cook's preference.

Make the sauce: In a saucepan, combine all the sauce ingredients and stir well over low heat until warmed and the sugar is dissolved. Pour into a bowl and refrigerate until needed.

Prepare the pork: In a small bowl, mix together the brown sugar, paprika, cumin, oregano, garlic, 2 teaspoons salt, and 1 tablespoon pepper. Rub the meat with half of the sugar/spice mixture. Put the meat into a large container and pour in 4 cups (32 fl oz/950 ml) cold water. Brine in the fridge overnight, turning the meat two or three times.
    Preheat the oven to 300°F (150°C/Gas Mark 2).
    Remove the meat from the brine and pat it dry with paper towels. Rub it with the remaining sugar/spice mixture. Set the pork in a large Dutch oven (casserole) skin-side up. Sprinkle the meat with ⅔ cup (5 fl oz/150 ml) of the vinegar, cover, and transfer to the oven. Bake for 3 hours.
    Add the remaining ⅔ cup (5 fl oz/150 ml) vinegar, cover, and continue to bake until the meat can be pulled apart with a fork, about 3 hours longer.
    Meanwhile, remove the sauce from the fridge and let it come to room temperature.
    Reserving the juices in the Dutch oven, remove the meat to a carving board. Discard the skin and shred the meat.
    Add the sauce to the Dutch oven and stir together with the pan juices. Ladle out about half of the sauce into a gravy boat. Add the pulled pork to the sauces in the pan and season with salt and pepper to taste.

Make the cabbage-apple slaw: In a small bowl, whisk together the yogurt, mayonnaise, vinegar, mustard, and chives.
    In a large bowl, combine the cabbage, carrot, and apple. Add the dressing and toss to coat.

To serve: Make sandwiches with the meat and coleslaw on corn bread. Serve the remaining sauce on the side for people to add to their sandwiches to taste.

Egg Foo Yung

 China

Preparation time: 30 minutes
Cooking time: 35 minutes
Serves: 4

For the gravy
Generous 1 cup (150 g) cornstarch
  (cornflour)
4 tablespoons oyster sauce
3 tablespoons tamari
2 tablespoons Shaoxing wine
1 tablespoon sesame oil
Freshly ground white pepper

For the egg pancakes
9 oz (250 g) ground (minced) pork
3 tablespoons sesame oil
1 tablespoon tamari
1 tablespoon oyster sauce
1 teaspoon sugar
5 tablespoons rice bran oil
2 cloves garlic, chopped
12 eggs
12 oz (350 g) bean sprouts, rinsed
8 shallots, thinly sliced
Sea salt and freshly ground
  white pepper

Though there may be a link to an ancient Chinese dish called egg foo yung, the restaurant dish that is served in many places across the world today is a product of the Chinese diaspora and may have been created by a Chinese immigrant to America. The stuffed egg pancake, whose name translates to "hibiscus egg," is filled with vegetables and pork (or shrimp) and smothered in a tasty gravy. Shaoxing Chinese rice wine is used in the sauce, which has an amber color, low alcohol content, and is widely used in marinades.

Make the gravy: In a medium bowl, stir together the cornstarch (cornflour), 2 cups (16 fl oz/475 ml) water, the oyster sauce, tamari, wine, and sesame oil and whisk until well combined and lump free. Season to taste with white pepper. Pour into a saucepan, bring to a simmer over medium heat, and stir until the sauce slightly thickens, 1–2 minutes.

Make the egg pancakes: In a large bowl, combine the pork, sesame oil, tamari, oyster sauce, and sugar and mix gently with a fork to combine.

In an 8-inch (20 cm) frying pan, heat 3 tablespoons of the rice bran oil over low heat. Add half of the garlic and cook until lightly browned, about 2 minutes. Add the pork mixture, increase the heat to high, and stir-fry for 13 minutes. Set aside to cool.

Break the eggs into a large bowl and whisk. Stir in the bean sprouts, shallots, pork mixture, remaining garlic, and salt and white pepper to taste. Mix well with a fork or use your fingers to crumble the meat very well.

In a 6 inch (15 cm) nonstick frying pan, heat the remaining 2 tablespoons rice bran oil over medium heat. Pour in enough egg batter to cover the bottom with a layer ½ inch (1.25 cm) thick. Cook until the underside is golden, 1–2 minutes. Flip and cook the other side, about 2 minutes.

Slide the egg pancake onto a plate and repeat until all the egg mixture is used. Serve the cakes topped with the gravy.

Pork-Stuffed Peppers in Tomato Sauce

 Austria

Preparation time: 20 minutes
Cooking time: 1 hour
Serves: 4

14 oz (400 g) pork loin,
    coarsely chopped
1 onion, finely chopped
1 egg
2 tablespoons Dijon mustard
Sea salt and freshly ground
    black pepper
4 red bell peppers
1 cup (8 fl oz/240 ml) passata
    (unseasoned tomato sauce)
½ cup (4 fl oz/120 ml) warm
    vegetable stock

Gefüllte Paprika is an Austrian dish of peppers stuffed with pork and cooked in tomato sauce. It is typically served with boiled potatoes. Unlike most other stuffed peppers, which are baked in the oven, these are actually braised on the stovetop. In German, the word *Paprika* is not a reference to the spice of that name in English, but is the word for the peppers themselves.

In a bowl, combine the meat, onion, egg, and mustard. Season with salt and black pepper. Mix well to evenly combine.

Halve the bell peppers lengthwise and pull out the core and seeds. Fill each pepper with the meat mixture.

Pour the tomato sauce into a large pan that can hold the peppers snugly and bring to a boil. Add the peppers filling-side up, then pour in the stock. Cover and simmer over low heat until the peppers are soft and the filling is cooked through, about 1 hour.

Serve hot.

Meatball Tagine with Eggs

Preparation time: 30 minutes
Cooking time: 50 minutes
Serves: 6

For the meatballs
1 lb (450 g) ground (minced)
    lamb or beef
1 small onion, grated
2 tablespoons chopped fresh
    parsley
1 tablespoon chopped fresh
    cilantro (coriander)
1 teaspoon ground cumin
Pinch of cayenne pepper
Sea salt and freshly ground
    black pepper

For the tagine
2 tablespoons extra-virgin olive oil
2 medium onions, chopped
2¼ lb (1 kg) tomatoes, chopped
2 cloves garlic, chopped
½ teaspoon ground cinnamon
½ teaspoon ground cumin
Pinch of cayenne pepper
Pinch of freshly ground black
    pepper
1 tablespoon chopped fresh
    parsley
6 eggs

Tagine is the name both of a type of stew as well as its traditional ceramic cooking vessel, which is used all over the Middle East and North Africa. The vessel consists of two parts: a shallow base and a cone-shaped lid, which is designed to capture the steam rising from the stew and channel it back down to add to the cooking juices. As it doesn't need a lid, this tagine is cooked in a cast-iron skillet. The meatballs can also be made with a mixture of beef and lamb.

Make the meatballs: In a bowl, combine the ground (minced) meat, onion, parsley, cilantro (coriander), cumin, cayenne, and salt and black pepper to taste. Roll into 1-inch (2.5 cm) balls.

Make the tagine: In a deep cast-iron skillet, heat the olive oil over high heat. Add the meatballs and sauté until browned on all sides, 4–5 minutes. Set the meatballs aside.

In the same skillet, combine the onions, tomatoes, garlic, cinnamon, cumin, cayenne, black pepper, and parsley. Cook until it has reduced to a thick sauce, about 30 minutes.

Add the meatballs to the sauce and simmer for 10 minutes. Make 6 indentations in the sauce and break an egg into each. Cook until the whites are set, about 5 minutes. Serve hot.

Herb, Bean, and Meat Stew

**Preparation time: 20 minutes,
  plus overnight soaking time
Cooking time: 2 hours
  30 minutes
Serves: 4**

6 tablespoons sunflower oil
⅓ cup (25 g) finely chopped
  fresh parsley
⅓ cup (12 g) finely chopped fresh
  cilantro (coriander)
½ oz (12 g) fresh fenugreek, finely
  chopped, or 2 teaspoons
  fenugreek seeds
3 scallions (spring onions), green
  tops only, finely chopped
1 onion, finely chopped
1 lb 5 oz (600 g) lamb or beef
  stew meat, cut into 2-inch
  (5 cm) cubes
1 tablespoon ground turmeric
Sea salt and freshly ground
  black pepper
1 cup (200 g) dried red kidney
  beans, soaked overnight in
  warm salted water and drained
3 dried black limes (see Note)
Crispy Saffron Rice (page 174),
  for serving

Ghormeh sabzi is considered the national dish of Iran. *Ghormeh* means "fried" and *sabzi* means "herbs." Combined with meat, these sautéed herbs are turned into a delicious stew. It is eaten with *tahdig*, a crunchy rice dish. The recipe calls for some ingredients that may be difficult to find: *limoo amani,* which are dried black limes, can be replaced with lemon juice or lime juice (see Note); and the fresh fenugreek leaves can be replaced by fenugreek seeds.

In a large frying pan, heat 4 tablespoons of the oil over medium heat. Add the parsley, cilantro (coriander), fenugreek, and scallions (spring onions) and sauté, stirring occasionally, for 3 minutes. Set aside.

In a large pot, heat the remaining 2 tablespoons oil over low heat. Add the onion and cook until golden, about 10 minutes. Add the meat and turmeric and season with salt and black pepper. Sauté for 6 minutes.

Add the beans, the fried herbs, black limes, and 2 quarts (2 liters) water. Bring to a boil over high heat, then reduce the heat, cover, and simmer over medium-low heat until the beans are tender, about 2 hours.

Serve the stew over the crispy rice.

Note: Dried black limes (*limoo amani*) are popular in Middle Eastern cuisine. If you can't find them, use 3 tablespoons lemon juice or the juice and grated zest of 1 lime.

Tangia Marrakchia

**Preparation time: 20 minutes,
   plus 20 minutes to season**
Cooking time: 4 hours
Serves: 4

2¼ lb (1 kg) boneless leg of lamb
   or beef chuck (roast), cut into
   4 or 5 chunks
1 onion, diced
Handful of fresh parsley, chopped
Grated zest of ½ lemon
2 tablespoons ground cumin
2 tablespoons ras el hanout
1 teaspoon powdered saffron
1 teaspoon ground turmeric
1 teaspoon sea salt
½ teaspoon freshly ground
   black pepper
½ teaspoon ground white pepper
6 cloves garlic, minced
1 cup (8 fl oz/240 ml) olive oil
7 tablespoons (105 g) butter
½ lemon, cut into wedges

A *tangia* is a terra-cotta amphora used in Morocco for the preparation of a tagine-like stew—though when cooked in this vessel, the stew is called a *tangia*. Typical of the city of Marrakech, the dish is also called both "bachelor's stew" and *bent r'mad*, which translates loosely to "daughter of ashes." Traditionally, the stew-filled pot was taken to a Moroccan public bath, where it was set in the ashes of the fire used to heat the bathing facility to slow-cook the meat. For this recipe, if you happen to own a *tangia*, you can cook it in a low oven.

In a large bowl, combine the meat, onion, parsley, lemon zest, cumin, ras el hanout, saffron, turmeric, salt, black pepper, and white pepper. Let it season for 20 minutes.

Place the seasoned meat in a Dutch oven (casserole) or tangia. Add the garlic cloves, oil, butter, lemon wedges, and water to cover. Cover the Dutch oven with the lid, or cover the top of the tangia with parchment paper and tie it around the top with kitchen twine to seal it. Make some holes in the paper with a fork to let the steam out.

Put the Dutch oven or tangia in a cold oven. Set the oven temperature at 275°F (140°C). Cook until the meat is tender, about 4 hours.

Churrasco

(DF) (NF)   **Ecuador**

**Preparation time: 10 minutes,
    plus 4 hours marinating time
Cooking time: 25 minutes
Serves: 4**

4 pork sausages
4 pork ribs
5 oz (150 g) pork loin, cut into
    4 slices
5 oz (150 g) beef sirloin, cut into
    4 slices
4 beef ribs
4 tablespoons extra-virgin olive oil
1 clove garlic, minced
2 teaspoons minced fresh cilantro
    (coriander)
1 teaspoon ground cumin
2 teaspoons paprika
Sea salt and freshly ground
    black pepper
Chimichurri sauce (page 312),
    for serving

Pretty much every country in Latin America has their version of *churrasco,* which is meat cooked on an outdoor grill (barbecue). This example from Ecuador is a mixture of sausages, ribs, and chunks of meat grilled and served with a chimichurri sauce. This dish can be embellished with fried eggs, fried potatoes or plantains, and salad. Please ensure the sausages you use contain no gluten.

In a large bowl, toss all the meat with the oil, garlic, cilantro, cumin, paprika, and salt and black pepper to taste. Refrigerate for 3 hours to marinate, then let marinate at room temperature for 1 hour.
  Prepare an outdoor grill (barbecue) and grill the meat for 15–25 minutes or until your desired doneness, pulling each type of meat off the grill as it's done. As they cook, transfer the meat to a serving bowl and cover with a lid to allow the steam to soften the meat.
  Serve with chimichurri sauce.

Bavarian Meat Loaf

(NF)   **Germany**

**Preparation time: 15 minutes,
    plus 1 hour 30 minutes chilling
    time
Cooking time: 1 hour 15 minutes
Serves: 4**

1 lb 5 oz (600 g) beef top round
    (topside), finely chopped,
    well chilled
11 oz (300 g) smoked bacon,
    finely chopped, well chilled
1 onion, chopped
1 teaspoon dried marjoram
1 tablespoon sea salt
Freshly ground black pepper
1½ cups (12 fl oz/355 ml) ice water
Butter, for greasing

This dish, made from beef or pork, is typical of Bavaria in Germany and it can be bought from any kiosk in Munich. It is usually served in slices, accompanied by sweet or spicy mustard. Its name, *Leberkäse,* literally means "liver cheese," but there is neither cheese nor liver among its ingredients.

In a large bowl, combine the beef, bacon, onion, marjoram, salt, and black pepper to taste. Add the ice water, then knead everything with your hands until the mixture is homogeneous. Cover the bowl and refrigerate for at least 1½ hours.
  Preheat the oven to 350°F (180°C/Gas Mark 4). Butter a 9 × 5-inch (23 × 10 cm) loaf pan.
  Transfer the meat mixture to the loaf pan and press it with your hands to make a uniform loaf. Bake until the meatloaf has a browned, crispy crust, about 1¼ hours.
  Cut into thick slices to serve.

Kentucky Burgoo

(DF) (NF)

Preparation time: 1 hour
Cooking time: 3 hours 30 minutes
Serves: 4

4 tablespoons canola
    (rapeseed) oil
1 lb (450 g) pork shoulder, cut into
    large pieces (3 inches/7.5 cm)
12 oz (350 g) chuck roast, cut into
    large pieces (3 inches/7.5 cm)
2 bone-in, skin-on chicken thighs
1 onion, chopped
2 cloves garlic, chopped
1 carrot, chopped
1 stalk celery, chopped
½ green bell pepper, chopped
Sea salt
1 cup (8 fl oz/240 ml) chicken
    stock
Generous ¾ cup (200 g) passata
    (unseasoned tomato sauce)
1 large yellow potato, peeled and
    diced
7 oz (200 g) frozen corn kernels,
    thawed
3½ oz (100 g) frozen lima beans
    (butter beans), thawed
Freshly ground black pepper

This thick, hearty stew is typical of Kentucky, but also the neighboring states of Illinois, Indiana, and Ohio. Like all stews, there are countless versions, but all have in common the use of at least three types of meat (often including game, such as venison), tomatoes, lima beans (butter beans), corn, and potatoes. It is a great dish to make ahead (in fact it's even better reheated the next day) and can be kept refrigerated for 3–4 days.

In a Dutch oven (casserole), heat 3 tablespoons of the oil over medium-high heat. Working in batches, add the different meats and brown on all sides. Set them aside in a bowl.

In the same pan, heat the remaining 1 tablespoon oil over low heat. Add the onion, garlic, carrot, celery, and bell pepper and cook until the vegetables are crisp-tender, about 10 minutes. Season with 1 teaspoon salt, then return the meat to the pot. Add the stock and tomato sauce and simmer over low heat until the meat is very tender, at least 2 hours.

Pull the meats out of the pot. Cut the pork and beef into small pieces. Bone the chicken thighs and cut the meat into small pieces. Return all the meat to the pot.

Bring to a boil. Add the potato, reduce to a simmer, and cook for 40 minutes to combine the flavors and thicken the sauce.

Add the corn and lima beans (butter beans), season with salt and black pepper to taste, and cook for 10 more minutes to heat through. Serve hot.

Awara Stew

**Preparation time: 30 minutes,
plus 24 hours soaking time
Cooking time: 2 hours 40 minutes
Serves: 8**

9 oz (250 g) salted pig tails
or dried pork
14 oz (400 g) awara paste
(see Note)
4 cups (32 fl oz/950 ml) hot
chicken stock
1 fresh chili pepper, minced
9 oz (250 g) smoked ham, sliced
9 oz (250 g) unsliced smoked
bacon, cut into chunks
1 lb (450 g) smoked chicken,
cut into chunks
5 oz (150 g) smoked cod, cubed
Sea salt
1 head green cabbage, cut into
large pieces
9 oz (250 g) fresh cucumber,
peeled, seeded, diced
9 oz (250 g) spicy pickled
cucumber diced
9 oz (250 g) eggplant, diced
9 oz (250 g) green beans,
chopped
¼ cup (12 g) chopped fresh chives
4 sprigs parsley, leaves only
2½ tablespoons fresh thyme
Freshly ground black pepper

Bouillon d'awara or *awara* broth, from French Guiana on the northeast coast of South America, is a dish with a multitude of meats and made with the intensely orange fruit of the *awara* palm.

Place the pig tails or dried pork in a bowl of water to cover and soak for 24 hours. Change to fresh water every 6 hours. Drain and rinse.

In a large pot, combine the awara paste and 1 cup (8 fl oz/ 240 ml) warm water and mix until the mixture is smooth. Add the pig tails. Place over low heat and cook until the meat is very tender, at least 2 hours.

Add the stock, chili pepper, smoked ham, smoked bacon, smoked chicken, smoked cod, and 1 tablespoon salt. Cover the pot and simmer for 15 minutes.

Meanwhile, in a pot of boiling water, blanch the cabbage for 3 minutes. Drain.

To the pot with the meats, add the cabbage, fresh cucumber, pickled cucumber, eggplant, and green beans and simmer until the vegetables are tender, about 20 minutes. Sprinkle in the chives, parsley, and thyme. Season to taste with salt and pepper. Serve hot.

Note: If you can't find awara paste, use 12 oz (320 g) oranges, peeled and left whole.

Choucroûte Alsacienne

(DF) (NF)

France

Preparation time: 15 minutes
**Cooking time: 2 hours
   35 minutes**
Serves: 4

4 oz (120 g) goose fat
2 onions, chopped
1 clove garlic, peeled
⅔ cup (5 fl oz/150 ml) Alsatian
   white wine
Generous ½ cup (4.2 fl oz/130 ml)
   meat stock
9 oz (250 g) smoked ham, sliced
4 Strasbourg sausages
1 lb 2 oz (500 g) sliced smoked
   bacon (streaky)
11 oz (300 g) beef liver, cubed
1¾ lb (800 g) pork loin, sliced
1 bay leaf
8 juniper berries
Sea salt and freshly ground
   black pepper
8 oz (240 g) canned sauerkraut,
   drained but not rinsed
8 yellow potatoes, peeled

Also known as *choucroûte garnie*, this is a dish of pork and cabbage, typical of Alsace in northeastern France. It's a very rich and savory dish, garnished with smoked and salted meats and sausage. Please ensure the sausages you use contain no gluten.

In a large Dutch oven (casserole), melt the goose fat over low heat. Add the onions and garlic and cook until softened, about 10 minutes.

Pour in the wine and stock, then add the meats, bay leaf, juniper berries, and salt and pepper to taste. Cover and simmer over low heat for 1½ hours.

Add the sauerkraut and cook for 10 minutes longer.

Set the whole potatoes on top of the mixture, cover, and cook for 40 minutes. Serve hot.

Meat and Corn Pie

Preparation time: 30 minutes
Cooking time: 1 hour
Serves: 4

3 tablespoons sunflower oil
2 onions, chopped
14 oz (400 g) ground
    (minced) beef
1 teaspoon ground cumin
Sea salt and freshly ground
    black pepper
3 eggs
3 tablespoons plus ⅓ cup
    (4.2 fl oz/125 ml) milk
3 cups (500 g) canned corn
    kernels
3 tablespoons (45 g) butter
1 teaspoon sugar
1 teaspoon chopped fresh basil
5 tablespoons raisins
15 black olives, pitted
    and chopped
Generous 1 cup (200 g) shredded
    roasted chicken

The *pastel de choclo* is traditionally made with *choclo*, which in the local Quechua language means "soft corn" and is the corn of the new season. Because actual *choclo* is very difficult to find, this pie is made with canned corn instead. *Pastel de choclo* is traditionally prepared in an earthenware pan called a *paila*.

In a large frying pan, heat the oil over medium heat. Add the onions and sauté until soft and translucent, about 5 minutes. Add the beef, cumin, and a pinch each of salt and pepper. Stir well, reduce the heat, and cook until the meat is browned and crumbled, about 12 minutes. Remove from the heat, pour off any liquid and fat from the pan, and set aside.

Meanwhile, place the eggs in a saucepan and cover them with cold water. Bring to a boil and cook for 9 minutes. Drain and cool them under cold running water. Peel the eggs, chop, and set aside.

In a food processor, combine 3 tablespoons of the milk and the corn and blend until smooth.

In a saucepan, melt the butter over low heat. Add a pinch of salt, the sugar, the remaining ⅓ cup (80 ml) milk, and the corn purée. Simmer until it's thick, about 5 minutes. Stir in the basil and remove from the heat.

Preheat the oven to 375°F (190°C/Gas Mark 5).

Spread the beef mixture in a 15 × 10-inch (38 × 25 cm) baking dish. Sprinkle with the chopped eggs, raisins, olives, and the shredded chicken. Spoon the corn mixture over the top, spreading to cover all the ingredients.

Transfer to the oven and bake until the surface is golden brown, about 40 minutes.

Stuffed Cabbage Rolls

(DF) (NF)

Romania

**Preparation time: 1 hour, plus
  45 minutes resting time
Cooking time: 2 hours
  30 minutes
Serves: 4**

Scant 1 cup (175 g) long-grain
  white rice
Salt
4 tablespoons extra-virgin olive oil
4 onions, finely chopped
4 carrots, finely chopped
4 oz (120 g) bacon, diced
12 oz (350 g) ground (minced)
  pork
12 oz (350 g) ground (minced)
  veal
2 eggs
¾ cup (6 fl oz/180 ml) passata
  (unseasoned tomato sauce)
2 teaspoons paprika
Freshly ground black pepper
1 large head Savoy cabbage
Juice of ½ lemon
2 cups (16 fl oz/475 ml)
  vegetable stock

Sarmale is a hearty and nutritious winter main course from Romania: These cabbage rolls are always present on the table for celebrations and anniversaries, and for Lent they are prepared with a meatless filling of rice and vegetables. The name of the dish comes from *sarma*, which are stuffed leaves of various sorts from Eastern Europe. (The category includes stuffed grape leaves, such as Dolmades, page 61.) Romanian *sarmale* are usually served with yogurt or sour cream, or with *mamaliga*, a kind of polenta.

In a saucepan, combine the rice, water to generously cover, and salt and bring to a boil over medium-high heat. Cook for 15 minutes. Drain and cool under cold running water, then drain again.

In a frying pan, heat 2 tablespoons of the oil over medium heat. Add the onions, carrots, and bacon and sauté until the bacon is lightly crisped, about 15 minutes. Let cool.

In a large bowl, combine the pork, veal, eggs, ½ cup (4 fl oz/ 120 ml) of the tomato sauce, the sautéed onion/carrot/bacon mixture, and the drained rice. Season with the paprika, salt, and pepper to taste. Knead carefully until the mixture is homogeneous, then let the filling rest for 45 minutes.

Pull off the 8 largest, nicest leaves from the outside of the head of cabbage (or you could use 16 smaller ones). Shred the rest of the cabbage.

In a large pot, bring 4 cups (32 fl oz/950 ml) water and the lemon juice to a boil. Add the cabbage leaves and parboil them for 30 seconds.

Drain well, then place them on a cutting board and cut out the thick base of the stalks in a thin triangular shape. Place 3 tablespoons of the filling on each cabbage leaf and roll up the leaf until it is sealed.

In a large pot, combine the rest of the cabbage and remaining 2 tablespoons oil. Arrange the rolls on top and cover with the stock and the remaining ¼ cup (2 fl oz/60 ml) tomato sauce. Simmer over low heat until the filling is firm, about 1 hour 45 minutes.

Set the rolls on a plate and drizzle with the sauce. Serve hot.

Meat, Vegetable, and Chickpea Stew

Preparation time: 30 minutes, plus overnight soaking time
Cooking time: 2 hours 30 minutes
Serves: 6

1 lb (450 g) beef heel muscle or bottom round (silverside)
1 Cornish hen (poussin), 14 oz (400 g), trimmed
1 ham bone
1 lb (450 g) carrots, chopped
7 oz (200 g) onions
9 oz (250 g) dried chickpeas, soaked overnight and drained
5 oz (150 g) pork belly
7 oz (200 g) morcilla or blood sausage (black pudding)
4 pork sausages
1 lb (450 g) medium yellow potatoes, peeled
Sea salt and freshly ground black pepper

Cocido madrileño is a Spanish meat and vegetable dish from the capital city of Madrid. Please ensure the morcilla and sausages you use contain no gluten.

In a large pot, combine the beef, hen, ham bone, carrots, onions, and cold water to cover. Bring to a boil over medium heat, then reduce to a simmer and cook for 30 minutes.

Add the chickpeas and cook until the chickpeas are tender, about 1 hour.

Add the pork belly to the pot and cook for 30 minutes.

Meanwhile, in a small pot, combine the morcilla with water to cover. Bring to a boil and cook until cooked through, about 30 minutes. Drain and cut the morcilla into 2-inch (5 cm) pieces.

Add the morcilla to the pot with the meat and chickpeas. Add the sausages, potatoes, and salt and black pepper to taste. Cook for 30 minutes more.

Scoop the meat and vegetables out of the broth and arrange together in a large serving platter. Moisten everything with a little broth. Serve the broth separately.

Spicy Stir-Fried Chicken

Preparation time: 15 minutes, plus 2 hours marinating time
Cooking time: 40 minutes
Serves: 4

3 tablespoons tamari
2 tablespoons rice vinegar
1 tablespoon curry powder
½ tablespoon sugar
1 small piece fresh ginger, peeled and grated
2 tablespoons sesame seeds, plus more for garnish
1 lb 5 oz (600 g) boneless, skinless chicken breasts, each cut into 8 chunks
4 tablespoons rice bran oil
1 large onion, sliced
1 red bell pepper, diced
2 yellow potatoes, diced
1 tablespoon gochujang (Korean chili paste)

Dakgalbi is a popular Korean stir-fried chicken dish—there is even a food festival dedicated to it in late August. The dish first appeared in the city of Chuncheon in the mid-twentieth century, when it was served in small and cheap taverns in the industrial part of the city. Today you can find it everywhere in Korea.

In a bowl, combine the tamari, vinegar, curry, sugar, ginger, and sesame seeds. Add the chicken and toss to coat. Cover and marinate in the fridge for at least 2 hours.

In a deep frying pan, heat the oil over high heat. Add the onion, bell pepper, and potatoes and cook until the bell pepper is crisp-tender, about 10 minutes. Add the chicken and gochujang, reduce the heat to medium, and stir-fry until the chicken is cooked through, about 15 minutes.

Serve hot, garnished with some more sesame seeds.

Pomegranate Chicken

Preparation time: 15 minutes
Cooking time: 1 hour 30 minutes
Serves: 4

7 oz (200 g) walnuts
1½ lb (700 g) boneless, skinless
 chicken thighs, cut into
 1-inch (2.5 cm) pieces
Sea salt and freshly ground
 black pepper
2 tablespoons extra-virgin olive
 oil, plus more for searing
 the chicken
1 teaspoon (5 g) unsalted butter
1½ yellow onions, diced
4 cloves garlic, roughly chopped
1 teaspoon ground cinnamon
1 teaspoon ground cumin
1 teaspoon ground turmeric
½ teaspoon grated nutmeg
Grated zest of 1 orange
2 cups (16 fl oz/475 ml)
 chicken stock
¼ cup (2 fl oz/60 ml)
 pomegranate molasses
2 tablespoons maple syrup
Crispy Saffron Rice (page 174),
 for serving
4 tablespoons pomegranate
 seeds, for serving

This centuries-old recipe for stew is said to come from the Caspian region of Iran. Originally, *fesenjān* was made with wild duck and small lamb meatballs, but nowadays it is usually made with chicken. Once difficult to locate, pomegranate molasses is now easily purchased, but if you don't have access to a store that sells it, you can boil unsweetened pure pomegranate juice until it is the thickness of molasses (treacle).

In a Dutch oven (casserole), toast the walnuts over medium-low heat, stirring occasionally, until golden, about 10 minutes. Set aside to cool. Grind the toasted walnuts in a food processor until finely ground.

Season the chicken with salt and pepper to taste. In the same Dutch oven, heat ½ inch (1.25 cm) oil over medium heat. Add the chicken and sear until golden, about 8 minutes. Remove from the pan and set aside.

Add the 2 tablespoons olive oil and the butter to the pan and heat over medium heat. Add the onions and sauté until golden, about 5 minutes. Add the garlic and cook until golden, about 4 minutes. Add the cinnamon, cumin, turmeric, nutmeg, and orange zest and cook for 2 minutes.

Add the stock, pomegranate molasses, maple syrup, 1½ teaspoons salt, the chicken, and ground walnuts and bring to a boil, while stirring. Cover, reduce the heat to low, and simmer, stirring every 15 minutes, until the liquid is well reduced, about 1 hour.

To serve, pour the stew over the rice and garnish with the pomegranate seeds.

Coq au Vin

Preparation time: 1 hour, plus overnight marinating time
Cooking time: 2 hours 15 minutes
Serves: 4

For the marinade and chicken
4 cups (32 fl oz/950 ml) full-bodied red wine, ideally Bordeaux
1 carrot, finely diced
1 shallot, left whole and stuck with 2 cloves
1 tablespoon fresh parsley leaves
1 tablespoon fresh rosemary leaves
½ tablespoon fresh thyme leaves
1 teaspoon black peppercorns
4 juniper berries
1 whole chicken (4½ lb/2 kg) trimmed and cut into serving pieces

For the stew
3 oz (80 g) dried porcini mushrooms
1 sprig rosemary
1 sprig thyme
1 sprig parsley
1 tablespoon lard or duck fat
4 shallots, chopped
4 cloves garlic, chopped
7 oz (200 g) unsliced bacon, cut into lardons
3 tablespoons Cognac, other brandy, or grappa
1 carrot, cut into ¼-inch (6 mm) slices
10 pearl (button) onions, peeled
Sea salt and freshly ground black pepper
1 tablespoon (15 g) unsalted butter

Chicken in red wine is a traditional and ancient French dish: Legend has it that it was served to Julius Caesar during the conquest of ancient Gaul, after he was offered a cockerel as a symbol of the honor of the Gauls. For the marinade you can replace the expensive Bordeaux with another equally full-bodied red wine.

Marinate the chicken*: In an airtight container large enough to hold the chicken, combine the wine, diced carrot, shallot, herbs, peppercorns, and juniper berries. Add the chicken to the marinade. Cover and refrigerate overnight.

For the stew: In a small bowl, combine the porcini mushrooms and 1 cup (8 fl oz/240 ml) hot water and set aside to rehydrate for 15 minutes.

Tie the herbs into a bundle.

Reserving the marinade, drain the chicken pieces.

In a Dutch oven (casserole), melt the lard over high heat. Add the chicken and the herb bundle and brown the chicken for 3–4 minutes per side. Remove the chicken to a plate and set aside. Discard the herbs.

To the same pan, add the shallots, garlic, and bacon and cook over high heat until the shallots are beginning to soften, about 2 minutes. Return the chicken to the pan. Pour in the Cognac and using a long fire lighter, carefully flambé and gently swirl the pan.

Strain the marinade and pour it into the pan. Add the sliced carrot, pearl (button) onions, the rehydrated porcini and their soaking liquid, salt and black pepper to taste, and ½ cup (4 fl oz/ 120 ml) water. Cover and simmer over low heat until the chicken thigh is tender, about 2 hours. Remove the chicken pieces from the pan and set on a serving dish.

Remove the pan from the heat and stir in the butter to melt. Pour the sauce over the chicken pieces. Serve hot.

Chicken Yassa

**Preparation time: 30 minutes,
plus 3 hours marinating time
Cooking time: 1 hour 45 minutes
Serves: 6**

3 chicken leg quarters (leg and
  thigh), about 11 oz (300 g) each
3 skin-on chicken breasts
  (about 1 lb/450 g each)
5 onions, halved and thinly sliced
1 habanero or Scotch bonnet
  pepper
½ cup (4 fl oz/120 ml) fresh
  lemon juice
5 tablespoons canola (rapeseed)
  oil or extra-virgin olive oil
2 tablespoons Dijon mustard
4 cloves garlic, minced
Sea salt and freshly ground
  black pepper
1½ cups (12 fl oz/350 ml)
  chicken stock
1¾ cups (350 g) short-grain
  white rice
11 oz (300 g) pitted green olives,
  sliced, for garnish

Originally from Senegal, chicken yassa is a comfort food recipe that is enjoyed all over West Africa. It is relatively easy to prepare, yet rich in flavor. Remember to allow plenty of time for the chicken to marinate: It's easier if you let it marinate overnight, making the preparation the next day faster. In addition, the longer marinating time tenderizes the chicken and gives it more flavor.

In a large bowl, combine the chicken and onions. Make a few slits in the habanero pepper and add it to the bowl. In a small bowl, whisk together the lemon juice, 4 tablespoons of the oil, the mustard, garlic, and ½ teaspoon salt. Pour over the chicken and toss to coat evenly. Cover the bowl and marinate in the fridge for a minimum of 3 hours or up to overnight.

Remove the chicken and the habanero from the marinade and set aside. Also set the onions and marinade aside.

In a large Dutch oven (casserole), heat the remaining 1 tablespoon oil over medium-high heat. Season the chicken with salt and black pepper. Working in batches, carefully place 3 pieces of chicken in the hot oil. Cook the chicken until browned on both sides, about 5 minutes. Set the chicken on a plate. Spoon most of the chicken fat out of the pot and repeat to cook the next batch of chicken.

Preheat the oven to 350°F (180°C/Gas Mark 4).

Add the onions and marinade to the pot and cook, stirring, over medium-high heat until beginning to soften, about 5 minutes. Cover the pot, reduce the heat to medium-low, and cook, stirring occasionally, until the onions are very soft and starting to caramelize, about 10 minutes.

Push the onions in the pot aside with a spatula. Carefully place the chicken pieces on the bottom of the pan, then spoon the onions on top of the chicken pieces. Add the reserved habanero to the pan, setting it in the middle. Pour the chicken stock into the pot and bring to a simmer over medium-high heat.

Cover the pot, transfer to the oven, and cook until the chicken is tender and the sauce is thickened, 1 hour 15 minutes to 1 hour 40 minutes.

Meanwhile, rinse the rice until the water runs clear. Pour it into a large saucepan. Add 3½ cups (28 fl oz/830 ml) cold water and let it sit for 30 minutes.

Bring the rice and water to a boil over high heat, then reduce the heat to medium, cover, and let cook for 5 minutes or until the water level is low enough for you to see the surface of the rice. Switch to low heat and let it simmer until there is no more water left, about another 10 minutes. Remove from the heat, uncover, and drape the pan with a cloth to absorb any steam.

To serve, divide the rice among plates and top with the chicken/onion mixture. Add sliced green olives to garnish.

Chicken Satay with Peanut Sauce

 (DF)

Preparation time: 15 minutes, plus 1 hour resting and marinating time
Cooking time: 15 minutes
Serves: 6

For the sambal pecal
12 oz (350 g) in-shell raw peanuts
6 tablespoons palm oil
4 dried chilies, seeded
5 scallions (spring onions), diced
1 clove garlic, chopped
3 lemon leaves, washed and sliced (see Note)
6 oz (175 g) solid palm sugar, cut into small pieces
1-inch (2.5 cm) cube seedless tamarind pulp
Sea salt

For the lime sauce
2 tablespoons tamari
Juice of 1 lime
2 fresh red chilies, diced
1 shallot, cut into chunks
2 tablespoons sugar
6 makrut lime leaves, cut into small pieces (see Note, page 33)

For the chicken
2 tablespoons tamari
2 teaspoons coriander seeds, freshly ground
1 teaspoon freshly ground white pepper
6 boneless, skinless chicken thighs, cut into small cubes

These chicken skewers, or *saté ayam,* are popular in Indonesia as well as Malaysia and Singapore and are served with a delicious peanut sauce called *sambal pecel.* In the countries of origin the skewers are a typical street food snack, but if served with cucumber wedges, red onion slices, and *nasi impit* (pressed rice cubes), they become a meal.

Make the sambal pecal: Shell the peanuts, but leave the peanut skins on. Rinse the peanuts and drain well, then pat them very dry on a paper towel.

In a wok, heat the palm oil to 300°F (160°C) on a deep-fry thermometer. Add the peanuts and fry for 2 minutes, stirring constantly, then remove from the wok and drain on paper towels. Set aside.

In the same oil, fry the dried chilies, scallions (spring onions), garlic, and lemon leaves for 2 minutes, then remove from the heat. Drain off the oil.

In a food processor, combine the peanuts, palm sugar, tamarind pulp, the chili/scallion mixture, and salt to taste.

Divide the mixture into 6 equal portions and roll into balls with wet hands. Wrap individually in plastic wrap (cling film) and store in the freezer until ready to use. (You will only need 1 portion of sambal pecal for the peanut sauce; the remainder can be stored in the freezer for up to 1 month.)

Make the lime sauce: In a bowl, combine the tamari, lime juice, red chilies, shallot, sugar, and makrut lime leaves. Mix thoroughly and let it rest for 1 hour.

Meanwhile, prepare the chicken: In a bowl, combine the tamari, ground coriander, and white pepper. Add the chicken and toss to coat. Cover the bowl and let marinate for 45 minutes.

If using wooden skewers on an outdoor grill (barbecue), soak them in water for at least 30 minutes before cooking.

Preheat an outdoor grill or grill pan (griddle pan) to high heat.

Thread the chicken onto skewers. Add them to the grill or grill pan and cook, turning them until each side is golden brown and crispy, about 10 minutes.

In a bowl, combine 1 ball of sambal pecel with 1 tablespoon hot water and stir to thoroughly melt, adding 1 or 2 more tablespoons hot water, if necessary, to obtain a smooth sauce.

Set the skewers on a plate and serve with a bowl of lime sauce and a bowl of peanut sauce.

Note: If you can't find lemon leaves, you can replace them with 1 stalk lemongrass, sliced.

Chicken and Taro Casserole

Preparation time: 30 minutes, plus 10 minutes resting time
Cooking time: 2 hours 40 minutes
Serves: 4

1 whole chicken (3¼ lb/1.5 kg), cut into serving pieces
Grated nutmeg
Sea salt and freshly ground black pepper
Juice of 2 lemons, plus 1 tablespoon for the chicken
1 stick plus 1 tablespoon (120 g) unsalted butter, plus more for greasing
1 lb (450 g) cooked chicken sausage links, sliced
2 onions, chopped
4 tomatoes, peeled, seeded, and chopped
3 cloves garlic, minced
1 habanero pepper
2 tablespoons chopped fresh parsley
4 cups (32 fl oz/950 ml) chicken stock
3 lb (1.4 kg) pomtajer, peeled, rinsed, and grated
Juice of 1 orange
1 tablespoon sugar

A beloved dish mostly reserved for birthdays and other special occasions, *pomtajer* (*pom* for short) is generally considered the national dish of Suriname. It's said that originally the recipe was a potato recipe brought to Suriname by Jewish immigrants who were forced to leave Portugal and Spain by the Spanish Inquisition. Once in South America, the potatoes in the dish were replaced by a local starchy root vegetable called *pomtajer*, which in English can be called taro, but is in a different botanical family. It can be quite difficult to source, so if you do not find *pomtajer*, you can replace it with grated potatoes or yuca (cassava) root. Please ensure the sausages you use contain no gluten.

Season the chicken with nutmeg, salt, and black pepper and rub all over. Put it in a bowl and sprinkle with 1 tablespoon of the lemon juice. Let it rest for 10 minutes.

In a Dutch oven (casserole), heat 4 tablespoons (60 g) of the butter over medium heat. Add the chicken pieces and chicken sausage and brown for 5 minutes. Remove the meat from the pan. Slice the chicken meat off the bones and set the meat aside.

To the same pan, add 3 tablespoons (45 g) of the butter and heat over low heat. Add the onions and cook until golden brown, about 5 minutes. Add the tomatoes, garlic, habanero, and parsley and put the chicken back in. Pour in the stock, cover, and simmer over low heat until the chicken is cooked through, about 30 minutes. Remove from the heat. Drain the cooking liquid into a bowl.

In a bowl, stir together the pomtajer, orange juice, lemon juice, and a little of the cooking liquid. Stir in the sugar.

Preheat the oven to 425°F (220°C/Gas Mark 7). Butter a 10-inch (25 cm) round baking dish.

Place half of the pomtajer mixture on the bottom of the baking dish. Spread the chicken mixture over and top with the remaining pomtajer mixture. Pour the reserved cooking liquid over the top and dot with the remaining 2 tablespoons (30 g) butter.

Cover with foil, transfer to the oven, and bake for 1 hour. Take the foil off, reduce the oven temperature to 375°F (190°C/Gas Mark 5), and bake until the filling is stewy and the top is firm, about 1 hour.

Chicken Molokhia

(NF)   **Egypt**

**Preparation time: 20 minutes,
plus 30 minutes soaking time
Cooking time: 1 hour 10 minutes
Serves: 4**

1¾ cups (350 g) short-grain
    white rice
1 whole chicken (3½ lb/1.5 kg)
1 large onion, finely chopped
1 sprig rosemary
1 cinnamon stick
1 bay leaf
14 oz (400 g) whole fresh
    molokhia
1 tablespoon minced garlic
1 tablespoon plus 1 teaspoon
    ground coriander
3 tablespoons (45 g) unsalted
    butter
Sea salt and freshly ground
    black pepper
½ teaspoon ground cinnamon
½ teaspoon ground cumin
¼ teaspoon sweet paprika

Molokhia or *mulukhiyah* are the leaves of a shrub (called jute mallow in English) that in the Middle East is cultivated as a vegetable. The word *molokhia* comes from a word that means "royalty," a reference to the fact that its use dates back to the time of the pharaohs. This dark green stew has a distinctive bitter taste and a viscous texture (think okra). It is usually served with chicken and white rice.

In a large saucepan, combine the rice and 2⅓ cups (18 fl oz/ 550 ml) water and let it sit for 30 minutes.

Place the chicken in a large deep pot. Sprinkle with the onion and add the rosemary, cinnamon stick, bay leaf, and 3 quarts (2.84 liters) water. Place a small plate on top of the chicken to keep it submerged and bring to a boil. Reduce to a simmer and cook over low heat until the chicken is cooked through, about 45 minutes.

Meanwhile, bring the rice and water to a boil over high heat. Reduce the heat to medium, cover, and cook until the water level is low enough to see the surface of the rice, about 5 minutes. Reduce to low heat, cover, and simmer until there is no more water left, another 10 minutes. Remove from the heat. Place a tea towel over the pan to absorb any steam.

Remove the chicken from the pot and place it on a plate to cool down. When cool enough to handle, cut into serving pieces. Strain the broth through a sieve into a heatproof bowl (discard the solids). Spoon off some of the fat.

Return 2 cups (16 fl oz/475 ml) of the broth to the pot. Add the molokhia to the pot and simmer for 10 minutes.

Put the garlic and 1 tablespoon of the ground coriander in a mortar and mash it with a pestle into a paste.

In a small frying pan, melt 1 tablespoon of the butter. Add the garlic paste and cook over medium-high heat until golden brown, about 1 minute. Add the fried paste to the molokhia and simmer for 5 minutes. Season to taste with salt and pepper.

In a small bowl, combine the remaining 1 teaspoon ground coriander, the ground cinnamon, cumin, paprika, and ½ teaspoon each salt and black pepper. Sprinkle the chicken all over with the spices.

In a large nonstick skillet, melt the remaining 2 tablespoons butter over high heat. Add the chicken and cook until the skin is crisp and golden, about 4 minutes.

To serve, divide the rice among four shallow soup bowls. Pour the molokhia over it and carefully place some chicken on top of the molokhia. Serve immediately.

Spiced Chicken Stew

Preparation time: 20 minutes
Cooking time: 1 hour 35 minutes
Serves: 4

1 whole chicken, (3¼ lb/1.5 kg),
    cut into quarters
Juice of ½ lemon
Sea salt and freshly ground
    black pepper
2 tablespoons niter kibbeh
    (see Note) or ghee
2 onions, finely minced
½ cup (4 fl oz/120 ml) sunflower oil
1–2 tablespoons berbere
    (see Note, page 251)
½ tablespoon minced fresh ginger
2 cloves garlic, minced
½ teaspoon ground cumin
4 eggs
Injera (page 153), for serving

Doro wat is a party dish in Ethiopia: It is served to particularly important guests and at weddings, when the bride has to demonstrate to her husband and guests that she is capable of perfectly dissecting a chicken into 12 parts. This dish is traditionally quite spicy. If you are not a fan of hot food, you don't have to miss out on this fabulously tasty chicken stew, just adjust the spiciness to taste. This recipe is a scaled-down version of a typical *doro wat.*

In a bowl, marinate the chicken with the lemon juice, 1 teaspoon salt, and black pepper to taste.

In a Dutch oven (casserole), heat the niter kibbeh or ghee over low heat. Add the onions and sauté until translucent, about 5 minutes. Cover, reduce the heat to very low, and cook until the onion has reduced to a paste, about 45 minutes. Add water if it's in danger of burning.

Add the oil, berbere, ginger, and garlic and fry until fragrant. Add the chicken and cook until partially cooked and the skin is crispy, about 20 minutes. Add the cumin, season with salt and black pepper, and cook until the chicken is cooked through, about 20 minutes longer. Add 2–3 cups (16–24 fl oz/475–710 ml) water if the mixture gets too dry.

Meanwhile, place the eggs in a saucepan and cover them with cold water. Bring to a boil over medium heat and boil for 9 minutes. Drain and cool them under cold running water. Peel the eggs.

Add the eggs to the stew and serve with injera.

Note: *Niter kibbeh* is a seasoned clarified butter a little like ghee, but cooked with lots of warm curry-style spices

Spicy Creamed Chicken

Preparation time: 40 minutes
Cooking time: 50 minutes
Serves: 4

Salt
4 yellow potatoes
2 eggs
4 cups (32 fl oz/950 ml) chicken
  stock
2½ lb (1.1 kg) boneless, skinless
  chicken breasts
3 fresh ají amarillo chilies,
  seeded, or 2 tablespoons ají
  amarillo paste
½ cup (4 fl oz/120 ml) sunflower oil
2 cloves garlic, chopped
1 onion, finely chopped
4 tablespoons milk
2 tablespoons (30 g) unsalted
  butter
2 tablespoons chopped walnuts
3 tablespoons grated
  Parmesan cheese
Cooked white rice, for serving
8 black olives, pitted

Ají de gallina, a name that literally means "hen's chili," is a spicy and creamy chicken dish. It is a combination of European influences (the walnut-thickened sauce, for example) and typical Peruvian ingredients, such as potatoes and ají amarillo. The ají is a brightly colored yellow chili pepper, which gives the dish flavor and an intense yellow color. It is difficult to find fresh outside Peru, but it is sold frozen as well as in paste form in jars.

In a pot of boiling salted water, cook the potatoes until firm-tender, about 30 minutes. When cool enough to handle, peel and cut into chunks.

Meanwhile, place the eggs in a saucepan and cover them with cold water. Bring to a boil over medium heat and boil for 9 minutes. Drain and cool them under cold running water. Peel the eggs and cut in slices.

In a large pot, bring the stock to a boil. Add the chicken and simmer over medium heat until just cooked through, about 15 minutes. When the chicken is cool enough to handle, pull it into shreds or bite-size pieces. Strain the broth and reserve 2 cups (16 fl oz/475 ml).

If using whole chilies, combine the chilies and 4 tablespoons of the oil in a food processor. (Alternatively, if using chili paste, combine the chili paste and 4 tablespoons of the oil in a small bowl.) Blend until smooth and creamy.

In a frying pan, heat the remaining 4 tablespoons oil over medium-low heat. Add the garlic, onion, and chili purée and cook until the onions are soft, about 5 minutes.

In the same food processor, combine the milk, butter, walnuts, and Parmesan and blend until smooth. Add the onion/chili mixture and blend for 1 more minute.

In a soup pot, combine the reserved chicken broth, chili/walnut cream, and the shredded chicken and bring to a boil over medium heat, stirring frequently.

Spoon the chicken mixture over rice and top with the yellow potatoes, eggs, and black olives.

Panang Chicken Curry

Preparation time: 30 minutes
Cooking time: 50 minutes
Serves: 6

For the Panang curry paste
3 oz (80 g) bird's eye chilies
  or serrano chilies, seeded
  and finely chopped
½ oz (10 g) fresh cilantro
  (coriander) root
1 stalk lemongrass, tough
  outer leaves removed and
  thinly sliced
1 tablespoon grated fresh
  galangal
2 cloves garlic, peeled and sliced
1 shallot, finely chopped
2 teaspoons shrimp paste
1 oz (30 g) unsalted roasted
  peanuts, grounded
1 teaspoon grated nutmeg
2 teaspoons coriander seeds
1 teaspoon ground cumin
½ teaspoon ground white pepper
1 teaspoon makrut lime
  grated zest

For the curry
2 tablespoons sunflower oil
1 lb 5 oz (600 g) boneless, skinless
  chicken breast, cut into 2-inch
  (5 cm) chunks
Sea salt and freshly ground
  black pepper
1 tablespoon coconut oil
1 onion, chopped
1 red bell pepper, thinly sliced
1 yellow bell pepper, thinly sliced
3 carrots, cut into matchsticks
4 oz (120 g) green beans,
  trimmed and cut in thirds
2 cloves garlic, chopped
1 can (13.5 fl oz/400 ml) full-fat
  coconut milk
1½ teaspoons coconut sugar
2 tablespoons peanut butter
1 tablespoon tamari
2 teaspoons fresh lime juice
Lime wedges, for squeezing

This traditional Thai curry gets its unique flavor from a very specific curry paste: The thick, red paste is made with chilies, galangal, garlic, shallot, lemongrass, coriander (seeds and root), shrimp paste, and peanuts (see Note). If the recipe turns out to be too spicy, add more coconut milk; if it is too salty, add lime juice; and if it is not salty enough, add a little fish sauce. The dish, which needs gentle cooking, can also be baked in the oven.

Make the Panang curry paste: In a mortar, combine the chilies, cilantro (coriander) root, lemongrass, galangal, and garlic. Grind with the pestle until the mixture becomes a paste. Add the shallot, shrimp paste, and peanuts. Keep working with the pestle until the mixture becomes a homogeneous paste. Add the spices and lime zest and stir to combine.

Make the curry: In a frying pan, heat the sunflower oil over medium heat. Add the chicken and brown on all sides for 5 minutes. Season with salt and black pepper. Set aside.

In a large Dutch oven (casserole), heat the coconut oil over medium heat. Add the onion and a pinch of salt and cook, stirring constantly, until softened and translucent (not browned), about 5 minutes.

Add both bell peppers, the carrots, and green beans and cook until beginning to soften, about 5 minutes. Add the garlic, 2 tablespoons of the curry paste, coconut milk, ½ cup (4 fl oz/ 120 ml) water, and coconut sugar and simmer over medium-low heat, frequently stirring, until the vegetables are crisp-tender, about 10 minutes. Add the chicken and cook until cooked through, about 15 minutes, adding water if the mixture looks too dry.

Remove from the heat and stir in the peanut butter, tamari, and lime juice. Season with a pinch of salt and serve with lime wedges for squeezing.

Note: You will only need 2 tablespoons of the curry paste for the curry. Transfer leftover curry paste to a container, cover with plastic wrap (cling film), making sure the plastic wrap is lying directly onto the surface of the paste, and store in the fridge for up to 1 week. If you want to shortcut the recipe, use a high-quality store-bought Panang curry paste.

Chicken Vindaloo

 (DF) (NF)

**Preparation time: 10 minutes,
   plus 4 hours marinating time
Cooking time: 30 minutes
Serves: 4**

2–4 dried red chilies, to taste,
   stemmed
1 teaspoon paprika
½ teaspoon ground cumin
½ teaspoon mustard powder
¼ teaspoon ground cinnamon
12 cloves garlic, peeled
4 inches (10 cm) fresh ginger,
   peeled and coarsely chopped
1 teaspoon sugar
½ cup (4 fl oz/120 ml) distilled
   white vinegar
1 lb 5 oz (600 g) boneless, skinless
   chicken breast, cut into 1½-inch
   (4 cm) chunks
2 tablespoons sunflower oil
1 onion, chopped
1 tablespoon tomato paste (purée)
Sea salt and freshly ground
   black pepper
Cooked basmati rice, for serving

The origin of vindaloo dates back to the sixteenth century, when the Portuguese settled in Goa, on the west coast of India. The term vindaloo actually comes from a mash-up of Portuguese words: *vinha* (wine) and *alho* (garlic). Over the centuries the basic Portuguese recipe for *carne de vinha d'alhos* (meat with wine and garlic) was adapted to its new surroundings to include the chilies and other spices of India. Today the dish is searingly hot and vinegar has replaced the wine, but the garlic is definitely still there.

In a small food processor, combine the chilies, paprika, cumin, mustard powder, cinnamon, garlic, ginger, sugar, and vinegar and blend until smooth.

In a bowl, toss the chicken with the spice paste. Cover and marinate in the fridge for at least 4 hours.

In a Dutch oven (casserole), heat the oil over high heat. Add the marinated chicken and cook until and browned on all sides, about 5 minutes.

Add the onion and tomato paste (purée) and stir well to combine. Add ½ cup (4 fl oz/120 ml) water (or more if you like the sauce to be thinner) and season with salt and black pepper. Cover, reduce the heat, and cook until the chicken is cooked through, about 25 minutes.

Serve the chicken with the cooked rice.

Red Curry with Chicken

Preparation time: 1 hour
Cooking time: 40 minutes
Serves: 6

For the red curry paste
1 shallot, chopped
1 stalk lemongrass, sliced
1 teaspoon white peppercorns
4 cloves garlic, peeled
3 fresh red chilies, chopped
½ teaspoon ground cumin
½ teaspoon ground ginger
1 tablespoon fresh cilantro
 (coriander) leaves
Grated zest of ½ makrut lime
2 tablespoons grated fresh
 galangal or ginger
1 teaspoon fine sea salt

For the curry
2 cups (16 fl oz/475 ml) full-fat
 coconut milk
4 tablespoons cornstarch
 (cornflour)
2 tablespoons coconut oil
1 lb 5 oz (600 g) boneless, skinless
 chicken thigh, sliced
2 scallions (spring onions),
 chopped
1 tablespoon grated fresh ginger
1 tablespoon chopped garlic
2 tablespoons tamari
3 tablespoons light brown sugar
10 Thai basil leaves
Cooked jasmine rice, for serving

The seasoning paste for this Thai curry is made from scratch here, but you can easily substitute a high-quality store-bought brand of red curry paste. The base consists of red chilies, garlic, ginger, onion, shallot, and other spices. The red curry paste is also great for seasoning vegetables, rice, and noodles.

Make the red curry paste: In a mortar, combine the shallot, lemongrass, white peppercorns, garlic, and chilies. Grind with the pestle until the mixture becomes a paste. Add the cumin, ground ginger, cilantro (coriander), lime zest, galangal, and salt. Keep working with the pestle until the mixture become a homogeneous and creamy paste.

Make the curry: In a small bowl, stir together 1 cup (8 fl oz/ 240 ml) of the coconut milk and the cornstarch (cornflour).
 In a Dutch oven (casserole), heat the coconut oil over medium heat. Add the chicken and cook until browned on both sides, about 5 minutes. Add the red curry paste, scallions (spring onions), fresh ginger, and garlic and stir for 2 minutes.
 Add the remaining 1 cup (8 fl oz/240 ml) coconut milk, the cornstarch/milk mixture, tamari, brown sugar, and basil. Bring to a boil and cook for 3 minutes. Reduce the heat to a simmer and cook until the chicken is cooked through, about 25 minutes. Add a few spoons of water if the mixture gets too dry.
 Serve the chicken with the cooked rice.

Roasted Partridge

Preparation time: 45 minutes
Cooking time: 45 minutes
Serves: 4

4 oven-ready partridges
  (about 9½ oz/275 g each)
4 sprigs thyme, plus more
  for garnish
8 juniper berries
Sea salt and freshly ground
  black pepper
4 tablespoons extra-virgin olive oil
2 tablespoons (30 g) unsalted
  butter, melted
8 slices (rashers) smoked bacon
1½ cups (120 g) sliced mushrooms

Roasted partridges are a popular dish in Canada. For the best results, let the bird air-dry uncovered in the fridge for up to 24 hours: This helps to make the skin crispier when it's roasted. Take the partridges out of the fridge to come up to room temperature (about 45 minutes) before roasting. This dish also goes really well with baked potatoes.

Preheat the oven to 400°F (200°C/Gas Mark 6).

Stuff each partridge cavity with a sprig of thyme and 2 juniper berries. Tie the ends of the drumsticks together with kitchen twine to close off the cavity. Season the partridges with salt and black pepper.

In a small bowl, stir together 2 tablespoons of the oil and the melted butter and brush the mixture all over the partridges. Drape 2 slices (rashers) bacon over each bird and place in a 7 × 11-inch (18 × 28 cm) baking pan.

Transfer to the oven and roast until the skin is crispy, about 40 minutes. Transfer the partridges to a plate, cover with foil, and keep warm while you finish preparing the dish.

Pour the pan juices into a small saucepan and simmer over low heat to reduce by half.

In a frying pan, heat the remaining 2 tablespoons oil over medium heat. Add the mushrooms and cook until browned, about 5 minutes.

Serve the partridges with the mushrooms and drizzle everything with the warmed pan juices.

Desserts and Sweet Treats

Baked Apples

Bulgaria

Preparation time: 15 minutes
Cooking time: 1 hour
Serves: 6

6 medium red apples
3 tablespoons (45 g) unsalted
   butter, at room temperature
1 cup (200 g) sugar
3 tablespoons chopped walnuts
Ground cinnamon
3 tablespoons honey, for serving

Very popular in Bulgaria, *pecheni yabalki* are delicious baked apples stuffed with nuts. Other variations on the stuffing include raisins soaked in brandy or the omission of the honey. Serve the apples with a scoop of vanilla ice cream. Once cooked, baked apples can be stored in the fridge for 2 days.

Preheat the oven to 350°F (180°C/Gas Mark 4).
   Core out the apples, but do not go all the way through. Leave a barrier at the bottom so the stuffing doesn't leak out.
   In a small bowl, thoroughly mix the butter, sugar, walnuts, and cinnamon to taste.
   Fill the apples with this mixture and place them in an 8-inch (20 cm) square baking pan. Bake until softened, about 1 hour.
   Serve hot, drizzled with a little honey.

Cloudberries with Whipped Cream

 (NF) (VT) (30) [5]   **Norway**

Preparation time: 10 minutes
Serves: 4

1 cup (8 fl oz/240 ml) heavy
   (whipping) cream
1 teaspoon vanilla extract
3 tablespoons superfine
   (caster) sugar
½ cup (160 g) cloudberry jam
Fresh cloudberries, for garnish

Multekrem is Norwegian dessert of fluffy, cloud-like mounds of whipped cream flavored with the aptly named cloudberries. Cloudberries are golden-amber berries that grow in very northern climes. Their tart flavor sweetens as the berries ripen. As they are not easy to find outside Scandinavia, you can replace them here with raspberry jam and fresh raspberries.

In a bowl, with an electric mixer, combine the cream, vanilla, and sugar and whip to soft peaks. Gently fold in the jam. Divide among dessert bowls and garnish each with berries.

Banana Split

Preparation time: 10 minutes
Serves: 4

4 bananas, halved lengthwise
½ pint (240 ml) vanilla ice cream
½ pint (240 ml) strawberry
  ice cream
½ pint (240 ml) chocolate ice
  cream
1 cup (250 g) canned crushed
  pineapple
10 fresh strawberries, sliced
½ cup (4 fl oz/120 ml) chocolate
  syrup
½ cup (4 fl oz/120 ml) heavy
  (whipping) cream, whipped
½ cup (70 g) chopped peanuts
12 maraschino cherries
  (cocktail cherries)

The banana split is a quintessentially American dessert that came into being in the early twentieth century, the same time that American "ice cream parlors" were becoming popular. A banana split is (as the name suggests) a banana that is split down the middle. Sitting on top of the split banana are three different scoops of ice cream. The toppings and sauces can vary considerably, though frequently there are fruit, nuts, whipped cream, and cherries. The banana split is such an iconic dessert that there are special elongated dessert bowls designed specifically to hold it.

Place 2 banana halves in each of four dishes, setting them a bit apart to make room for the ice cream. Place one scoop of each flavor of ice cream in a row between the bananas. Divide the pineapple, strawberries, and chocolate syrup over the ice cream. You can put only one type of topping on each scoop, or you can mix and match.

Dollop each scoop of ice cream with whipped cream and sprinkle with the nuts. (Alternatively, you can sprinkle with the nuts first and then put on the whipped cream.) Place a cherry in the middle of each dollop of whipped cream. Serve immediately.

Bananas in Coconut Milk

Preparation time: 10 minutes
Cooking time: 10 minutes
Serves: 4

Scant 3¼ cups (25.4 fl oz/750 ml)
  full-fat coconut milk
4 barely ripe bananas,
  sliced crosswise
3 tablespoons cane sugar
Pinch of sea salt

Kluay buad chee is a very simple dessert of bananas gently simmered in lightly sweetened coconut milk. It's important to use green (barely ripe) bananas here because you want them to hold their shape when cooking. The little bit of salt balances the sweetness of the sauce and the richness of the coconut milk.

In a small saucepan, bring the coconut milk to a boil over medium heat. Carefully slip the banana slices in, reduce the heat, and simmer for 5 minutes, stirring occasionally.

Stir in the sugar and salt and cook for 5 minutes longer. Serve warm.

Lemon Syllabub

Preparation time: 20 minutes
Serves: 4

1½ cups (12 fl oz/355 ml) heavy
    (whipping) cream
½ cup (100 g) superfine (caster)
    sugar
5 tablespoons dry white wine
Grated zest and juice of 1 lemon
20 strawberries, sliced or diced,
    for garnish

A dessert that dates back to the sixteenth century, syllabub was originally made by combining cream and wine or cider, which curdled the cream. In later versions of the dessert, the mixture was whipped to a froth and served in a glass, with the soft curds rising to the top.

In a bowl, with an electric mixer, combine the cream and sugar and whip to soft peaks. Stir in the wine, half of the zest, and all the lemon juice. Pour the mixture into four champagne coupe glasses and garnish with the remaining zest. Top with strawberries and serve.

Dulce de Leche

Preparation time: 5 minutes
Cooking time: 3 hours
Makes 1 cup (240 ml)

4 cups (32 fl oz/950 ml) milk
1½ cups (300 g) sugar
1 vanilla bean, split lengthwise
½ teaspoon baking soda
    (bicarbonate of soda)

Dulce de leche is popular all across Latin America, but legend has it that it was invented in Argentina in the nineteenth century by a cook who forgot that a pot of milk and sugar was on the stove. The happy accident produced a deeply caramelized and rich "milk candy" that is great in all types of baked goods and just straight up on ice cream. The dulce de leche can be stored in the fridge for up to 1 month.

In a 1½-quart (1.5 liter) saucepan, combine the milk and sugar. Scrape the vanilla seeds in and add the pod, too. Bring to a simmer over medium heat and cook, stirring occasionally, until the sugar has dissolved. Add the baking soda (bicarbonate of soda) and stir to combine. Turn the heat to very low and cook for 1 hour. Stir occasionally, but do not re-incorporate the foam that rises to the top.

Fish out the vanilla pod and simmer the mixture until it turns a dark caramel color, about 2 more hours. It will have reduced to about 1 cup (8 fl oz/240 ml). Strain the mixture through a fine-mesh sieve and pour into a sealed container.

Ovos Moles

Preparation time: 20 minutes
Cooking time: 10 minutes
Makes: 8

2½ cups (500 g) sugar
6 egg yolks, lightly beaten
2 tablespoons ground cinnamon

Ovos moles are a traditional dessert from the Aveiro district in Portugal, where they are baked in fanciful molds with shapes such as shells, fish, and crabs. The recipe was apparently invented by some thrifty nuns who used egg whites to starch their clothes and were thus left with a large number of egg yolks. To protect these delicate treats, the commercial versions are often coated with a light wafer.

Position an oven rack in the upper third of the oven and preheat the oven to 500°F (260°C/Gas Mark 10).

In a saucepan, combine the sugar and 1 cup (8 fl oz/ 240 ml) water. Bring to a boil and simmer until the mixture reaches 340°F (170°C) on a candy thermometer; the mixture should be a light caramel color. Remove from the heat and let cool to room temperature.

Add the egg yolks to the caramel, return the pan to low heat, and cook, whisking, for 5 minutes. Stir in the cinnamon.

Pour into 8 small ramekins 1½ inches (4 cm) in diameter and 1½ inches (4 cm) deep. Bake until lightly browned, about 2 minutes. Then serve.

Coconut-Vanilla Custard

Preparation time: 20 minutes,
 plus 4 hours chilling time
Cooking time: 1 hour 5 minutes
Serves: 8–10

1 tablespoon coconut oil or
   cooking spray
8 eggs
¾ cup (145 g) superfine
   (caster) sugar
Pinch of sea salt
5 cups (40 fl oz/1.2 liters) milk
1 teaspoon vanilla extract
1 teaspoon coconut extract

Khanom maw kaeng is a simple custard-style Thai dessert, beloved all around the country. It can be stored, covered, in the fridge for 3 days.

Preheat the oven to 350°F (180°C/Gas Mark 4). Grease an 8-inch (20 cm) square baking pan with coconut oil or cooking spray.

In a bowl, whisk together the eggs, sugar, and salt.

In a saucepan, warm the milk over medium heat (do not boil). Whisking constantly, slowly pour the hot milk into the egg mixture. Whisk in the vanilla and coconut extracts. Pour the custard into the prepared baking pan.

Set the baking pan of custard in a roasting pan and set the roasting pan on a pulled-out oven rack. Pour enough hot water into the roasting pan to come about 1 inch (2.5 cm) up the sides of the baking pan.

Bake until a skewer inserted in the center of the custard comes out clean, about 1 hour.

Let cool, then refrigerate for 4 hours before serving.

Baked Coconut Custards

**Preparation time: 10 minutes,
  plus 30 minutes resting time
  and 3 hours chilling time
Cooking time: 25 minutes
Serves: 4**

Butter, for the ramekins
Scant ½ cup (80 g) superfine
  (caster) sugar, plus more
  for the ramekins
7 egg yolks
Scant ½ cup (40 g) unsweetened
  shredded (desiccated) coconut
¼ cup (60 ml) condensed milk
¼ cup (60 ml) full-fat coconut milk
Boiling water

Quindim is a very popular dessert in Brazil and is similar to a Portuguese custardy sweet called *brisa do lis*. The Portuguese recipe contains ground almonds while the Brazilian one uses coconut. The coconut rises to the top during baking and becomes a "crust" for the little custards when they are inverted. Feel free to decorate the custards by drizzling with some melted chocolate or sprinkling with more coconut.

Preheat the oven to 350°F (180°C/Gas Mark 4). Grease four 4-ounce (120 ml) ramekins with butter and dust with sugar.
 Strain the yolks through a fine-mesh sieve into a bowl. Stir in the sugar, shredded (desiccated) coconut, and both milks and stir to combine.
 Divide the custard mixture among the prepared ramekins. Set the ramekins in a 7 × 11-inch (18 × 28 cm) baking pan. Set the baking pan on a pulled-out oven rack. Pour enough boiling water into the baking pan to come two-thirds of the way up the ramekins.
 Bake until a toothpick inserted in the center of a custard comes out clean, 20–25 minutes. Remove from the bain-marie and let the custards cool for 3–4 minutes.
 To unmold, run a knife around the edges of the ramekins to loosen the custards, then invert the ramekins onto a plate Let cool for 30 minutes, then refrigerate for at least 3 hours before serving.

Catalan Cream

 Spain

Preparation time: 10 minutes
Cooking time: 15 minutes, plus
3 hours chilling time
Serves: 4

2 cups (16 fl oz/475 ml) plus
   5 tablespoons milk
Grated zest of 1 lemon
1 cinnamon stick
½ cup (100 g) superfine
   (caster) sugar
3 tablespoons (25 g) cornstarch
   (cornflour)
4 egg yolks
Granulated sugar, for sprinkling

Crema catalana, with its rich custard and crackly sugar topping, is very similar to a crème brûlée—and in fact there are those from Catalonia who insist that crème brûlée is the copycat. Unlike crème brûlée, the Catalan version is a cinnamon-scented custard and is cooked on the stovetop instead of being baked. To make the sweet crust, sugar is sprinkled over the chilled custards and is then caramelized with a kitchen torch or broiled (grilled), but the traditional method of doing this is to super heat a special iron (see Note) over a flame and then let the radiant heat caramelize the sugar.

In a saucepan, combine 2 cups (16 fl oz/475 ml) of the milk, the lemon zest, cinnamon stick, and ¼ cup (50 g) of the superfine (caster) sugar. Bring to a boil, stirring often.

In a small bowl, add the remaining 5 tablespoons milk to the cornstarch (cornflour) and stir to combine.

In a medium bowl, whisk together the yolks and remaining ¼ cup (50 g) superfine sugar, then whisk in the cornstarch mixture. Whisking constantly, very gradually pour the hot milk into the egg yolk mixture. Pour the mixture back into the saucepan and bring to a bubble over low heat. Stir constantly until it's creamy, thick, and smooth, 2–3 minutes.

Pour the cream into four 6½-ounce (200 ml) ramekins, cover with plastic wrap (cling film) and refrigerate until firm, about 3 hours.

Dust the tops of the custards with granulated sugar, then caramelize them with a kitchen torch and serve immediately. (Alternatively, you can put the custards on a sheet pan and run under a very hot broiler/grill.)

Note: Special long-handled caramelizing irons are frequently sold in a set with shallow ceramic custard molds for making *crema catalana*.

Floating Islands

Preparation time: 20 minutes,
  plus 1 hour freezing time
Cooking time: 20 minutes
Serves: 4

1 cup (120 g) confectioners'
  (icing) sugar
4 eggs, separated
6 tablespoons sugar
1 tablespoon potato starch, rice
  starch, or cornstarch (cornflour)
1½ cups (12 fl oz/355 ml) milk
1 cup (8 fl oz/240 ml) heavy
  (whipping) cream
1 vanilla bean, halved lengthwise

In France, this delicious meringue dessert is called *œufs à la neige*, or "snowy eggs." It can also be called *îles flottantes,* hence the translation to Floating Islands in English. This simple confection is a poached "island" of meringue floating on a sea of rich crème anglaise.

In a saucepan, combine the confectioners' (icing) sugar with 2 tablespoons water. Cook over medium heat, without stirring, until it turns a light brown caramel color.

Set a sheet of parchment paper on a work surface. Dip a spoon into the caramel and let it fall off the spoon onto the parchment paper as you move the spoon to create spirals. Chill the caramel decorations in the freezer for 1 hour.

In a bowl, with an electric mixer, whisk the egg whites with 2 tablespoons of the sugar to stiff peaks.

In a heatproof bowl, beat the yolks with the remaining 4 tablespoons sugar and the starch until the mixture is silky.

In a saucepan, combine the milk and cream. Scrape in the vanilla seeds and add the pod, too. Bring to a boil over medium heat, then reduce the heat to a simmer.

With 2 large spoons, make a quenelle of the egg white mixture and place it carefully on the surface of the boiling milk. Turn and roll it gently for 2 minutes per side, then remove it with a skimmer and place on a plate. Repeat to make 3 more quenelles.

Remove the vanilla pod. Whisking constantly, slowly stream the hot milk/cream mixture into the egg yolks. Then return the mixture to the saucepan and cook over very low heat, constantly whisking, until the crème anglaise is silky and soft, 4–5 minutes.

Divide the crème anglaise among four dessert bowls, float a quenelle of meringue on top and decorate with caramel spirals.

Lucuma Meringue Torte

**Preparation time: 1 hour,
  plus 1 hour chilling time
Cooking time: 1 hour 30 minutes
Serves: 6**

6 eggs whites, at room
  temperature
1½ cups (290 g) superfine
  (caster) sugar
2 tablespoons confectioners'
  (icing) sugar
2½ cups (20 fl oz/590 ml)
  heavy (whipping) cream
6 tablespoons lucuma powder
Fresh or dried fruits, for
  decorating

A traditional Peruvian dessert, three layers of meringue are stacked and frosted with a whipped cream flavored with *lucuma*, a native fruit that grows in the Andean valleys. When unripe, the fruit is very starchy, but it gets sweeter as it ripens and in its fully ripe state is a deep orange (loaded with beta-carotene) and not overly sweet, more on the level of a sweet potato. The flesh can be dried and ground to a powder to be used as a nutrition supplement as well as a cooking ingredient.

Preheat the oven to 210°F (100°C).

Cut out four 9-inch (22 cm) rounds of parchment paper.

In a bowl, with an electric mixer, whip the egg whites to stiff peaks. Continuing to whip, gradually add 1 cup (195 g) of the superfine (caster) sugar and continue beating on medium speed for 5–6 minutes or until the mass is silky and glossy. Add the confectioners' (icing) sugar and mix gently to combine.

Place 2 parchment paper rounds on each of two sheet pans. Fit a piping bag with a round tip (nozzle) and fill the bag with the meringue. Starting at the outside of each round, pipe concentric circles of meringue all the way in to the center.

Transfer the pans to the oven and bake until the surface of the meringue is shiny, at least 1½ hours. Turn off the oven, prop the oven door ajar, and let the meringue cool in the oven.

In a well-chilled bowl, with an electric mixer, whip the heavy (whipping) cream on high speed to firm peaks, then reduce the speed and slowly add the lucuma powder and the remaining ½ cup (95 g) superfine sugar. Whisk for 30–60 seconds on high speed to incorporate.

Assemble the torte: Set 1 meringue layer on a cake plate and frost with one-quarter of the lucuma cream. Add 2 more meringue layers, frosting each with a quarter of the lucuma cream. Set the final meringue layer on top and frost with the remaining lucuma cream. Refrigerate for 1 hour before serving.

Decorate with fresh or dried fruits just before serving.

Pavlova

(NF) (VT)

Preparation time: 30 minutes
Cooking time: 2 hours
Serves: 4

6 egg whites, at room
  temperature
Pinch of salt
1 teaspoon vanilla extract
1 tablespoon cornstarch
  (cornflour)
1⅓ cups (250 g) plus 2 tablespoons
  superfine (caster) sugar
1 tablespoon apple cider vinegar
  or white wine vinegar
1½ cups (12 fl oz/355 ml)
  heavy (whipping) cream
Favorite fresh fruits:
  blueberries, kiwi (peeled
  and sliced), strawberries
  (halved), raspberries

This delicious dessert was created (and named) in honor of the Russian prima ballerina Anna Pavlova who in the 1920s toured Australia and New Zealand. In fact, the question of whether the pavlova originated in Australia or New Zealand has been a matter of debate between the two nations for many years. Pavlova is a perfect dessert for special occasions, especially in the summer when there is an abundance of colorful seasonal fruit. The meringue ring should be crunchy on the outside and soft and fluffy on the inside, but should stay snowy white and not browned. You'll know to take it out of the oven when cracks start to form on the surface.

Preheat the oven to 475°F (245°C/Gas Mark 9).

In a bowl, with an electric mixer, whip the egg whites with the salt to stiff peaks. Continuing to whip, add the vanilla, cornstarch (cornflour), and 1⅓ cups (250 g) of the superfine (caster) sugar, 1 tablespoon at a time. Then whip in the vinegar.

Draw an 8-inch (20 cm) circle on a sheet of parchment paper (trace around a cake pan). Set the parchment paper drawing-side down (it should show through the paper) on a sheet pan. Spread the meringue just inside the circle, gently pushing into the middle of the mixture to make a depression into the center and a higher border all around.

Transfer the sheet pan to the oven and immediately reduce the oven temperature to 225°F (110°C/Gas Mark ¼). Bake for 2 hours. Turn off the oven, prop the oven door ajar, and let the meringue cool in the oven.

In a bowl, with an electric mixer, whip the cream with the remaining 2 tablespoons sugar to firm peaks.

Top the meringue with the whipped cream and decorate with fresh fruit. Serve immediately.

Daifuku Mochi

Preparation time: 15 minutes
**Cooking time: 2 hours 30
   minutes**
Makes: 20 mochi

⅔ cup (120 g) dried adzuki beans
5 cups (40 fl oz/1.2 liters)
   boiling water
Scant 1 cup (175 g) packed
   light brown sugar
1¾ cups (280 g) sweet rice flour
1 cup (200 g) superfine (caster)
   sugar
Potato starch or cornstarch
   (cornflour), for dusting
20 strawberries

This traditional Japanese treat is a sweet rice shell filled with a sweetened adzuki bean paste called *anko*. The word *daifuku* literally means "good luck" and *mochi* is the Japanese name for a sticky rice cake made with glutinous rice. To make mochi the old-fashioned way, cook the rice with sugar and then pound it in a mortar to make a smooth dough. Luckily, you can get the same effect in a shorter time by starting with sweet rice flour.

In a saucepan, combine the adzuki beans and 2½ cups (20 fl oz/ 590 ml) of the boiling water. Let simmer for 5 minutes. Drain the beans, clean the pan, return the beans to the pan, and add the remaining 2½ cups (20 fl oz/590 ml) boiling water. Cover and simmer until the beans are very soft, about 2 hours, adding water as needed to keep the beans submerged.

Drain the beans and return to the pan. Add the brown sugar and stir constantly over medium-high heat for 10 minutes; you will see a sort of dough form. It will be ready when it looks shiny but still loose. This is the anko. Transfer it to an airtight container and set aside.

In a heatproof bowl, stir the sweet rice flour with ¾ cup (6 fl oz/180 ml) water until a dough forms. Set up a steamer with a steamer basket or insert big enough to hold the bowl. Place the bowl with the rice dough in the steamer and steam for 20 minutes.

Transfer the steamed dough to a pot. Add about ⅓ cup (65 g) of the superfine (caster) sugar and stir constantly over medium heat until the sugar is completely dissolved. Continue adding the sugar ⅓ cup (65 g) at a time.

Transfer the dough to a cutting board dusted with starch. Roll the dough to a ⅜-inch (1 cm) thickness. Cut into 20 pieces.

Scoop out about 1 tablespoon (½ oz/15 g) of the anko and with starch-dusted hands roll into a ball (the anko is particularly sticky). Make a hole in the ball of anko and fill with a strawberry. Continue to stuff balls of anko.

Wrap each ball in a piece of rice dough and seal.

Set the mochi, seam-side down, on a serving plate.

Steamed Rice Dumplings

Preparation time: 45 minutes
Cooking time: 30 minutes
Serves: 4

For the dough
3¾ cups (600 g) sweet rice flour
1 cup (8 fl oz/240 ml) warm water

For the chaku
12 oz (350 g) molasses sugar
  or muscovado sugar
2 tablespoons ghee
2 tablespoons sesame seeds,
  ground to a powder
1 tablespoon ground cardamom
2 tablespoons coconut flour

For assembly
½ cup (4 fl oz/120 ml) sesame oil,
  for greasing
1 cup (8 fl oz/240 ml) khoa
  (dried condensed milk)

Yomari are Nepalese steamed dumplings made with sweet rice flour. Their name loosely translates to "a loved delicacy" (from *mari*, which means "delicacy," and *yo*, which means "to like"). And it is in fact not only popular in Nepal, but central to an important festival that celebrates the end of the rice harvest. The stuffed dumplings have a highly distinctive shape (sort of like a cross between an elongated radish and a sea creature) and are stuffed with a variety of sweet fillings, including a taffy-like candy called *chaku*.

Make the dough: Place the sweet rice flour in a large bowl. A little at a time, knead in the lukewarm water until a soft but consistent dough that easily separates if you pull it is formed. Set aside.

Make the chaku: Heat a deep pan over high heat until hot. Stir in the molasses sugar, ghee, sesame powder, cardamom, and coconut flour. Reduce the heat to medium and stir until the molasses sugar is fully melted and perfectly combined into a thick mixture. Set aside.

Assemble the yomari: Take 2 tablespoons (about 40 g) of dough, grease your hands with some sesame oil, and roll the dough into a ball. Still rolling between your hands, form a cone shape about 5 inches (10 cm) long with a pointed top. Dip your finger into the sesame oil and start at the wide end of the cone to dig a hole into the cone. Then widen the opening by pinching the dough at the same time as you rotate the cone, leaving a wall about ¾ inch (1 cm) thick. You'll end up with something like a thick-walled ice cream cone.

Fill half of the cones with khoa (dried condensed milk) and half with the chaku, about 2 tablespoons filling for each cone. The filling should come only about halfway up in the insides of the cone. Pinch the top edges above the filling together to close off the dumpling and squeeze into a thick stem (it will now look like a radish with a stem coming off it). Flatten the top of the "stem," divide it in half, and pinch it into two little "ears."

Set up a steamer. Grease a steamer rack with 2 tablespoons sesame oil. Steam the dumplings over medium heat until the surface is lightly translucent and the texture is chewy, 15–20 minutes. Remove the dumplings from the steamer and let them cool down before serving.

Baked Rice Pudding

Preparation time: 30 minutes
Cooking time: 2 hours
40 minutes
Serves: 6

1½ tablespoons (20 g) unsalted
   butter, plus more for
   the baking dish
3½ cups (28 fl oz/830 ml) milk
1¼ cups (285 ml) heavy
   (whipping) cream
Zest strips from ½ lemon
1 vanilla bean, split lengthwise
½ cup (100 g) short-grain rice
   (see Note)
2 tablespoons sugar
Freshly grated nutmeg

A comforting homestyle dessert, baked rice pudding is generally served hot, but can also be served cold (and makes a very fine breakfast). The pudding can be eaten plain, but to make it extra special you can serve it with preserves, fresh fruit, or fruit coulis. Cinnamon is often used instead of nutmeg. For a vegan version, make this with a plant milk; use full-fat coconut milk for the same level of richness.

Preheat the oven to 300°F (150°C/Gas Mark 2). Butter an 8 × 11-inch (20 × 30 cm) baking dish 3 inches (8 cm) deep.
   In a saucepan, stir together the milk, butter, cream, and lemon zest. Scrape in the vanilla seeds and add the pod. Heat over very low heat, stirring, until it is warm.
   Remove from the heat and let it rest for 5 minutes, then pluck out the vanilla pod and lemon zest.
   Place the rice and the sugar into the prepared baking dish, then pour in the warmed milk. Sprinkle a little nutmeg all over the top.
   Transfer the dish to the oven and bake until the pudding is thick and the top is nicely browned, about 2½ hours.

Note: In the UK, you can buy something called "pudding rice," which is a nice starchy rice that works perfectly in this recipe.

Argentine Rice Pudding

 Argentina

Preparation time: 20 minutes
Cooking time: 1 hour 30 minutes
Serves: 6

Generous ¾ cup (175 g)
   short-grain rice
1 cup (8 fl oz/240 ml) milk
Zest strips from 1 lemon
1 cinnamon stick
Butter and rice flour,
   for the baking dish
1 egg
4 tablespoons sugar
Ground cinnamon

Arroz con leche has all the flavors and comfort of a rice pudding, but has a firm texture and cuts like a cake. It can double as a delicious breakfast or snack, and is a family favorite.

In a saucepan, bring 1½ cups (12 fl oz/355 ml) water to a boil over medium heat. Add the rice and cook for 15 minutes, then set aside.

In a separate saucepan, combine the milk, zest strips, and cinnamon stick. Bring to a simmer over medium heat, then remove the cinnamon and zest and let the milk cool to room temperature.

Preheat the oven to 325°F (165°C/Gas Mark 3). Grease a 10-inch (25 cm) square baking dish with butter and dust with rice flour.

In a bowl, whisk together the egg and sugar, then whisk in the milk. Finally, stir in the rice and season with cinnamon to taste.

Pour the mixture into the prepared baking dish and bake for 45 minutes. Reduce the oven temperature to 250°F (120°C/Gas Mark ½) and bake until the liquid is completely absorbed and the top is lightly browned, about 30 minutes longer.

Remove from the oven and let cool before serving.

Egyptian Rice Pudding

Preparation time: 25 minutes, plus 15 minutes soaking time and 1 hour chilling time
Cooking time: 30 minutes
Serves: 4

¾ cup (150 g) short-grain rice
3¼ cups (26 fl oz/770 ml) milk
5 tablespoons sugar
1 tablespoon cornstarch (cornflour)
3½ oz (100 g) pistachios or other nuts, lightly crushed, for serving

Roz bel laban—loosely "rice milk"—is a dessert enjoyed all over North Africa and the Middle East. We've topped it off with pistachios, but for a nut-free version, use cinnamon and raisins. And coconut milk can replace some of the dairy milk. The short-grain rice ("pudding rice" in the UK) makes a nice, creamy pudding. The pudding should be chilled before serving.

Wash the rice thoroughly. Soak it for 15 minutes, then drain and transfer to a pot. Add the milk and sugar. Bring to a simmer over medium heat, stirring, then reduce the heat to low and simmer for 20 minutes.

In a bowl, stir 4 tablespoons water into the cornstarch (cornflour). Add to the pudding while stirring vigorously to incorporate. Let simmer for 10 minutes.

Divide the rice pudding among four dessert bowls. Sprinkle with the crushed pistachios. When cooled, refrigerate for at least 1 hour or overnight to chill before serving.

Cheesecake with Raisins

Preparation time: 20 minutes, plus 1 hour chilling time
Cooking time: 50 minutes
Serves: 8

1½ lb (700 g) quark cheese, fromage frais, or fromage blanc
⅔ cup (100 g) ricotta cheese
5 eggs
3½ tablespoons sugar
½ cup (80 g) potato starch
4 tablespoons (60 g) unsalted butter, melted, plus 1 tablespoon for greasing
1 cup (8 fl oz/240 ml) sour cream
½ teaspoon vanilla extract
Grated zest and juice of 2 lemons
5 tablespoons raisins, soaked in warm water for 30 minutes and drained
6 oz (175 g) candied cherries (or other favorite candied fruit)

In Russia, *zapekanka* is often served at teatime, accompanied by sour cream and fresh berries. Its name translates to "casserole" and it can also be made as a savory dish. You can switch up the dried fruit in the cake to whatever you fancy.

In a bowl, with an electric mixer, beat together the quark, ricotta, and eggs. Beat in the sugar, potato starch, melted butter, sour cream, and vanilla until smooth. Refrigerate the cheesecake batter for 1 hour.

Preheat the oven to 375°F (190°C/Gas Mark 5). Grease a 9-inch (23 cm) springform pan with the remaining butter.

Stir the lemon zest, lemon juice, raisins, and cherries into the cheesecake batter. Pour the batter into the prepared springform.

Bake until golden brown, about 50 minutes. Remove from the pan and let it cool.

Ricotta Cake

Preparation time: 40 minutes
Cooking time: 1 hour 30 minutes
Serves: 8

10 tablespoons (5 oz/150 g)
    unsalted butter, melted,
    plus extra for the pan
2 tablespoons potato starch,
    plus extra for the pan
8 eggs, separated
2 cups (400 g) superfine
    (caster) sugar
2¼ lb (1 kg) ricotta cheese
1 tablespoon vanilla sugar
Juice of ½ orange
Juice of ½ lemon
1½ teaspoons baking powder

Polish *sernik* ("cheesecake") rises quite high during baking, but will sink back down as it cools, and, like many cheesecakes, does a final bit of slow cooking in a turned-off oven. If preferred, serve it decorated with melted chocolate, berry compote, or caramel sauce.

Preheat the oven to 325°F (165°C/Gas Mark 3). Grease a 12-inch (30 cm) springform pan with butter and dust with potato starch.

In a bowl, with an electric mixer, whisk the egg yolks and superfine (caster) sugar until pale yellow and frothy. Add the ricotta and thoroughly combine. Add the melted butter, potato starch, vanilla sugar, orange juice, lemon juice, and baking powder and mix well.

In a clean bowl, with an electric mixer, whip the egg whites to stiff peaks. Fold the egg whites into the ricotta mixture. Pour the batter into the prepared pan.

Transfer to the oven and bake for 1 hour. Turn off the oven and let the cake rest for 30 minutes inside the oven, without opening the door.

Remove from the oven and let it cool down before removing the pan's sides. Leave the cheesecake on the springform base or carefully transfer it to a serving plate. Serve warm.

Paskha

Preparation time: 40 minutes, plus 12 hours chilling time
Serves: 4

1¾ sticks (7 oz/200 g) unsalted butter, at room temperature
½ cup (4 fl oz/120 ml) sour cream
½ cup (100 g) superfine (caster) sugar
2 teaspoons vanilla extract
Pinch of sea salt
1¾ lb (800 g) tvorog (see Notes), quark, or fromage frais, lightly drained to remove liquid
½ cup (4 fl oz/120 ml) condensed milk
1½ oz (40 g) nuts, crushed or in chunks
Candied fruits, crumbled cookies, or chocolate chips, for decoration

Paskha is a pyramid-shaped cheesecake that is baked for Russian Orthodox Easter. In fact its name actually means "Easter" and the word is related to the French *Pâques*, Italian *Pasqua*, and Spanish *Pascua*. During Holy Saturday celebrations, this cake is brought to churches to be blessed. It is baked in a special mold and is decorated with traditional religious symbols, including the Cyrillic letters X and B: initials of the phrase "Christ is risen," the traditional Easter greeting.

In a bowl, beat together the butter, sour cream, sugar, vanilla, and salt until thoroughly combined. Beat in the tvorog and mix well. Add the condensed milk and beat until smooth, 4–5 minutes.

Line a 5½ × 7-inch (14 × 18 cm) paskha mold (see Notes) with moistened cheesecloth (muslin) and set it in a large bowl with the wide opening up. Fill the mold with the batter, fold the cheesecloth over the top, cover the cheesecloth with a plate, and put weights (at least 2 lb/1 kg) on the plate. Place the bowl with the paskha mold in the fridge for at least 12 hours to drain.

Remove the plate and weights and discard the liquid in the bowl. Unwrap the top of the cheesecake and invert the mold onto a serving plate. Remove the sides of the mold.

Sprinkle with the nuts. Add candied fruits, cookie crumbs, or chocolate chips all around the pyramid base.

Notes: Tvorog is a fresh Russian cheese similar to quark or fromage frais (or farmer cheese in the U.S.).

Paskha molds are easily found online. Old-fashioned molds are made of wood, but modern-day molds are plastic. You can make the cake without the mold, but you do have to put the mixture in something that will let the liquid drain off, such as a sieve lined with cheesecloth set in a bowl. As with the paskha mold, you will need to cover the cheesecloth with a plate and add some weights on top.

Vanilla Flan

Mexico

**Preparation time: 20 minutes,
  plus 4 hours chilling time
Cooking time: 1 hour 10 minutes
Serves: 6**

1 cup (200 g) sugar
2 cups (16 fl oz/475 ml) milk
4 eggs
1 teaspoon vanilla extract
Pinch of sea salt

Flan arrived in Mexico with the Spanish conquistadors in the sixteenth century. Today *flan de vainilla* is one of the most popular Mexican desserts, and Mexicans associate it with home cooking.

Preheat the oven to 350°F (180°C/Gas Mark 4).

Have ready six 5¼-ounce (160 ml) custard cups. In a small heavy-bottomed saucepan, combine ½ cup (100 g) of the sugar and ¼ cup (2 fl oz/60 ml) water and stir over low heat until the sugar is light golden in color. Increase the heat to medium and boil, without stirring but swirling the pan occasionally, until the sugar caramelizes, about 10 minutes. Divide the caramel among the custard cups. Quickly swirl the cups to coat the bottoms and partway up the sides with the caramel.

In a medium saucepan, combine the milk and remaining ½ cup (100 g) sugar and stir over low heat until the sugar dissolves. The milk will be lukewarm.

In a medium bowl, whisk the eggs. Whisking constantly, slowly stream the warm milk mixture into the eggs. Whisk in the vanilla and salt. Pour the mixture through a sieve into the individual custard cups.

Arrange the custard cups in a large baking pan. Set the baking pan on a pulled-out oven rack and pour enough hot water into the pan to come halfway up the sides of the cups.

Bake until set but still a little jiggly in the center, about 50 minutes.

Remove the custard cups from the bain-marie and let stand for 30 minutes. Refrigerate until cold, at least 4 hours and up to 24.

To serve, dip the custard cups, one at a time, into a heatproof bowl half-filled with hot water, then release the custard from the edges with a small knife and invert each flan onto a serving plate.

Milk Flan

**Preparation time: 20 minutes,
    plus overnight chilling time
Cooking time: 2 hours
Serves: 4**

¾ cup (150 g) sugar
3 eggs
1 can (14 fl oz/400 ml)
    condensed milk
¾ cup (6 fl oz/175 ml) milk
1 tablespoon vanilla extract

Venezuelan *quesillo* (or "little cheese") has no cheese in it, but is a flan that develops airholes as it bakes, making it look like Swiss cheese. You can also bake *quesillo* in individual molds, adjusting the cooking time according to their size.

Preheat the oven to 290°F (140°C/Gas Mark 2).

In a small saucepan, combine the sugar and 2 tablespoons water and cook over medium heat until it caramelizes. Remove from the heat and pour into a 10-inch (25 cm) cake pan 2 inches (5 cm) deep, and let the caramel cool on the bottom of the pan.

In a bowl, with an electric mixer, beat the eggs, condensed milk, milk, and vanilla for 5 minutes. Pour the mixture into the cake pan over the caramel.

Set the cake pan in a roasting pan on a pulled-out oven rack. Pour enough hot water into the roasting pan to come halfway up the sides of the cake pan with the flan.

Bake until firm and lightly browned on top, about 2 hours.

Remove from the oven. Remove the cake pan from the hot water and let cool, then refrigerate overnight until well chilled.

To serve, invert the flan out of the pan onto a serving plate, so the caramel is on top.

Steamed Layer Cake

 (DF) (VG) (VT)

**Preparation time: 30 minutes,
plus 3 hours cooling time
Cooking time: 45 minutes
Serves: 4**

20 fresh pandan leaves,
   cut into small pieces
2½ cups (300 g) tapioca starch
Scant 1¼ cups (175 g) rice flour,
   plus more as needed
Generous 1 cup (8.5 fl oz/250 ml)
   coconut milk
4 drops jasmine essence
1⅓ cups (250 g) superfine
   (caster) sugar

Khanom chun is a beautiful dessert from Thailand that is served
at auspicious occasions such as wedding ceremonies. Pandan
leaves give the dish a sweet and delicate aroma; the leaves can
be found both fresh and dried in Asian stores.

In a blender, combine the pandan leaves and ½ cup (4 fl oz/
120 ml) water and blend until they form a paste. Set a fine-mesh
sieve over a bowl and pour the paste into it, pressing on the
solids to extract as much juice possible.

In a large bowl, combine the tapioca flour and rice flour.

In a saucepan, combine 1 cup (8 fl oz/240 ml) water, the
coconut milk, jasmine essence, and sugar. Set over medium-low
heat until the sugar is fully melted. Pour the contents of the pot
into the flour bowl and stir carefully to avoid lumps.

Pour half the batter into a separate bowl. Stir the pandan
juice into one of the bowls. Add a little rice flour to the pandan
bowl to thicken the batter to the same consistency as the other
half. You will now have a white batter and a green batter.

Set up a steamer. With a ladle, spoon a thin (about
1⁄16 inch/2 mm) layer of the white batter into a 5-inch (12.5 cm)
square heatproof container. Place it in the steamer basket
and steam until it's set and no more moisture is on the surface,
about 5 minutes. Pour a thin layer of green batter over the
cooked white batter and steam the same way and for the same
time. Repeat this process, alternating colors, until you have
cooked 8 layers.

Let cool for at least 3 hours at room temperature. To serve,
cut into squares.

Desserts and Sweet Treats

397

Apple Pastila

(DF) (NF) (VT) [5]   **Russia**

Preparation time: 30 minutes
Cooking time: 4 hours
   30 minutes
Makes: 24 squares

2 lb (900 g) sweet green apples
½ cup (170 g) honey
1 egg white
3 tablespoons confectioners'
   (icing) sugar

Pastila are traditional Russian fruit-based tea cakes. The name comes from the Latin *pastillus*, which means "lozenge."

Preheat the oven to 375°F (190°C/Gas Mark 5).

Using a small, sharp knife, score around the circumference of each apple. Place the apples in a 9 × 13-inch (23 × 33 cm) baking pan. Add 2 inches (5 cm) water to the bottom and bake for 30 minutes. Remove the apples from the oven, but leave the oven on.

Reduce the temperature to 212°F (100°C). Line an 8 × 12-inch (20 × 30 cm) baking pan with parchment paper.

When the apples are cool enough to handle, peel and core the apples and cut them into chunks. In a food processor, puree the apple chunks. Add the honey and process to thoroughly combine. Transfer to a bowl.

In a bowl, with an electric mixer, whip the egg white to stiff peaks. Fold the egg white gently into the apple puree. Pour the mixture into the lined baking pan and bake until set and lightly browned, at least 4 hours.

Let the pastila cool, then sprinkle it with the confectioners' (icing) sugar and cut into 2-inch (5 cm) squares for serving.

Tuscan Chestnut Cake

**Preparation time: 20 minutes,
plus 30 minutes soaking time
Cooking time: 40 minutes
Serves: 6**

¼ cup (50 g) raisins
3 tablespoons extra-virgin olive
oil, plus more for the pan
2⅔ cups (300 g) chestnut flour
½ teaspoon sea salt
⅓ cup (50 g) pine nuts, toasted
Scant ½ cup (50 g) crushed
walnuts
3 tablespoons chopped fresh
rosemary

Castagnaccio is a simple cake made with chestnut flour, nuts, and dried fruits that is often served with fresh ricotta cheese.

In a small bowl, soak the raisins in water for 30 minutes. Rinse and drain.

Preheat the oven to 350°F (180°C/Gas Mark 4). Generously grease a 10-inch (26 cm) cake pan with oil.

In a large bowl, combine the chestnut flour and salt. Whisking constantly, stream in 1½ cups (12 fl oz/355 ml) cold water, mixing thoroughly to avoid lumps. The batter will be thin. Stir in the oil. Stir in half each of the raisins, pine nuts, walnuts, and rosemary.

Scrape the batter into the prepared pan. Sprinkle the remaining raisins, pine nuts, walnuts, and rosemary on the surface. Bake until the surface has some cracks, about 40 minutes.

Let cool and serve. The cake can be kept for 2–3 days at room temperature or 5 days in the fridge.

Flourless Chocolate Cake

Preparation time: 40 minutes
Cooking time: 45 minutes
Serves: 6

1½ sticks (6 oz/170 g) unsalted
  butter, at room temperature,
  plus more for the pan
1½ tablespoons (25 g) potato
  starch, plus more for the pan
1½ cups (180 g) confectioners'
  (icing) sugar, plus 2 tablespoons for dusting
½ vanilla bean, split lengthwise
5 eggs, separated, at room
  temperature
Pinch of salt
6 oz (170 g) dark chocolate,
  grated
Generous ½ cup (80 g) almonds,
  finely chopped
Generous ½ cup (80 g) hazelnuts,
  finely chopped
2 tablespoons unsweetened
  cocoa powder
1 teaspoon baking powder

Depending on which origin story you believe (and there are many), the *torta caprese,* from the Italian island of Capri, might be the result of a mistake (a baker in the 1920s forgot to add flour to a cake recipe) or possibly simply a cake designed to showcase almonds, an ingredient typical of that part of Italy. Any way you look at it, the cake is delicious, soft, and creamy.

Preheat the oven to 350°F (180°C/Gas Mark 4). Butter an 8¼-inch (21 cm) round cake pan that is 3⅛ inches (8 cm) deep. Dust the pan with potato starch.

In a bowl, combine the softened butter and ¾ cup (90 g) of the sugar. Scrape the vanilla seeds into the bowl. With an electric mixer, beat at high speed for 4 minutes. Add the egg yolks and salt and mix for 5 more minutes.

In a separate bowl, stir together the chocolate, almonds, hazelnuts, potato starch, cocoa powder, and baking powder.

In a third bowl, with clean beaters, beat the egg whites with the remaining ¾ cup (90 g) sugar until stiff peaks form. Fold half of the egg whites into the butter/egg yolk mixture and stir gently. Add half of the chocolate/nut mixture, then the remaining whites again, and then the remaining chocolate/nut mixture. Gently mix all the ingredients until perfectly smooth.

Scrape the batter into the prepared pan and bake until the surface is dry and lightly cracked, about 45 minutes.

Let the cake cool in the pan on a wire rack. Invert the cake onto a serving plate and dust with the remaining sugar.

Cinnamon Cookies

**Preparation time: 30 minutes,
plus 1 hour chilling time
and 20 minutes cooling time
Cooking time: 15 minutes
Makes: about 30 cookies**

For the dough
2 egg whites
2 teaspoons fresh lemon juice
1 cup (130 g) confectioners'
    (icing) sugar
2¼ cups (250 g) coarse almond
    flour (coarsely ground almonds)
1 tablespoon ground cinnamon
1 teaspoon ground or grated
    fresh ginger
Pinch of sea salt
1 vanilla bean, halved lengthwise
2 tablespoons rice flour,
    for dusting

For the glaze
1½ cups (170 g) confectioners'
    (icing) sugar
1 egg white
1 teaspoon lemon juice

The name of these sweet cookies, *Zimsterne*, means "cinnamon stars." They are mostly served at Christmas and are sold in the annual Christmas markets of Switzerland (as well as those in Austria and Germany). To give the cookies their traditional rustic appearance, the almond flour must be coarse. This texture contrasts beautifully with the smooth sugar glaze.

Make the dough: In a bowl, with an electric mixer, whip the egg whites and lemon juice to stiff peaks. Whisking constantly, add the confectioners' (icing) sugar a little at a time until the mixture is glossy.

In a bowl, combine the almond flour, cinnamon, ginger, and salt. Scrape in the vanilla seeds and mix thoroughly. Add the beaten egg whites and stir well. Cover the bowl with plastic wrap (cling film) and refrigerate for at least 1 hour.

Preheat the oven to 325°F (165°C/Gas Mark 3). Line a sheet pan with parchment paper.

On a surface dusted with rice flour, roll out the dough to ½ inch (1.25 cm) thick. Cut out cookies with a 2-inch (5 cm) star-shaped cutter.

Set the cookies on the lined sheet pan and bake until lightly browned, about 15 minutes; start checking at 8 minutes. Let the cookies cool completely on a wire rack, about 20 minutes.

Make the glaze: In a small bowl, stir together the confectioners' (icing) sugar, egg white, and lemon juice until the mixture is homogeneous and silky.

Drizzle the glaze over each cookie (about 1 tablespoon per cookie), letting it drip down the sides to cover the whole surface, and spreading it out with the help of a toothpick (cocktail stick). Let the glaze dry.

Amaretti

(DF) (VT)

Italy

**Preparation time: 1 hour, plus
overnight chilling time**
Cooking time: 20 minutes
Makes: about 50 cookies

⅔ cup (7½ oz/200 g) blanched
  almonds
Bitter almond extract
Generous ¾ cup (150 g) superfine
  (caster) sugar
Generous 1 cup (130 g)
  confectioners' (icing) sugar
1 teaspoon baker's ammonia
  or baking soda (bicarbonate
  of soda)
2 oz (50 g) egg whites

Amaretti are little cookies that are very popular throughout most of Italy, with many regional variations: soft, sprinkled with sugar, or crunchy. They are perfect for a sweet break or for teatime.

Preheat the oven to 400°F (200°C/Gas Mark 6). Line a sheet pan with parchment paper.

Spread the blanched almonds on the lined sheet pan and toast in the oven for a few minutes. Transfer to a food processor, add 1 drop of bitter almond extract, and chop. Add the superfine (caster) sugar and confectioners' (icing) sugar and process to finely chop.

Transfer the mixture to a sieve set over a large bowl. Return the coarse portion in the sieve to the food processor and process it again. Sieve it again into the bowl. Keep doing this until there are no fragments left in the sieve.

Add the baker's ammonia or baking soda (bicarbonate of soda), egg whites, and a few drops of bitter almond extract and stir until evenly combined. Cover the bowl with a clean cloth and refrigerate overnight to firm up the dough.

Preheat the oven to 340°F (170°C/Gas Mark 3). Line a sheet pan with parchment paper.

Scoop the dough into ½-tablespoon (10 g) amounts and roll into balls. Press them in the center to flatten just slightly. Arrange on the lined sheet pan.

Bake until browned, about 20 minutes. Let cool.

Scottish Macaroons

Preparation time: 30 minutes, plus 4 hours freezing time and 2 hours chilling time
Cooking time: 30 minutes
Makes: 20 macaroons

2 medium white potatoes
4 cups (480 g) confectioners' (icing) sugar
2 cups (200 g) unsweetened shredded (desiccated) coconut
11 oz (300 g) dark chocolate, chopped

In spite of its name, a Scottish macaroon has nothing to do with other cookies of the same name, which are usually made with almonds or other nuts. These are chocolate and coconut coated bars with a fondant-like filling made with mashed potatoes. Macaroon bars come originally from Glasgow, where they have been produced commercially since 1931. This recipe makes them in the traditional bar shape, but if you'd prefer smaller pieces, you can roll the filling into small balls before coating. At room temperature the macaroons get very soft, so store them in an airtight container in the fridge. They will keep for 10 days.

In a medium saucepan of boiling water, cook the potatoes until firm-tender, about 25 minutes. Drain and when cool enough to handle, peel, transfer to a large bowl, and thoroughly mash.

Add the confectioners' (icing) sugar to the potatoes 1 tablespoon at a time and stir until the mixture is stiff and without lumps. Line an 8 × 6-inch (20 × 15 cm) rectangular dish with parchment paper. Using the back of a spoon, spread the dough into an even layer about 1 inch (2.5 cm) thick.

Put the dish into the freezer for 2½ hours.

Pull the potato layer out of the dish and quickly cut it into 20 bars. Line a larger dish with parchment paper, arrange the bars in the dish, and freeze for 1½ hours more.

Meanwhile, in a dry frying pan, toast the coconut flakes over medium heat, stirring constantly, until golden brown. Remove them immediately from the pan and let them cool. Spread out in a shallow dish.

When the bars have frozen, melt the chocolate in a microwave-safe bowl in the microwave. (Alternatively, melt the chocolate in a heatproof bowl set over a pan of simmering water.)

Remove the bars from the freezer and dip them, one at a time, into the chocolate and then roll them in the coconut flakes.

Return the bars to the lined baking dish and refrigerate for 2 hours to set up the chocolate.

Macarons

Preparation time: 45 minutes, plus 25 minutes drying and cooling time
Cooking time: 25 minutes
Makes: 20 macarons

1⅔ cups (200 g) confectioners' (icing) sugar
1¾ cups (200 g) almond flour (ground almonds)
3 eggs, separated, at room temperature
1 cup (200 g) superfine (caster) sugar
Food coloring
5½ oz (160 g) white chocolate, chopped
¼ cup (60 ml) heavy (whipping) cream
1 vanilla bean, halved lengthwise

These French sweets made with almond flour (ground almonds) have achieved world-wide popularity, in part because they tend to be so colorful, often with a contrasting color of filling. The ingredients are simple, but the technique has some aspects that must be strictly observed for the best results. In particular, it is essential to weigh the ingredients exactly, gently fold in the egg whites, and let the macarons sit for at least 10 minutes to develop a "skin" (which helps give them a good shape).

In a bowl, stir together the confectioners' (icing) sugar, the almond flour (ground almonds), and half of the egg whites. Stir to thoroughly combine until the mixture is smooth and lump-free.

In a bowl, with an electric mixer, start whisking the remaining half of the egg whites. At the same time, in a small saucepan, combine the superfine (caster) sugar and 4 tablespoons water and heat over low heat to 245°F (118°C). With the mixer running, pour the hot syrup into the egg whites while continuing to whip. Add your chosen food coloring and continue mixing until the color is homogeneous. (If you want to make macarons in several colors, spoon the meringue into separate bowls before mixing in the colors.)

Add the meringue to the bowl with the almond dough and gently fold together, taking care to deflate the meringue as little as possible. If you want to have different colored macarons, divide the dough into different bowls and add 1 color for each one.

Line a sheet pan with parchment paper. Fit a piping bag with a ½-inch (1 cm) plain tip (nozzle). Fill the piping bag with the mixture and squeeze to create ¾-inch (2 cm) discs on the lined sheet pan. Let them dry at room temperature for 10 minutes.

Meanwhile, preheat the oven to 325°F (160°C/Gas Mark 3).

Bake the macarons until they develop a rough-looking bottom layer called the "foot," about 15 minutes.

In a heatproof bowl set over a pan of simmering water, melt the chocolate. Add the cream, scrape in some vanilla seeds to taste, and stir until smooth. Let the ganache cool for 15 minutes.

Spread the ganache on the flat side of a macaron. Top with another macaron flat-side down to make a sandwich. Repeat with all the macarons.

Crispy Tapioca and Guava Bars

(VT)
Brazil

**Preparation time: 30 minutes,
plus 1 hour cooling time**
Cooking time: 45 minutes
Makes: 12 bars

1¾ sticks (7 oz/200 g) unsalted
  butter
¼ cup (50 g) sugar
Sea salt
Scant 1¾ cups (200 g) tapioca
  starch
8 oz (225 g) guava paste, cut into
  ¼-inch (6 mm) slices
6 tablespoons (50 g) coconut flour
¼ cup (50 g) packed brown sugar

This confection is typical of northeastern Brazil and uses the starch of the yuca (cassava) root. There are two types of tapioca starch: sour (fermented briefly) or sweet. Either can be used, depending on what the toppings will be.

Preheat the oven to 350°F (180°C/Gas Mark 4). Line a sheet pan with parchment paper.

In a bowl, with an electric mixer, beat together 8 tablespoons (120 g) of the butter and the sugar for 3–4 minutes or until fluffy. Beat in ½ teaspoon salt and 1¼ cups (150 g) of the tapioca starch until a cohesive dough forms.

Tip the dough onto the lined sheet pan and press the dough into a 10 × 14-inch (25 × 35 cm) baking pan. Places the slices of guava paste all over the dough layer.

In a food processor, combine the coconut flour, brown sugar, a pinch of salt, and the remaining 6 tablespoons (90 g) butter and scant ½ cup (60 g) tapioca starch. Process to fine crumbs.

Sprinkle the mixture over the top of the guava layer.

Transfer to the oven and bake for 45 minutes, or until golden. Let cool for at least 1 hour. Cut into 12 bars.

Coconut and Peanut Bars

(DF) (VG) (VT) (30) [5]
Tanzania

Preparation time: 10 minutes
Cooking time: 20 minutes
Makes: 12 bars

2 cups (16 fl oz/475 ml) coconut
  water
1⅓ cups (250 g) packed light
  brown sugar
6 cardamom pods, lightly
  crushed with your fingers
  and seeds removed
Small pinch of sea salt
Generous ¾ cup (120 g) roasted
  peanuts, coarsely chopped
1¼ cups (120 g) unsweetened
  shredded (desiccated) coconut

Kashata is a traditional Tanzanian sweet. Buying unsalted roasted peanuts simplifies the recipe, but you can toast raw unsalted nuts in a saucepan until they begin to brown.

Spread a sheet of parchment paper on a work surface.

In a saucepan, combine the coconut water, brown sugar, cardamom seeds, and salt. Bring to a simmer over medium-high heat, stirring until the sugar has dissolved. At this point, stop stirring (to avoid crystallization of the sugar) and only swirl the pan around. Continue to cook for 16 minutes, or until the mixture is the consistency of golden syrup.

Add the peanuts and shredded coconut and mix well until everything clumps up together, but the mixture is still moist.

Spread the coconut/peanut mixture onto the parchment paper and lightly tap the mixture into a square layer about ⅜ inch (1 cm) thick, trying not to push the mixture too much.

Let cool. When it is firm, cut with a knife into 12 diamonds or squares.

Desserts and Sweet Treats

Fudge Balls

Brazil

Preparation time: 20 minutes
Cooking time: 50 minutes
Makes: 24 fudge balls

4 cups (32 fl oz/950 ml) milk
¾ cup (6 fl oz/175 ml) heavy
 (whipping) cream
1½ cups (300 g) sugar
⅛ teaspoon kosher (flaked) salt
4 tablespoons unsweetened
 cocoa powder, sifted
Pinch of sea salt
2 tablespoons (30 g)
 unsalted butter, plus more
 for rolling balls
Chocolate sprinkles

Brazilian *brigadeiros* are small balls of fudgy chocolate rolled in sprinkles—usually chocolate, but you can use multicolored sprinkles for a brighter effect (especially for children's birthday parties). If making these treats in the hot weather, store them in the fridge.

In a saucepan, combine the milk, cream, sugar, and kosher (flaked) salt. Heat over medium heat, stirring occasionally, until the mixture begins to simmer, about 12 minutes. Let it simmer for 30 minutes, stirring constantly. It will turn foamy. Keep stirring and cooking until the foam subsides.

Mix in the cocoa powder, sea salt, and butter. Heat over medium-low heat, stirring constantly, until it thickens so much that your spatula can only move slowly through it, about 5 minutes. Let the mixture cool to room temperature.

Pour chocolate sprinkles on a plate. Grease your hands with a little butter. Take half a tablespoonful of chocolate mixture and roll into a little ball. Roll the ball in the sprinkles. Repeat until you have used up all the fudge mixture.

Fudge

United States

Preparation time: 15 minutes, plus 2 hours cooling time
Cooking time: 15 minutes
Makes: 20 squares

1½ cups (12 fl oz/355 ml) condensed milk
½ cup (4 fl oz/120 ml) milk
2 cups (400 g) superfine (caster) sugar
1 stick (4 oz/115 g) unsalted butter

It's unclear who invented fudge, but the U.S. is known for it and happily claims credit for the delicious candy. The best known fudge is made with chocolate, but the category includes many versions without chocolate, such as this simple version, which when made with brown sugar is called penuche.

Line a 10-inch (25 cm) square baking pan with parchment paper.
In a large nonstick saucepan, combine the condensed milk, milk, sugar, and butter and heat over low heat, stirring constantly, until the mixture is perfectly smooth. Bring to a boil and simmer until the mixture reaches 239°F (115°C) on a candy thermometer, about 10 minutes.
Remove the pan from the heat and let it rest for 5 minutes, then pour it into a large bowl and vigorously whisk for 10 minutes until it thickens.
Pour the mixture into the lined pan, pressing it carefully with a spatula or the back of a tablespoon.
Let it cool for at least 2 hours, then cut it into 20 squares.

Coconut Burfi

India

Preparation time: 5 minutes, plus 4 hours setting time
Cooking time: 15 minutes
Makes: 16 squares

2 tablespoons ghee
2 tablespoons crushed cashews
2 cups (16 fl oz/475 ml) milk
14 oz (400 g) unsweetened shredded (desiccated) coconut
1 cup (200 g) superfine (caster) sugar

Burfi is a type of milk candy from South India and comes in a whole host of flavors. Some are made with nuts, some with chickpeas, some with chocolate, and even some with carrots. All *burfis*, however, start out with a sweetened milk base.

Grease an 8-inch (20 cm) square baking pan with ½ tablespoon of the ghee.
In a frying pan, heat 1 tablespoon of the ghee over medium heat. Fry the cashews and set aside.
In a saucepan, combine the milk and coconut over medium heat and cook, stirring, until the milk has reduced by half. Add the sugar and cook until it starts to become a light syrup. Add the remaining ½ tablespoon ghee and keep stirring until the mixture comes away from the edges of the pan, 5–7 minutes.
Spread the mixture evenly into the prepared pan. Press down with a spatula. Sprinkle the cashews on top. Press lightly so they stick to the burfi.
Let it cool and set for about 4 hours, then cut into 16 squares.

Sweet Rice Cake Balls

(DF) (VG) (VT)

Korea

Preparation time: 1 hour,
 plus overnight soaking time
Cooking time: 1 hour
Serves: 4

¾ cup (150 g) adzuki beans,
 soaked in water overnight,
 drained, and rinsed
1 teaspoon superfine (caster)
 sugar
¾ teaspoon ground cinnamon
½ teaspoon vanilla extract
Sea salt
2 cups (300 g) sweet (glutinous)
 rice flour
⅔ cup (125 g) plus 2 tablespoons
 light brown sugar
½ cup (4 fl oz/120 ml) boiling
 water
2 tablespoons black sesame seeds
2 tablespoons matcha green
 tea powder
2 tablespoons unsweetened
 shredded (desiccated) coconut

These traditional Korean treats, called *gyeongdan*, have sweetened red bean paste inside. Korean tradition has it that red beans in food can drive out evil spirits, so these bean-stuffed rice cakes were often served on a baby's first birthday, to ensure a long and healthy life. The balls can be rolled in all sorts of ingredients; in addition to the three suggestions listed here, they can also be coated with toasted soy powder or powdered yellow or green beans.

In a medium pot, combine the soaked beans with water to cover. Bring to a boil over high heat and cook for 10 minutes. Reduce the heat and simmer until soft, about 30 minutes. Drain the beans. Mash them in a bowl with a spoon (or mash in a blender) to get a paste. Return the paste to the pot and add the sugar, cinnamon, vanilla, and salt to taste. Mix over low heat for 1 minute to thoroughly combine.

In a medium bowl, combine the rice flour, 1 teaspoon salt, and ⅔ cup (125 g) brown sugar. Add the boiling water and mix with your hands until you obtain a dough. Set the rice cake dough aside in a plastic bag.

In a small dry frying pan, toast the black sesame seeds until they pop. Set aside.

In a separate bowl, stir together the matcha green tea powder with the remaining 2 tablespoons brown sugar.

Put the rice cake dough on a cutting board and roll into a rope 1½ inches (4 cm) thick. Cut the rope into 1½-inch (4 cm) chunks. Roll each chunk into a little ball. Press your thumb in the middle of the ball and put ½ teaspoon bean paste in the middle. Fold the dough around the filling and roll back into a smooth ball. Make sure to seal the dough. Repeat the process until all the dough and bean paste are finished.

Set up a bowl of ice and water. Bring a large pot of water to a boil. Working in batches, cook the rice balls until they rise to the surface, about 5 minutes. Scoop them into the ice bath to cool down. Drain well.

Roll the cooked rice balls in either the toasted sesame seeds, the matcha/sugar mixture, or the shredded coconut. Roll until they are completely covered.

Serve each person 3 balls, each with a different coating.

Coconut Balls

**Preparation time: 10 minutes,
  plus 2 hours freezing time and
  30 minutes chilling time
Makes: 20 coconut balls**

11 oz (300 g) fresh coconut, grated
4 tablespoons honey
3 tablespoons virgin coconut oil
1 teaspoon vanilla extract
Pinch of salt
3 oz (80 g) dark chocolate,
  roughly chopped

These delicious Thai sweets are made from fresh coconut, which should be easily available already cut up at Asian stores and well-stocked grocery stores. Should you happen to get hold of a whole coconut, though, here's how to open it: Make holes in two of the "eyes" of the shell with a corkscrew or screwdriver and pour the coconut water out of one of the holes into a glass. Firmly tap the coconut shell all around the equator with a hammer until it cracks in half. With a sharp knife, cut the coconut flesh into pieces and pry them off the shell. Use a vegetable peeler to pull off the hard brown skin.

In a food processor, combine the coconut, honey, oil, vanilla, and salt and pulse together.

Line a sheet pan with parchment paper. Divide the mixture into 20 portions and roll into little balls. Place the balls on the lined pan and freeze until hard, at least 2 hours.

In a heatproof bowl set over a pan of simmering water, melt the chocolate. Dip each ball halfway into the chocolate, then return to the lined pan, and refrigerate to set the chocolate before serving.

Honeycomb Toffee

**Preparation time: 15 minutes,
  plus 1 hour cooling time
Cooking time: 4 minutes
Makes: 12 ounces (340 g)**

Sunflower oil, for greasing
⅔ cup (140 ml) golden syrup
1 cup (200 g) superfine
  (caster) sugar
3 tablespoons baking soda
  (bicarbonate of soda)

This crunchy, sweet confection is perfect sprinkled over (or into) ice cream or yogurt. It is a fun recipe to make with children, who will be amazed by the drama of the foaming caramel. In New Zealand its original name was "hokey pokey."

Line a 6-inch (15 cm) square pan with foil and grease the foil with oil.

In a saucepan, thoroughly stir the syrup and sugar together. Set over medium heat, without stirring, until the mixture reaches 300°F (150°C) on a candy thermometer, about 3–4 minutes.

Remove from the heat and add the baking soda (bicarbonate of soda), whisk, and quickly pour the mixture onto the greased foil in an even layer. Let it cool, then smash it into many pieces.

Dried Apples

Preparation time: 15 minutes
Cooking time: 4–5 hours
Makes: 5 oz (150 g) dried apples

1 lb (450 g) your favorite apples,
    washed, cored, and thinly sliced

In the Czech Republic, *křížaly* can be either apples or pears, and depending on the specific variety will be more or less sweet. The dried fruit can be eaten as a snack, sprinkled over yogurt or added to muesli, or added to vanilla ice cream for dessert. For this recipe, you will need an oven that goes down to 160°F (70°C); if your oven can't go that low, an alternative option would be to use a food dehydrator to dry the apple slices. Watch that the fruit doesn't turn dark as that means it has been dried too far.

Preheat a convection (fan-assist) oven to 160°F (70°C). Line a sheet pan with parchment paper.

Arrange the apples on the lined sheet pan. Set in the oven and bake, flipping the slices every 30 minutes, with the oven door ajar, for 2 hours.

Bake until the slices are fully dried and crisp (they will crack, not bend), 2–3 hours longer.

Halvah

(DF) (VT)

Preparation time: 40 minutes, plus overnight cooling time
Cooking time: 10 minutes
Makes: 2¼ pounds (1 kg)

1 cup (5¼ oz/150 g) hulled
   sesame seeds
5 tablespoons sesame oil
½ teaspoon kosher (flaked) salt
11 oz (350 g) honey
12 oz (300 g) pistachios
5 oz (150 g) dried cranberries

This dense sesame-based candy comes in many flavors and consistencies, but here we make an Israeli version sweetened with honey and studded with pistachios and cranberries.

In a large dry frying pan, toast the sesame seeds over medium heat, stirring constantly, until they are fragrant and slightly golden, about 5 minutes.

Pour the toasted sesame seeds into a mortar or food processor. Let the seeds cool down for 1 minute, then mash them with a pestle or process them in the food processor until you reach a crumbly paste. Add 4 tablespoons of the sesame oil and process again for 3 minutes or until you reach the consistency of a smooth sauce. Add the salt and process until it has been evenly combined. Transfer the paste to a small pot and set aside. This is the tahini.

In a small saucepan, heat the honey over medium heat to 240°F (115°C) on a candy thermometer or until it reaches the "soft ball" stage. To confirm, drop a bit of honey into a glass of cold water. If it forms a sticky and soft ball that flattens when removed from the water, you have reached the perfect temperature. Remove the honey from the heat.

Set the pot of tahini over low heat and bring to 120°F (50°C).

Grease a 7 × 4-inch (18 × 10 cm) rectangular dish at least 2 inches (5 cm) deep with the remaining 1 tablespoon sesame oil.

Pour the tahini into the honey and mix with a wooden spoon, off the heat, for 3 minutes or until perfectly combined. Add the pistachios and cranberries and continue to mix for 8 minutes or until the mixture becomes stiff.

Pour the mixture into the prepared dish. Let it cool to room temperature. Cover tightly with plastic wrap (cling film) and refrigerate overnight or for up to 36 hours. During this time sugar crystals will form.

Remove from the fridge. Cut the halvah into slices to serve. Store leftovers wrapped tightly in plastic in the fridge, where it will keep for up to 2 months.

Peanut and Rice Bites

 Liberia

Preparation time: 15 minutes
Cooking time: 5 minutes
Makes: 24 bites

Scant 1 cup (150 g) rice flour
2 cups (300 g) unsalted peanuts
⅓ cup (120 g) sugar

Traditionally, this confection takes a lot of time and effort because the peanuts and rice were pounded by hand. This recipe takes a shortcut (the food processor), which makes this three-ingredient candy a snap.

In a dry frying pan, toast the rice flour over medium-low heat, stirring frequently, until lightly browned, about 5 minutes.

In a food processor, combine the peanuts and sugar and process to a loose, pebbly sand. Add the toasted rice flour and blend until the mixture holds its shape without crumbling. It will take time, about 10 minutes or more. Keep blending and checking. The idea is to release enough of the peanut oils to make a nut butter that will bind the dough so it won't crumble when cut into pieces.

Press the mixture into a 6-inch (15 cm) square baking pan. Cut into 24 squares. (If it crumbles, put it back into the food processor and blend longer.)

Sesame Seed Candy with Peanuts

 Cyprus

Preparation time: 10 minutes
Cooking time: 20 minutes
Makes: about 1¾ pounds (795 g)

2 tablespoons sunflower
 or other vegetable oil
3⅓ cups (400 g) confectioners'
 (icing) sugar
2 tablespoons honey
½ teaspoon vanilla extract
1 teaspoon distilled white vinegar
5 tablespoons sesame seeds
12 oz (350 g) skin-on peanuts

Pastellaki is a traditional peanut and sesame candy from Cyprus with ancient roots: Homer mentions a honey and sesame sweet that was offered to wedding guests, a custom that continues today on some Greek islands. The original recipe made a caramel from carob, but in modern times this is replaced with sugar.

Line a sheet pan with parchment paper and grease the paper with the sunflower oil.

In a nonstick saucepan, combine the sugar, honey, vanilla, and 5 tablespoons water. Mix thoroughly and bring to a boil over medium heat, without stirring, for 10 minutes or until you reach a temperature of 250°F (120°C) on a candy thermometer and the mixture caramelizes.

Add the vinegar and stir carefully. Add the sesame seeds and peanuts, stirring constantly over high heat until the mixture is lightly browned, 8–10 minutes. Pour the mixture onto the greased parchment paper and let cool.

Break into pieces and serve.

Almond Brittle

**Preparation time: 10 minutes,
plus 1 hour cooling time
Cooking time: 15 minutes
Makes: 2¼ pounds (1 kg)**

3 cups (600 g) sugar
1 tablespoon (15 g) unsalted butter
1 lb (450 g) blanched almonds,
toasted

In Spain this sweet is called *turrón de guirlache*. *Turrón* is a category of candy studded with nuts, and *guirlache* is the Spanish spelling of the French word *grillage*, which means "roasting"—in this case a reference to the toasted almonds. It is typically a Christmas candy and is sometimes also prepared with dried fruit.

Set a sheet of parchment paper on a marble or stainless steel surface or a sheet pan.

In a large stainless steel saucepan, combine the sugar and butter and simmer over low heat until caramelized, 10–15 minutes. As with any caramel, it is essential to avoid stirring the sugar with a spoon. You can swirl the pot, but only slightly, without touching the contents.

Add the almonds to the caramel and stir carefully to thoroughly combine. Pour the almond mixture onto the parchment paper and level with a silicone spatula, giving it a roughly square or round shape. Let it cool for at least 1 hour. (You can also pour the mixture into a 9-inch/23 cm square or round pan lined with parchment paper.)

Break the turrón with your hands into rough pieces or use a knife to break into slices or wedges.

Index

Phaidon Press Limited
2 Cooperage Yard
London E15 2QR

Phaidon Press Inc.
65 Bleecker Street
New York, NY 10012

phaidon.com

First published 2022
© 2022 Phaidon Press Limited
Published under license from
Dalcò Edizioni S.r.l. © Dalcò Edizioni

ISBN 978 1 83866 313 1

A CIP catalogue record for this book
is available from the British Library
and the Library of Congress.

Text by Cristian Broglia/© Dalcò
Edizioni S.r.l.
Photography by Infraordinario Studio
for Dalcò Edizioni S.r.l.

Commissioning Editor: Emily Takoudes
Project Editor: Clare Churly
Production Controller: Lily Rodgers
Designed by Evi O. Studio

Printed in China

Phaidon would like to thank Vanessa
Bird, Lucia Carletti, Paolo Dalcò,
Ilaria Ferrarini, Lee Graham, Fatima
Khawaja, Giulia Malerba, Cristiana
Mistrali, João Mota, Claire Rogers,
Marta Santacatterina, Margherita
Scorletti, Kate Slate, Ellie Smith,
Caroline Stearns, Ana Teodoro, Emilia
Terragni, Elena Vaga, and Karen Wise.

Dalcò Edizioni S.r.l. and the author
would also like to thank the following
chefs for their assistance: Deniz Aysev,
Chris Campbell, Florin Dumitrescu,
Bernard Fournier, Cesare Gasparri,
Omar Hussein, Angela Kim, Pierre
Joseph Limoujoux, Curtis Clemet
Mulpas, Antonio Passarelli, Altin Prenga,
Barbara Ross, Mildred Navarrete
Salazar, Renzky Kurniawan Saputra,
Basanta Sapkota, Filtarau Sebastian,
Tomoyuki Sekiguchi, Stephan Vaccaro,
Felipe Valente, Yara Marzia Vitalba,
Jarno Winberg, and Yadira Zacarias.

Recipe Notes

— Butter is unsalted, unless specified otherwise.
— Eggs are assumed to be large (US)/medium (UK) and preferably organic and free-range.
— All milk is whole (full-fat) milk, unless specified otherwise.
— Herbs are fresh, unless specified otherwise.
— Individual fruits and vegetables, such as onions and pears, are assumed to be medium sized, unless specified otherwise, and should be peeled and/or washed.
— When using the zest of citrus fruit, buy unwaxed or organic.
— Cooking and preparation times are for guidance only, as individual ovens vary.
— If using a convection (fan) oven, follow the manufacturer's instructions concerning oven temperatures.
— When deep-frying, heat the oil to the temperature specified, or until a cube of bread browns in 30 seconds. After frying, drain fried foods on paper towels.
— When sterilizing jars for preserves, wash the jars in clean, hot water and rinse thoroughly. Heat the oven to 275°F/140°C/Gas Mark 1. Place the jars on a sheet pan and place in the oven to dry.
— Exercise a high level of caution when following recipes involving any potentially hazardous activity including the use of high temperatures and open flames and when deep-frying. In particular, when deep-frying, add food carefully to avoid splashing, wear long sleeves, and never leave the pan unattended.
— Some recipes include raw or very lightly cooked eggs, meat, or fish, and fermented products. These should be avoided by the elderly, infants, pregnant women, convalescents, and anyone with an impaired immune system.
— Bitter almonds can be poisonous if consumed in large quantities. Though they have slightly less flavor, almond and bitter almond extract can be used as substitutes.
— Calcium hydroxide (also known as pickling line or slaked lime) is a colorless crystal or white powder most commonly used for clarifying, binding, and pickling. Unprotected exposure can cause chemical burns so take extreme care when using and do not allow to come into contact with skin.
— When no quantity is specified—for example of oils, salts, and herbs used for finishing dishes or for deep-frying—quantities are discretionary and flexible.
— All spoon and cup measurements are level, unless otherwise stated. 1 teaspoon = 5 ml; 1 tablespoon = 15 ml. Australian standard tablespoons are 20 ml, so Australian readers are advised to use 3 teaspoons in place of 1 tablespoon when measuring small quantities.
— Cup, metric, and imperial measurements are used in this book. Follow one set of measurements throughout, not a mixture, as they are not interchangeable.
— Always check labels of condiments and other pre-prepared ingredients and choose a brand that is gluten-free.